D1468865

DISARRAY IN WORLD FOOD MARKETS

A QUANTITATIVE ASSESSMENT

TRADE AND DEVELOPMENT

A series of books on international economic relations and economic issues in development

Edited from the National Centre for Development Studies, Australian National University, by Helen Hughes

Advisory editors
Juergen Donges, *University of Cologne*
Peter Lloyd, *Department of Economics, University of Melbourne*
Gustav Ranis, *Department of Economics, Yale University*
David Wall, *Department of Economics, University of Sussex*

Other titles in the series
Achieving Industrialization in East Asia, Helen Hughes (ed.)
The China–Hong Kong Connection: The Key to China's Open Door Policy, Yun-Wing Sung
New Silk Roads: East Asia and World Textile Markets, Kym Anderson (ed.)

DISARRAY IN WORLD FOOD MARKETS

A QUANTITATIVE ASSESSMENT

ROD TYERS and KYM ANDERSON

Faculty of Economics and Commerce,
Australian National University, Canberra
and
Economic Research and Analysis Unit,
General Agreement on Tariffs and Trade, Geneva.

CAMBRIDGE
UNIVERSITY PRESS

Published by the Press Syndicate of the University of Cambridge
The Pitt Building, Trumpington Street, Cambridge CB2 1RP, UK
40 West 20th Street, New York, NY 10011-4211, USA
10 Stamford Road, Oakleigh, Melbourne, Victoria 3166, Australia

© Cambridge University Press 1992
First published 1992

Printed in Hong Kong by Colorcraft

National Library of Australia cataloguing in publication data
Tyers, Rodney.
Disarray in world food markets: a quantitative assessment.
Bibliography.
Includes index.
ISBN 0 521 35105 7.
1. Food industry and trade. 2. International trade. I. Anderson,
Kym. II. Title. (Series: Trade and development).
338.19

Library of Congress cataloguing in publication data
Tyers, Rodney
Disarray in world food markets: a quantitative assessment / Rod
Tyers and Kym Anderson.
(Trade and development)
Includes bibliographical references and index.
ISBN 0-521-35105-7
1. Food industry and trade—Government policy. 2. Produce trade–
Government policy. 3. Agriculture and state. 4. Agricultural
price supports. 5. Food prices—Government policy. 6. Commercial
treaties. 7. International economic relations. I. Anderson, Kym.
II. Title. III. Series: Trade and development (Cambridge, England)
HD9000.6.T934 1992
382′.456413—dc20
91-37379
CIP

A catalogue record for this book is available from the British Library

ISBN 0 521 35105 7 hardback

To D. Gale Johnson, without whose encouragement this book may never have been written

Contents

List of Figures

List of Tables

Preface

Public discussion of the crisis in international agricultural trade that has developed over the past two decades has been greatly aided by a number of major studies. Foremost among these is Professor D. Gale Johnson's seminal book *World Agriculture in Disarray*, first published in 1973. This book was among the first to point out the problems caused by inward-looking agricultural policies in an increasingly interdependent world. Many worthy studies followed as gyrations of increasing amplitude were observed in world food prices. In 1985, a group of specialists on the problem were drawn together by the World Bank to prepare the *World Development Report 1986*. In the course of that project we were encouraged to extend our earlier work on policies affecting world trade in temperate agricultural products in ways which ultimately led to the completion of this volume. We are particularly indebted to Professor Johnson for this encouragement. Many of his ideas are reflected in our work. We have even borrowed the word 'disarray' from the title of his book. It is our contention that the concerns to which he applied this term in 1973 are even more problematic today.

The centrepiece of the book is the estimation of the economic effects of policies which distort food markets and their incidence across countries and among groups within countries. At the time of writing, ours is one of a number of studies with this aim. But, it remains the only one which incorporates both the dynamic properties of food markets, including the role of food stocks, and an assessment of the degree to which distortionary policies serve the purpose of insulating domestic agents from fluctuations in the international market place.

This book adds further to the current literature by complementing the analysis of the effects of food policies with a quantitative review of long-term trends in world food market behaviour and an extensive examination of the reasons why governments choose to implement distortionary policies. The latter follows on from the 1986 study by Kym Anderson, Yujiro Hayami and others (*The Political Economy of Agricultural Protection*). In addition, we have included an examination of some of the reforms which have been proposed in the Uruguay Round of multilateral trade negotiations which began in September 1986.

Rod Tyers and Kym Anderson

Acknowledgements

Our joint work on the international economics of agriculture has extended over more than a decade. It began at a conference on food security at the East-West Center's Resource Systems Institute in Honolulu in 1980, for which a mathematical model of world food trade was constructed by Rod Tyers, in collaboration with Professor Tony Chisholm. After much modification and updating, that model forms the essential core of the analysis presented in this book. The initial development of the model was greatly aided by the generous support of the Director of the Resource Systems Institute, the late Professor Harrison Brown. His successor, Professor Seiji Naya, has also offered valuable support and advice in the course of our work, facilitating our participation at subsequent conferences on related topics. In addition, we are grateful for external funding in 1980 and 1981 from the Economic Research Service of the United States Department of Agriculture.

In the mid-1980s our research continued at the Australian National University, with the support of the National Centre for Development Studies and the Department of Economics in the Research School of Pacific Studies, and with help from the Department of Foreign Affairs and Trade of the Australian Government. Professors Helen Hughes, Peter Drysdale and Ross Garnaut were strongly supportive of the continuation of the work at the Australian National University. In 1985, particular encouragement from Professor D. Gale Johnson and support from the World Bank (associated with our contribution to the Bank's *World Development Report 1986*) facilitated a further update and extension of our trade-modelling work and cemented our intention to write this book.

In the late 1980s this work continued at the Department of

Economics at the University of Adelaide as a project of the Centre for International Economic Studies. During this period we received external support for particular papers on topics covered by this book from the International Food Policy Research Institute, the International Agricultural Trade Research Consortium, the Centre for International Food and Agricultural Policy at the University of Minnesota, the OECD Development Centre, the World Bank, the Australia–Japan Research Centre and the Australian Department of Foreign Affairs and Trade.

We are particularly grateful for the comments and suggestions offered by numerous colleagues in addition to those mentioned thus far. An incomplete list includes Richard Cornes, Wally Falcon, Rod Falvey, John Freebairn, Frank Jarrett, Gordon Rausser, Martin Ravallion, Ammar Siamwalla, Alberto Valdes and Brian Wright. Special thanks are due to Peter Lloyd who offered numerous comments and suggestions on our first complete draft. Invaluable research assistance has been provided over the years by Melissa Gibbs, Christina Jancovic, Eric Saxon, Suthad Setboonsarng, John Souter, Helen Wickens, Berhanu Woldekidan and by Prue Phillips and her staff from the International Economic Data Bank at the Australian National University. We are also much indebted to Debbie Beckman who cheerfully word processed and re-processed the various drafts of the manuscript.

Few books are written without strong support from authors' families and this one is no exception. To our wives and children we offer our sincere thanks.

Finally, we note with sadness the death in 1991 of Roger Revelle, a great American scientist, teacher and mentor. It was his guidance and commitment, while Professor at Harvard University, which cemented the senior author's interest in food and agricultural policy.

Abbreviations and Glossary

ASEAN	The six member countries of the Association of Southeast Asian Nations (Brunei, Indonesia, Malaysia, the Philippines, Singapore and Thailand)
Australasia	Australia and New Zealand
CAP	Common Agricultural Policy of the European Community
Centrally planned Europe	The USSR plus Eastern Europe.
CPE	Centralled planned economy
East Asia	Northeast and Southeast Asia
Eastern Europe	The eight (currently or formerly) centrally planned economies of Albania, Bulgaria, Czecho-slovakia, DPR (East) Germany, Hungary, Poland, Romania, Yugoslavia
EC or EC–12	European Community of twelve member countries (Belgium, Denmark, Federal Republic of(West) Germany, France, Greece, Ireland, Italy, Luxembourg, the Netherlands, Portugal, Spain and the United Kingdom)
EC–10	The above countries minus Portugal and Spain (the most recent entrants)

EFTA	European Free Trade Association of six member countries (Austria, Finland, Iceland, Norway, Sweden and Switzerland)
EFTA-5	EFTA minus Iceland
GATT	General Agreement on Tariffs and Trade
IFPRI	International Food Policy Research Institute
MTN	Multilateral trade negotiations
NICs	Newly industrializing countries
North America	Canada and the United States
Northeast Asia	Japan, Hong Kong, South Korea, Taiwan, and, in some contexts, also mainland China
Southeast Asia	The six member countries of ASEAN and, in some contexts, also the centrally planned economies of Indo-China
Western Europe	EC-12 plus EFTA-5
Uruguay Round	The eighth round of multilateral trade negotiations launched by the GATT in Punta del Este in September 1986 and due for completion in the early 1990s.

Symbols

n.a. not applicable
..   not available
–   zero or insignificant

Introduction and Summary

If 'disarray' was an apt description of world food markets when D. Gale Johnson wrote his seminal book two decades ago, it is an even more appropriate term today. In the United States, the government has been paying farmers to cease producing grain and to slaughter cows; in Europe, farmers are subsidized to produce more grain and livestock; yet in some malnourished countries, farmers are discouraged from producing food by their governments' price-depressing policies. Many food-deficit countries have restrictions on agricultural imports, thereby raising food prices for their consumers while denying countries with a strong comparative advantage in food production the opportunity to exploit their full potential. National economic welfare is reduced in rich and poor countries alike, and those individuals within countries which do benefit from these policies are few in number and are rarely the most needy.

Why another study of these issues?

These sorts of statements have been made in many scholarly books, as well as in reports by various national and international agencies and, increasingly, by the media. So what new ground is being covered by the present study? At least five contributions to the debate are worth emphasizing at the outset.

A common presumption is that government intervention to support and stabilize food prices in advanced industrial countries is necessary to ensure farmers a stable income that keeps pace with non-farm incomes. Chapter 1 shows that indeed international food prices have been on a long-term downward trend in real terms, that they fluctuate substantially around this long-term trend, and that the degree of fluctuation in the 1970s and 1980s has been much more severe than in earlier decades. Poor countries, too, insulate their domestic markets from fluctuations in international prices but, in their case, it is mainly to protect urban consumers, who spend as much as half their income on food and therefore prefer food prices to be low and stable. The irony is, however, that government intervention to stabilize and, in the case of individual countries, to raise domestic food prices *contributes* to the low and unstable prices in international food markets which that intervention is aimed to offset. That is, if all industrial countries reduced their food price supports, the international price of food would rise; and, if all countries were to reduce their insulation from international food markets simultaneously, many countries would enjoy more stable domestic food prices than at present and very few would suffer significantly less stable prices. One of the important contributions of the modelling results reported in the present study is the ability to show the extent to which different countries are affected in these ways by current policies, as well as to estimate the effects on trade and on the economic welfare of various groups in those and other countries.

A second contribution of the study is the ability to show that intervention in food markets by governments of industrial countries that had been growing steadily since the 1950s, accelerated from the mid-1970s and similar patterns of inter- vention began to spread to newly industrializing countries. This growth in agricultural protectionism, together with the use of export subsidies by Western Europe to dispose of surpluses, prompted the United States to retaliate in the mid-1980s with the introduction of its own Export Enhancement Program. Unfortunately, this retaliation by the United States has had little impact on the European Community and has rubbed salt into the wound for other agricultural exporting countries by way of depressing even further the price of food in international markets. This protection growth and its effects on prices, trade, government budgetary outlays and economic welfare have been quantified using our model of world food markets, and the results are presented in some detail.

A further development in the 1980s that has the potential to affect world food markets significantly is the move by centrally planned economies (CPEs) to reform their policies. China's rapid growth in agricultural output in the early 1980s certainly put downward pressure on international prices for some farm commodities (most notably cotton), and there have been fears expressed that Eastern Europe and the USSR might do the same in the 1990s. A third contribution of the present study is its analysis of the likely effects of these developments on world food markets. This involves examining the possibility that the reforms in the CPEs may well generate income growth which thereby expands their food and animal feed demands more rapidly than the expected increases in their domestic production. Accordingly, the study draws on modelling results to provide an indication of the possible price and quantity effects that China's growth may have in the 1990s.

It is not surprising that the combination of these developments—and the embarrassingly large increase in the fiscal costs of food policies in the US and EC—has brought food policies to the forefront of trade discussions and has placed agriculture high on the agenda for the eighth round of multilateral trade negotiations launched in Punta del Este in September 1986 (the so-called Uruguay Round). These negotiations have been extremely difficult, however. One reason is that there are strong political forces at work: there are arguments in advanced industrial economies for the continuation of high levels of support for farmers, in developing countries arguments for low food prices, and, in both rich and poor countries, arguments for intervention to stabilize domestic food prices. A fourth contribution of this study is the shedding of light on the political reasons behind the adoption of economically costly farm policies. It examines the likely effects not only of a total liberalization of such policies but also of phased partial liberalizations which are more feasible politically and yet also more equitable and less costly than present policies.

Finally, a fifth contribution concerns the reluctance of many developing countries to support the inclusion of agricultural trade negotiations in the Uruguay Round. In part, this reluctance is because the governments of those countries fear they will be required to abandon their own policies (which keep domestic food prices low and stable). Ironically, such policies are in place because the relatively small non-farm sector is very influential in the polity of poor agrarian economies. However, another reason for food-importing developing countries not supporting agriculture's inclusion in the Uruguay Round is that they assume that liberalization in industrial countries would make them worse off by raising international food prices and hence raising their food import bill. The present study examines this issue also, and throws considerable doubt on the assumption that such developing economies would be worse off economically from liberalization by industrial countries.

Outline and summary

In short, the three key purposes of this book are to quantify the increasing extent and changing pattern of disarray in world food markets, to explain why such distortionary policies are adopted, and to quantify the effects of existing policies and of less-costly alternative approaches to achieving policy goals.

The study begins with a brief summary of the changing anatomy of world food markets. International food prices are shown to have been on a long-run downward trend throughout this century, falling at a rate of 0.5 per cent per year relative to prices of industrial products. While they have always fluctuated more than industrial product prices, the extent of fluctuation has been especially large in the past two decades, during which they have changed from twice to half their trend value before returning close to trend again. The direction of international food trade has also changed markedly in recent decades. Industrial market economies accounted for a little over half of both world food imports and world food exports in the early 1960s. But, by the mid-1980s, they accounted for only 40 per cent of food imports and 70 per cent of food exports. In other words, industrial countries switched from being slight net importers to massive net exporters of food during those 25 years, while the opposite happened for developing countries.

The long-run decline in real food prices in international markets—and the decline in the relative importance of agriculture as an economy grows—is in part simply a function of the low income elasticity of demand for food. This has contributed to food demand expanding less rapidly than food supplies, as explained in the final section of Chapter 1. The fluctuations in food prices are also partly due to the natural phenomenon of seasonal fluctuations. However, these are by no means the sole reasons for the declining and unstable international prices of food products. A major additional cause is the increasing interference by governments in domestic food markets and in food trade, particularly in industrial countries.

It is true that such government intervention has been a common practice for centuries, but, during the past two or three decades, a number of new features have emerged in the pattern of distortions to agricultural incentives which are further depressing and destabilizing international food prices, raising the industrial countries' dominance in food markets and lowering world economic welfare. Among the important new features, discussed in more detail in Chapter 2, are the following:

- the growth of agricultural protectionism in advanced industrial economies since the 1950s (particularly when expressed in terms of its effect on value added rather than merely on the gross value of farm production);
- the spread of agricultural protectionism to a number of rapidly growing middle-income economies;
- the increased emphasis on using fluctuations in volumes of trade (rather than in stocks or consumption) to stabilize domestic markets, the effect of which is to increase the volatility of international food prices;
- the evolution in highly protected economies, most notably the European Community (EC), of food surpluses which are dumped in foreign markets with the help of variable export subsidies; and
- the use of retaliatory subsidies by the largest food exporter, the United States, in an attempt to raise its farmers' incomes and retain their share of foreign markets threatened by the EC's subsidized exports.

Evidence is presented in Chapter 2 on the extent of the rise in protection in industrial and rapidly growing middle-income countries, as well as on the extent of policy discrimination against agriculture in poorer economies and of insulation of domestic from international markets in rich and poor countries alike.

Why do rich countries tend to set prices of farm products above international levels (sometimes several-fold) while poor countries tend to do the opposite, when farmers are a far smaller proportion of the voting population in the former than in the latter? Does this mean all countries will gradually change their policies increasingly in favour of farmers as their economies develop? Why are some commodities assisted more than others? And why is it that the governments of both rich and poor countries choose to insulate (to varying extents) their domestic markets from international food price fluctuations? These are questions that need to be answered if we are to estimate quantitatively the effects of current and prospective policies. Any analysis of the international impacts of policy reform must account sensibly for trends in the pressures driving governments to intervene in food markets. Furthermore, it is important to represent properly the way the food policies of one country respond to changes in those of another country or country group. Generally, until we understand *why* governments adopt the policies they do, we remain poorly equipped to suggest ways in which societies might achieve their objectives more efficiently.

Chapter 3 seeks to explain the observed pattern and nature of food policies by examining the benefits of intervention to different groups and the costs of influencing the policy-making process. The analysis in that chapter suggests that, in both rich and poor countries, on a per capita basis, the losers are likely to lose little relative to the benefits accruing to those who are already gaining from existing policies. This applies both to the trend level of domestic food prices relative to international food prices (the protection component of food policy) and to the extent to which policies insulate domestic markets from the volatility of international food prices. It suggests a strong need to include both of these aspects of food policy behaviour in any model of food markets.

To understand the effects of these policies (and of structural changes) on world food markets, it is helpful to start by drawing on standard economic theory. This is done in Chapter 4 to determine the parameters on which the direction and magnitude of effects depend. In the majority of cases the directions of effects will be clear *a priori* but, as that chapter illustrates, not only the magnitude but even the direction of some of the effects over time can be determined only by quantifying the relevant parameters and using an empirical simulation model of world food markets.

What is required is a dynamic, stochastic, multi-commodity model of world food markets. Ideally, markets for all other goods and services should also be included in what would then become a global general equilibrium model. In practice, however, this could be achieved only at great expense or by suppressing much of the commodity detail among the various interdependent food and feed markets. The model used here is a revised and updated version of a partial equilibrium model that was first developed by Tyers (1984, 1985). Initially the model included only grain and meat but it was expanded to include dairy products and sugar for the preparation of a background paper for the World Bank's *World Development Report 1986*. It has been further updated and revised for the purposes of this volume, and is detailed in Chapter 5 and Appendix 1. The model has the following distinguishing features:

- it is global in coverage, involving 30 countries or country groups spanning the world, so that international as well as domestic effects of policy, or structural changes in one or more countries or commodity markets, can be determined endogenously;
- it incorporates the cross-effects in both production and consumption between the interdependent grain, livestock product and sugar markets;
- it has a dynamic mode, in which the effects of policy or structural changes in a particular year can be simulated for every subsequent year, as well as a static equilibrium mode which can simulate the effects of those changes after any desired degree of adjustment;
- it is stochastic in that production uncertainty and hence price variability is included via probability distributions associated with each commodity's production level;
- stockholding behaviour is endogenous, based on empirical analysis of stock level responses to price and quantity changes in each country;
- policy is endogenous to the extent that price transmission equations are used to incorporate the two key features of each country's food price policies: the protection component, which raises the trend level of food prices faced by domestic producers and consumers around which prices fluctuate, and the stabilization component, which allows trade fluctuations to limit the degree to which domestic prices change in response to shifts in domestic supply or in international prices; and

- it is able to estimate not only the price and quantity effects of policy or structural changes in world food markets but also the effects on economic welfare.

Following the description of the simulation model, the rest of the study is largely concerned with its use in quantifying the effects of existing and prospective policies and structural changes on world food markets and welfare. This begins in Chapter 6 with an empirical analysis aimed at quantifying the effects of current policies. Specifically, it reports estimates of the price, quantity and economic welfare effects of distortions to world food markets as they existed in 1980–82 and as they are forecast by the model to 1990 and 2000 (assuming the policy trends of the 1980s continue unreformed). A major finding is that not only are the costs of current protectionist policies in industrial countries very high in terms of economic welfare forgone, but they are escalating over time. If current policies were to remain in place through the 1990s, their annual cost to the industrial economies and globally would be more than double what it was in the early 1980s. These policies are also becoming increasingly inefficient in transferring welfare to low-income farmers. To boost the income of the poorest 30 per cent of farmers in industrial countries by, say, $1,000 it is costing consumers and taxpayers in those countries more than $10,000 via current policies. This is largely because current price-based protectionist policies tend to bestow benefits in proportion to production, so large farmers receive most of the transfer.

Another important effect of the current policies of industrial countries is that they not only depress the average level of food prices in international markets (through reducing those countries' excess demand for imports) but they also increase the year-to-year instability of prices in those markets. This comes about because current policies tend to cause the country's food trade to fluctuate in order to maintain a stable domestic market for food. The combined effect of many industrial countries adopting such policies is that international food prices were depressed by one-seventh in the early 1980s and the year-to-year variation of those prices was about 50 per cent higher than it otherwise would have been. By the 1990s these effects will be about half as large again if current policies continue.

Thus the effects of these protectionist policies are not restricted to the countries imposing them. On the contrary, food-exporting countries such as Argentina, Australia, New Zealand and Thailand are hurt badly, particularly by the policies of the European Community. The EC often argues that the international price-depressing effect of its policies helps consumers in poor countries, and indeed helps them more than it harms farmers in those countries, because developing countries as a group are net importers of temperate staple foods. That view is called into question in this study and is found wanting. It is true that developing countries as a group are net importers of food staples, but they would be net exporters in the absence of the protectionist policies of industrial countries. Furthermore, since developing countries' own policies tend to discriminate against agriculture, higher food prices in poor countries resulting from less farm protection in industrial countries, and assuming that at least some of any international price change would be transmitted domestically by developing countries) would tend to draw back some of the resources in the protected industrial sector for socially more productive use in the agricultural sector. Together, these two factors are sufficient, according to our results, to demonstrate that current food policies of industrial countries are harming rather than helping developing countries in the 1990s in the narrow economic welfare sense of income forgone. This is especially so if it is assumed that farm productivity growth is positively correlated with the level of producer prices.

If a broader definition of welfare is used, which incorporates equity, risk and food security concerns, then the harm done to people in poor countries by continuing with agricultural protectionism in rich countries is even greater. In terms of equity, it must be remembered that the majority of people in developing countries—especially poorer folk—are members of farm households and are net sellers of staple foods, while the net buyers of food are mainly relatively affluent urban consumers. Hence the price-depressing effect of agricultural protection in industrial countries almost certainly worsens the inequality of spending power within poor countries. Secondly, given the importance of food in poor agrarian economies, both producers and consumers of food are likely to prefer food prices to be more rather than less stable through time. Thus, the welfare of all people in poor countries is reduced by the greater international market instability resulting from farm protection policies of industrial countries. Thirdly, since these policies reduce food self-sufficiency in poor countries from above to below 100 per cent, they reduce their perceived food security.

It is true that developing countries' own policies also affect welfare, as well as distorting the international market for food. Since their policies tend to discriminate against agriculture, they amplify the effects on domestic welfare of industrial country policies. They also contribute to the instability of international food markets because their policies insulate their domestic market to some degree from fluctuations in international food markets. Our results suggest that their policies may be contributing more to the instability of those international markets than industrial country policies. Indeed, the combined effect of domestic market insulation in both groups of countries is so large that if they were simultaneously to cease insulating their domestic markets, international (and hence domestic) food prices would fluctuate less than has been the case historically in their (partially insulated) domestic markets. The perceived need for any one country's insulating policies exists only because of the destabilizing effect internationally of other countries' insulating policies! Thus, the probability that developing countries will adopt less interventionist policies towards agriculture would be higher if industrial countries themselves were less interventionist.

The increasing chaos in international food markets is prompting lightly distorted economies to pressure heavily distorted ones to reform their policies. As a result, numerous reform proposals have been advocated as part of the 1986–92 Uruguay Round of multilateral trade negotiations under the auspices of GATT. These have typically suggested partial and gradual liberalizations of food markets in industrial countries. In order to explore the domestic and international effects of such proposals over the 1990s, Chapter 7 presents results from the dynamic version of our world food model for two scenarios. The main scenario involves the gradual reduction of the agricultural protection levels of 1990 in industrial countries such that, by the year 2000, they are only half as large as in 1990 and hence close to the level of the early 1980s.

As one would expect, such a reform would raise international food prices and reduce their instability, thereby boosting welfare in lightly assisted food-exporting countries. However, two surprising results emerge. One is that, even though food production levels in liberalizing countries are projected to be lower than they otherwise would have been, they are nevertheless higher than they were in 1990. Thus, despite the considerable extent of the liberalization in this scenario, its negative influence on production each year in almost all cases is less than the assumed exogenous growth in production due to normal technological changes in these countries. Even in Japan, where some absolute reduction in grain output is projected to occur in a scenario of partial liberalization, there is an expansion in livestock production (due to the lower price of feedgrain and lower profitability of grain production) the value of which more than offsets the reduction in grain output. Moreover, the scenario modelled does not allow for any reduction in the extent to which the Japanese government encourages farmers to direct paddy land to non-rice production. If that incentive were gradually eliminated, the results suggest that rice production may well continue to be sufficient to meet domestic requirements even at lower domestic prices. This is part of the second surprising result to emerge from this partial and phased liberalization exercise, namely, that, for many of the food items that are politically sensitive because of food security concerns, self-sufficiency would not plummet but rather remain close to 100 per cent. These results suggest that there is less cause for concern about the domestic political effects of gradually reforming the agricultural policies of rich countries than is sometimes assumed.

Before turning finally, in Chapter 9, to discuss the policy implications of these and earlier findings, Chapter 8 addresses the vexed question of the impacts that reforms in the (formerly) centrally planned economies may be expected to have on world food markets in the 1990s. Since China is the most populous of those economies and has already had a decade of partial market reform, most of the chapter assesses its experience and prospects. The raising of farm product prices, the legislation of free food markets and the introduction of the household responsibility system in the countryside soon after the reforms began in late 1978, enabled a massive 80 per cent expansion in China's agricultural output over a decade. But, since real incomes roughly doubled over that period, food consumption also rose dramatically—especially of luxuries such as livestock products which require a more intensive use of grain feeding. As a result of the rapid expansion of its economy, China's self-sufficiency in farm products is falling as its comparative advantage switches from primary products to light manufactures.

The macroeconomic problems of the late 1980s in China, and the Tiananmen Square incident in May–June 1989, brought that reform process and rapid economic growth to a halt, at least temporarily. If the moves toward a more open economy are to be resumed, it is feasible that incomes in China could again double over the next decade. On the other hand, if the recent return to heavy-handed central control continues, China's economic growth in the 1990s may be only half as large as it was during Mao's time. The implications of these two different scenarios are explored in Chapter 8 using our world food model. The optimistic scenario involves faster food consumption growth but also faster food production growth. The net effect on food self-sufficiency is thus much the same as for the pessimistic scenario, which is a slight fall over the 1990s of about half a per cent per year. Because of the larger absolute amount of imports in the optimistic scenario, however, international food prices would be higher in this case, but only by as much as an estimated 5 per cent.

The other major centrally planned Asian economies are Vietnam and North Korea. Being extremely densely populated, they will lose their comparative advantage in agriculture if they open up their markets and grow rapidly. Vietnam, which is still extremely poor, could begin this process by expanding its rice exports—particularly if the reform process there were to be like China's and, at the outset, were to involve much greater liberalization of agricultural rather than industrial markets. But, like its neighbours Thailand and China, its comparative advantage would gradually switch to light manufactures, if its capital stock were to grow rapidly, and it would very likely join the ranks of the next generation of newly industrializing Asian economies and eventually become a net food importer. That same pattern of change would occur even faster for a reforming North Korean economy.

The eventual pattern of trade specialization of the East European and USSR economies, should they open up in a substantial way in the 1990s, is more difficult to assess. The assessment is difficult partly because they do not have the extreme factor endowment ratios of East Asian economies, again in part because their economies have been grossly distorted for so long that present production and trade patterns provide little guide to their natural comparative advantages, and partly because their trade will be affected to some as-yet-unknown extent by the preferential access they are likely to have to markets of numerous Western economies. About all that can be said with reasonable certainty is that, in the short run, the impact of any substantial reforms will be to destabilize international food markets to some extent as their domestic markets struggle towards new equilibria. This underlines the need to bring greater stability to international food markets by reforming the agricultural policies of industrial market economies in the 1990s.

After summarizing the main findings from the study, the final chapter draws out some of the policy implications for industrial, developing and centrally planned economies. It concludes on a somewhat optimistic note by looking at recent developments that are helping to weaken the tendency for agricultural protection to continue growing inexorably, and closes with some suggestions for further research.

ONE

*WORLD FOOD MARKETS AND
THEIR BEHAVIOUR*

1

Changing Patterns of World Food Prices, Production and Trade

One of the striking features of world food markets is that the international price of food relative to industrial products has been on a long-run downward trend throughout this century. Food prices have always fluctuated considerably around that long-run trend, which is perhaps not unexpected given the vagaries of the weather. But, since the 1960s, two other features have become significant. First, the extent of fluctuation in international food prices has increased considerably in recent times, when falling transport and communication costs would lead one to expect the opposite; and second, the share of industrial market economies in world food exports has risen while centrally planned and developing economies have become increasingly dependent on food imports despite rapid growth in the latter's production of food.

This chapter begins by documenting these features of world food markets. It then examines the extent to which they can be explained by natural economic forces and finds the standard explanations wanting in some respects. This suggests that unnatural forces, namely government policy interventions, are also influencing these markets, evidence for which is then sought in Chapter 2.

To keep the task manageable, this study is restricted to the main staple foods of agricultural origin (as distinct from marine origin) which are internationally traded and frequently the

Table 1.1: Shares of various commodities in the value of world food[a] trade, 1980 to 1982 (per cent)

	Industrial market economies		Developing economies		World
	Exports	**Imports**	**Exports**	**Imports**	
Wheat	14	7	2	20	10
Coarse grain	11	9	3	9	9
Rice	2	1	6	7	3
Ruminant meat	7	6	3	4	6
Non-ruminant meat	4	3	1	3	3
Dairy products	10	6	-	9	8
Sugar	4	7	17	11	8
Total of above	**52**	**39**	**32**	**63**	**47**
(Share of food in all agricultural trade	76	72	74	77	75)
(Share of food in all commodity trade	9	9	9	10	9)

[a] Food is defined as SITC 0, 1, 22 and 4; non-food agriculture is SITC 2 less 22, 27 and 28.

Source: Food and Agriculture Organisation, *Trade Yearbook*, Rome, 1983.

subject of trade disputes. These are the various grains, edible livestock products and sugar.[1] In what follows, these will be often sub-divided into seven commodity groups: wheat, coarse grain, rice, meat of ruminants (cattle and sheep), meat of non-ruminants (pigs and poultry), dairy products and sugar. As Table 1.1 shows, these products account for about half the value of world trade in raw and processed food, which in turn is about three-quarters of all agricultural trade and one-tenth of global trade in all commodities. These staple foods are the principal sources of nourishment in rich and poor countries alike, both directly and indirectly via the feeding of grain to animals. While the grains dominate in trade, livestock products dominate in the value of production and consumption. Even in developing economies, where people are less able to afford the relative luxury of meat and dairy products, those products account for 40 per cent of the value of food consumption at domestic prices (Table 1.2).

Table 1.2: Shares of various commodities in the value of food production and consumption at domestic prices, major country groups, 1985 (per cent)

	Wheat	Coarse grain	Rice	Ruminant meat	Non-ruminant meat	Dairy products	Sugar	Total
Industrial market economies								
production	9	14	4	21	24	24	4	100
consumption	5	14	4	23	25	24	5	100
Centrally planned Europe								
production	11	15	1	13	17	39	5	100
consumption	13	17	1	14	18	29	9	100
Developing economies								
production	14	14	26	10	13	15	8	100
consumption	16	14	23	10	13	17	8	100
World								
production	11	14	12	15	19	24	6	100
consumption	11	15	11	16	18	22	7	100

Source: See Appendix 2.

1.1 The long-run decline and increasing fluctuations in world food prices

The empirical evidence on the long-run trend in the price of primary products relative to manufactures has been the subject of debate for decades. The issue was brought to a head by Prebisch's (1964) claim that the trend was definitely downward, a claim that stimulated more extensive empirical studies. While the issue cannot yet be considered closed, the weight of available evidence strongly supports the view that food prices at least have been steadily declining this century relative to industrial product prices.[2] One comprehensive set of price series for the period since 1900 has been compiled by the World Bank (Grilli and Yang 1988). For the subset of commodities of interest in this study, namely the traded staple foods (grains, meats, dairy products and sugar), the Bank's real price index shows a clear downward trend of about 0.5 per cent per year (Figure 1.1).

In addition to a real decline over the long term, it is evident from Figure 1.1 that the relative price of food in international markets has fluctuated substantially from year to year around the declining trend. This might be expected, given that supplies are dependent on the vagaries of the weather. However, with rapidly declining real costs of domestic and international transportation and communication over the past one hundred years and the consequent closer integration of the world economy, one might expect these price fluctuations to have diminished over time. Yet, if anything, the opposite is true. In particular, international food prices since World War II appear to have become more unstable, with their levels changing during the past two decades from twice to half their trend value and back to trend again. This has been of concern to rich and poor countries alike. It is one of the reasons governments look to intervene to insulate their domestic markets from the rest of the world. As will become clear in subsequent chapters, however, the irony is that such policy action simply worsens this problem for other countries.

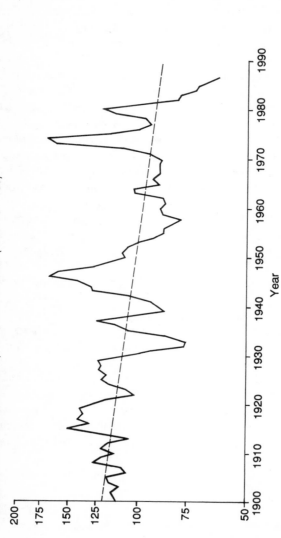

Figure 1.1: Real international food prices, 1900 to 1987[a] (1977-79 = 100)

[a] An index of export prices in US dollars for cereals, meats, dairy products and sugar, deflated by the US producer price index (primarily for industrial products), with weights based on the importance of each product in global exports, 1977-79.

Source: Authors' calculations based mainly on price series made available by the World Bank's Economic Analysis and Projections Department (see Grilli and Yang 1988).

1.2   The increasing dominance of industrial countries in world food exports

In the early 1960s, industrial market economies accounted for almost 60 per cent of world food imports and for a little over half of world food exports. By the mid-1980s, however, they accounted for only 40 per cent of food imports and 70 per cent of exports. In other words, these countries switched from being minor net importers to massive exporters of food. This has come about partly because the USSR has become more dependent on food imports, but mainly because of changes in poorer economies. The contribution of developing economies to world food exports fell from 35 to 25 per cent between the early 1960s and the mid-1980s while their share of imports rose from 27 to 41 per cent (Figures 1.2 and 1.3).

Figure 1.2:   The distribution of world food trade, 1961–64 and 1983–86

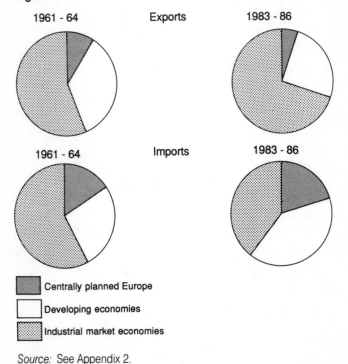

1961 - 64   Exports   1983 - 86

1961 - 64   Imports   1983 - 86

⬛ Centrally planned Europe

◻ Developing economies

▦ Industrial market economies

Source: See Appendix 2.

Figure 1.3: Food self-sufficiency[a] in industrial market economies, centrally planned Europe and the developing economies, 1961-64 and 1983-86

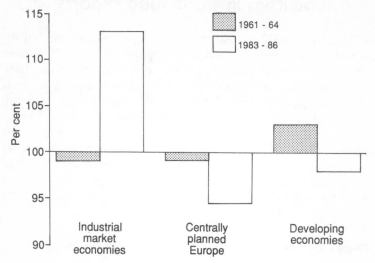

a Production as a percentage of consumption of grains, meats, milk products and sugar, each valued at their average price in international markets in 1980-82.
Source: See Appendix 2.

Much of this change in world food trade occurred in the 1970s. Between the periods 1970-74 and 1983-86 the volume of food imported by industrial market economies increased by only one-tenth whereas it doubled for both developing economies and centrally planned Europe. Moreover, the changes were not concentrated in any one commodity market. As is clear from Table 1.3, these same overall trends apply also to almost every one of the seven individual food commodity groups shown.

To begin to understand these trends, it is necessary first to look at underlying changes in food production and consumption in each of these country groups. Figure 1.4 reveals that the explanation does *not* lie in slow production growth in developing and centrally planned economies. In fact, food production in those economies has increased substantially more than it has in industrial market economies. Rather, the explanation is that consumption growth in the former country groups is outstripping production growth, whereas the opposite is true in industrial countries. Even the growth in food consumption

Table 1.3: World trade shares and food self-sufficiency of industrial market economies, centrally planned Europe and the developing economies, 1961–64 and 1983–86 (per cent)

	Wheat	Coarse grain	Rice	Ruminant meat	Non-ruminant meat	Dairy products	Sugar	Total[a]
Industrial market economies								
Share of world exports								
1961–64	83	62	34	56	77	91	10	56
1983–86	90	80	33	76	72	95	14	70
Share of world imports								
1961–64	29	77	36	79	84	68	64	58
1983–86	16	32	44	57	68	59	38	40
Self-sufficiency[b]								
1961–64	139	98	100	97	99	103	69	99
1983–86	182	122	115	106	102	108	87	113
Centrally planned Europe								
Share of world exports								
1961–64	8	12	1	10	19	7	3	9
1983–86	3	3	1	6	14	4	-	9
Share of world imports								
1961–64	22	11	12	12	9	4	21	16
1983–86	25	26	8	12	10	6	34	20
Self-sufficiency[b]								
1961–64	98	103	37	100	101	100	85	99
1983–86	88	92	84	97	102	99	72	94

(continued)

Table 1.3 (continued)

	Wheat	Coarse grain	Rice	Ruminant meat	Non-ruminant meat	Dairy products	Sugar	Total[a]
Developing economies[c]								
Share of world exports								
1961–64	8	26	66	33	5	3	87	35
1983–86	7	18	67	18	13	2	86	25
Share of world imports								
1961–64	50	12	52	10	7	28	16	27
1983–86	58	43	48	31	22	35	28	41
Self-sufficiency[b]								
1961–64	81	105	102	105	100	96	135	103
1983–86	82	93	102	96	99	91	119	98

a The aggregate percentages for the seven commodity groups shown are weighted averages with weights based on average prices in international markets in 1980-82.
b Production as a percentage of consumption.
c Includes high-income, oil-exporting countries of the Middle East.
Source: See Appendix 2.

per capita has been about twice as fast in developing and centrally planned economies as in industrial countries, as shown by the shaded areas of Figure 1.4. This has been especially so in the 1970s: between the periods 1970–74 and 1983–86 per capita consumption of these foods increased 25 per cent for developing countries but rose only 6 per cent for industrial market economies and 10 per cent for centrally planned Europe. Again, this development is occurring in virtually all of the seven commodity groups, not merely in a subset of them (Table 1.4).

Within the industrial country group, it is useful to consider three sub-groups: (i) the traditional food exporters of Australia, Canada, New Zealand and the United States; (ii) the more densely populated countries of Western Europe; and (iii) very densely populated Japan. Figure 1.5 shows that food production has grown much more rapidly in the latter two sub-groups since the early 1960s. Food and feed consumption has also grown more rapidly in Western Europe and especially Japan. The

Figure 1.4: Increase in food production and consumption, total and per capita, major country groups, 1961–64 to 1983–86[a]

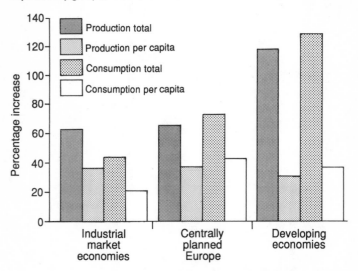

a The percentage by which production (consumption) in 1983–86 exceeded production (consumption) in 1961–64 of grains, meat, milk products and sugar, each valued at their average price in international markets in 1980–82.
Source: See Appendix 2.

Table 1.4: Increase in production and consumption of various foods in industrial market economies, centrally planned Europe and the developing economies,[a] 1961–64 to 1983–86 (per cent)

	Wheat	Coarse grain	Rice	Ruminant meat	Non-ruminant meat	Dairy products	Sugar	Total
Industrial market economies								
Production	94	79	74	41	92	23	64	63
Consumption	48	44	51	29	86	17	32	45
Centrally planned Europe								
Production	42	73	515	80	101	55	21	67
Consumption	58	93	270	86	100	57	43	74
Developing economies								
Production	210	93	102	59	310	88	96	120
Consumption	205	118	103	74	310	98	123	131

[a] The percentage by which production (consumption) in 1983–86 exceeded production (consumption) in 1961–64. The final column shows the changes in the aggregate for these products, each valued at their average price in international markets in 1980–82.

Source: See Appendix 2.

Figure 1.5: Increase in food production and consumption, various industrial economies, 1961-64 to 1983-86[a]

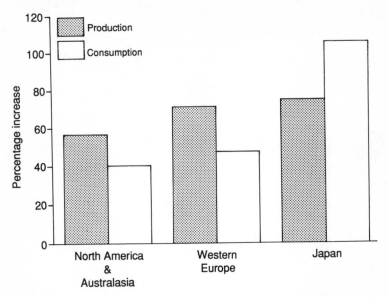

[a] The percentage by which production (consumption) in 1983-86 exceeded production (consumption) in 1961-64 of grains, meat, milk products and sugar, each valued at their average price in international markets in 1980-82.
Source: See Appendix 2.

impact of these changes on each sub-group's net exports is illustrated in Figure 1.6. Australasia and North America account for a little over half of world exports of these foods (net of their imports) but that share is little different now from what it was three decades ago. Japan's share of world food imports grew considerably in the decade to the early 1970s, but fell somewhat in the subsequent decade so that its share is now one-sixth. Western Europe, however, has shown a dramatic turnaround, from accounting for about 40 per cent of world food imports in the early 1960s to now contributing almost 10 per cent of world *exports* (net of its imports). Again, these changes apply to each of the main food product groups and are not simply accounted for by one or two commodities. Overall, Western Europe's food self-sufficiency changed from 90 per cent in 1961-64 to 105 per cent in 1983-86.

Figure 1.6: Shares of various industrial market economies in world food trade, 1961–64, 1970–74 and 1983–86

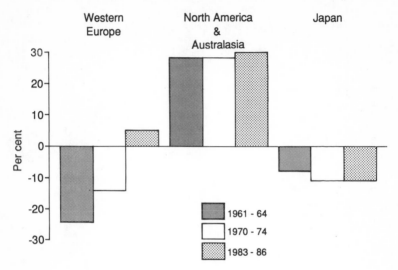

a Quantities valued at average international prices in 1980–82.
Source: See Appendix 2.

It is not surprising that food consumption is growing less rapidly in the higher income countries. One would expect food consumption growth to be lower there for at least three reasons: slower population growth, slower income growth and a lower income elasticity of demand for food. Since the early 1960s, population growth in industrial countries has been only one-third as fast, and real per capita income growth only two-thirds as fast, as in developing countries (see World Bank 1988). Moreover, because consumers tend to spend a less than proportionate and declining share of their income on food as their incomes rise (the income elasticity of demand for food is less than unity and declines as incomes increase), food consumption would grow more slowly in industrial countries even if its population and per capita income growth rates were the same as for developing countries. This is especially true of the relatively high-protein foods being examined in this study, because developing country consumers substitute them for low-protein non-tradable starchy foods, such as rootcrops, as their incomes rise and urbanization increases.

Similarly, within the industrial country group, one would expect Japan, the lowest income country in that group in 1960 and the one whose income has grown fastest, to enjoy the fastest increase in food consumption, whereas such an increase would not be expected for Australasia and North America which had the highest incomes in 1960 and the highest levels of per capita food consumption. In 1961–64, Japan's grain, meat, milk and sugar consumption per person was in total only one-third that for Australasia and North America, and even Western Europe's was only three-quarters of the latter's.

With respect to production, the adoption in developing countries of imported and/or newly developed technologies is largely responsible for the fast growth in their food production. A glance at Table 1.5 suggests that Western Europe and Japan have not been able to expand their arable land area but, like the developing countries, they have improved their grain yields per hectare and their livestock output at faster rates than Australasia and North America.

Table 1.5: Growth in grain and livestock output,[a] yield and harvested area, major country groups, 1959 to 1985 (per cent per year)

	Grains			Meat and milk production
	harvested area	yield per hectare[b]	output	
Australasia and North America	0.9	1.8 (3.5)	2.8	1.5
Western Europe and Japan	-0.3	2.5 (4.3)	2.2	3.9
All industrial market economies	0.5	2.0 (3.7)	2.6	1.6
Centrally planned Europe	-0.1	2.2 (2.0)	2.1	2.9
Developing economies	0.7	2.7 (1.9)	3.3	2.5

[a] Grain output is measured in tonnes and livestock product output is aggregated by valuing production at constant 1980–82 international prices.

[b] Average yields in 1985 are shown in parentheses in tonnes per hectare.

Sources: The area and yield data are from the Food and Agriculture Organisation, *Production Yearbook*, Rome, various issues; the output data sources are detailed in Appendix 2 to this volume.

Within the industrial country group, why has food production grown so rapidly in Western Europe and Japan? Being much more densely populated than Australasia and North America they have less comparative advantage in food production (Anderson 1983c). Moreover, for reasons explained in the next section, one might expect their more rapid industrialization and income growth to have been accompanied by less rapid growth in agricultural production. As we will see in Chapter 2, much of the explanation for the opposite finding has to do with the relative decline in farmers' real market prices in North America, Australasia and in many developing countries, a decline that has been offset in Western Europe and Japan through increased assistance to their own farmers.

1.3   Reasons for the relative decline in food prices and changes in comparative advantage[3]

Before turning to examine the pattern of price distortions in different countries and its effect on international prices and trade (Chapter 2), it is helpful first to generalize the likely effects of industrialization and economic growth at home and abroad on the fortunes of a country's farm sector and on its food self-sufficiency in the absence of government intervention. We proceed in stages.

Consider first a closed economy with only two sectors, agriculture and non-agriculture. If productivity growth is occurring equally rapidly in both sectors, supply curves would shift out at the same rate, as in Figure 1.7. Here we assume the two supply curves coincide initially, and hence they also coincide subsequent to the productivity growth. But, because people typically spend a declining proportion of their income on food as their incomes increase, demand grows less for agricultural products than for other goods. Thus, the demand curves are shown in Figure 1.7 to shift to the right to different extents in the two sectors. The net result of these two sets of changes is as follows: output of both sectors rises, but less so for agriculture, and the price of agricultural products falls

Figure 1.7: Changes in supply of and demand for agricultural and non-agricultural goods in a growing economy[a]

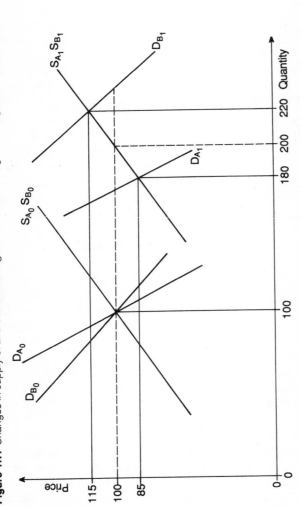

[a] D_A (D_B) is the demand curve for agricultural (non-agricultural) goods, while S_A (S_B) is the supply curve for agricultural (non-agricultural) goods.

Source: Adapted from Johnson (1973:Figure 5.2).

relative to the price of non-agricultural products (the moreso the relatively price inelastic is the demand for food). Hence the share of agriculture in aggregate national product falls.

In the illustrated example, agriculture's initial share of GDP was 50 per cent. After the equi-proportional productivity growth has taken place in the two sectors, the increase in the quantities supplied would be the same if prices for the two sets of goods remained unchanged. However, the growth in incomes that results from this productivity growth leads to the demand for agricultural goods shifting less than that for non-agricultural goods. Equilibrium in the two markets requires that agricultural output expands only 80 per cent and non-agricultural output 120 per cent in the case illustrated, and that the price of agricultural goods falls 15 per cent while that of non-agricultural goods rises 15 per cent. Thus agriculture's share of GDP becomes: 85 x 180/((85 x 180) + (115 x 220)) = 38 per cent, compared with 50 per cent initially.

This model is appropriate not only for a closed national economy but also for the world economy as a whole; that is, it suggests that international prices for agricultural products relative to non-agricultural products are likely to decline over time as the world economy grows. This is indeed what has happened, as we have seen from Figure 1.1 above.[4]

The effects of these tendencies in a closed economy can be seen also from Figure 1.8, where AB represents the production possibilities today and U captures the community's preferences in the sense that society would be indifferent about consuming at any of the points along U. The tangency point E is the equilibrium outcome where supply equals demand for both agricultural and all other goods. The equilibrium price of all other goods in terms of agricultural goods is given by the slope of price line 1.

Suppose productivity growth or factor expansion then shifts the production possibility curve out. If it shifts that curve out equi-proportionately, to A'B', the growth in income that accompanies that productivity growth will lead to a new equilibrium at E', where the share of income spent on agricultural products is less than before. Even though the *quantity* of food consumed may have risen (from F to F'), the quantity of other goods consumed has risen by a larger proportion (from M to M'). This is a direct result of the assumption that food has an income

Figure 1.8: Effects of agricultural and non-agricultural growth in a closed economy

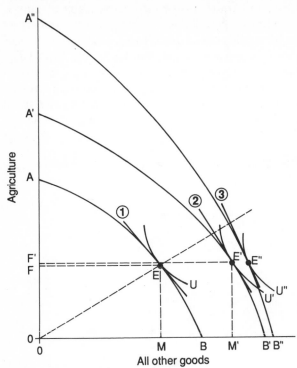

Source: Adapted from Anderson (1987).

elasticity of demand that is less than unity. As a result of this change, the equilibrium price of all other goods relative to agricultural goods has increased (price line 2 is steeper than price line 1). Thus, in this simple model with no intermediate inputs, since national product is price times quantity summed over all products, agriculture's share of national product must have fallen. And it could fall even more if the increase in productive capacity is greater in agriculture than in other sectors. In that case the move could be from E to E″ rather than to E′, where price line 3 is even steeper than price line 2.[5]

But what of the case of an open agrarian economy which can trade all of its products internationally at those terms of trade? Suppose the domestic terms of trade in this agrarian economy are given by the slope of line 1 in Figure 1.9 (assuming the economy to be closed to foreign trade), and that the international terms of trade are given by the slope of line 3. Then, if this economy opened itself to international trade, the production point would shift from E to E_0. The importance of agriculture would increase and the country would export E_0T units of agricultural produce and with the foreign exchange proceeds would import TC_0 units of other goods. If growth occurred in this economy but not elsewhere, agriculture's share of national product would rise or fall depending on whether

Figure 1.9: Effects of growth in an open economy producing and consuming only tradable goods

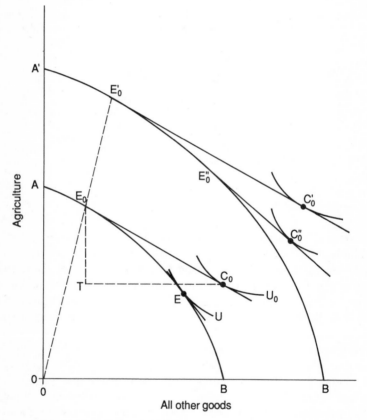

Source: Adapted from Anderson (1987).

that growth was biased toward farm or non-farm production. If that growth was sectorally unbiased, agriculture's share would remain unchanged, as at E'_0 in Figure 1.9. However, if growth also occurred in the rest of the world in the manner depicted in Figure 1.8, the international terms of trade would have deteriorated and so E''_0 rather than E'_0 would be the new equilibrium. More generally, if economic growth is occurring abroad, the agricultural sector of a small open economy would decline unless that economy's own growth is sufficiently biased towards agriculture for the quantity changes to more than offset the adverse change in the terms of trade. This agricultural bias in growth would have to be even stronger in a large open economy because its own contribution to world agricultural exports would depress the terms of trade even further.

The above model assumes all products are tradable internationally. In reality, however, a large part of each economy involves the production and consumption of non-tradable goods and services. These are items for which the costs of overcoming barriers to trading internationally—especially transport costs—are prohibitively expensive. The price of non-tradables is determined by domestic demand and supply conditions because, in equilibrium, the quantity of non-tradables demanded, unlike tradables, has to equal the quantity supplied. If one were to combine the two tradable sectors considered above into one super-sector of tradables, then the above conclusion that agriculture's share of GDP is likely to decline over time is even stronger if it can be demonstrated that the share of tradables in GDP is also likely to decline in growing economies.

Available evidence suggests that the income elasticity of demand for services (which make up the vast majority of non-tradables) is well above unity in developing countries and tends to converge towards unity as incomes grow.[6] In other words, any increase in income for developing countries leads to a more than proportionate increase in the demand for services, which in turn means the demand for tradable goods tends to grow less than proportionately. So, if productivity growth is equally rapid for non-tradables as for tradables, but demand for non-tradables expands more rapidly while demand for tradables expands less rapidly than aggregate output, both the price and quantity of non-tradables relative to tradables will increase.[7] Thus, the share of tradables in GDP declines.

Figure 1.8 can be used to illustrate the above point simply by changing the axes from 'agriculture' to 'tradables' and from 'all other goods' to 'non-tradables'. Sectorally unbiased growth would cause the equilibrium point to switch from E to E'. The real exchange rate appreciation (the increase in the price of non-tradables relative to tradables as given by the slopes of the price lines through E and E') and the larger increase in the quantity of non-tradables relative to tradables that are produced, can then be seen from the diagram. If production possibilities expanded more in the tradables super-sector than in non-tradables,[8] it would be even more likely that the tradables' share of GDP would decline, as illustrated in Figure 1.8 by the move to point E".

Since the earlier discussion suggests agriculture's share of tradables' production is likely to decline in a growing economy, and since this discussion suggests that the super-sector's share of tradables in a growing economy is also likely to decline, it appears even more likely that agriculture's share of total GDP— tradables plus non-tradables—will decline over time. For that *not* to happen, agricultural growth has to be sufficiently greater than growth in other sectors so as to offset the effects of the decline in the relative price of agricultural goods.[9] In the extreme case of productivity growth being confined solely to the non-farm tradables sector, we know from the standard booming-sector theory that the farm sector is highly likely to shrink not only relatively but also in absolute terms. Agriculture in that case loses mobile resources both directly, as resources are attracted into the booming sector, and indirectly because the increasing national income expands the demand for non-tradables and so mobile resources are drawn from agriculture to non-tradables also (Corden 1984; Neary and van Wijnbergen 1985).

The above reasoning is sufficient also for explaining the decline in agriculture's share of employment, unless labour productivity growth is much slower in agriculture than in other sectors. Where labour productivity has been growing *more* rapidly on farms than in non-farm jobs, as appears to have been the case at least in industrial countries during recent decades, there is even more reason to expect agriculture to become a less important employer.

One might also expect agriculture's share of exports to decline with economic growth, but this tendency is likely to be weaker than that for agriculture's shares of GDP and employment. To explore this, consider again a small economy within an open global economy in which the international price of agricultural goods relative to other goods is declining over time because productivity growth in the rest of the world is not biased strongly enough against agriculture to offset the effect of the relatively slow growth in food demand. If this small economy is not growing, then clearly the share of agriculture in exports will decline: the price change would discourage domestic food production and encourage domestic food consumption, while the opposite would occur in the domestic market for non-farm tradables. If this economy **is** growing and if its productivity growth is sectorally unbiased, then this tendency for agriculture's share of exports to fall would be weakened because domestic demand would grow less rapidly for food than for non-food products. It would be weakened further if productivity growth was faster in agriculture than non-agriculture in this economy. The latter two considerations somewhat reduce the probability that agriculture's share of exports will decline as an economy grows.

This theory has strong empirical support from both cross-sectional and time series evidence.[10] The negative relationship between agriculture's shares of gross domestic product (GDP), employment (EMP) and exports (EXP) on the one hand, and income per capita (YPC) on the other, are very significant statistically. These shares are also negatively associated with population density per unit of agricultural land (PDA), although significantly so only for the export share equation. This is clear from the following regression equations, from Anderson (1987), which are based on World Bank data for 1981 for 70 countries with populations in excess of 1 million (t-values in parentheses):

$$GDP = 87 - 9.2\ln YPC, \qquad \bar{R}^2 = 0.80 \qquad (1.1)$$
$$(6.7)$$

$$EMP = 179 - 18.5\ln YPC, \qquad \bar{R}^2 = 0.80 \qquad (1.2)$$
$$(16.6)$$

$$EXP = 152 - 9.5\ln YPC - 8.5\ln PDA, \quad \bar{R}^2 = 0.45 \qquad (1.3)$$
$$(5.1) \qquad (4.7)$$

1.4   Changes in food self-sufficiency as an economy grows

What determines whether a country is a net agricultural exporter or importer at a point in time? And how will that position change with economic growth at home and abroad? In other words, in terms of Figure 1.9, what determines whether E_0 is to the left or right of C_0 and hence E, and whether E''_0 is to the left or right of C''_0?

The standard theory of comparative advantage suggests that, under various assumptions (including no distortions to producer incentives), a country tends to export commodities which require relatively intensive use of the country's relatively abundant factors of production. In the decade following World War II, empirical tests failed to support this model of comparative advantage in its simplest form, giving rise to numerous attempts to modify the theory to make it more applicable to the real world. Many of the earlier modifications have been synthesized by Johnson (1968) in his Wicksell Lectures. He suggests that the two-sector, two-factor, Heckscher–Ohlin–Samuelson model is more applicable, at least for manufactured goods, if capital is defined broadly to include not only physical capital equipment but also human skills, social capital, technological and organizational knowledge, and natural resources, while labour is defined in the narrow sense of human labour time availability. The relative capital intensity of different activities is then reflected in flow terms by relative value added per unit of labour time input. A country's exports would then be more intensive in the use of capital broadly defined in this way, the larger the country's availability of various forms of capital relative to the number of workers. Balassa (1979), Garnaut and Anderson (1980), Balassa and Bauwens (1988) and others have shown that this theory is consistent with the evidence on the changing pattern of comparative advantage in manufactures.

Krueger (1977) has further modified the model to allow it to better explain trade in primary products as well.[11] This modification separates out natural resources from Johnson's broad definition of capital, and integrates the model with the Ricardo-Viner specific-capital model that has become popular again (following Jones 1971). The model then becomes one of an economy with two tradable sectors, producing primary products and manufactures, and three factors of production: natural resources (which are specific to the primary sector), capital (which is specific to the manufacturing sector), and labour (which is used in both sectors, and is intersectorally mobile and exhibits diminishing marginal product in each sector). In this model, at a given set of international prices, the real wage rate is determined by the overall per worker endowment of natural resources and capital, as in the Johnson synthesis, while the pattern of comparative advantage between manufactures and primary products is determined by the relative endowments of man-made capital and natural resources.

An underdeveloped country with little capital will produce mostly primary products and export them (in raw or lightly processed form) in exchange for manufactures. As the availability of industrial capital per worker expands, wages increase and labour is attracted to the manufacturing sector. The country gradually changes from being predominantly a primary producer to being predominantly an exporter of (non-resource-based) manufactured goods, with the capital intensity of manufacturing activities increasing over time. Labour begins to be attracted to manufacturing at an earlier stage of economic development, and the non-resource-based manufactured goods initially exported use unskilled labour relatively more intensively the lower the country's natural resources per worker and hence the lower the initial wage rate. This is because the low wage will give the resource-poor country an international comparative advantage initially in labour-intensive, standard-technology manufactures.

The fact that capital is required in addition to natural resources and labour in primary production strengthens the conclusion that densely populated countries which are poor in natural resources will begin manufacturing at an earlier stage of capital availability per worker than resource-rich countries. Capital is a complement to natural resources, especially at early stages of economic development, because it is needed initially to clear land (or develop mine sites). Only after farm land is highly developed does capital become a substitute for agricultural land. The greater a country's agricultural land and mineral resource endowments per worker, the greater the share of its available capital used in primary production than manufacturing and hence the higher the productivity of that capital in the primary sector, at a particular level of capital per worker.

Also, the fact that capital is internationally mobile allows the possibility of a country proceeding faster along its path of economic growth than its domestic savings rate alone would allow. These changes in comparative advantage can proceed even more rapidly when barriers to foreign capital inflow are lowered.

The demand for food increases with population and per capita income while the demand for industrial raw materials increases with industrial production. Thus, relatively rapid increases in a country's GNP and manufacturing output raise domestic demand relative to overseas demand for primary products and hasten the country's switch from being a net exporter to being a net importer of primary products.

The country's comparative advantage in agricultural products compared with minerals and energy products depends largely on the ratio of agricultural land to mineral resources in the country relative to the rest of the world. The higher that ratio, the more capital is likely to be attracted to agriculture rather than to the mining sector, and the more likely it is that the country's primary exports are dominated by agricultural products and/or that its primary product imports are dominated by minerals and energy. A shock, such as a domestic minerals discovery or an increase in the international price of minerals, however, would reduce that country's agricultural comparative advantage (Corden 1984).

Three important assumptions implicit in this analysis require qualification. One is the assumption that no intermediate goods and services are used in production. This would matter little if the value-added share of output (value of production minus value of intermediate inputs) was constant or changed at the same rate in each sector, and if the sectoral source of those intermediate inputs remained constant over time. As it happens, however, the value-added share of output typically falls but falls faster for agriculture than for industry as economic development proceeds (Johnson 1973:Ch. 4; Anderson 1987: Table 2), and the non-farm sectors typically provide a large and increasing proportion of agriculture's purchased intermediate inputs. Both of these facts add to the reasons for expecting agriculture's share of GDP and employment to decline in a growing economy.

The second implicit assumption is that markets for primary factors of production and intermediate inputs are not distorted by government policies, when in fact they often are. The greater the degree of such distortions, the smaller will be the aggregate output and the more difficult it is to predict the way the economy would move should some of those markets be freed up (Bhagwati 1971; Lloyd 1974). The difficulty is compounded if the economy had been closed to foreign technology inflows for a long time because the opportunities for rapid productivity growth, through relaxing the import ban on new technologies, may differ markedly across sectors.

The third important assumption is that markets for final products are free of distortionary intervention by government and adjust readily to new equilibria as market circumstances change with economic developments at home and abroad. However, governments typically do also intervene in product markets, usually in ways that—as we shall see in the next chapter—discriminate against agriculture in poor countries and in favour of farmers in rich countries. Insofar as a country gradually changes its policies from a regime which effectively taxes agriculture to one which subsidizes it, this will slow the relative decline of the agricultural sector, especially its share of GDP measured at current domestic prices. Indeed, it could even reverse the decline in agricultural self-sufficiency, as Figure 1.6 above shows has happened in Western Europe during the past two decades.

1.5 Conclusions

It is not too surprising that the international price of food relative to industrial products has been on a long-run downward trend, given the relatively low and declining income elasticity of demand for food. The fact that global productivity growth in agriculture is faster than in the non-farm sector adds to that tendency. Nor is it surprising that food prices fluctuate around their long-run trend, given the vagaries of the weather. What *is* surprising is that food prices have fallen so much since their last major peak in 1973, and that the extent of fluctuations around the long-run trend has, if anything, increased when the decline in transport and communications costs would lead one to expect fluctuations to decrease.

Also requiring explanation is the fact that advanced industrial countries, particularly those of Western Europe, have increased their self-sufficiency in staple foods while developing countries have become net importers of grain and livestock products, despite relatively rapid growth in the latter's production of food. The above theory does alert us to the possibility that a country's food self-sufficiency could increase or decrease in the course of its own and other countries' economic growth, depending on the sectoral biases in the growth in production and consumption. But, the dramatic extent of the changes in food self-sufficiency shown in Figure 1.3 suggests that more than the normal uninterrupted forces of supply and demand are at work in these markets.

These changes in both the time path of international food prices and the food self-sufficiency of industrial market economies, *vis-à-vis* developing and centrally planned economies, could be explained by an increased degree of intervention in food markets by national governments and, in particular, by an increase in agricultural protectionism. It is therefore appropriate to examine next the trends in patterns of government intervention in food markets.

Notes to Chapter I

[1] The main omitted food and feed product group is edible oil, particularly that from soybean. Since it and the other sources of animal feeds, such as corn gluten, cassava and citrus pellets, are generally subject to far fewer distortions than the commodities focused on in this study (see OECD 1987, 1988), their inclusion would not alter the major conclusions from the analysis to follow. Soybean is omitted because its market interacts very strongly with the markets for palm oil, olive oil and rape-seed, and so to include one requires including them all.

[2] See, for example, Spraos (1980), Sapsford (1988) and Grilli and Yang (1986). One of the perennial contentious issues is the extent to which quality adjustments have been properly made in compiling price indices of manufactured goods.

[3] This section draws on Johnson (1973:Ch. 5) and Anderson (1983c, 1987), where the arguments are laid out more fully.

[4] This conclusion, that the real price of agricultural products in terms of non-agricultural products is likely to decline as does

agriculture's share of GDP, is made even stronger if, in addition to relatively slow demand growth, agriculture is assumed to have a faster rate of supply growth or technical change than the non-farm sector. Classic writings which have drawn on these facts to explain agriculture's relative decline in a closed economy include those by Schultz (1945:Chs. 3-5) and Kuznets (1966:Ch. 3) as well as Johnson (1973:Ch. 5). For evidence that total factor productivity growth has been faster in agriculture than in other sectors in the United States since the 1930s, see Baumol *et al.* (1985), Jorgenson (1988), and Williamson and Lindert (1980). The latter study, and Williamson's (1985) parallel study on Britain, suggest that, in earlier periods, productivity growth in agriculture lagged behind that of the modern sector of the economy. This is claimed to be often the case in developing countries also (Kelley and Williamson 1984:70 and Appendix), although less so where so-called green revolutions have occurred as in India (see Becker, Mill and Williamson 1986). However, this does not necessarily mean that agricultural growth lags behind that of the non-farm sector in *aggregate*, because the latter includes the typically slow-growing traditional service sector.

[5] As pointed out in Anderson (1987), in principle, E″ may be above rather than below the ray OE extended in the biased growth case, in which case it is conceptually possible that agriculture's share of GDP could rise. For that to happen, the growth bias would have to be extremely favourable to agriculture such that the increase in the ratio of farm to non-farm output more than offsets the decrease in the ratio of farm to non-farm product prices. Incidentally, Figure 1.8 could be used to describe the world economy as a whole, in which case it indicates we should expect a decline in agriculture's terms of trade in international markets.

[6] See, for example, Lluch, Powell and Williams (1977); Kravis, Heston and Summers (1983); Summers (1985); Theil and Clements (1987).

[7] Strong cross-country evidence that the price of non-tradables relative to tradables increases with real incomes is provided in Kravis and Lipsey (1988).

[8] Available evidence suggests that, in fact, productivity growth has probably been slower in services than in other sectors. See, for example, Clark (1957). If capital was used relatively more intensively in the tradables sector and the expansion in capital per worker was the reason for the outward shift in the production possibility curve, this too would lead to an outcome such as E″ (Rybczynski 1955). As with the earlier discussion of Figure 1.8, there are some extreme conditions under which the non-tradable

sector's share of GDP would not fall, but they are unlikely to eventuate (Anderson 1987).

⁹ Since the fitted trend in Figure 1.1 declines at 0.5 per cent per year, agricultural value added during this century would have had to grow at an average rate of more than 0.5 per cent per year just to offset the decline in agriculture's terms of trade.

¹⁰ Since many empirical studies are available with such evidence, only a small sample of evidence is presented here. For more detailed evidence, see for example Kuznets (1971), Chenery and Syrquin (1975), and Chenery, Robinson and Syrquin (1986).

¹¹ See also Deardorff (1984), Leamer (1984) and Eaton (1987).

2

Distortionary Policies Affecting Food Markets

Governments have been intervening in food markets for centuries. McCalla (1968) notes that agricultural protectionism goes back at least to the fifteenth century. Certainly in Western Europe and the United Kingdom the extent of intervention has been very considerable during the past two centuries (Tracy 1982; Kindleberger 1951, 1975), and has become so more recently in East Asia (Anderson 1983b; Anderson, Hayami *et al.* 1986).

This chapter seeks to show that the extent of agricultural protection from import competition in advanced industrial economies—which has been growing more or less steadily for a century or more—has accelerated since the 1950s and has spread to many rapidly developing, middle-income economies. At the same time, policies in poor countries have tended to discriminate against the agricultural sector. The chapter also documents the extent to which most countries, both rich and poor, tend to insulate their domestic food markets from the vagaries of international food price fluctuations and thereby tend to export some of the instability caused by fluctuations in their own domestic production. As we shall see, this combination of increasing protectionism and insulation has contributed significantly to the downward trend and increasing fluctuations in international prices of food as well as to the increasing importance of (especially West European) industrial countries in world food exports.

2.1   The growth of agricultural protection in industrial countries

Much publicity has been given to the fact that, in the 1980s, both the European Community and the United States spent large and increasing sums of taxpayers' money on subsidies for agriculture. While data on such subsidies make striking headlines and help to focus the public's and the politicians' minds on their farm policies, they provide only a very crude indication of the extent of overall assistance to the farm sector or of distortions to food prices facing consumers.

To see why this is so, consider Figure 2.1 which depicts a small economy's market for food products. If OP_w is the international price at the country's border for food (relative to the price of other tradable goods) then it would also be the domestic price in the absence of price-distorting policies.

Figure 2.1: A small economy's market for food products

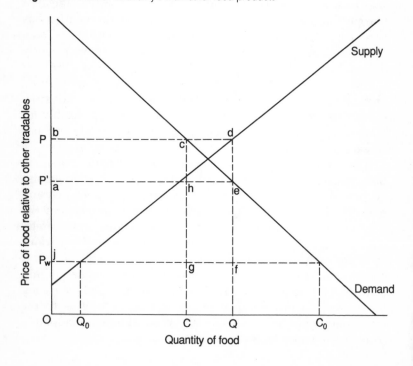

Production would be OQ_0, consumption OC_0 with Q_0C_0 units imported. Suppose, however, that the government decides farmers should receive price OP. At that price OQ units would be produced in the absence of any other distortions. If OP is also the price charged to domestic consumers, then OC will be consumed which leaves CQ to be otherwise disposed of. Typically such surpluses are sold abroad, where they fetch price OP_w per unit. The export subsidy required to finance such sales is PP_w per unit, or area cdfg in total. The large sum represented by area cdfg is a very poor indicator of the extent of distortion to food prices, however, because it only represents the transfer from taxpayers to farmers. There is also the transfer of area bcgj from domestic consumers to farmers which is not directly visible.[1] The budgetary cost would be a smaller proportion of the total transfer from consumers and taxpayers to producers, the smaller the proportion of production that is exported. If that proportion were 5 per cent, the treasury payment would be only one-twentieth of the total transfer.

Alternatively, instead of exporting CQ, it would be possible to dispose of all local production OQ domestically if the consumer price were set at OP', below the producer price OP. This would require a consumer price subsidy of PP' per unit, or area abde in aggregate. Again, to focus solely on the implications for the government's budget of this food policy would be misleading: it would suggest taxpayers are subsidizing consumers when in fact consumers are paying area aefj more for consuming OQ units of food, and farmers are receiving area jbdf more for producing those units, than they would in an open undistorted economy.

Clearly, a much more meaningful way of indicating the extent to which government policies are distorting food markets is to compare the domestic consumer and producer prices with prices at the country's border. That, together with information on the slopes of the demand and supply curves in Figure 2.1, can then provide a far better idea of the effects of those food policies.

By the mid-1980s, agricultural prices in international markets (measured relative to industrial product prices) were 30 per cent below their early 1960s level. They also declined by 30 per cent in Australasia and North America during that 25-year period, reflecting the fact that domestic prices in these traditional food-exporting countries followed closely the changes in export prices. In Western Europe and East Asia, however, domestic agricultural prices relative to industrial prices changed little over this period of declining international terms of trade for agriculture. Compared with Australasia and North America, the domestic terms of trade for agriculture in Western Europe and East Asia improved by more than one-third (Table 2.1). This dramatic difference in trends in incentives facing producers is largely responsible for the faster growth in food production and net export surpluses in Western Europe and Japan than in Australasia and North America, as depicted above in Figures 1.5 and 1.6. The final two columns of Table 2.1 confirm that the associated levels of agricultural protection have grown substantially in Western Europe and East Asia compared with Australasia and North America. Production on the protected farms would have been boosted both directly (since farmers will produce more the higher their output price) and indirectly in the sense that at higher (and more stable) producer prices there is a higher expected return from generating and adopting new technologies or adapting existing technologies from abroad.

To examine the extent of protection by industrial countries more closely, individual commodity price series were compiled for each industrial country (and for most sizable developing countries), and these were compared with food prices at the country's border (the fob export price or the cif import price, depending on whether the country would export or import the product in the absence of distortionary food policies). The percentage by which domestic producer prices plus marketing margins exceed border prices is known as the nominal rate of protection.

Obtaining exact measurements of the nominal rate of protection is always difficult, even for relatively homogeneous products such as foodstuffs. The differing qualities of products to which available price data refer and the presence of data on marketing margins are but two of the problems associated with using even this simplest indicator of the extent of distortions. A further problem is that, since food price and trade policies typically ensure that domestic prices fluctuate less than international prices, estimated rates of protection tend to be higher in years of low international prices than in years of high international prices for food. The estimates summarized in Figure

Table 2.1: Indices of agricultural prices relative to industrial prices in industrial market economies and international markets, 1961 to 1987[a] (1961–64 = 100)

	Domestic Prices					International Prices	Column (1) Column (6)	Column (5) Column (6)
	Australasia and North America	European Community-10	European Free Trade Associations	Japan	ALL WESTERN EUROPE AND EAST ASIA[b]			
	(1)	(2)	(3)	(4)	(5)	(6)	(7)	(8)
1961-64	100	100	100	100	100	100	100	100
1965-69	100	101	105	124	104	99	101	105
1970-74	109	99	104	128	104	100	109	104
1975-79	95	106	102	131	110	89	108	124
1980-84	80	97	96	114	100	83	98	121
1985-87	70	90	98	122	96	70	99	136

[a] The 'domestic prices' columns show the changes in the prices received by farmers in each country group relative to the price received by producers of other tradables (as reflected in the industrial wholesale price index in those countries). The 'international prices' column shows the changes in the index of prices of agricultural exports from industrial market economies relative to the index of prices of manufactured exports from industrial market economies.

[b] The EC-10, EFTA and Japan, plus Spain and Portugal and the newly industrializing economies of Korea and Taiwan.
Source: Prices received by farmers and agricultural export prices are from the Food and Agriculture Organisation, *Production Yearbook and Trade Yearbook,* Rome, various issues; industrial wholesale prices are from the International Monetary Fund, *International Financial Statistics,* Washington D.C., various issues; export prices for manufactured goods are from the World Bank, *Commodity Trade and Price Trends,* Washington D.C., various issues. In the case of Korea and Taiwan, however, the sources were Economic Planning Board, *Major Statistics of Korean Economy,* Seoul, various issues and Council for Economic Planning and Development, *Taiwan Statistical Data Book,* Taipei, various issues.

2.2 refer to 1980-82, which was a period over which average international food prices roughly followed the trend of Figure 1.1. Given the very much lower international prices since the early 1980s, the rates in Figure 2.2 are underestimates of more recent protection.[2]

The key point to note from Figure 2.2 is that, while governments in virtually all industrial countries assist their farmers, the extent of protection in 1980-82 was relatively low in North America and especially Australasia but it was high in the European Community, even higher in the other countries of Western Europe (a fact that is often not recognised outside Europe), and extremely high in Japan. In 1980-82, food prices were, on average, 50 per cent above international levels in Western Europe while in Japan they were 150 per cent above. These differences across countries ensure that if all industrial countries reduced their agricultural protection levels, the resulting increase in international food prices may be sufficient to cause an expansion in production of some agricultural products in the less protected markets of those countries.

Moreover, assistance to farmers in many of these industrial countries has been increasing over time. Assistance in Europe emerged last century when industrial development there and agricultural export expansion in the Americas began to reduce the competitiveness of European farmers. It was boosted in the Depression of the 1930s and again during the period of rapid industrial growth from the 1950s onwards. One study estimates that the average nominal rate of agricultural protection in Western Europe increased from 38 per cent in 1956/57 to 47 per cent in 1963/64 and 62 per cent in 1968/69 (Gulbrandsen and Lindbeck 1973:38), during which time assistance to the manufacturing sector was much lower and was being reduced. This is part of a long-run trend towards assisting agriculture relative to manufacturing (Table 2.2). Manufacturing protection in Western Europe has, in contrast to agricultural protection, been reduced further over the past two decades. This has been a consequence of both the Kennedy and Tokyo Rounds of multilateral GATT negotiations and the formation of the European Community and the European Free Trade Association. Tariffs on Western Europe's imports of manufactures fell from an average of 12 per cent in 1958 to 10 per cent in 1968 and to less than 7 per cent by 1972 (Balassa 1975:Table 2.4). They

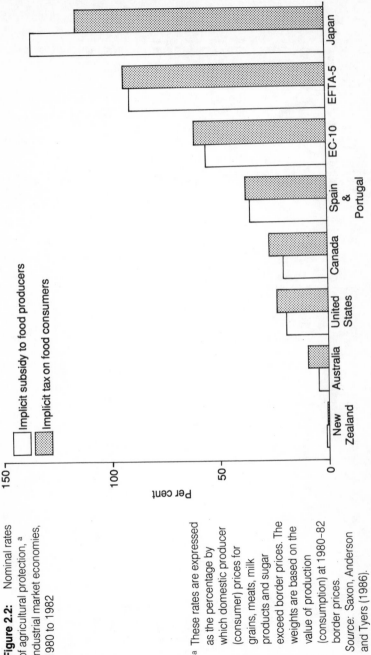

Figure 2.2: Nominal rates of agricultural protection, [a] industrial market economies, 1980 to 1982

[a] These rates are expressed as the percentage by which domestic producer (consumer) prices for grains, meats, milk products and sugar exceed border prices. The weights are based on the value of production (consumption) at 1980–82 border prices.

Source: Saxon, Anderson and Tyers (1986).

Table 2.2: Estimated nominal rates of protection to agriculture and manufacturing in Western Europe, 1902 to 1963[a] (per cent)

	Foodstuffs				Industrial manufactured goods			
	1927	1931	1956	1963	1902	1927	1931	1960–62
Austria	17	60	30	27	..	21	28	18
Belguim	12	24	25	41	13	12	13	13
Finland	58	102	97	75	..	18	23	..
France	19	53	34	44	34	26	29	19
Germany	27	83	40	60	25	19	18	8
Italy	25	66	44	63	27	28	42	20
Spain	45	81	40	36	76	63	76	..
Sweden	25	39	40	60	23	21	24	8
Switzerland	22	42	76	84	7	18	22	9
Average	**27**	**68**	**41**	**53**	**33**	**28**	**33**	**14**

a Import tariffs, except for 1956 and 1963 which refer to the rate of producer price support.
b Averages are rather crudely obtained using 1950 populations as weights.

Sources: Liepmann (1983:413) except for the 1902 estimates which are from Little, Scitovsky and Scott (1970:162) and for 1956 to 1963 which are from Gulbrandsen and Lindbeck (1966).

have fallen further during the 1970s following the conclusion of the Tokyo Round of negotiations. Non-tariff import barriers have increased for some manufactured commodities, but the overall rate of protection to manufacturing has fallen considerably.

The policy trend in East Asia has been even more pronounced. At the turn of the century, when Japan first became a net importer of food, a tariff on rice imports was introduced and the relatively heavy taxation of the agricultural sector began to be lowered. Around 1905, the nominal rate of protection for rice was less than 20 per cent, but it rose to more than 30 per cent during World War I and to more than 60 per cent by the late 1930s. Following reconstruction in the years after World War II, the average nominal rate of grain and meat protection in Japan rose even more rapidly, from around 50 per cent in the late 1950s to 100 per cent in the early 1970s and to 150 per cent in the early 1980s. Assistance to Japanese manufacturers, on the other hand, has been modest by comparison and, as in Europe, has been decreasing rather than increasing (Anderson 1983b).

An even more rapid switch in incentive structures has occurred in South Korea and Taiwan since their liberation from Japan following the Pacific War. During the 1950s, both embarked on an import-substituting industrialization drive which involved not only substantial protection from import competition for domestic manufacturers but also low prices for agricultural products. Then, in the early 1960s, these countries switched the basis of their development strategy away from import substitution towards export-oriented industrialization. The trade and payments liberalizations ensured that both agriculture and manufacturing faced relatively undistorted prices through the mid-1960s. By the late 1960s, however, farmers in Korea and Taiwan—like their counterparts in Japan in earlier decades—felt the effects of the relative decline in agriculture predicted by the theory presented in the previous chapter. They sought to resist this decline, arguing successfully for assistance via price supports and protection from import competition. As a consequence, nominal rates of grain and meat protection rose from negative levels in the 1950s, and from close to zero in the mid-1960s, to high positive levels in the 1970s and early 1980s (when they reached around 150 per cent for Korea and

50 per cent for Taiwan). Meanwhile, assistance to manufacturing in those economies fell to a low level in the early 1960s and has remained there (Hong 1979; Nam 1981; Anderson 1983b; Anderson, Hayami *et al.* 1986).

Similarly, a number of oil-exporting developing countries, which enjoyed rapid economic growth and structural change during the decade following the first petroleum price hike in 1973, have, like the rapidly industrializing, resource-poor countries of Northeast Asia, adopted policies to protect farmers from the increased import competition that necessarily accompanies the currency appreciation associated with a booming export sector. According to estimates compiled by the World Bank (1986:64–5), agricultural protection by the early 1980s had become quite high in Mexico, Nigeria and Yemen, for example, while in Saudi Arabia it is extremely high. Even in Indonesia, the taxation of agricultural exports has been reduced and the domestic-to-international price ratio for basic foodstuffs rose considerably from the early 1970s (Booth 1984, 1985).

In North America, on the other hand, agricultural protection rates did not grow significantly until after the mid-1980s; and, apart from a brief period in New Zealand in the early 1980s, no significant agricultural protection growth has occurred in Australasia. It is the Australasian manufacturing sector which is heavily protected from import competition. Australia and New Zealand did not participate in the earlier GATT rounds of manufacturing tariff reductions, but they did unilaterally reduce manufacturing protection (Australia from the mid-1970s, New Zealand in the mid-1980s when agricultural support was also reduced) so that their average effective rates of assistance to manufacturers in the late 1980s were well below those of the early 1970s (Industries Assistance Commission 1983, 1987; Sandrey and Reynolds 1990; OECD 1990a).

Further evidence of the growth of nominal agricultural protection rates is available from time-series data summarized in Saxon, Tyers and Anderson (1986). Those data suggest that during the decade 1965–74, the average rate of protection in industrial countries for grain, livestock products and sugar was 21 per cent (Table 2.3). But, during 1975–83 (which Figure 1.1 confirms was a period covering both high and low international prices), this nominal protection rate averaged 28 per cent, or one third higher. Consistent with Table 2.1, these data show

Table 2.3: Trends in average nominal protection rates for food products, selected industrial countries, 1965[a] to 1983 (per cent)

	1965–74	**1975–83**
Japan	110	161
EC–10[b]	38	51
EFTA–5[c]	62	89
United States	6	7
Canada	5	12
Australia	3	-
New Zealand	14	-
Weighted average	**21**	**28**

[a] Averages compiled based on time series data, for grains, edible livestock products and sugar. Consolidation across commodities is by averaging producer-to-border price ratios, using as weights the commodity shares of the value of output at border prices.
[b] The European Community of 10 (excluding Spain and Portugal).
[c] The European Free Trade Association, which includes Austria, Finland, Norway, Sweden and Switzerland.
Source: Saxon, Anderson and Tyers (1986).

that the protection increases have been concentrated in Western Europe and Japan.

Moreover, agricultural protection has increased even further since the early 1980s. The Saxon, Anderson and Tyers series have not been updated beyond 1983, but more recently, the US Department of Agriculture (USDA) in Washington D.C. and the Organization for Economic Cooperation and Development (OECD) in Paris have compiled estimates for the 1979–89 period of producer and consumer subsidy equivalents for food products in selected industrial countries. These two sets of estimates, summarized in Table 2.4, provide very similar numbers and suggest the extent of protection in the second half of the 1980s was about one-third greater than in the early 1980s.[3]

Even in countries where nominal protection has not increased, the *effective* rate of assistance to value added by farmers (net of purchased inputs), and hence the incentive to expand farm output, tends to have risen. This can be explained in the following way. If there are no distortions acting on input prices, the effective rate of protection is defined simply as the nominal rate of output protection divided by the value-added share of

Table 2.4: Producer subsidy equivalents of food policies in selected industrial countries, 1979 to 1988 (per cent)

	OECD estimates				USDA estimates	
	1979–81	1982–84	1985–86	1987–88	1982–84	1985–86
Australia	9	14	15	11	11	12
Canada	24	29	42	50	25	39
EC-10	37	33	45	46[a]	30	44
EFTA-5	..	53[b]	67[c]	68	..	..
Japan	57	63	71	76	70	74
New Zealand	18	27	26	11	30	19
United States	16	22	34	38	22	30
Weighted average	**29**	**31**	**43**	**47**	**31**	**41**

[a] EC-12.

[b] 1979–85. The EFTA weighted average is derived using as weights the value added in agriculture in each of the five member economies.

[c] 1986 only.

Source: OECD (1988) and Mabbs-Zeno *et al.* (1988).

output measured at free-trade prices (Corden 1971). According to the data in Table 2.5, the value-added share of output in industrial countries (measured at actual rather than free-trade prices) has been declining much more rapidly for agriculture than for manufacturing, especially in the European Community, as farmers have become more dependent on purchased inputs such as fertilizer, pesticides and machinery[4]. The relative decline in this share would be even greater if measured at free-trade prices, given the growth in nominal agricultural protection mentioned in the previous paragraph. Together, these facts suggest effective rates have been rising more rapidly than nominal rates of protection for agriculture relative to that for manufacturing, especially in Western Europe where the value-added share of farm output has fallen substantially. It is this steady increase in effective assistance to farmers which has been largely responsible for the generation and diffusion of new farm technologies which in turn have boosted food production in and exports from Western Europe.

Turning to distortions affecting individual commodity markets, these are detailed for seven food commodity groups in Table 2.6. They show that rice is the most protected of these

Table 2.5: Value-added share of agricultural (manufacturing) production measured at domestic prices, industrial market economies, 1963 to 1983[a] (per cent)

	1963-65	1970-73	1975-78	1980-83
Australia	38 (41)	33 (40)	33 (42)	30 (38)
Austria	.. (..)	70 (40)	68 (37)	66 (35)
Canada	43 (..)	38 (33)	29 (33)	22 (33)
EC-10[b]	65 (39)	57 (41)	51 (40)	46 (39)
Japan	.. (33)	62 (34)	62 (32)	54 (30)
Korea	.. (..)	80 (39)	77 (36)	67 (33)
New Zealand	.. (40)	63 (38)	53 (33)	45 (33)
Norway	59 (39)	52 (37)	52 (31)	50 (28)
Sweden	55 (44)	54 (38)	53 (37)	48 (34)
Taiwan	64 (..)	56 (..)	54 (..)	50 (..)
United States	42 (46)	43 (46)	37 (43)	34 (42)
Weighted average[c]	**48 (40)**	**49 (41)**	**43 (41)**	**39 (38)**

[a] Manufacturing sector shares are shown in parentheses; in the final column they refer only to 1980. Because of different statistical methods used, shares are not comparable across countries as they are over time for each country.

[b] Weighted average for France, FR Germany and the United Kingdom for manufacturing shares, with weights based on 1980 value of manufacturing production.

[c] Weights based on 1980 value of agricultural (manufacturing) production at domestic prices.

Source: Anderson (1987).

commodities in industrial countries (due almost entirely to Japan's influence), followed by dairy products and sugar. Coarse grains, which are a major input into the livestock sector in most industrial countries, are relatively lightly protected so as not to offset too much the nominal protection provided to meat and milk producers. These differences across commodities in each country's rates of protection add to the welfare cost of protection. This is because, in addition to more resources in total being devoted to food production in protected economies than would be the case without protection, total economic output in these economies is restrained because resources are consequently under-allocated to less protected, and usually more efficient, industries.[5]

In summary, then, the domestic terms of trade for agriculture

Table 2.6: Nominal protection coefficients (domestic-to-border price ratios) for various food commodities, industrial market economies, 1980 to 1982[a]

	Wheat	Coarse grain	Rice	Ruminant meat	Non-ruminant meat	Dairy products	Sugar	WEIGHTED AVERAGE
Australia	1.05	1.00	1.15 (1.70)	1.00	1.00	1.30 (1.40)	1.05 (1.40)	1.05 (1.10)
Canada	1.15	1.00	1.00	1.10	1.10	1.95	1.25	1.19 (1.26)
EC–10	1.40 (1.45)	1.40	1.40	1.95	1.25	1.75 (1.80)	1.50	1.55 (1.60)
EFTA–5	1.65	1.55	1.00	2.30	1.40	2.45	1.55	1.90 (1.93)
Japan	3.90 (1.25)	4.30 (1.25)	3.35 (2.90)	2.80	1.50	2.90	3.00 (2.60)	2.33 (2.14)
New Zealand	1.00	1.00	1.00	1.00	1.00	1.00	1.00	1.00 (1.00)
Spain and Portugal	1.35	1.30	1.15	1.65	1.10	1.75	1.65	1.35 (1.36)
United States	1.15 (1.00)	1.00	1.30 (1.00)	1.10	1.00	2.00	1.40	1.18 (1.23)
Weighted average	**1.25 (1.29)**	**1.13 (1.13)**	**2.52 (2.43)**	**1.50 (1.53)**	**1.18 (1.18)**	**1.88 (1.93)**	**1.48 (1.58)**	**1.41 (1.49)**

[a] Domestic producer prices divided by the border price, except values in parentheses which refer to the domestic consumer price divided by the border price if it differs from the producer-to-border price ratio, after allowing for appropriate marketing margins. The weighted averages are calculated using 1980–82 production (consumption) at border prices as weights. The nominal rate of protection is 100 times the producer-to-border price ratio minus 100. Estimates have been rounded to the nearest 5 per cent except for weighted averages.

Source: Saxon, Anderson and Tyers (1986).

improved in Western Europe and East Asia during a period when they deteriorated in Australasia and North America and in the international marketplace. High levels of protection have been sustained for decades in the former group of countries, and finally, these high levels of protection have accompanied relatively stable domestic food prices (discussed in Section 2.3 below). It is therefore not surprising that food production growth has been relatively rapid in Western Europe and Japan. Because high and rising domestic prices for food also would have reduced the rate of growth of food consumption, it is even less surprising that those countries have increased their share of world food exports and reduced their food import dependence, thereby putting downward pressure on international food prices.

2.2   Food price distortions in developing economies

The decline in the share of developing countries in world food exports has occurred despite relatively rapid growth in their food output. As noted in the discussion of Figures 1.2 to 1.4 earler, this is in part because, at low levels of income and given prices, food consumption expands almost as rapidly as income grows. Food demand in developing countries has simply out-stripped supply over the past three decades. Nevertheless, the fact that the average grain yield in developing countries is still only half that in industrial market economies suggests that great scope remains for production growth in these countries. Indeed, it has become a popular generalization that developing countries discourage food production and suppress the growth of food output through the imposition of 'cheap food policies' (see Peterson 1979).

The comparisons of domestic prices with border prices in the time series provided in Saxon, Anderson and Tyers (1986), suggest that, while producers of specific commodities are clearly taxed in many developing countries, this generalization tends not to apply across all the traded food staples which are the focus of this study. From the period averages in Table 2.7, a general pattern of producer taxation is apparent in Latin America, in the majority of sub-Saharan African countries and

Table 2.7: Estimated nominal direct rates of agricultural protection in developing economies[a], 1965 to 1983 (per cent)

	1965–74	1975–83
Argentina	−34	−25
Brazil	−34	−1
Mexico	19	26
All Latin America	**−24**	**−10**
Egypt	28	29
Nigeria	109	128
Other sub-Saharan Africa	−13	−7
All Africa and Middle East	**3**	**8**
Bangladesh	9	−8
China	5	−9
India	9	−7
Indonesia	−21	36
Korea, Rep.	50	160
Pakistan	26	11
Taiwan	20	39
Thailand	−25	−10
All developing Asia	**4**	**−1**
All developing economies	**−2**	**−2**

a   Averages compiled based on time-series data for grains, edible livestock
    products and sugar. Consolidation across commodities is by averaging
    producer-to-border price ratios using as weights the commodity shares of the
    value of output at border prices. These ratios are derived by converting border
    prices to domestic currencies at official exchange rates. Since those rates are
    typically overvalued (often very substantially), the above numbers need to be
    treated as upper-bound estimates.
Source: Saxon, Anderson and Tyers (1986).

in some Asian countries. But, in some developing countries, particularly Northeast Asia's newly industrializing economies and the petroleum exporters, protection of food producers is high and growing. In general, however, the picture is one of direct price distortions which discourage rather than encourage the production of food.

This direct comparison of producer and border prices ignores indirect distortions of incentives which, in developing countries tend to be relatively large. First, many developing countries have non-convertible currencies or official exchange rates that are overvalued, so foreign exchange has to be rationed among importers. In countries which export food products, this reduces the relative price of food in the domestic market and discourages production. If food is imported, the effect on relative prices depends on the priority given to food imports in the allocation of foreign exchange: where this priority is high, the relative domestic price of food can be further suppressed below its free-trade value. This form of distortion is particularly important in the centrally planned economies, in sub-Saharan Africa and in some South Asian countries.

Secondly, even where the exchange rate is not distorted directly, the imposition of export taxes and import tariffs or quotas in other tradable sectors affects the equilibrium level of an economy's exchange rate. Protection of import-competing manufacturing sectors, for example, reduces imports and hence the demand for foreign currency, causing the home currency to appreciate.[6] Taxation of non-food primary exports, on the other hand, reduces the domestic supply of foreign currency and so depreciates the home currency.

Accurate and consistent estimates of the changes in aggregate food production incentives that are due to these potentially off-setting effects are, unfortunately, not available for all the developing countries. It is therefore difficult to draw a precise picture of the full extent of the disincentives facing farmers in developing countries. However, a rough estimation for a selection of 18 developing countries can be made from a recent World Bank study. That study focused on the indirect impact of industrial and exchange rate policies on agricultural incentives. As shown in Table 2.8, it found their impact to be very substantial, reducing farmers' gross returns by about one-quarter on average. The indirect effect of all *non-food* policies on *food* producers would probably be somewhat less than this, as many of the non-food agricultural sectors and mining sectors of developing countries are directly taxed at the point of export. But, the final two columns of Table 2.8 suggest the extent of that offset may be small by comparison with the disincentive effect of industrial protection and exchange rate overvaluation: direct taxation of non-staple farm products for the country and commodity shown averages only half the rate of indirect taxation caused by non-farm policies.

Table 2.8: Estimated nominal indirect rates of taxation of agricultural production due to industrial and exchange rate policies and nominal direct rates of taxation of non-staple farm products, selected developing countries, 1975-79 and 1980-84 (per cent)

	Indirect rate of taxation		Direct rate of taxation[a]		
	1975-79	**1980-84**	**1975-79**	**1980-84**	
Argentina	16	37			
Brazil	32	14			
Chile	-22	7			
Colombia	25	34	7	5	(coffee)
Cote d'Ivoire	33	26	31	21	(cocoa)
Dominican Rep.	18	19	15	32	(coffee)
Egypt	18	14	36	22	(cotton)
Ghana	66	89	-26	-34	(cocoa)
Korea	18	12			
Malaysia	4	10	25	18	(rubber)
Morocco	12	8			
Pakistan	48	35	12	7	(cotton)
Philippines	27	28	11	26	(copra)
Portugal	5	13			
Sri Lanka	35	31	29	31	(rubber)
Thailand	15	19			
Turkey	40	35	-2	28	(tobacco)
Zambia	42	57	-1	-7	(tobacco)
Unweighted average	**24**	**27**	**12**	**14**	

[a] Blank entries signify data absent in source.
Source: Krueger, Schiff and Valdes (1988).

Notwithstanding the presence of these policies which in-directly affect food markets, it is useful to examine the ratio of domestic to international prices of the seven food commodity groups in this study, since the *differences* between these ratios are not greatly affected by overvaluation of a country's currency and non-food sectoral policies. Notice from Table 2.9 that, for each of the commodity markets shown, the distortions imposed in developing countries are substantially lower than those in industrial countries (see Table 2.6). Rice production is taxed in most developing countries (with the notable exceptions of Korea and Taiwan), while the direction in which the other grain

Table 2.9: Nominal protection coefficients (domestic-to-border price ratios) for various food commodities, developing economies, 1980 to 1982[a]

	Wheat	Coarse grain	Rice	Ruminant meat	Non-ruminant meat	Dairy products	Sugar	WEIGHTED AVERAGE
Egypt	0.60	0.70	0.50	1.50	1.50	1.60	0.65	0.92 (0.88)
Nigeria	1.95	2.05	1.70	1.95	1.70	2.30	1.50	1.93 (1.88)
South Africa	1.60	1.15	1.00	1.10	1.00	2.05	0.90	1.21 (1.24)
Other sub-Saharan Africa	1.05	0.95	1.00	0.75	0.75	1.20	0.55	0.87 (0.89)
Other North Africa and Middle East	1.20	1.20	1.20	1.00	1.00	1.80	1.00	1.24 (1.23)
Bangladesh	1.00 (0.90)	1.00	0.95 (0.90)	0.90	0.90	1.30	0.60	0.95 (0.91)
China	1.45 (1.30)	1.15 (1.10)	0.85 (0.80)	0.70	0.65	2.35	1.15 (1.60)	0.98 (0.95)
India	1.00 (0.95)	1.00	0.90 (0.85)	1.00	1.00	1.50	0.80	1.01 (0.99)
Indonesia	1.00 (1.50)	1.30	1.10 (0.85)	1.80	2.00	1.60	2.65	1.30 (1.15)
Korea, Rep.	2.45 (1.45)	2.30 (1.30)	2.50 (2.40)	3.75	2.50	2.95	1.00 (2.90)	2.59 (2.35)
Pakistan	0.90	0.90	0.75	1.00	1.00	1.65	0.70	1.04 (1.06)
Philippines	1.00	1.15	1.00	1.60	1.40	1.70	0.80	1.11 (1.15)
Taiwan	2.10 (1.00)	2.10 (1.00)	2.65	2.50	1.15	2.80	1.00	1.66 (1.57)
Thailand	1.00	1.00	0.90	0.95	0.90	1.60	1.00(1.50)	0.93 (1.00)
Other Asia	0.85	0.95	0.75	0.90	0.80	1.30	0.75	0.81 (0.81)

(continued)

Table 2.9 (continued)

	Wheat	Coarse grain	Rice	Ruminant meat	Non-ruminant meat	Dairy products	Sugar	WEIGHTED AVERAGE
Argentina	0.90	0.85	0.80	0.85	0.90	0.85	0.85	0.86 (0.86)
Brazil	1.05	0.90	0.80	0.80	0.90	1.25	0.75	0.88 (0.90)
Cuba	0.70	0.80	0.80	0.60	0.65	0.90	0.50 (1.00)	0.56 (0.76)
Mexico	1.00	1.40 (0.95)	0.90	1.00	1.20	2.35	0.70	1.34 (1.24)
Other Latin America	1.00	1.00	0.90	0.90	1.00	1.50	0.85	1.00 (1.02)
Weighted average	**1.20 (1.13)**	**1.10 (1.08)**	**0.93 (0.88)**	**0.94 (0.97)**	**0.86 (0.86)**	**1.60 (1.61)**	**0.84 (1.00)**	**1.03 (1.03)**

[a] Domestic producer price divided by the border price, except values in parentheses which refer to the domestic consumer price divided by the border price (not shown if the same as the producer-to-border price ratio). The weighted averages are calculated using the value of 1980-82 production (consumption) at border prices for weights. These ratios are derived by converting border prices to domestic currencies at official exchange rates. Since those rates are typically overvalued (often very substantially), the above numbers need to be treated as upper-bound estimates.

Source: Saxon, Anderson and Tyers (1986).

markets are distorted is mixed, averaging a little above zero using official (typically overvalued) exchange rates to convert border prices to domestic currency. Meat and sugar distortions are also mixed in direction, but producers of these commodities are taxed on average. Finally, in the important market for dairy products, producers are highly protected both in industrial and developing countries. Only New Zealand and some Latin American countries are identified as exceptions to this general tendency.

2.3   The insulation of domestic food markets

The international markets for agricultural commodities are notorious for the instability of relative prices through time. Simple comparisons of domestic with border prices in many industrial and developing countries yield rates of nominal protection which are high when world prices are low and which decline when world prices rise again. This reflects the fact that domestic food markets are insulated so that domestic prices change more sluggishly than international prices.

In countries with insulated markets, changes in relative international prices are not fully transmitted to domestic markets. Domestic agents are therefore less exposed to changes in international scarcity values, and the burden of adjustment to international price shocks is shed, at least in part, onto other countries. Furthermore, domestically generated instability due to fluctuating yields is often accommodated by varying the volume of net food trade. This appears 'unfair' particularly where it results from policies in countries such as the USSR, whose agricultural output fluctuates widely from year to year. Countries such as this therefore 'export' domestic market instability without sharing in the adjustments to it which must be made by producers, consumers and stockholders in the rest of the world (Johnson 1975; Blandford 1983).[7]

A crude index of market insulation is the degree to which domestic market prices are more stable through time than prices at the border. From an examination of the time series of prices in Saxon, Anderson and Tyers (1986), the tendency for relative domestic prices to be more stable in both industrial and developing countries is readily established. Table 2.10 lists ratios of coefficients of variation of domestic and international prices measured about log-linear trends. A ratio of less than 100 per cent means domestic prices are more stable than international prices. This is the case for a substantial majority (about 80 per cent) of countries and commodities listed in the table.

This index of relative price stability tends to underestimate the degree of market insulation, however. Changes in relative domestic prices can result from policy changes (sustained increases in protection, for example) and be entirely unrelated to international price movements. A better measure is the elasticity of price transmission, identified as a policy parameter by Bredahl *et al.* (1979). It is possible to estimate such elasticities of this type from the available time-series data. Before doing so, however, it is useful to review some of the means by which domestic markets are insulated.

Sources of market insulation

Even in the absence of intervention by governments in domestic commodity markets, domestic prices can be only partially responsive to changes at the border. This situation can arise where marketing margins are large; that is, where infrastructural costs, which include the costs of domestic transportation, processing, packaging and marketing, constitute a substantial share of the cost of producing and delivering an imported product to domestic markets or a domestically produced product to the border for export. Consider the case of an imported product where domestic value added beyond the farm gate is half the domestic wholesale price, and the border price rises by half while unit infrastructural costs remain constant. The proportional change in the domestic wholesale price is then one quarter—just half the proportional change in the border price. In this case, the elasticity of price transmission is 0.5 and the domestic market is partially insulated.

Taking a similar approach to the case of an exported product, we would conclude that large marketing margins would result in the opposite of insulation. A change in the export price would result in a larger than proportional change in the domestic producer price. Large marketing margins can result in market

Table 2.10: Index of relative domestic price stability, selected countries, 1961 to 1983[a] (per cent)

	Wheat	Maize	Barley	Rice	Cattle meat	Sheep meat	Pig meat	Poultry meat	Milk products	Sugar
Industrial Market Economies										
Australia	82 (35)	92	87 (57)	76 (56)	95	163	92 (133)	72	66 (72)	71 (26)
Canada	119	130	119	n.a.	53	95	92	160 (100)	63	68
EC-10	35 (36)	45	45 (49)	40 (45)	26 (27)	46 (54)	86	66 (74)	42 (63)	18 (13)
EFTA-5	40 (41)	63	43	n.a.	16 (15)	69 (72)	88	73	56	17 (20)
Japan	77 (81)	122	85 (89)	44	80	n.a.	78	118	68	43 (46)
New Zealand	70	75	55	n.a.	141	135	81 (106)	106	100	n.a.
Spain & Portugal	25 (79)	52 (57)	50 (96)	49	27	57	99	77	55	24 (90)
United States	125	102 (107)	-	95 (123)	81 (74)	114 (132)	143 (132)	138	33 (31)	41 (46)
USSR	38	35	32	33	-	-	-	-	39	60
Africa										
Egypt	79	80	98	62	93	89	-	111	80	59
Nigeria	58	77	85	65	51	96	-		85	
South Africa	32	51	42	n.a.	61	90	-	96	55	44
Other sub-Saharan Africa	56 (81)	101 (45)	58	63	62	62	56	115	58	40

(continued)

Table 2.10 *(continued)*

	Wheat	Maize	Barley	Rice	Cattle meat	Sheep meat	Pig meat	Poultry meat	Milk products	Sugar
Asia										
Bangladesh	162 (208)	267	143	138 (112)	82	159	-	138	112	60
China	90	130	73	50	82	-	90	-	81	57
India	82 (64)	100 (110)	80 (115)	78 (82)	55	79	-	-	67	33 (54)
Indonesia	n.a.	-	-	97 (92)	80	n.a.	125	106	103	96
Korea, Rep.	81 (52)	69	64 (79)	48 (57)	75	n.a.	63	111	72	100
Pakistan	100 (108)	111 (158)	103 (107)	62 (133)	36	-	-	-	74	23 (80)
Philippines	100	36	-	36 (47)	106	-	125	-	103	49 (66)
Taiwan	60 (51)	76 (113)	111 (114)	46 (40)	80	n.a.	82	87	153	61 (23)
Thailand	n.a.	103 (94)	n.a.	53	33	n.a.	68	87	77	50 (53)
Latin America										
Argentina	75	80	75	73	83	88 (107)	88 (90)	83	80	70
Brazil	98	109	93	96	137	114	89	113	124	83
Mexico	88	86 (95)	85	104	99	124	70	89	78	65

[a] Ratio of the coefficient of variation of the domestic producer (consumer) price to the coefficient of variation of the corresponding border price, both deflated by the domestic GDP deflator, measured around log-linear trends and expressed as a percentage. The consumer price stability index is shown only when it differs from the producer price stability index.

Source: Derived from the price data reported in Saxon, Anderson and Tyers (1986).

insulation, however, even in the export case. If we make the reasonable assumption that unit infrastructural costs increase with the volume of exports, then a rise in the export price would tend to increase the volume and hence increase these costs, reducing the share of the border price increase which is passed through to producers. A decline at the border, on the other hand, reduces the volume and hence the marketing margin, again reducing the proportional change in the domestic producer price relative to that at the border. By similar reasoning, it is readily seen that volume-dependent infrastructural costs such as these add to the insulation of domestic prices in the case of imported products.

Another contributor to market insulation is the 'pipeline lag'. Where many months elapse between the purchase of food products and their eventual delivery, domestic prices can appear to respond sluggishly following changes in corresponding international market prices.

It must also be emphasized that the appearance of market insulation is, in part, a statistical phenomenon arising from the non-homogeneity of food commodity aggregates. Even grains such as rice and wheat are aggregates of many distinct and imperfectly substitutable varieties and grades within varieties. Insufficient data are available, however, to ensure that our comparisons of domestic with border prices are always specific to single varieties or grades. Thus, even where marketing margins are very small and there are no distortions, statistical estimates are likely to suggest the presence of some market insulation.

For all these reasons, a part of the relative stability of domestic food prices which is evident from Table 2.10 can be explained in terms of 'natural' market insulation. This natural insulation is especially significant in markets where transportation, storage and processing costs are comparatively high, such as those for livestock products and sugar. It is even more significant in developing countries where internal transportation services are poor and climatic conditions make storage more costly. Thus, even in a world without distortions, we would expect domestic food prices in developing economies to respond more sluggishly and less completely to changes in international prices than those in industrial economies. Furthermore, we expect this natural insulation to be greatest in the countries which combine comparative poverty with vast hinterlands, such as China, India, Bangladesh, Pakistan and Brazil. We return to this point later in the book when discussing the effects of multilateral liberalization.

Nevertheless, a great deal of observed market insulation is due to government intervention. Even where differing trade policy instruments give rise to the same average rate of protection, their effects on the relative stability of domestic prices may differ considerably. Simple specific tariffs and export taxes or subsidies, for example, distort the proportional changes transmitted to domestic markets in response to changes in prices at the border. Their *ad valorem* counterparts, on the other hand, preserve proportional changes but distort the absolute magnitudes of border price changes (Zwart and Meilke 1979). Binding quotas would insulate the domestic market totally, but prevailing policy regimes generally involve more than just one such instrument.

Agricultural policies almost always employ instruments designed to be adjusted through time. Notorious among such instruments is the system of variable levies and export restitutions which were adopted as part of the Common Agricultural Policy (CAP) of the European Community. In this case, the domestic market price is determined by agreement among agricultural ministers and a levy is imposed on imports or a restitution paid to exporters. This is routinely adjusted so that consumers and producers always face the same domestic price (Sampson and Snape 1980; Koester and Tangermann 1986). The degree to which this policy insulates domestic markets is therefore dependent, first, on the responsiveness of the political process by which the domestic price is determined relative to international food price changes and, second, on associated changes in European exchange rates.

In many countries, monopoly control over international trade in important food commodities is given to government agencies. These agencies typically use trade as a means of managing domestic supply and, therefore, of maintaining domestic prices at desired levels. In industrial countries, such agencies include Japan's Food Agency and the Wheat Boards of Australia and Canada. In developing countries, key examples are the Food Corporation of India, the National Logistics Agency of Indonesia (BULOG) and the National Food Authority of the Philippines.

In all cases, these agencies are empowered to maintain relatively stable domestic prices. A re-examination of the relative price stability thus achieved is therefore desirable.

Measuring market insulation

The approach adopted here to measure market insulation stems from a suggestion by Abbott (1979). The degree to which border price changes are transmitted to the domestic market can be estimated by comparing domestic with border prices in time series using regression analysis. To do this, we employ a Nerlovian lagged adjustment model (Nerlove 1972). It is assumed that there is, in association with any value of the border price P_t, a 'target' domestic price p^*_t, towards which policy ensures that the actual price p_t moves only sluggishly. In turn, proportional changes in this target price might respond imperfectly, even in the long run, to corresponding changes in the border price. If all prices are expressed in logarithms, the target domestic price then has the following relationship with the border price:

$$p^*_t = p_0 + \phi^{LR} (P_t - P_0) \tag{2.1}$$

where, ϕ^{LR} is the long-run price transmission elasticity and the values of p_0 and P_0 are the domestic and border prices in some base period. In the short run, the domestic price adjusts only partially to any change in the target domestic price:

$$p_t - p_{t-1} = \delta (p^*_t - p_{t-1}) \tag{2.2}$$

where the parameter δ gives the fraction of the ultimate adjustment which takes place in any one year. By substituting equation (2.1) into equation (2.2) to eliminate the unobservable target price, the following reduced form suitable for fitting to data is obtained:

$$p_t = \delta (p_0 - \phi^{LR} P_0) + (1-\delta) p_{t-1} + \delta\phi^{LR} P_t \tag{2.3}$$

where, again, if the prices are expressed in logarithms, the short-run (same year) elasticity of price transmission is simply:

$$\phi^{SR} = \delta\phi^{LR} \tag{2.4}$$

An important characteristic of this model is the separate identification of the elasticity of price transmission in both the short run and the long run. If the objective of policy is to hold the level of protection constant on average but to stabilize the domestic price (around the trend of the border price), then we expect the value of ϕ^{SR} to be less than one (though more than zero). Its long-run counterpart, however, must in this case be unity. Values of ϕ^{LR} differing from unity imply that the market is insulated not only against short-run fluctuations in the international price but also against any long-run trend in the world market. One significant implication of this is that the level of protection implied by the policy will drift through time. In particular, if the trend of the world market is towards lower international food prices, incomplete price transmission in the long run implies growth in protection (or reduction in effective taxation) of the food sector.

Another important characteristic of this model is that the degree of insulation against increases in border prices is the same as that against decreases in border prices. This symmetry need not apply to domestic price movements, particularly where the insulation is policy-induced. As we discuss in the next chapter, where producer interests are strongest politically (as they tend to be in industrial countries), it is easier for governments to raise domestic prices than it is to lower them. Where farmers' interests are weakly represented (as in many developing countries), the opposite is true. We leave direction-dependent models of market insulation for further research, however, and retain the simple formulation above throughout the analysis presented in this book.[8]

A complete set of the price transmission elasticities estimated in this way is provided in Appendix 2. Their pattern is illustrated in the subset listed in Table 2.11. All the countries included in that table appear to have highly insulated domestic markets for the period examined (1961–1983). The principal exception is the United States, where no insulation is apparent in the markets for wheat, coarse grains and the meats of pigs and poultry. During the 1980s, however, US grain policy changed such that a majority of farmers participated in programs which guaranteed a fixed output price. The US short-run producer price transmission elasticities for wheat and coarse grains were therefore near zero in the late 1980s.

In all the other countries listed in Table 2.11, insulation is considerable, particularly in the short run. The important role

Table 2.11: Estimated producer (consumer) elasticities of price transmission[a], selected countries

		Wheat	Coarse grain	Rice	Ruminant meat	Non-ruminant meat	Dairy products	Sugar	WEIGHTED AVERAGE
EC-10	Short run	0.09 (0.10)	0.24 (0.13)	0.11	0.09 (0.02)	0.08 (0.62)	0.08	0.20	0.17
	Long run	0.20 (0.16)	0.58 (0.26)	0.46 (0.22)	0.14 (0.04)	0.98 (0.76)	0.30	0.30	0.38
Japan	Short run	0.20 (0.06)	0.02 (0.20)	0.06 (0.03	0.10	0.49 (0.47)	0.03	0.00	0.24
	Long run	1.00 (0.25)	0.12 (1.00)	0.55 (0.12)	0.24	0.63 (0.86)	0.08	0.00	0.47
United	Short run	1.00	1.00	0.30 (0.71)	0.60 (0.21)	1.00	0.07 (0.06)	0.43 (0.37)	0.70
States	Long run	1.00	1.00	0.55 (1.00)	0.61 (0.53)	1.00	0.36 (0.18)	0.49 (0.37)	0.78
Argentina	Short run	0.80	0.70	0.56	0.58 (0.77)	0.43 (0.66)	0.34	0.00	0.61
	Long run	1.00	0.80	0.56	0.63 (0.90)	0.46 (0.80)	0.35	0.00	0.70
Brazil	Short run	0.42	0.57 (0.35)	0.16 (0.26)	0.44	0.72	0.54	0.24	0.45
	Long run	0.79	1.00 (0.42)	0.46 (0.32)	0.60	0.77	0.54	0.90	0.67
China[c]	Short run	0.44 (0.05)	0.54 (0.10)	0.35 (0.05)	0.48 (0.05)	0.17 (0.10)	0.10 (0.05)	0.19 (0.05)	0.19
	Long run	0.60	0.87 (0.70)	0.58 (0.40)	0.66 (0.50)	0.25 (0.20)	0.16 (0.10)	0.23 (0.20)	0.48
India[c]	Short run	0.15	0.14	0.17	0.15	0.15	0.15	0.09	0.15
	Long run	0.90	0.80	0.26	0.40	0.60	0.25	0.20	0.42

(continued)

Table 2.11 (continued)

		Wheat	Coarse grain	Rice	Ruminant meat	Non-ruminant meat	Dairy products	Sugar	WEIGHTED AVERAGE
Nigeria	Short run	0.23	0.31	0.22	0.18	0.40	0.30 (0.34)	0.05	0.26
	Long run	0.64	0.53	0.52	0.42	0.60	0.40	0.30	0.50

[a] The table lists producer price transmission elasticities with the corresponding consumer elasticities provided in parentheses only when the two differ. Estimates are derived from time series analysis on the interval 1961–83.

[b] Averages are weighted by the value of production (consumption) at border prices.

[c] Only incomplete analyses of consumer price series were possible for China and India. Data that are available on Chinese urban consumer prices, however, suggest they are much more insulated than producer prices. The consumer elasticities listed for China are 'guesstimates' only.

Source: Based on estimates of equations (2.3) and (2.4) in the text using price data from Saxon, Anderson and Tyers (1986).

of marketing margins in developing countries is hinted at by the tendency of price transmission elasticities to be lower for livestock products and sugar than they are for grains. No such tendency is apparent in the industrial countries, although domestic markets for dairy products and sugar tend to be highly insulated in all countries. Although all price transmission elasticities are larger in the long run, the majority remain substantially less than unity, confirming that domestic food markets have been insulated not only against short-run fluctuations but also against the (generally downward) long-run trend of prices in international food markets.

2.4 Conclusions

The pattern of distortions affecting world food markets has three key characteristics. First, industrial country governments tend to assist the agricultural sector relative to other sectors of their economy while developing country governments tend to discriminate against farmers. Second, as economies grow, there appears to be a tendency for them to move gradually away from effectively taxing to increasingly assisting agriculture relative to other sectors, the rate of this change being most rapid in the economies with the fastest growth, structural change and declining agricultural comparative advantage. Third, all countries tend to be insulated to some extent—often to a very considerable extent—from fluctuations in international food prices. An important effect of insulation from longer-run trends in the presence of a long-run decline in international food prices is to guarantee automatically that domestic-to-border price ratios rise over time, as we observe happened in a dramatic way during the 1980s.

The reasons for policies having these characteristics is the subject of the next chapter. Before turning to that, it is illuminating to note the extent of statistical significance of the above-mentioned distortion pattern. In the econometric work of Honma and Hayami (1986), for example, almost 70 per cent of the variation in protection rates, in a sample of 15 industrial countries and a time series comprising 6 five-year intervals, is accounted for by differences in agriculture's comparative advantage, agriculture's share in the total economy, the international terms of trade between agricultural and manufactured commodities, membership of the EC and food security considerations associated with non-military alliance. Moreover, that study shows that the very high protection rates in East Asia are predicted reasonably well by their model, and concludes that those rates are primarily associated with comparatively rapid rates of structural change rather than other characteristics which might be peculiar to those countries.

An earlier study by the present authors adds further weight to the argument. Using the protection estimates for 1980–82 presented above in Tables 2.6 and 2.9, Anderson and Tyers (1986) regressed the nominal protection coefficient against an index of agricultural comparative advantage as well as against an index of relative per capita income, to obtain:

$$NPC = 0.22 + 0.11Y - 0.51CA \qquad\qquad (2.5)$$
$$(8.7)\ \ (5.6)\ \ (-10.7)$$

$\bar{R}^2 = 0.83$, SER = 0.14, F = 66, n = 30 observations

where NPC is the log of the weighted average of the nominal protection coefficients for traded staple food products in 1980–82, Y is the log of the ratio of an economy's per capita income to the global average per capita income in 1982, and CA is the log of what the food self-sufficiency ratio would be in the absence of the country's food price distortions (as estimated by the model described in Chapter 5).

These results are highly significant statistically, reinforcing earlier evidence for both the negative relationship between protection and comparative advantage and the positive relationship between protection and income per capita.

The relationship between protection and comparative advantage[9] is clearly evident from Figure 2.3. Also plotted in that figure are the predicted levels of protection when the level of income per capita is, respectively, one-tenth, the same as, and ten times the global average. Of the two bands thus delineated in the figure, the higher-income band is occupied mostly by industrial countries, while the lower-income band contains primarily developing countries. Exceptions to this pattern are developing countries with a strong comparative disadvantage in food production, namely Korea and Taiwan

Figure 2.3: Relationship between agricultural protection and an index of
comparative advantage in agriculture, 1980 to 1982[a]

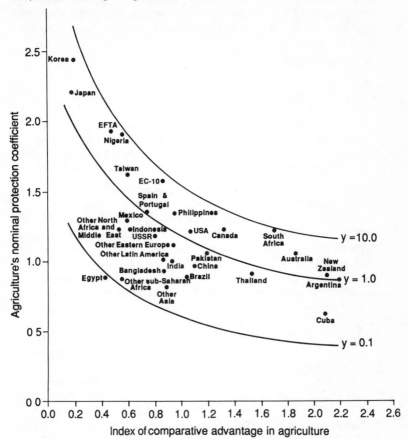

[a] The index of agricultural protection is the weighted average ratio of domestic
producer prices to border prices for grains, meats, dairy products and sugar,
from Tables 2.6 and 2.9; the index of comparative advantage is the ratio of what
the value of domestic production of these products would be to what the value
of their domestic consumption would be in the absence of the country's food
price distortions (as estimated by the model described in Chapter 5 below). The
fitted curves shown correspond to the indicated ratios of national per capita
income to its global average, y.
Source: Adapted from Anderson and Tyers (1986).

(whose high protection is associated with relatively little agricultural land per capita) and Nigeria (where comparative advantage in food production declined rapidly with the onset of the petroleum boom in the 1970s and early 1980s). The next chapter seeks reasons for this pattern of protection and its changes through time.

Notes to Chapter 2

[1]   As will become clear in Chapter 4, the net gains and losses to producers and consumers due to food policies are not precisely these rectangular areas, but, if the more precise methodology were to be used, it would not alter the main point being made here.

[2]   The considerably higher protection rates of the mid-1980s are reflected in the final column of Table 2.1 above. The estimates in Figure 2.2 are conservative also in the sense that they do not include the subsidy equivalent of the numerous forms of assistance provided to farmers that do not affect product prices. Among such measures are subsidies for fertilizer, irrigation water, credit and other inputs, income and fuel tax concessions, direct income support for farm households, subsidies to agricultural marketing services, research and extension support, and the like. These are much more difficult to quantify than policies affecting producer prices, and difficult to attribute to individual products. Thus, no attempt has been made to include their effects, in producer price subsidy equivalent terms, in the protection rates used in this study. There has, however, been a recent attempt by the United States Department of Agriculture (Mabbs-Zeno *et al.* 1988) to estimate the effects of such policies in 1982–86 on aggregate producer subsidy equivalents for industrial market economies. That attempt suggests that nominal rates of protection obtained simply by comparing domestic with border prices, as in the present study, may be underestimating the producer subsidy equivalent of all policies by as much as one-third. This provides a further reason for treating the results in this study as lower-bound estimates for the commodities included. See also the estimates by the OECD (1988 and subsequent updates).

[3]   The producer subsidy equivalent includes not just domestic-to-border price comparisons, as in Figure 2.2, but also as many of the other explicit and implicit subsidies and taxes affecting producer incentives as are quantifiable. It is conceivable, therefore, that a producer subsidy equivalent could be higher or lower than the nominal rate of protection at the border.

4   This phenomenon, of purchased inputs in agriculture becoming more important over time, is not confined to industrial economies. The following data on kilograms of chemical fertilizer used per hectare of arable land (World Bank 1986:180–1) show that the use of fertilizer has grown even more rapidly in developing and centrally planned economies than in industrial market economies:

	1970	1983
Low-income economies	18	66
Middle-income economies	21	44
Centrally planned Europe	64	122
Industrial market economies	99	123

5   Where resources are re-allocated depends, among other things, not only on the extent of changes in effective protection rates but also in the degree of substitutability in production between resource use in different industries (Corden 1971; Lloyd 1974).

6   For more evidence that policies—especially non-agricultural policies—in developing economies tend to discriminate against farmers, see for example, Little, Scitovsky and Scott (1970), Balassa and Associates (1971), Schultz (1978), Peterson (1979), Lutz and Scandizzo (1980), Bale and Lutz (1981), Bates (1981), World Bank (1983, 1986) and Krueger, Schiff and Valdes (1988).

7   To the extent that market instability is undesirable, stable international markets can be seen as international public goods. This is an example of the more general phenomenon discussed by Kindleberger (1986). Countries which 'export' instability are therefore 'free riding'. This issue is discussed further in the next chapter.

8   The work of Roe, Shane and Vo (1986) is encouraging as far as our model is concerned, however, in that it finds that short-run price transmission elasticities remain comparatively stable through time, at least in the markets for wheat and rice (the former in particular).

9   For a discussion of the use of the self-sufficiency ratio compared with other indicators of comparative advantage, see Bowen (1983).

3

Reasons for the Pattern of Food Price Distortions

This chapter is concerned with why it is that so many governments intervene heavily in markets for food products. Specifically, it seeks to explain, first, why rich countries tend to provide assistance to farmers while in poor countries policies tend to discriminate against agriculture, and, second, why most countries, rich and poor alike, tend to insulate their domestic markets from fluctuations in international food prices. In so doing, it also seeks to explain important variants to these general characteristics, particularly the fact that countries which have a strong comparative advantage (disadvantage) in food production tend to protect and insulate their markets less (more) than countries which do not. An important corollary to the first rule also needs explaining. This is the fact that policy regimes of growing economies tend to change gradually from effectively taxing farmers to increasingly subsidizing them, so that agricultural protectionism increases fastest in the fastest growing economies. This tendency seems paradoxical given that, during the course of economic development, the proportions of national votes and wealth in the countryside decline relative to the proportions employed in urban sectors producing tradable goods.

Understanding the reasons for these phenomena is an important part of policy analysis. Until economists know why the pattern of distortionary policies evolves in this way, they will be poorly equipped to suggest more efficient ways to achieve society's development objectives. Such an understanding is also required to enable us to include policy endogenously in a model for forecasting and estimating the effects of policy developments on production, consumption and trade trends in growing economies (such as the model described in Chapter 5).

Traditional attempts to rationalize these policies are typically unconvincing or at best insufficient. For example, the claim that agricultural protection and higher food prices are needed in industrial countries to transfer income to poor farmers looks hollow when the majority of such transfers from consumers goes to the wealthiest 20 per cent or so of farmers (US Government 1987). Similarly, food security concerns may be a part of the explanation for agricultural protection in food-importing industrial countries, but they cannot justify the high level of food prices in those countries which subsidize agricultural exports year after year. The need to raise government revenue in poor countries may help explain why their exports of primary products in these developing countries are taxed, assuming costs of collecting taxes by less distortionary means are much higher; but why then are those countries' imports not also taxed, instead of—as is so often the case—being subjected to quantitative restrictions or prohibitions which do not raise tax revenue? Almost no country has sufficient monopoly power in international markets to justify, on the grounds of maximizing national income, the high level of trade taxes so often imposed— particularly when the prospect of retaliation by trading partners is taken into account.

The first section of this chapter seeks to explain these differing patterns of price distortions by building on the economic theory of regulation developed by Stigler (1975), Peltzman (1976) and others. More specifically, it adopts a political market perspective in which various interest groups are seen to affect the demand for and supply of both agricultural and industrial price and trade policies. This perspective suggests that one of the major factors determining the policy regime is the extent to which different groups expect to gain or lose from its effects on prices and hence on incomes. Another factor is the relative political power of these various groups, which is a function of their share of votes and of wealth, as well as the relative costs to them of collective action, which in turn determines their efficiency in pressuring policy makers and influencing social preferences. A third factor, autonomous social preferences, also affects the policy outcome.

The chapter begins by describing a simple model of the political market for price-distorting policies. It then examines differences between rich and poor countries both in the distributional effects of distorting the relative price of food and in the political power of key vested interest groups. Together, these two sets of factors go a long way towards explaining the typical policy regimes of poor agrarian economies and rich industrial economies. The degree to which differences in social preferences, which themselves can be influenced by interest-group activity, contribute to the observed policy biases is then briefly reviewed. Using the same basic framework, the analysis then addresses the question of why both rich and poor countries choose to insulate their domestic markets from fluctuations in international food prices.

3.1 Why agriculture is subsidized in rich countries and taxed in poor countries[1]

The focus throughout this section is on explaining the inter-sectoral pattern of distortions among tradable sectors, or, more narrowly, between agriculture and industry. This distinguishes it from the now considerable literature aimed at explaining the intra-sectoral pattern of distortions, as well as from the literature which has focused simply on explaining why we have pro-tectionist policies in general rather than free trade.[2] It also distinguishes it from those previous partial equilibrium studies which have tended to examine only the interests and political power of producers and consumers of products whose price is to be distorted (see, for example, Balisacan and Roumasset (1987) and Honma and Hayami (1986) in the case of food price distortions). Most consumers are also factor-owning producers and taxpayers, so it is the effects of policy on their net after-tax real income position which needs to be determined. In addition to farmers (either as owner-occupiers or as landlords and landless labourers) and industrial capitalists, there are capital owners in the non-tradable sector and non-farm workers to consider. Moreover, the price of non-tradables will adjust to a change in the price of a tradable product. Hence, there is a need for a general equilibrium model with three sectors (two producing tradables and one producing non-tradables) and several groups of productive factors for determining the income distributional effects of price distortions.

The political market for price-distorting policies: a conceptual framework

Following Downs (1957), assume the political leadership behaves so as to maximize its chances of remaining in office. The government need not be democratically elected, but it is assumed that the leadership is contestable. One way for the government to obtain political support is to supply policies which assist particular groups. Such policies typically harm others, however, so the amount of assistance provided (which conceptually could be positive or negative) is limited to the point where the marginal gain in political support from the group being assisted is equal to the marginal political cost in terms of the reduced support from other groups. Of course price-distorting policies would not be implemented in a political environment where everyone voted on each policy issue, where no considerations other than the distributional effects of the policy determined the outcome, and where information on the costs and distributional consequences of the policy was available at no cost. This is because the deadweight welfare costs associated with distortionary policies would ensure it was always possible for the potential losers from a policy to bribe the potential gainers not to seek that policy. But, in practice, these ideal conditions do not hold, hence the need to examine the extent to which different groups gain or lose from particular policies and their costs of getting together to become informed and to influence policy makers.

The marginal preparedness of a group to pay for increased assistance is assumed to decline as the amount of assistance increases. This is because more assistance encourages new firms to enter the industry thereby spreading the benefits to new entrants and worsening the free-rider problem of collective lobbying action by the group (Olson 1965). Similarly, the marginal political cost of assisting that group increases with the amount of assistance because, at higher levels of inter-vention, the government loses support from more and more groups for whom the adverse effects of the policy exceed the costs of getting members together to voice their opposition. Thus, it is possible to conceptualize a political market with a downward-sloping demand curve for a policy which assists a particular group, and an upward-sloping supply curve repre-

senting the leadership's marginal political cost of providing that
assistance policy. The currency of payment is political support
for the government, which includes, but is not limited to, cash
contributions to electoral campaigns.[3]

Suppose the economy has just three sectors: two (agriculture
and industry) producing final tradable goods and one producing
non-tradable goods and services. Final-product export proceeds
are used to import intermediate inputs and perhaps some
additional quantities of one of the two final products that are
tradable. One way to quantify the amount of assistance to a
sector provided by price and trade policies is to use the partial-
equilibrium effective protection coefficient (EPC) concept. The
EPC is defined as one plus (minus) the proportion by which
government policies directly raise (lower) value added in that
sector. This coefficient is thus a positive number which exceeds
(is less than) unity for a particular sector when policies directly
discriminate in favour of (against) that sector.

This simple political market for assistance to a sector is
illustrated in Figure 3.1. The vertical axis measures the 'price',
in terms of political support, of a unit of effective protection
to a tradable sector, while the horizontal axis measures the
'quantity', in terms of the effective protection coefficient, for
this tradable sector relative to a given EPC for the other tradable
sector. Of particular interest here is why the demand and supply
curves for assistance to agriculture tend to intersect to the left
of unity on the horizontal axis for poor agrarian economies,
and to the right of unity in rich industrial countries, as illustrated
in Figure 3.1; and (though not illustrated in the figure) why
those for industry tend to intersect more to the right of unity
for developing compared with those for advanced industrial
countries.

Such a political market framework is able to accommodate
both the (positive or negative) benefits from assistance policies
and the costs of collective information-gathering and lobbying
by groups favouring or opposing assistance to a sector. It is
also able to accommodate (via the supply side) any special social
preferences, fiscal characteristics and the like which affect this
market. An examination of the factors affecting these demand
and supply curves could also uncover the reason why some
price-distorting policy instruments are used more than others,
why effective protection for agriculture relative to industry

Figure 3.1: The political market for government assistance to agriculture[a]

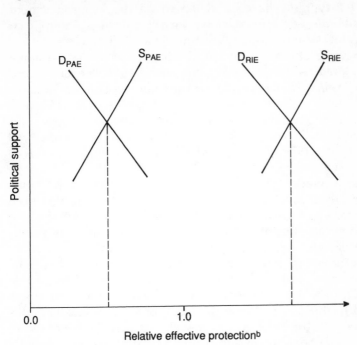

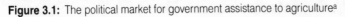

a D and S refer to the demand and supply curves; PAE and RIE refer to a poor
  agrarian economy and a rich industrial economy.
b The relative protection index is defined as the effective protection coefficient
  (EPC) for agriculture relative to a given EPC for the industrial sector. Thus an
  index in excess of (less than) unity indicates that government policy is effectively
  assisting (taxing) agriculture relative to the industrial sector.

increases in the course of a country's economic development,
and why protection coefficients differ between countries with
similar income levels. The most obvious factors to focus on first
are those which determine who gains and who loses from price-
distorting policies.

Income distributional effects of price-distorting policies

There are many ways to analyse the distributional and other
effects of policy-induced changes to producer incentives and
consumer prices, depending on the assumptions one is prepared

to tolerate. Trade theorists, following Stolper and Samuelson (1941), typically have concentrated on the long-run general equilibrium effects of trade taxes on factor incomes. These effects suggest results which are incompatible with the actual behaviour of interest groups: the Stolper–Samuelson relationship predicts that, in an economy with two mobile factors, one factor will gain but the other will lose from assisting an industry. Yet, there are numerous cases where both labour *and* capital owners in an industry lobby for its protection (Magee 1980). Such behaviour *is* predicted, however, by a model formalized by Jones (1971, 1975) and Mussa (1974) in which capital is assumed to be sector-specific and only labour is mobile intersectorally. While, in practice, both factors are less than perfectly mobile in the short run (and, in the long run, even capital is somewhat mobile through depreciation and redirection of new investments), the assumption that capital is sector-specific and labour is mobile intersectorally is sufficiently realistic for the medium term to be adopted here. Appendix 3 extends the Jones (1975) version of that model to include a non-tradables sector which produces both intermediate inputs and final products. While the inclusion of non-tradables adds realism to the Jones–Mussa model, it makes the equations of change rather complex and ensures that the directions of effects depend on the values of key parameters. To draw clear conclusions about the income distributional effects of distortionary policies, it is therefore necessary to adopt representative parameter sets for a poor agrarian economy and a rich industrial economy.

In the process of economic growth, there are at least five sets of parameters whose changes have important influences on the effects of price and trade policies. One is the distribution of labour across sectors: 60 per cent of workers are assumed to be employed in agriculture and 10 per cent in manufacturing in the poor country while, for the rich country, the shares are 3 and 30 per cent, respectively. Another critical parameter is the distribution of expenditure of different groups between the three sets of final products. In the poor country, food accounts for around half of household expenditure (in opportunity-cost terms for semi-subsistence farmers), while, in the rich country, its share is smaller than that for manufactures, and non-tradables are the dominant expenditure items.

A third important set of parameters relates to the much more rapid growth (from a low base) in the use of purchased inputs, including capital items, in agriculture compared with other sectors as economic growth proceeds. Subsistence farmers purchase very few intermediate inputs and employ little capital at early stages of development. Even the land used in traditional agriculture often has only modest capital value before the advent of systematic irrigation, the building up of nutrients via chemical fertilizer applications, and the like. On the other hand, agriculture in advanced industrial countries tends to be more intensive than other sectors in the use of purchased intermediate inputs and physical capital. Thus labour's share of value added and the value-added share of output are assumed for agriculture to be only half as large in the rich country as in the poor country, while the differences for other sectors are more modest.

The fourth set of parameters, which differs significantly between a poor agrarian country and a rich industrial one, concerns the pattern of trade specialization. Poor countries' exports tend to be dominated by primary products and perhaps a few light manufactured final products while imports are dominated by intermediate goods, as noted above in Section 1.3 of Chapter 1. By contrast, rich industrial countries tend to have a comparative advantage in manufactured goods and all but the most land abundant will import agricultural products in the absence of distortions.

Lastly, in poor agrarian countries, farmers typically pay no income tax because the cost of collecting it would exceed the revenues raised. Hence, real incomes of the relatively small urban sector of such countries are more sensitive to changes in the demand for tax revenue than is the case in rich countries, despite the fact that the latter have an overall rate of taxation double that of the former.

Given these and related assumptions about values for the relevant parameters (summarized in Table A.12 in Appendix 3) it is possible to generate representative effects of price and trade policies on factor rewards, output, employment, tax revenue and the real incomes of different groups in the two archetype countries. These effects obviously depend on the parameter values chosen, but the following inferences are robust for a wide range of feasible values for those parameters. For the moment, assume that the policy choice set is confined to trade taxes–cum–subsidies on final products, effects of which are summarized in Table 3.1.

When the relative price of the output from one of the sectors rises, because of the imposition of a trade tax-cum-subsidy, wages must rise to attract labour to the now more profitable sector. The wage rise will tend to be larger, the larger the share of employment in the expanding sector. The rise in product price and wages will also result in a higher price for non-

Table 3.1: Elasticities of factor rewards, the price of non-tradables, real incomes, and sectoral output and employment with respect to a trade policy induced change in the price of agricultural or industrial products

			Poor agrarian economy	Rich industrial economy
I	**Elasticity of factor rewards and non-tradables prices with respect to a change in:**			
	(a)	Agricultural product prices		
		1. Agricultural capital	1.45	3.69
		2. Industrial capital	-3.13	-0.20
		3. Other capital	0.93	0.09
		4. Wages	1.06	0.11
		5. Price of non-tradables	0.80	0.08
	(b)	Industrial product prices		
		6. Agricultural capital	-0.40	-1.81
		7. Industrial capital	4.82	1.73
		8. Other capital	0.32	1.21
		9. Wages	0.14	1.28
		10. Price of non-tradables	0.21	0.95
II	**Elasticity of real incomes of different groups with respect to a change in:**			
	(a)	Agricultural product prices		
		11. Farmers	0.37	2.29
		12. Industrial capitalists	-4.30	-0.32
		13. Other capitalists	-0.24	-0.03
		14. Non-farm workers	-0.25	-0.06
	(b)	Industrial product prices		
		15. Farmers	-0.21	-1.99
		16. Industrial capitalists	4.43	0.43
		17. Other capitalists	-0.06	-0.08
		18. Non-farm workers	-0.03	0.04

			Poor agrarian economy		Rich industrial economy	
III	**Elasticity of sectoral output and employment, and of tax revenue with respect to change in:**					
	(a)	Agricultural product prices				
		19. Agricultural output, employment	0.28	0.40	1.25	3.58
		20. Industrial output, employment	-2.93	-4.19	-0.16	-0.31
		21. Nontradables output, employment	-0.01	-0.02	-0.00	-0.00
		22. Tax revenue	0.00	(-1.60)[a]	0.00	(0.16)[a]
	(b)	Industrial product prices				
		23. Agricultural output, employment	-0.38	-0.55	-1.08	-3.09
		24. Industrial output, employment	3.28	4.68	0.22	0.44
		25. Nontradables output, employment	0.12	0.18	-0.04	-0.07
		26. Tax revenue	0.00	(-0.14)[a]	0.00	(-1.76)[a]

[a] The elasticities in parentheses show the tax revenue effect if income tax rates were not changed.

Source: Authors' calculations derived using equations (A3.23) to (A3.29) and (A3.32) of Appendix 3 to this volume together with the parameter values in Table A.12 of Appendix 3, assuming that a trade tax-cum-subsidy is used which changes the producer and consumer price of one of the final tradable products by the same proportion.

tradables since the former shifts out the demand curve in the market for non-tradables and the latter shifts up the supply curve. The non-tradables price rise will be larger the larger the share of expenditure on the tradable product whose price has risen and hence the larger the income-compensated cross-elasticity of demand for non-tradables. Hence, if agricultural product prices rise, wages and the price of non-tradables rise substantially in the poor agrarian economy while they rise only a little in the rich industrial economy, and conversely for a rise in industrial product prices (rows 4, 5, 9 and 10 in Table 3.1).[4] The more the wage rises, the less the boost to specific factor rewards in the expanding tradable sector and the greater the reduction in specific factor rewards in the contracting sector(s). Hence a rise in agricultural product prices boosts returns to agricultural capital less, and harms returns to industrial capital much more, in the poor agrarian economy than in the rich industrial economy, and conversely for a rise in the industrial product prices (rows 1,2,6 and 7 of Table 3.1).

The net effects on real incomes of farmers, industrial capitalists, owners of non-tradables capital and non-farm workers are summarized in part II of Table 3.1. These real income effects depend on the assumption that farmers supply their own labour as well as capital, and that capitalists have a different expenditure pattern from workers and farmers because they are assumed to be richer (see Table A.12 in Appendix 3).

These real income effects shed considerable light on the political economy of trade policy in poor countries compared with rich countries. A 10 per cent reduction in agricultural product prices relative to industrial product prices in the poor agrarian economy, due to a tax on agricultural exports, would reduce farmers' real incomes by less than 4 per cent but would boost industrialists' real incomes by 43 per cent (see the elasticities in rows 11 and 12 of Table 3.1).[5] At the same time, such a trade policy would boost real after-tax incomes of other capitalists and workers by about 25 per cent, assuming income tax rates were to be adjusted to ensure no net change in overall tax revenues. Moreover, unemployed people would benefit much more than workers if they continued to remain unemployed, because of the lower price not only of food but also of non-tradables: a 10 per cent drop in agricultural prices would lower their cost of living by about 8 per cent. Similarly, a rise in the price of industrial products in the poor country has a very large positive effect on real incomes of industrial capitalists, only a minor negative effect on farm incomes, and almost no effect on incomes of other capitalists and workers (rows 15 to 18). It would even have little negative effect on unemployed people, since the flow-on effect of industrial protection on the price of non-tradables is relatively minor and the cost of living for such people is in any case primarily determined by food prices. Indeed, unemployed people may favour an industrial protection policy in the belief that it would boost the number of available jobs.[6]

For the rich industrial economy, on the other hand, a 10 per cent increase in agricultural product prices would boost real farm incomes by 23 per cent, while lowering incomes of industrial capitalists' by only 3 per cent, and of other capitalists and non-farm workers by less than 1 per cent. A rise in industrial product prices would again do the opposite: it would hurt farmers seven times more than it helps industrial capitalists, while real incomes of other capitalists and workers would hardly be affected if full tax adjustment were to occur (see second column in part II of Table 3.1).

These factor owners are not the only groups with vested interests in price and trade policies, however. A not insignificant source of lobbying on sectoral policy issues comes from within the government's bureaucracy. Insofar as the career prospects of officials in the agricultural and industrial development ministries are positively related to output and employment in the sector they serve, the intensity of their support for or against a policy might be expected to be positively related to the sectoral output and employment effects of that policy. As shown in part III of Table 3.1, the proportional changes in output and employment in the poor country (resulting from distorting agricultural product prices relative to industrial product prices) are much smaller for agriculture than for industry, whereas the opposite is true in the rich country. (Non-tradables output and employment changes are close to zero in both cases.) As well, because agriculture is the dominant export sector in the absence of distortions in the poor country, and industry dominates in the rich country, trade tax revenue is enhanced greatly if agricultural exports are taxed in the poor country (an elasticity of 1.6—see line 22 of Table 3.1), whereas in the rich country they are enhanced by protecting farmers from import competition. Conversely, it is much easier to finance an industrial export subsidy in the poor country than in the rich country, given the size difference in their industrial sectors.[7] For these reasons, finance ministry officials, concerned with maintaining tax revenues in a environment where raising income tax rates is difficult, would tend to support a trade policy regime which is biased against the agricultural export sector of the poor country and in favour of import-competing farmers in the rich country.

In short, these simulations suggest that, other things being equal, the potential gross benefits to farmers and agricultural bureaucrats who successfully seek agricultural price supports or oppose industrial protection in poor countries are less than one-sixth the benefits to individuals in corresponding groups in rich countries. Furthermore, industrial capitalists and closely associated bureaucrats each have ten times more incentive to seek policies which assist manufacturing and reduce agricultural prices in poor countries than do individuals in corresponding groups in rich countries. Moreover, in the poor country, the per capita benefits to industrial capitalists from a trade policy regime that favours manufacturing at the expense of agriculture are more than ten times the costs that the policy regime imposes on farmers. The difference in distributional effects is not quite as extreme in the rich industrial country, but even there farmers would gain five or more times as much as industrial capitalists would lose *per capita* from a trade policy regime which favoured agriculture at the expense of manufacturing, according to this model.

These per capita distributional effects are only part of the story, however. To determine their impact on the policy outcome one also needs to consider the political power of vested interest groups to translate into action those incentives to influence policy.

The political power of vested interest groups

A group's political power is presumably a function of its vote contribution, its economic strength as indicated, for example, by its share of national income, and its efficiency in getting members together to become informed and to lobby. We now consider each of these in turn.

(i) Voting contribution of different interest groups

Perfectly informed voters might be expected to support or oppose a distortionary policy more vigorously the larger the percentage by which their real income is raised or lowered by that policy. If, in addition to being perfectly informed, voters had the opportunity (but no compulsion) to vote on each policy issue, then a crude indication of the strength of each group's aggregate voting behaviour could be obtained by multiplying the elasticities in part II of Table 3.1 by the proportion of votes each group represents. The sign of the sum of such weighted elasticities also provides a rough indication of the likely net voting outcome. These indicators are presented in part 1 of Table 3.2.

In this simplified polity of perfect voter information, (single-issue elections and no compulsion to vote), this indicator suggests that, in the poor country, the weight of the farmers' vote relative to that of the industrial capitalists' vote should be sufficient to more than offset the relative smallness of the income effects per farmer of a trade policy regime which favours the industrial sector at the expense of agriculture. What is surprising, however, is not that the summed vote-weighted elasticities for the poor economy are more than zero (0.068) for agricultural price support and less than zero (–0.091) for industrial price support, but that these sums are quite small, suggesting that the skewed income distributional effects of those trade policies are almost sufficient to offset the opposite asymmetry in the distribution of votes. Indeed, for the rich industrial country, the asymmetry in effects on income *is* just sufficient to offset the opposite voting asymmetry: the sum of the vote-weighted elasticities is 0.004 for an agricultural protection policy and -0.014 for industrial price support. This means that, if votes were all that influenced the policy determination process and voters were fully informed

Table 3.2: Indicators of aggregate gross incentives for groups to influence trade policy decisions

		Poor agrarian economy	Rich industrial economy
I	**Elasticity of real incomes of different groups[a], multiplied by the group's share of votes[b], with respect to a change in:**		
	(a) Agricultural product prices		
	1. Farmers	0.214	0.066
	2. Industrial capitalists	–0.043	–0.005
	3. Other capitalists	–0.007	–0.001
	4. Non-farm workers	–0.096	–0.056
	Total	**0.068**	**0.004**
	(b) Industrial product prices		
	5. Farmers	–0.122	–0.058
	6. Industrial capitalists	0.044	0.006
	7. Other capitalists	–0.002	–0.003
	8. Non-farm workers	–0.011	0.041
	Total	**–0.091**	**–0.014**

(continued)

Table 3.2 *(continued)*

		Poor agrarian economy	Rich industrial economy
II	**Elasticity of real incomes of different groups[a], multiplied by the group's share of GDP[c], with respect to a change in:**		
(a)	Agricultural product prices		
	9. Farmers	0.222	0.092
	10. Industrial capitalists	-0.129	-0.054
	11. Other capitalists	-0.021	-0.007
	12. Non-farm workers	-0.070	-0.033
(b)	Industrial product prices		
	13. Farmers	-0.125	-0.080
	14. Industrial capitalists	0.135	0.074
	15. Other capitalists	-0.005	-0.020
	16. Non-farm workers	-0.007	0.024

a   Elasticities of real income are taken from part II of Table 3.1.
b   The distributions of votes are based on sectoral employment shares from Table A.12 of Appendix 3 to this volume and on the assumptions that all, and only, farmers, urban capitalists and non-farm workers are eligible to vote and that there is one capitalist per ten (twenty) workers in each of the non-farm sectors in the poor (rich) country. The four groups' proportions of votes are 0.577, 0.010, 0.029 and 0.384 for the poor country and 0.029, 0.014, 0.032 and 0.925 for the rich country.
c   Shares of national income are derived from the first and the final rows of Table A.12. For the four groups listed they are 0.60, 0.30, 0.09 and 0.28 for the poor country and 0.04, 0.17, 0.248 and 0.542 for the rich country.

and more inclined to vote for or against a policy the more it affected their income, there would be a close match in both the poor country and the rich country in votes for and against a trade policy regime which favoured one of the tradables sectors at the expense of the other, despite the skewed distribution of votes in the two different types of countries.

In practice, of course, it is costly for voters to become informed about effects of policies (especially the indirect effects) on their real incomes. Moreover, voters do not have the opportunity to vote for or against each policy, but instead have to vote for a package of policies among which price and trade policies are but a small part. These facts of political life ensure that not just the voting size but also the economic size of different vested interest groups has an influence on the policy outcome.

(ii) Economic size of different interest groups

In order for the government and opposition parties to go to the electorate to persuade voters of the virtues of their party's policy package, the party needs resources. As Brock and Magee (1980) and others point out, these can be obtained by including in the package some policies which benefit a minority even though they reduce national income and the welfare of the majority. Such a strategy is possible wherever the political support gained from that favoured minority exceeds that lost from the disadvantaged majority. The latter is likely to be smaller relative to the former the stronger the group's relative economic strength (i.e. the larger its share of national resources and hence income), because, other things being equal, this affects the aggregate gross economic benefit of the policy to that group. Not only will the demand curve in the political market diagram in Figure 3.1 be further to the right the larger that aggregate benefit, but also the supply curve will be lower since some of the potential benefits of the policy to the group could be spent on disseminating selective information on the virtues to society of the policy, thereby reducing opposition to it.

An indication of the aggregate benefit to different groups of raising agricultural or industrial product prices via trade taxes-cum-subsidies is summarized in part II of Table 3.2. It shows the product of the elasticities reported in part II of Table 3.1 and the group's share of national income.[8] This index suggests that capitalists in the non-tradables sector are affected relatively little in aggregate terms. With regard to farmers and industrial capitalists in the rich country, this indicator suggests farmers have slightly more incentive to influence trade policies in their favour than do industrialists, although non-farm labour has a reasonably strong incentive to support the industrial capitalists' lobbying efforts. In the poor country, farmers have slightly less aggregate incentive to oppose an industrial protection policy than industrial capitalists have to demand it, but farmers would lose considerably more than industrialists would gain in aggregate from a lowering of agricultural prices. This latter asymmetry is consistent with the finding that farmers in poor countries tend to have been much more successful in preventing the imposition of direct disincentives for agriculture than they have been in preventing policies which indirectly disadvantage them (see Krueger, Schiff and Valdes (1988)).

Clearly, the indicators in part II of Table 3.2 bring us even closer to understanding why industrialists tend to be assisted more and farmers assisted less or even taxed indirectly, in poor economies compared with rich ones. This is especially so in view of the likelihood that the group benefitting directly from a policy is likely to be more informed about that effect than those who are affected indirectly. However, there is a further important set of factors affecting the incentive to lobby for favourable policies, namely those that determine the relative efficiency of different groups in acting collectively.

(iii) Costs of collective action by vested interest groups

In a poor agrarian economy, the costs of getting farmers to act collectively to become informed and lobby for a more favourable policy regime tend to be prohibitively high. Collective action is expensive to organize because of the difficulty of preventing free-riding due to the large number of small, poorly educated producers who find it costly to get together because of low quality rural transport and communications infrastructure. By contrast, urban capitalists in poor countries are relatively well-educated, politically articulate, small in number, have larger sales per firm than farmers, and are often located in the large cities in easy reach of people in government. Hence their costs of becoming informed and lobbying are comparatively low (Olson 1986).

In the course of a country's economic development, however, the costs of collective action decrease more for farmers than for urban capitalists. In part, this is because the differences between urban and rural education, transport and communications infrastructure tend to narrow with economic growth. Also, the positive effect of the increase in numbers of industrial and service sector firms on the lobbying strength of urban capitalists tends to be more or less offset by an increase in their free-rider problem of acting collectively. In addition, numerous industries graduate from import substitution to export status and perhaps also become direct investors abroad. Manufacturers' associations therefore become less inclined to seek manufacturing protection policies since that is against the interests of their more competitive, more successful members.

Even more importantly, with the process of development there emerges a way for farmers to reduce substantially their free-rider problem. As farmers gradually commercialize their activities, they perceive income earning opportunities in the supplying of off farm inputs and the marketing of farm output. They also often fear exploitation by the middlemen who emerge to supply these services. Thus, farmer associations or cooperatives form and act as input-buying and output-selling groups for the purpose of increasing farmers' bargaining power with middlemen. In some cases, farmer cooperatives even become a substitute for middlemen. Discounts for members on purchased inputs and marketing fees are offered to encourage producers to join.[9] Once established, these organizations are able to lobby on behalf of farmers at relatively low cost, despite the large number of relatively small farm firms still involved in agriculture. Furthermore, established farm cooperatives have a vested interest in lobbying not only on behalf of farmers but also on their own behalf. This is also true for the new groups of manufacturing and service industries producing farm inputs and processing farm outputs where these activities are not undertaken by farm cooperatives (Bolin, Meyerson and Stahl 1986; George and Saxon 1986). This adds considerably to the effective demand for policies favourable to agriculture in advanced industrial economies, especially as input and output volumes tend to keep expanding even as the number of farmers diminishes.

What about non-farm workers? Their costs of collective action in some poor economies, along with those of the unemployed, are demonstrably low enough to encourage collective action in the form, perhaps, of urban riots. They tend to support policies which favour industry and keep down food prices. This is what might be expected from the signs of the elasticities in Tables 3.1 and 3.2 in the case of agricultural policy, but not in the case of industrial protection. An explanation for the latter anomaly may be that urban workers give more weight to the direct effects of industrial policies in boosting jobs in urban areas. It is, of course, in the interests of industrial capitalists to emphasize these direct effects of policies and quietly to ignore the indirect effect such policies have in reducing the demand for labour and hence wages.

In rich industrial countries, urban workers are well organized into unions and therefore enjoy relatively low costs of collective action. The indicators in Table 3.2 would suggest workers should be against—but only mildly so—the typical trade policy regime in which agriculture is assisted relative to manufacturing. The absence of strong opposition from them may partly be because they find it more profitable to invest their resources in wage bargaining with employers and wage arbitration tribunals. But, it may also be due to their views on non-economic effects of trade policy, to which we now turn.

Social preferences and price-distorting policies

Social preferences of society can also have an important influence on policy outcomes. In poor agrarian economies, the desire to industrialize is typically strong because industrialization is perceived to be related to modernization and affluence and to result in a more 'balanced' economy (Johnson 1965). As well, in states which have recently gained their independence from a capitalist power, the ruling elite often has socialist tendencies which include inclinations to reduce the economy's dependence on trade with rich industrial countries, provide urban consumers with cheap food and housing, and develop state-financed, import-substituting industrial projects (Bates 1981). Funds for the latter can be raised most cheaply by trade taxes which, for countries with a comparative advantage in agriculture, will also contribute to the government's goals of being less agrarian and less trade-dependent. The larger these social benefits of taxing manufactured imports and agricultural exports are perceived to be relative to the perceived costs of trade taxes, the lower will be the political costs of such a trade policy regime as reflected in the supply curve in Figure 3.1.

As an economy industrializes, however, the 'balanced economy', nationalistic and self-reliance motivations for assisting the import-substituting infant industrial sector gradually disappear. So too does the need to depend heavily on trade taxes to raise government revenue and to redistribute welfare, because of a relative decline in the costs of collecting and dispersing government funds by more direct means. In addition, if the economy loses its comparative advantage in agricultural products in the course of industrial development, the earlier concern by society to promote manufacturing may be displaced by a concern to boost agricultural output for food security reasons.

During this century, productivity growth and demand changes have been such that the trend in the international price of farm products relative to industrial products has been downwards, a trend that has been exacerbated by the growth of agricultural protection.[10] Since many urban people in industrial countries have a fondness toward farmers, perhaps because of the perceived virtues of country life and the fact that their recent ancestors were farmers, their sense of fairness is aroused when farm output prices are not keeping up with inflation and farmers are having to leave the land (in part *because* of their sector's labour productivity growth and the protectionist policies of other rich countries). So, when farm lobbyists direct media attention to the plight of small farmers in 'left-behind' regions, few groups in advanced industrial societies actively oppose agricultural protection policies that will merely slow the declines in real food prices and farm employment. Indeed, urban groups may judge that, if the agricultural sector were to shed labour too rapidly, political instability would result which, in addition to being undesirable for its own sake, may be perceived to be more detrimental to economic growth in the non-farm sectors than the comparative-static deadweight costs of the price distortions. In any case, urban groups may see agricultural protection as a social insurance policy of a sort they themselves may feel the need to draw on at some future date (Corden 1974: 320–1; Eaton and Grossman 1985).

Finally on social preferences, both producers and consumers appear to prefer prices of (especially necessary) products to be more rather than less stable over time. The fact that international prices for farm products gyrate much more than prices for manufactured products is often used to justify policy intervention at a country's border. Once a price stabilization scheme is legitimized in principle, the administrative task of deciding on the trend level of prices around which to stabilize is subjected to the same pressures from interest groups as discussed above, since there is always uncertainty *ex ante* about that medium-term trend level. Thus, the social preference for stable food prices in an environment of fluctuating international prices simply makes it less costly politically for a government to intervene to distort farm product prices below or above the international trend level.

Why are first-best policy instruments not used

In view of the asymmetries in the costs of people getting together and becoming informed about the effects of sectoral policies, it is not difficult to understand why first-best policy instruments are not used to achieve particular objectives. Of special significance is the higher cost of information to potential opponents of a sectoral assistance policy when a covert second-best—or nth-best—instrument is used instead of a direct payment. However, it is illuminating to examine also the distributional effects of more direct instruments than trade policies. The most obvious instruments to consider are producer price subsidies for both tradable products in the rich country and food consumer and industrial producer subsidies in the poor country.[11]

Producer price subsidies for agriculture (column (3) of Table 3.3) are shown to have almost the same distributional effects on real after-tax incomes in the rich industrial country as does agricultural protection at the border. They presumably are not used to support farmers, despite their smaller deadweight cost than import taxes, simply because the extent of the transfer to farmers would be more obvious. Column (4) of Table 3.3 shows the effects of industrial producer price support policies. Again this more direct policy instrument would hurt farmers less and help industrialists more than would a trade policy instrument, but again it has a more negative effect on the real incomes of other urban groups as well as being overt.

To estimate the elasticities for an agricultural consumer price subsidy, it is assumed that farmers are ineligible for the subsidy. Thus, the effect on their real income is mainly due to the small changes in the price of non-tradables and in wages, which are negligible (column (5) of Table 3.3). Urban workers would gain but at the expense of urban capitalists, who lose because they are cross-subsidizing through their taxes the greater proportional implicit income transfer to that lower-income group (which spends a larger share of its income on food). Thus, the extent to which such subsidies are used rather than (or in addition to) agricultural export taxes, would depend on the

Table 3.3: Elasticities of real incomes with respect to various policy induced changes in the price of agricultural or industrial products

	Price-raising agricultural trade policy[a] (1)	Price-raising industrial trade policy[b] (2)	Agricultural producer price subsidy[c] (3)	Industrial producer price subsidy[c] (4)	Urban food consumer price subsidy[c] (5)
Poor agrarian economy					
Elasticity of real after-tax incomes of:					
Farmers	0.37	-0.21		-0.06	-0.01
Industrial capitalists	-4.30	4.43		4.40	-0.27
Other capitalists	-0.24	-0.06		-0.35	-0.45
Non-farm workers	-0.25	-0.03		-0.23	0.13
Rich industrial economy					
Elasticity of real after-tax incomes of:					
Farmers	2.29	-1.99	2.29	-1.82	
Industrial capitalists	-0.32	0.43	-0.35	0.73	
Other capitalists	-0.03	-0.08	-0.06	-0.28	
Non-farm workers	-0.06	0.04	-0.03	0.04	

a   From (a), part II, Table 3.1.
b   From (b), part II, Table 3.1.
c   Based on the modifications to equations (24) to (28) that are mentioned after equation (29) in Appendix 3 to this volume. In the case of column (5) it is the agricultural purchases of only urban people that are subsidized, that is, farmers continue to pay (typically in opportunity cost terms) the world price for their food.

Source: Authors' calculations based on the equations and parameters in Appendix 3.

relative political power of the three urban groups. Evidently, in some poor countries where urban workers (and the unemployed) have sufficient power, it has been in the government's interest to raise tax revenue to subsidize urban food consumption.[12] In such circumstances perhaps, other additional policy instruments have been used to compensate urban capitalists for the negative effect on them of food subsidies.

Possible extensions to the analysis

The above analysis could be extended in a number of ways. One is to modify the extreme factorial assumptions of the model outlined in Appendix 3; for example, to allow capital to be partially mobile between sectors (Diamond 1982; Grossman 1983), to allow for minimum wage laws and the urban unemployment it can induce (Harris and Todaro 1970; Corden and Findlay 1975), and to allow for some sector specificity to the human capital associated with labour (Baldwin 1984). Insofar as labour is imperfectly mobile and some capital can move between sectors, the elasticities of factor rewards reported in Table 3.1 overstate the extent of change that would take place. If workers have above average union strength and can thereby extract above equilibrium wages in a particular sector, or if they have sector-specific skills (as do farmers), the incentive for them to lobby for assistance to their own particular sector would be greater than otherwise, other things being equal (Becker 1983: 383). The latter is especially important when employment in that sector is declining absolutely, as happens in agriculture once a country graduates from middle income status,[13] because then all the benefits from assistance which slow that decline accrue to existing producers (Hillman 1982). Different assumptions concerning the taxing of factor incomes could also be introduced, including the deadweight costs of income taxation which Browning (1987) and others have identified as being significant.

Another extension could be to include more explicitly the reactions of other groups to any single group's lobbying demands.[14] What determines the proportion of farmers' lobbying funds which is devoted to demanding assistance policies for agriculture rather than to opposing policies favourable to industrialists or other groups? To help answer this, we need a general equilibrium model of the political market for which a Cournot–Nash equilibrium outcome could be determined. This would also shed light on why trade policy instruments rather than more direct redistributive instruments, such as income transfers or producer price subsidies, are used,[15] and why we simultaneously observe policies which subsidize an industry's output but tax some of its inputs or vice versa.[16]

A third extension would be to include the administrative and legislative arms of government more explicitly in the analysis than has been possible above. In addition to bureaucrats wanting to enhance their welfare, for example through expanding the size of their agency, politicians could be considered as an interest group over and above their role as arbiters of conflicting private interest groups.[17] Finally, lobbying itself involves resources, represented in Figure 3.1 by areas under the demand curves (see Anderson 1978). Integrating this fact into the analysis is unlikely to change the conclusions, but it would shed light on the extent of lobbying activity to expect in different circumstances (see Findlay and Wellisz 1982, 1983; Young and Magee 1986).

Implications of the analysis for the pattern of distortions

Even though the above involves a highly simplified model of the political process, it nevertheless helps explain why distortionary price and trade policies in poor agrarian economies are biased in favour of manufacturing and against agriculture, whereas the opposite intersectoral bias tends to prevail in rich industrial countries. Moreover, over time and within any group of countries, there will be a tendency for the policy regime to undergo a number of changes. First, it changes gradually in favour of agriculture as the economy grows (particularly if growth is accompanied by a decline in agricultural comparative advantage); second, it tends to favour farmers relative to industrialists at a lower per capita income level, the lower the agricultural comparative advantage of this compared with similar income countries; and, third, it changes faster the faster the growth of the economy and the faster the decline in its agricultural comparative advantage. This is indeed what has happened among the advanced and newly industrialized countries in recent decades. As can be seen from the first three columns of Table 3.4, nominal protection for agriculture is low in the relatively lightly populated, food-exporting countries of North America and Australasia, reasonably high in Western Europe and very high in the densely populated, food-importing industrial economies of East Asia. The proportional increases in the nominal protection coefficients for agriculture are similarly ranked, with protection growing fastest in rapidly growing East Asia where agricultural comparative advantage has declined substantially, and least in slow growing North America and Australasia which have maintained a strong comparative advantage in agriculture.

3.2   Why both rich and poor countries insulate their domestic food markets

This section takes the same approach to the market-insulating components of agricultural policy as is taken in the previous section for the pure protection components; that is, it first examines public interest explanations for market insulation and, where these are weak, it investigates whether the relative stability of domestic prices yields comparatively large increases in the welfare of influential groups.

Conceivably, a public interest case exists for stabilizing domestic prices if at least some agents are risk averse and if price fluctuations impair the welfare of these agents to an extent which dominates the effects on others. Certainly, it is safe to assume that most agents are averse to risks that are significant in relation to their average income (Newbery and Stiglitz: 1981, Ch.7). However, as our analysis subsequently demonstrates, where agents are averse to income risk, their welfare is not necessarily reduced by price fluctuations. This fact differentiates the analysis of the price-stabilizing component of food policy from the pure protection component, since the private welfare gains from pure protection are intuitively more obvious. But, even if price stabilization were universally welfare improving, the appropriate policy response would not necessarily be market insulation through distortions at the border. We return to this latter point in the next section.

In all countries some agents can be expected to have stronger preferences for price stability than others. Since we observe market insulation in both developing and advanced industrial countries, the arguments of the previous section would lead us to hypothesize that this preference would be strongest among the groups with most apparent influence over agricultural policy in each case, namely, consumers and industrial capital owners in developing countries and farmers in industrial countries. What, then, are the directions of the welfare impacts of price stabilization on these groups?

The simple Marshallian analysis of Waugh (1944) suggests that, in the dominant case where the source of the price fluctuations is not shifts in demand, consumers lose from the stabilization of the prices they face. This result stems simply from the downward-sloping nature of demand curves: a price decline increases welfare by more than a price rise of equivalent magnitude decreases it. Symmetrical fluctuations in price therefore raise average consumer welfare. This tendency of consumers to prefer price fluctuations persists in the more comprehensive analyses of Turnovsky, Shalit and Schmitz (1980) and of Newbery and Stiglitz (1981: Ch. 9). Their results suggest that consumers prefer price stability only when they are substantially averse to income risk and when their demand is relatively inelastic.

To complement the early Marshallian analysis of Waugh, the effects of price stabilization on producers were examined by Oi (1961) and Massell (1969). The principal result of these studies, that producers lose from stabilization where the source of disturbances is not the supply side, and gain from it otherwise, does not survive more comprehensive analyses such as those of Wright (1979) and Newbery and Stiglitz (1981: Ch.5,6,11). These latter studies take account of some important special characteristics of primary (and particularly crop) production, including lags in supply response which necessitate that production decisions are based on expected future prices. The way in which these expectations are formed and the extent of farmer aversion to risk are key determinants of production behaviour and of farmer preferences for price stability. When they are taken into account, the direction of these preferences is also ambiguous.

In a closed economy, prices fluctuate in such a way as to offset, at least to some degree, the effects of fluctuations in

Table 3.4: Indicators of agricultural protection, comparative advantage and economic growth in industrial countries, 1960–88

	Agricultural protection indicators						Comparative advantage indicators			Real growth per capita (% p.a.) in:	
	Nominal protection coefficient for agriculture[a]			Relative price of agricultural products domestically as a % of relative agricultural price internationally (1961–65 = 100)[b]			Hectares of agricultural land per capita, 1985[c]	Food production as a percentage of food consumption, valued at border prices, 1985[d]	Labour productivity growth in agriculture relative to the total economy, 1960–85[e]	Gross domestic product, 1960–85	Value added in industry, 1960–85
	1965–75	1975–83	1988	1960–69	1970–79	1980–87					
	(1)	(2)	(3)	(4)	(5)	(6)	(7)	(8)	(9)	(10)	(11)
North America and Australasia	1.10	1.15	1.40	101	108	99	3.57	125	2.41	2.1	1.7
Western Europe[f]	1.40	1.55	2.35	102	108	119	0.37	106	1.67	2.7	2.6
Japan, Korea and Taiwan	1.90	2.50	3.75	108	135	161	0.05	78	0.88[g]	5.9	7.9

a   Proportion by which domestic prices exceed border prices for grains, meats, dairy products and sugar. The values for 1988 are estimates based on the authors' earlier projections from their model of world food trade (Tyers and Anderson 1988b).

b   Domestic prices are based on the ratio of indices of prices received by farmers (FAO) and wholesale prices of industrial products (IMF). International price indices for agricultural and industrial products also are from the FAO and IMF.

c   Land used for crops (annual and perennial) and pastures.

d   Production and consumption of grains, meats, dairy products and sugar are aggregated using the border prices at which each country trades (or would do under free trade).

e   Real growth in value added per employee in agriculture as a ratio of real growth in value added per employee in the total economy.

f   The twelve member countries of the European Community plus the five member countries of the European Free Trade Association.

g   Refers to Japan only.

Sources: Agricultural protection coefficients are from Tables 2.1 and 2.2 of Chapter 2, and Tyers and Anderson (1988). Other indicators are based on data from the Food and Agriculture Organisation, *Production Yearbook and Trade Yearbook*, Rome, various issues; Organisation for Economic Cooperation and Development, *Historical Statistics 1960-1985*, Paris, 1987; and International Monetary Fund, *International Financial Statistics: Prices Supplement*, Washington D.C., 1986.

output. Price stabilization is therefore welfare reducing for risk-averse farmers with inelastic supply in the short run, because it destabilizes income. However, one aspect of the price stabilization issue not well covered by the studies we have reviewed concerns the origin of price risk in the more prevalent open economies. In practice, much of this risk originates outside the agricultural sector, from changes in macroeconomic policy or intervention in other sectors, and from fluctuations in international market prices. Other things being equal, then, price stabilization policies are likely to be opposed by such farmers only in open economies whose production is sufficiently large to influence international prices.

Of course, it is possible to reduce the risks faced by farmers without direct intervention by governments in commodity markets. This risk can be shared with other agents through insurance programs and futures markets, and it can be reduced through the supply of better information concerning potential sources of risk. In countries where information is plentiful and where efficient markets exist for risk sharing, the cost to farmers of price instability is comparatively low. Nevertheless, except where international prices are significantly responsive to domestic output, even farmers fortunate enough to face these conditions can be expected to prefer price stabilization.

Other agents also have a stake in price stabilization. In poor countries, where expenditure on food absorbs a large share of worker income, non-agricultural wages tend to fluctuate in order to compensate for food price changes. This compensation can be achieved through wage indexation or through payments in kind, such as have been made to government and other workers in Indonesia (Amat 1982) and Sri Lanka (Edirisinghe 1982). Food price fluctuations therefore increase the expenditure risk of government agencies and the military, and the profit risk of industrial capital owners. Governments and parastatal agencies with monopolies over imports of particular commodities can also gain from reductions in domestic price instability through partial insulation of domestic markets. This is because the revenue gained, when imports are drawn from a depressed international market and sold at higher prices domestically, exceeds that lost when world prices are high and imports must be resold at a loss.

A simple model with market insulation

The ambiguous nature of the consumer and producer welfare effects of price stabilization means that the preferences for price stability of these predominant groups remain matters for empirical analysis. As a test of our earlier hypothesis regarding the welfare impacts of market insulation, it is therefore useful to measure these effects in some illustrative cases. To do so we use an elementary model of a single open commodity market which is detailed mathematically in Appendix 4.

The model might apply to the market for a key food commodity such as rice. It assumes that the focus country is a small trader in the commodity and therefore cannot influence the level of the international price.[18] That price is, however, subject to random disturbances due to fluctuations in demand and supply in the wider international market. Domestic production of the commodity is also subject to random disturbances such as might be caused by weather and pest infestation. Together, these two sources of randomness generate the price and income risk from which the government seeks to insulate domestic agents.

To focus only on market-insulating policies, we consider the pure insulation case, in which the domestic price of the commodity is stabilized around the mean of the corresponding international price. This might be achieved using a tariff or import subsidy which is annually adjusted, as in the case of the European Community's variable levies and export restitutions, or by manipulation of import levels by a state trading monopoly in order to achieve desired levels of the domestic price. The task is made easy in the model by the assumption that the mean of the international price is constant. In this case, a government might readily implement a partial insulation policy by setting the domestic price in any year such that its deviation from the mean is a fixed fraction of the deviation observed in the international market. To simulate this, the model uses a linear price transmission equation of the type introduced in Chapter 2.

A key assumption in the model concerns the income of non-agricultural workers. Workers in developing countries are compensated for food price fluctuations by either having their wages indexed or receiving payments in kind. In industrial countries, on the other hand, food expenditure is small in relation to income and no such relationship exists between wages and food prices.

Thus, the model provides a simple framework for calculating changes in price and income risk associated with insulating interventions by the government. The corresponding impacts on the welfare of each group of agents included in the model can then be calculated as functions of the parameters of the price transmission equation. To complete this calculation, however, we must specify a measure of aversion to risk. The most convenient is the coefficient of relative risk aversion, R, introduced by Pratt (1964) and Arrow (1965); it relates to the elasticity of the marginal utility of income, a measure of the curvature of the utility function. Its values are found from empirical studies to vary with income and with the size of risks (in relation to income). Risk-neutral individuals have values of R near zero, while the corresponding values for risk-averse individuals range up to two for sizeable risks (Newbery and Stiglitz 1981: Ch. 7).

With this information it is possible to derive approximate expressions for the welfare impacts of market insulation in terms of each group's level of price and income risk, their average incomes and their coefficients of relative risk aversion. As presented in Appendix 4, each expression indicates the gain, as a proportion of group income, which would accrue from a partial insulation of the domestic market.

Impacts of insulation in archetypical poor and rich economies

Here we take the approach of the previous section and examine the effects of market insulation on the real incomes of different groups in two archetypical economies. This time, however, it is sufficient to use the simpler model of a single open commodity market, discussed above and detailed in Appendix 4. While, again, the effects obviously depend on the parameter values chosen, it remains useful to compare the characteristics of two small open economies, as summarized in Table 3.5. One is a poor economy which imports the commodity, say rice, and the other is a rich industrial country which exports it. In the poor

Table 3.5: Illustrative rice market parameters for archetypical poor and rich economies

	Poor economy	Rich economy
Coefficient of variation of border price	0.20	0.20
Coefficient of variation of production	0.10	0.10
Expenditure shares of: farmers	0.50	0.10
workers	0.20	0.10
Price elasticity of demand[a]: farmers	0.50	0.00
workers	0.10	0.00
Income elasticity of demand of: farmers	0.50	0.00
workers	0.10	0.00
Share of output consumed by farmers	0.67	0.08
Net imports as a share of production	0.33	-0.20
Ratio of gross revenue from domestic commodity production to national income	0.19	0.08
Share of national income to: farmers	0.25	0.07
workers	0.62	0.60
industrial capital	0.13	0.33
Government revenue as a share of national income	0.20	0.40

[a] Price elasticities of demand are defined positive. See Appendix 4.
Source: Judgemental parameter values based on the pattern of the parameters in Appendices 2 and 3 to this volume and on the World Bank (1988).

economy, farmers consume half the rice but earn only a quarter of national income. Workers consume the rest and receive wages which are compensated for rice price fluctuations. They and industrial capital owners earn three-quarters of the national income. Household incomes differ between farmers and workers and, therefore, so do their rice consumption parameters.

In the rich industrial economy, on the other hand, farmers consume only a small fraction of their total output and earn a small share of the national income. Their household incomes are similar to those of workers, however, and they are therefore assumed to exhibit the same consumption behaviour. For purposes of illustration, we assume all agents in both the poor and the rich economies are risk averse. We assign a value of R=2 to poor-country agents and to farmers in the rich country, whose risks stemming from price fluctuations are significant in relation to their net income. Food price risk is less significant for consumers and taxpayers in the rich economy, however, so we assign to them a value of R=1.

The empirical estimates of market insulation presented in the previous chapter suggested that such insulation is generally partial (price transmission elasticities are between zero and unity) in both poor and rich economies. For convenience, therefore, we examine the welfare impacts of a partial insulation which reduces the coefficient of variation of the domestic price by half (transmitting to the domestic market only half of any change in the international price). These impacts are readily calculated from equations derived in Appendix 4. The results are listed in Table 3.6.

Farmers are comparatively indifferent to market insulation in the poor country but could be expected to favour it in the rich country. This is primarily because farmers in the poor economy consume a relatively large share of their production of food. Their gain from revenue stabilization is largely offset by losses which stem from their relatively elastic consumer behaviour. In the rich country, on the other hand, farmers commit little of their income to food and the revenue (and hence income) stabilization effects are dominant.

Non-agricultural workers in both the poor and the rich country are generally indifferent to market insulation. In the poor country this is because worker income is assumed to be adjusted for food price changes through wage indexing or partial

Table 3.6:   Benefits from partial insulation in archetypical poor and rich economies[a]

	Poor economy	Rich economy
Farmers	0.20	4.00
Workers	−0.05	0.02
Industrial capital owners	2.70	0.00[b]
Government revenue	0.60	0.00

[a]   Per cent of average group income or of government expenditure

[b]   This value is zero since, while wages in the poor country are assumed to be adjusted for food price changes, they are not adjusted in the rich country. Industrial profits are therefore not significantly affected by food price risk.

Source: Calculations based on equations (A4.21) through (A4.25) in Appendix 4 and on the parameters listed in Table 3.5.

payments in kind.[19] In the rich country it is because demand is inelastic and workers spend only a small share of their income on food.

Food market insulation is clearly favoured by industrial capital owners in the poor country. This is because payments to labour dominate the value added in the non-agricultural sector. Fluctuations in these payments therefore result in substantial profit risk. In the rich country, capital owners are indifferent to food price stabilization because worker income tends not to be compensated for short-term changes in food prices and, in any case, the non-agricultural sector is less labour intensive.

The government revenue effects are dominated by shifts in mean revenue due to the partial insulation policy. These revenue gains depend primarily on the elasticity of domestic consumer demand in the short run. Since this elasticity is comparatively high in developing countries, the revenue effects of partial stabilization are positive and significant there.

In both cases there are net gains nationally from the insulation, a fact which supports the public interest explanation for insulating policies. The results do, however, bear out the hypothesis that the most influential group has the most to gain from market insulation in each case. The gains to industrial capital owners and to government revenue are dominant in the poor country, where industry tends to be protected at the expense of agriculture and where the cost of collecting revenue by means other than trade distortions is especially high. In the rich country, on the other hand, where agriculture tends to be protected at the expense of other sectors, farmers have the dominant interest in price stabilization.

The above illustration suggests that there is indeed a public interest case for the insulation of food markets in both rich and poor countries. This is supplemented by private interest pressures, since relatively influential groups stand to gain the most from insulation and can be expected to lobby aggressively in its favour. Since no group of agents in the domestic economy would appear to lose significantly, governments tend not to find it politically costly to justify market-insulating policies to non-beneficiaries.

Other reasons for market insulation

There are other important reasons for the prevalence of market insulation. One stems from two general characteristics of market-insulating policies. First, such policies always separate domestic from border prices and hence distort domestic incentives, at least in the short run; second, because the current and future trend of international market prices is uncertain, there is no obvious and undisputed target level at which domestic prices should be set in order to achieve the objective of comparative stability. The process by which the domestic price is set is therefore subject to lobbying by vested interests. The cost of substantially distorting domestic prices away from border prices is reduced because governments can claim that the distortion is temporary, pending the return of border prices to 'trend' levels.

Because, for the reasons detailed in Section 3.1, the lobbying and propagandizing effort of farmers in industrial countries is stronger than that of groups which lose from high food prices, this process tends to be captured by farm interests. Similarly, in the poor countries, the initially well-intentioned separation of domestic markets from international markets by governments averse to food price risk and wage risk reduces the political costs of policies which ensure that the trend of domestic prices is below that at the border (see Bates 1981 for numerous African examples).

Irrespective of this bias, in the long run, market insulation tends to foster increases in the trend of domestic prices relative to border prices and to mitigate against the negative price distortions which have occurred in developing countries. This is because relative world food prices have been declining, as Figure 1.1 shows, and can be expected to continue to decline for the reasons outlined in Section 1.3 of Chapter 1. High levels of protection therefore result where governments adopt the comparatively undisputed policy of market insulation and simply take no action to change the relative price of food in the domestic market. Wide fluctuations in international prices make their true trend difficult to estimate in the short run, leaving proponents of lower relative food prices with a comparatively weak case. This also helps to explain the tendency, documented in the previous chapter, for nominal rates of protection to increase in both developing and industrial countries.

There are therefore several reasons why food markets are insulated. The pure insulation components of food policies benefit influential minorities without significantly hurting the majority. Once in place, they reduce the cost to governments of more redistributive price distortions favouring those minorities.

Nevertheless, even where insulating policies are not accompanied by protection, it would be improper to leave the impression that such policies are desirable from the standpoint of *world* welfare. They involve the shedding of risk through international food markets. Although our analysis in this chapter has emphasized the small country case, the insulation of food markets by large numbers of small countries must increase the instability of international prices (Bale and Lutz 1981; Sampson and Snape 1980; Blandford 1983). When risk is shed in this way by some countries, it must be borne by others. The cost of market insulation policies is therefore the burden of foreigners, the interest group with the least voice in domestic politics. It is to this issue which we now turn.

3.3 Liberal trade as an international public good

In his presidential address to the American Economic Association in 1985, Charles Kindleberger highlighted a number of public goods the exchange of which transcends national boundaries. In general, public goods are those from which non-paying consumers cannot be excluded. In addition, consumption by one additional consumer does not diminish the supply of the goods available to others. They are typically underproduced, since consumers with free access to such goods are unlikely to contribute fully to the cost of their supply. Such goods are generally produced by national governments, which require consumers to contribute to the cost of their provision through the taxation of domestic income and expenditure.

In the international sphere no government exists to ensure that such contributions are made. Yet, a number of important international public goods exist on which the smooth functioning of international commerce depends. Kindleberger's list includes:

> . . . an open trading system, including freedom of the seas, well-defined property rights, standards of weights and measures that may include international money or fixed exchange rates, . . . consistent macroeconomic policies in periods of tranquility, and a source of crisis management when needed. By the last I mean the maintenance of open markets in glut and a source of supplies in acute shortage, plus a lender of last resort in acute financial crisis. (Kindleberger 1986: 7–8)

The emphasis on 'fairness' in recent international trade debates stems in part from a concern that the burden of the supply of public goods such as these is not being borne equitably. Few countries can be expected to be willing to contribute more than a 'fair share' based on agreements as to the nature of fair contributions. Such agreements include the General Agreement on Tariffs and Trade (GATT), one general objective of which is to assure signatories that their contributions to the supply of international public goods will be matched to some acceptable extent by those of others (Runge *et al.* 1989). It is when such agreements are incomplete in coverage or ineffective in enforcing obligation and liability that the undersupply of international public goods becomes a serious problem.

These circumstances have prevailed in international food markets through the 1980s. Trade in food has been plagued by exceptions and waivers to the GATT since its inception. Despite the fact that many of these have been at the behest of the United States, that country has nevertheless largely underwritten international food trade by exposing its own vast domestic market to comparatively undistorted international price signals in times of both surplus and shortage. In agricultural trade, as in other aspects of its international relations, the United States has played the role of 'hegemonic power' using its economic and political strength to extract reciprocal commitments from other trading countries which are sufficient to ensure the expansion of gains from trade (Kindleberger 1986). Since the 1970s, however, the decline in the relative economic power of the United States and the rise of the European Community and Japan, with their highly distorted agricultural sectors and the EC's subsidized food exports, has heightened the perception in the United States that food trade has become increasingly unfair. This is one reason for the increases in protection accorded to United States' farmers following the Food Security Act of 1985 (addressed further in Chapter 6).

In explaining the present pattern of distortions in international food trade, it is useful to extend Kindleberger's list of international public goods to include a number of behavioural characteristics of international markets which stem from domestic distortions. In the case of food markets, two such characteristics stand out. The first of these is the stability of international prices. Net suppliers of international price stability are countries which expose their domestic agents to international price movements and/or carry stocks which fluctuate in such a way as to make them net absorbers of international quantity fluctuations. The stability they supply benefits countries which trade in food products but whose net imports or exports fluctuate so as to insulate their domestic markets. They might be seen as net consumers of the risk-spreading capacity of world food markets, which constitutes the international public good. The individual small country can use trade to insulate domestic food markets without significantly increasing the risk to which other countries are exposed. But, as large numbers of such countries adopt similar policies, the classical problem of congestion in the consumption of the public good arises. International prices become more unstable and the cost of foreign exchange risk, to which new consumers are exposed, increasingly offsets their gains from opening their economies to trade.

The second behavioural characteristic of international markets is the level of international food prices. If we temporarily ignore the ever-declining number of countries which appear to value low food prices (those developing countries which still keep domestic food prices below international prices), then it is also possible to view the level of average international food prices as a public good. The higher the border prices, the more the economic cost of maintaining high domestic food prices is reduced. Protectionist countries consume the food while it is supplied by countries with comparatively undistorted economies or which subsidize food consumption. As more and more countries adopt protectionist policies the problem of congestion arises and international food prices fall.

The extent to which countries free ride (or, in the terminology of Cornes and Sandler 1986, 'easy ride') can be crudely quantified by comparing measures of their consumption and their contribution to the supply of these goods. Countries whose production has fluctuated widely but whose domestic consumption and stock levels have not offset those fluctuations are net consumers of international food market risk-spreading. The Soviet Union, the European Community and China are most prominent in this group for traded staple food products. Their standard deviations of net trade in such food products, measured about a geometric trend over the period 1961 to 1983, are the highest of all countries included in our study, ranging between US$1 billion and US$2 billion. At the same time, adjustments by consumers and stockholders have been suppressed in all three economies by market insulating policies— their average short-run food price transmission elasticities are all less than 0.2 (Table 2.11 and Table A1, Appendix 2).

The greatest beneficiaries from the maintenance of higher rather than lower average international food prices, on the other hand, are economies which have levels of domestic production and consumption which are high by world standards and which have trade policies ensuring that domestic food prices are kept well above border prices. It is these economies which increase global excess supply by reducing imports (or expanding exports) and hence place the greatest burden on countries whose farmers and consumers are not shielded by protection policies and must carry the costs of adjustment. Most prominent among the free-riding economies, as we detail in Chapter 6, are the European Community and Japan.

Thus, a number of economies, including the large centrally planned economies, the EC and Japan, have become increasingly prominent in recent years as beneficiaries from an orderly international trade in food products that has been underwritten to a considerable extent (at least prior to the mid-1980s) by the United States. Market insulation and protection policies have been made easier in these economies by the resulting capacity of their governments to impose at least part of the cost of these policies on foreigners. Furthermore, the inevitable consequence of this practice is an increase in world food market disarray which in turn has caused a widespread diminution of confidence in the gains from trade in food products and thus has reduced further the domestic political cost of food market distortions.

Research on liberal agricultural trade by Runge *et al.* (1989) suggests that what is required is the assurance that a critical mass of countries demonstrate a willingness to submit to GATT principles (principles which have been extended with increased rigour in their coverage of agricultural trade). Such an assurance will reduce the political costs of similar commitments by other countries. The widespread recognition that the gains from participation in international food trade will decline still further should no such assurance be forthcoming, led to agriculture being placed high on the agenda of the Uruguay Round of multilateral trade negotiations. The success of these and subsequent negotiations will be enhanced by the provision of estimates of the magnitudes of these gains from freer trade in food. It is to this end that we have assembled the behavioural model presented in Chapter 5. But, before turning to that quantitative assessment, it is helpful first to review qualitatively the way in which various government policy instruments impact on markets and thereby affect economic welfare, at home and abroad.

Notes to Chapter 3

[1] This section draws heavily on Anderson (1989).

[2] See Baldwin (1985), Anderson and Baldwin (1987) and the references therein on attempts to explain inter-industry differences in manufacturing protection in various industrial countries. Fewer attempts have been made to explain inter-industry differences in agricultural price distortions, but two such studies are Anderson (1978) and Gardner (1987). Among the recent papers that have focused on explaining the existence of tariffs rather than free trade are those by Baldwin (1982), Brock and Magee (1978, 1980), Findlay and Wellisz (1982, 1983), Magee (1980), Magee, Brock and Young (1989), Mayer (1984), Wellisz and Findlay (1984), and Young and Magee (1986). See also the earlier paper on nineteenth-century agricultural trade policy in Europe by Kindleberger (1951).

[3] This partial equilibrium conceptualization of the political market thus incorporates, via the supply curve, the political opposition from all other groups to the lobbying actions of any particular

group seeking assistance. In practice, the reaction of opposing groups may also include seeking more assistance for their own group. Thus the demand and supply curves need to be specified for particular levels of assistance in other sectors.

4 If the prices of both tradable products were to change by the same proportion, the net changes in the price of non-tradables and in factor rewards would not be the same (that is, the elasticities for each variable would not sum to unity). This differs from what Lerner's (1936) symmetry theorem leads us to expect for a model without intermediate inputs. The reason is that when intermediate inputs are included and are used more in some sectors than others, a given product price change, resulting from a policy change, generates different changes in effective assistance for the various sectors.

5 The elasticity of real farm income assumes farms are owner occupied. If farmers also sold part of their labour services they would be affected less than suggested in row 11 of Table 3.1 (their elasticity would be closer to that of non-farm workers). On the other hand, if as landlords they hired farm labour they would be affected more than suggested. The real income elasticity for a landlord with a spending pattern equivalent to urban capitalists and not subject to income tax would be 0.79 in response to an agricultural product price rise (–0.79 for a price fall) and 0.64 in response to an industrial product price rise, compared with the 0.37 and 0.21 shown in Table 3.1 for the owner-occupying farmer in the poor agrarian economy. This difference helps explain Krueger's (1989) finding that government policies tend to discriminate less against agriculture in countries with a more skewed distribution of farm land ownership.

6 The belief that jobs are created by industrial protection policy is very common but is not well founded, especially when the reasons why people drift to the city are taken into account (see Corden (1974: Ch.6) and Corden and Findlay (1975)). An obvious extension of the present analysis would be to include wage distortions and Harris-Todaro type unemployment in the model in Appendix 3.

7 Notice that the sector producing final industrial products in the poor country is a slight net exporter. This is because the agricultural sector's exports alone are insufficient to pay for the imported intermediate inputs in this simulated economy. It would only take a small change in assumed parameter values to make it an import-competing sector, however.

8 Notice that the values in part II of Table 3.2 sum to zero (apart from rounding errors). This is necessarily the case for the model presented in Appendix 3 because technically it refers to infinitesimally small changes from equilibrium.

9 The ingenuity of farmer cooperatives in finding ways to entice membership is quite remarkable. See, for example, Olson (1965), George and Saxon (1986) and Bolin *et al.* (1986) for examples in the United States, Japan and Sweden, respectively.

10 As reported in the discussion of Figure 1.1 in Chapter 1, a recent study found that, between 1900 and the mid-1980s, international prices for foods other than beverages declined on average by 0.5 per cent per year (and non-food agricultural prices declined by 0.8 per cent per year), relative to industrial product prices (Grilli and Yang 1988). See also Spraos (1980) and Sapsford (1985).

11 It should be kept in mind that the raising of taxes for distributing subsidies itself introduces welfare-reducing distortions (Browning 1987). Price subsidies need not, therefore, be always superior to border distortions.

12 See, for example, Byerlee and Sain (1986) and Peterson (1979).

13 During the period from 1960 to 1981, the number of people employed in agriculture in industrial countries declined at an average rate of 2.8 per cent per year (OECD 1983), reasons for which are outlined in Section 1.3 of Chapter 1.

14 See Findlay and Wellisz (1983) for a diagrammatic analysis of such reaction functions for a two-sector economy. See also Becker (1983).

15 Becker (1983, 1985) has argued that, other things being equal, we should observe redistributive policy instruments which impose the lowest deadweight costs on the economy. Presumably part of the reason for trade policies being used as a redistributive device is that they provide more covert forms of assistance than do direct payments since the latter have to appear in the finance ministry's annual budget papers. This makes it more costly for potential opponents to determine the adverse effects on them of those policies. In poor agrarian economies there is also the problem that raising and dispersing revenue other than via trade taxes involves relatively high administrative costs. This is part of the reason for the bias in assistance towards import-competing and against export industries in these countries especially.

16 For an analysis of some reasons for the plethora of sometimes contradictory policies affecting farmers in industrial counries, see

Rausser (1982) and Rausser and de Gorter (1989). The issue has also been raised in the context of developing countries by Krueger (1989). The model in Appendix 3 could be extended to include domestically produced tradable intermediate inputs for computing the distributional effects of input price or trade policies to compare with the effects of a similar rate of effective assistance to a sector via output price or trade policies.

[17] Apart from wanting to be elected or re-elected, the objectives of politicians might include securing jobs for family members or friends in government assisted firms or organizations and promoting party ideology. On the role of ideology, personality and party, see Peltzman (1984) and Kalt and Zupan (1984). See also Brennan and Buchanan (1985).

[18] Extensions to this simple model by Gibbard and Tyers (1990) yield the same general pattern of results when countries have production or consumption large enough to influence world prices.

[19] The effect of total wage indexation is essentially to annul the benefits to risk-averse workers from price stabilization. The losses caused by the Waugh–Oi–Massell effects then dominate, though these are negligible compared with the mean income of workers.

TWO

EFFECTS OF FOOD MARKET DISTORTIONS

4

The Theory of Food Market Distortions: A Graphical Approach

The types of distortionary policies discussed in Chapters 2 and 3 can be assessed qualitatively using simple diagrams to represent international food markets.[1] We use this approach at this juncture to illustrate possible effects of food market distortions so as to prepare the reader for some results from our subsequent quantitative analysis which might otherwise appear paradoxical. Such results arise, in particular, from the analysis of partial reforms which lead to a transition from one set of distortions to another. For example, distortions remain where insulating policies ensure that international price shocks are imperfectly transmitted to the domestic market or where the removal of distortions specific to one market or sector is not accompanied by liberalization in others. Of interest are the effects on quantities produced, consumed and traded, and on the distribution of income, government revenue and national and global economic welfare. For the most part the analysis assumes that agriculture is a small part of each economy. Changes in food markets therefore do not affect other parts of the economy in ways which have a secondary impact on the food sector. The last section of the chapter discusses the implications of relaxing that assumption.

We begin with the simplest possible case of a small country and a single commodity market before considering the large country case involving several interrelated markets. The chapter combines points of theory with qualitative applications to issues such as the impacts on net food-importing developing countries of liberalization in industrial countries and of 'reforms' such as the European Community's producer levies.

4.1 Distorting a single commodity market in a small country

Suppose a small economy is able to import grain at price P_w and its domestic demand and supply curves are as in Figure 4.1. In the absence of distortions, P_w would also be the domestic price and this economy would produce OQ domestically, import QC and consume OC units per year. Gross income from grain production would be OajQ, of which OzjQ is the variable cost and the residual is a return to the farmer's labour and capital assets.

It may be that the government wishes to raise farm incomes, however, and to do so more covertly than by a direct transfer. One of the ways to do that is to provide a price subsidy which raises the producer price to P. This would encourage QQ' extra production which would reduce imports to Q'C, and it would raise gross income from grain to ObcQ', of which QjcQ' is extra variable costs and area abcj is the boost in net farm income. The cost to the treasury of providing that price subsidy is PP_w/P_wO per unit produced, or the area abci. This treasury outlay is more than the net gain to farmers, by area cij which represents the extra cost associated with producing quantity QQ' domestically rather than importing it. Thus, while a price subsidy can be a means of boosting farm incomes, it reduces national economic welfare. It also involves an explicit government handout which will appear in the government's annual budget papers.

For reasons discussed in the previous chapter, overt handouts are less likely to be provided than covert ones. The same net farm income boost could be achieved using a tariff on imports instead of an explicit producer price subsidy. In that case, though, not only the producer price but also the consumer price would be raised to P in Figure 4.1. Hence, in addition to the production effects, domestic consumption would fall to OC' and imports would be reduced to Q'C'. Consumer welfare is therefore lowered by area abef because consumers buy less grain and have to pay more per unit for it. A major attraction to the government of the tariff instrument over the producer price subsidy as a means of raising farm income is that, while the latter involves a government budgetary outlay, the tariff *raises* government revenue, equal to area cegi. The net impact on the

Figure 4.1: Effects of price distortions in a small economy

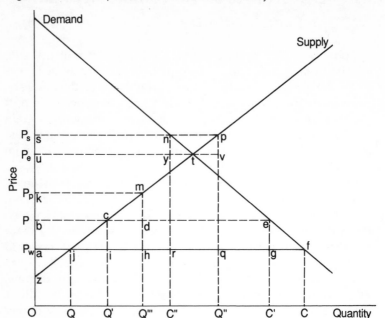

national economy, therefore, is the producer gain (area abcj) plus the revenue gain (area cegi) minus the consumer loss (area befa), which is a negative amount equal to the area of the two triangles cij and efg. It exceeds the net loss in the producer price subsidy case which is just cij. That is, even though taxpayers as well as grain producers are better off when a tariff is imposed, their gain is insufficient to compensate the loss imposed on consumers. In net national economic welfare terms, this instrument of farm income support is inferior to direct subsidies or producer price support, because of the extra triangular deadweight loss efg.

The government might be tempted to use the tariff revenue to raise the producer price even further by way of a price subsidy in addition to the tariff. For example, if P_p was such that area bkmd equalled area degh, then all of the tariff revenue on $Q'''C'$ imports could be spent to encourage production of OQ''' units by way of a producer price subsidy of P_pP per unit on top of the tariff of PP_w per unit. In that case the benefit of intervention for producers would be not just area abcj but also area bkmc, while the net effect on government revenue would be zero. Thus this revenue-neutral tariff plus producer price subsidy scheme would have a larger net economic welfare cost to the country than just the tariff: it would be the sum of the two triangular areas jmh (instead of jci) and efg.

If the tariff was sufficient to raise the domestic price to P_e in Figure 4.1, domestic production would equal domestic consumption and imports would thereby be eliminated completely. In that case the producer gain would be area autj, the consumer loss would be area autf, there would be no government tariff revenue and hence national economic welfare would be reduced by area tfj. Clearly, the higher the tariff, the larger the redistribution of welfare from consumers to producers and the larger this small economy's net loss in economic welfare.

Should the government desire an even higher price for producers than P_e, it would be necessary to add a subsidy to that price or, more commonly, to subsidize exports. An export subsidy of P_sP_w per unit exported would increase the domestic consumer price as well as the producer price to P_s so that consumption shrinks to OC″ and production expands to OQ″; the difference, C″Q″, is then exported. The treasury cost of the subsidy is area npqr, the consumer loss would be even greater than at the autarchic price P_e (namely area asnf) but the producer gain would be further increased (to area aspj compared with free trade). The export subsidy—which would need to be supported by an equally high tariff or a prohibition on imports to prevent importing for subsequent subsidized export—thus adds further to the extent of redistribution from consumers to producers and also now from taxpayers to producers. It is also even more expensive than just a tariff in terms of net national economic welfare, the loss (compared with free trade) being area jpq plus area nfr.

Note that the higher (lower) the world price, the less (greater) the extent of tariff or producer price subsidy needed to raise the domestic price to a particular level and hence the smaller (larger) the welfare and distributional effects of intervention. If the world price was slightly above P_e, for example, in which case the country would be a net exporter under free trade, then only a small producer price subsidy or export subsidy would be needed to raise the producer price to P_s.

The above cases all assume that the government considers the domestic price should be above the international price. As we saw in the previous two chapters, this is quite often the case in advanced industrial countries. In poor agrarian economies, on the other hand, governments often seek to set the domestic price of food below international levels. This distortion also reduces net welfare, but in this case it redistributes welfare from producers to consumers. If P_s in Figure 4.1 was the international price and P_e the domestic price (achieved by imposing an export ban or tax of P_sP_e), producers would lose area uspt, consumers would gain area usnt, and there would be no export tax revenue because exports would be reduced to zero, so the net loss to the economy would be area npt.

All of these cases assume the country's share of the world market for this commodity is too small for changes in its domestic market to influence the international price. They also assume this commodity market is too small a part of the country's total economy for changes in it to alter the foreign exchange rate. In the next section the first of these two assumptions is dropped.

4.2 Distorting a single commodity market in a large country

Consider now a country which is a net exporter of grain and is a sufficiently large participant in the world grain market to face an excess demand curve that is upward sloping rather than horizontal. In order to analyse the effect of distorting this economy's grain market we must look simultaneously at its domestic market and the international market, as in Figure 4.2.

Suppose, as in Section 4.1, that this country wants to raise its domestic price from the international price level P_w to P, and chooses to do so by introducing an export subsidy. The quantity of its exports expands from CQ(=OX) to C'Q'(=OX') which drives down the international price to P'_w. Thus an export subsidy of PP'_w is required per unit, or a total export subsidy equal to area acef. The gain to producers is area cijd while the loss to consumers is area cghd. The latter loss is less than the

Figure 4.2: Effects at home and abroad of export price distortions in a large economy

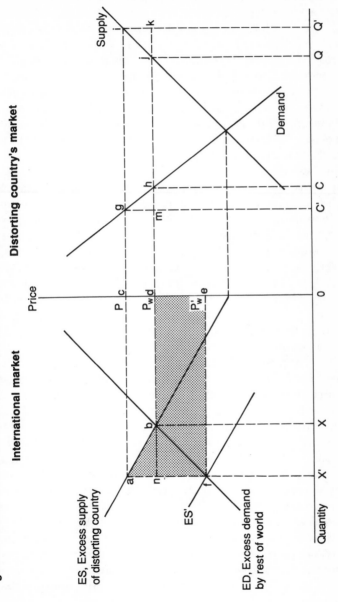

former gain by area gijh, which is equivalent to area acdb. But taxpayers have to pay area acef as an export subsidy, so the net loss to this country is the shaded area abdef. Some of that loss (area bdef) is transferred to foreigners who, as net importers, enjoy a lower price for their imports; the rest (area abf) is a pure net loss globally of which the upper part, area abn, equals area ghm plus area ijk, and the lower part, area bfn, is the corresponding sum of triangles in the diagram (not shown) for the demand and supply curves for the rest of the world. In short, the large exporting country has more to lose than a small country from raising its domestic price a given amount above the free-trade international price, because its own policy action depresses the international price and so confers benefits to the rest of the world at the distorting country's expense.

The case of a large country which is a net importer rather than an exporter can be similarly analysed, using Figure 4.3. If that country's government raises the domestic price from the free-trade level of P_w to P by way of a tariff, domestic production will increase from OQ to OQ' and consumption will decrease from OC to OC'. Hence imports will shrink from QC to Q'C' or, in terms of the international market, from OM to OM'. This shrunken excess demand (it is as if the distorting country's excess demand curve in the international market has shifted to ED') leads to overseas suppliers competing to push down the international price to P'_w. Thus a tariff of PP'_w is required by the country to raise its domestic price to P, and the tariff revenue so generated is area ebcf (which is equivalent to area mnrk). Producer welfare in the distorting country is increased by area jkba and consumer welfare is reduced by area jkcd. But whether this country's net economic welfare is reduced or increased depends on whether area abcd (or area krsj) exceeds or is less than area ebcf (or area mnrk). It is more likely to be reduced the more inelastic is the country's excess demand curve and the more elastic is the rest of the world's excess supply curve, and hence the less the country's own policy actions can influence the international price. This is the standard optimal trade tax argument, which means that it is possible for a large country to improve its national economic welfare by taxing its trade—up to a point. Note, however, that world economic welfare, and hence welfare of the rest of the world as a bloc, is necessarily lowered by this tariff: global welfare

Figure 4.3: Effects at home and abroad of import price distortions in a large economy

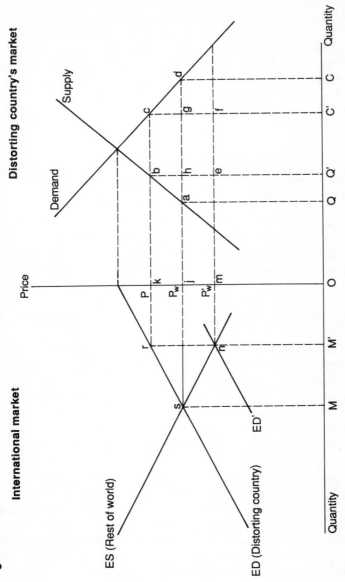

is lowered by area nrs, and the rest of the world is worse off by area mnsj.

Both of these large country cases can of course be analysed in reverse for a policy which reduces rather than increases the domestic price of this good. An export tax in the first case, for example, may—if it is small enough—actually increase national welfare for the taxing country while still worsening welfare in the rest of the world and globally. An import subsidy in the second case, on the other hand, necessarily worsens welfare for the subsidizing country as well as for the rest of the world as a bloc.

4.3   Domestic effects of international price changes: some apparent paradoxes

In general, when a large country subsidizes exports or taxes imports and the international price is lowered, other net importing countries are better off (because it improves their terms of trade, other things being equal) while other net exporting countries are made worse off. Several qualifications to this general rule should be noted, however. First, if a country switches from being a net exporter to being a net importer because of the lowering of the international price, it is possible for that country to be better rather than worse off as a consequence of the change. This is illustrated for a small open-economy in Figure 4.4. If the international price of the commodity in question falls from OP_w to OP'_w, the country switches from being an exporter to being an importer of this good. Producers lose area hjbf and consumers gain area hjag, so that the net welfare effect is negative only if area abc exceeds area cgf. Clearly, if the price falls sufficiently, the area of the lower triangle will exceed that of the upper triangle. That is, the country will be better off because the consumer welfare gain exceeds the producer welfare loss. The country will then import $Q'C'$ units instead of exporting CQ units. Simply switching to become a net importer is not necessarily sufficient to ensure being better off, however, as can be seen at OP''_w where area cde is clearly less than area abc.

Figure 4.4: Effects on a small open economy of a fall in the international price of a commodity

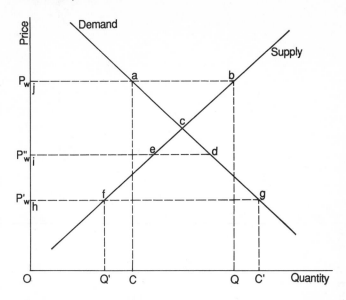

A second qualification to the rule that a net exporting (importing) country loses (gains) from a lowering of the international price, is necessary if that country is large and allows less than complete transmission of that price change (and thereby introduces a domestic distortion). This is illustrated in Figure 4.5 for the case of a large exporting country. Given the shrinkage in excess demand in the international market due to protection by some other economy which is a large importer of this good (see Figure 4.3), the large exporter which fully transmits the price fall (from OP_w to OP'_w) would be worse off by area aghc (which is equivalent to area jkim) in Figure 4.5. Its exports would fall from OX to OX'. However, if only part of the international price fall is transmitted to the exporting country, say P_wP, then exports will fall only to OX" in which case the international price will be depressed further, to OP''_w. For this exporting country, the net economic welfare loss will be even greater in the presence of a price-insulating policy than in its absence: it is given by area agdbf rather than just area aghc (the difference, fchdb, is shaded). The policy instrument required to maintain a domestic price of P is an export subsidy

Figure 4.5: Effects of a reduction in international demand on a large exporting economy

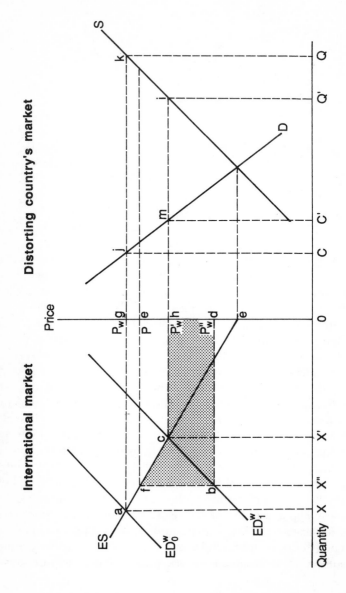

of PP″$_w$ per unit (as well as a ban or equally high tariff on imports to avoid entrepot trade taking advantage of the export subsidy). This larger economic welfare loss due to the market-insulating policy comprises a transfer to foreigners of area chdb plus a deadweight global welfare loss of area bcf.

Global deadweight welfare losses, such as area bcf in Figure 4.5, result when a previously undistorted large importing country chooses to transmit only part of an international market shock.[2] The main point of this example is that market-insulating policy regimes are distortionary when international price shocks occur. Unless domestic agents derive substantial risk-reduction benefits from the insulation (along the lines discussed in the previous chapter), such policies reduce aggregate welfare in the insulating country. Once again, however, risk reduction at home, where it is achieved by this means, only serves to amplify the shock faced by other countries (in Figure 4.5 the international price fall is amplified from $P_wP'_w$ to $P_wP''_w$). In general, global welfare is impaired by insulating policies, the more so where agents in all countries are averse to the risk of price shocks.

A third qualification (to the rule that net exporters (importers) of a good lose (gain) from a drop in its international price) is

Figure 4.6: Effects of an international price shock on a small economy that distorts its domestic market

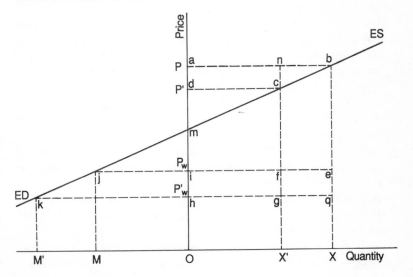

required if those countries already sufficiently distort their
domestic market for that good to have reversed the direction
of trade.[3] In the case illustrated in Figure 4.6, a small country,
whose excess supply (or demand) curve is shown as ED-ES,
would be a net importer under free trade. At price OP_w, for
example, imports would be OM. But this country chooses to
protect producers to an extent which requires the domestic
price to be raised to OP. Imports are banned and an export
subsidy is provided of PP_w per unit. The direction of trade is
reversed and it becomes a net exporter of OX. Now, consider
the impact on this distorted economy of an international price
shock. Imagine that the international price falls, say because
protection is raised in another country. The effect on domestic
welfare then depends on whether it fully transmits that shock
to the domestic market. If it does, then welfare improves despite
the fact that, for an exporter, the price decline represents an
adverse shift in its terms of trade. If it fully insulates the home
market, domestic welfare will decline.

To see this, consider the relevant areas in Figure 4.6. The
export subsidy has reduced net economic welfare in this country
by area jbe. This is made up of the export subsidy payment
to foreigners, area abei, plus the net loss in consumer and
producer surplus, area jmi less area mab. If the international
price falls to P'_w and this drop is fully transmitted to the domestic
market so that the domestic price falls to P' (where $PP' = P_w P'_w$),
the deadweight welfare loss associated with the country's export
subsidy remains unchanged: areas jbe and kcg are identical.
But, the international price fall itself adds to the country's
welfare. If the market was undistorted, this country would
benefit by area ihkj from the price fall which is the consumer
gain net of the producer loss. In the presence of the export
subsidy/import ban, the consumer gain net of the producer loss
is a negative value, area abcd, but offsetting that is the reduction
in the treasury outlay on export subsidies which is a saving
of area nbef. The net gain is therefore equivalent to area cbef
less area fghi which, as Tyers and Falvey (1989) show, is
equivalent to area ihkj. That is, if there is full transmission of
the international price change to the domestic market, the
welfare effect in the presence of an export subsidy is the same
as in the absence of an export subsidy: the country thus gains
from a price fall even though it is, because of the subsidy, a

net exporter rather than a net importer.

At the other extreme, if none of the international price fall is transmitted domestically to this distorted economy, producer and consumer welfare is unchanged but the treasury has to outlay $P_wP'_w$ more per unit exported in export subsidies. Thus, the economy is worse off by area eqhi. Intermediate cases of partial transmission are therefore ambiguous, and it becomes an empirical question as to whether an imperfectly insulating economy gains or loses in the presence of a distortion which has reversed its direction of trade.

4.4 The effects on net importing developing countries of liberalization in industrial countries

Figure 4.7 depicts the conventional view of what would occur in a developing country's food market if the advanced industrial countries liberalized their protectionist policies towards food trade. An unequivocal effect of such a reform is that food prices in international markets would rise.[4] Suppose that, following the international price rise, the domestic producer and consumer prices in a food-importing developing country rose from P_0 to P_1. (Throughout, the P's refer to the price of food relative to the price of other products. For the moment assume there are no distortions or externalities in the developing country.) Producer surplus would then rise by area abfg while consumer surplus would fall by area acdg. The net welfare loss to this economy therefore is seen as area bcdf. Note, though, that the food import bill would be greater only if the price elasticity of excess demand for food is less than unity.

However, it need not be the case that this developing country continues to be a net food importer. Suppose, for example, that the post-liberalization price is P_2 rather than P_1. In that case, it is possible that this economy's welfare loss would be less than if the price rose only to P_1. The required condition is that area fde is less than area eih, and the net loss in this case is area bce less area eih. It therefore follows that if the international price rose sufficiently, this country could be a net beneficiary. If it rose to P_3, for example, the net gain in economic welfare

Figure 4.7: Partial equilibrium effects on a small open economy of a higher international price of food

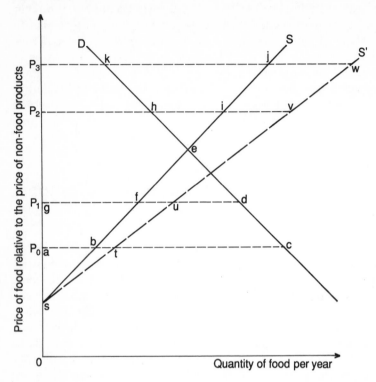

would be area ejk less area bce. Food would be a net contributor instead of a net drain on foreign exchange earnings.[5] Whether a food-importing developing country is better or worse off following an increase in the international price of food is thus an issue that has to be resolved empirically and cannot be inferred simply by observing the pre-liberalization net food trade situation.

Of course, an undistorted developing country, which is a net food exporter at the pre-liberalization price, gains unequivocally from any price rise resulting from liberalization abroad. If P_2 and P_3 were the pre- and post-liberalization prices, for example, then the net economic welfare gain to that exporting country would be area hijk if the price change were fully transmitted. (If none of the change were transmitted to the domestic market, the gain would be confined to the government revenue generated by the necessary export tax, which is hi times the international price rise P_2P_3.)

The argument does not end here, however, because the above comparative static view ignores the dynamics of innovation. It is likely that the rate of induced technical change in a sector is positively related to the sector's expected mean level of profitability (Ruttan 1982; Alston, Edwards and Freebairn 1988). It is probably also negatively related to the expected variability of profits through time. Therefore, the permanent reduction of industrial country protection which would, on the one hand, lower domestic food price levels (and perhaps their stability) in industrial countries and, on the other, increase the level and stability of food prices in developing countries, is likely to boost agricultural productivity growth in developing countries while slowing it down in industrial countries.

The welfare effects of this can be seen in Figure 4.7 if it is assumed that the rise in the international price of food and the greater stability of that price level has been transmitted to the domestic market of the developing country and has induced a shift in that country's food supply curve from S to S'. In the case of a food-importing developing country faced with a rise in the price of food from P_0 to P_1, consumer welfare is still reduced by area acdg but producer welfare is increased not only by area abfg but also by area suf less the amortized cost to domestic producers of the research which generated the shift in the supply curve. It is possible that the gain in producer welfare could outweigh the loss in consumer welfare in this dynamic case, *even if the country were to remain a net food importer*. This would be the case if area suf minus the amortized cost of research exceeded area bcdf, which, other things being equal, is more likely the larger the price-induced shift in the supply curve relative to the cost of the investment required to generate that shift.

For the food-exporting developing country, dynamic considerations simply add further to their positive net benefit from the international food price rise, raising it by area swj to area swkhi, if P_2 and P_3 were the pre- and post-liberalization prices of food internationally and domestically.

So far it has been assumed that developing countries do not distort their own food markets. Given that they do, in fact, pursue distorting policies, the economic gains to developing countries could be even greater if those distortions were also removed. In the case of foods grown in temperate zones, developing countries typically keep the domestic price level lower than in industrial countries, and in some cases it is well below the international price level even when converted at official exchange rates. Thus, whether a liberalization of food policies in developing countries, on top of an industrial-country liberalization, would raise further or dampen the rise that would otherwise take place in the international price of food, is an empirical question. What is unequivocal, however, is that if developing countries reduced their market-insulating behaviour as part of their reform, the instability of international food prices would be reduced more than if only industrial countries were to liberalize. While the extent of price fluctuations might increase in the liberalizing developing countries, which currently have the most insulated food markets, it would fall in what are currently the more open, less insulated economies.

Whether an individual developing economy would be made worse off or better off from the combined effect of the inter-national price change and its own food policy liberalization is also an empirical question. The answer depends on two things: whether it would be a net importer in the absence of its own distortionary food policy (as distinct from its food trade situation with its current food policy in place) and the extent of any liberalization of its own food policy (over the range from zero to complete liberalization).[6] Figure 4.8, which parallels Figure 4.6 in the previous section, illustrates this.

In Figure 4.8, ED is the excess demand curve for food (the horizontal difference between the supply and demand curves in Figure 4.7). Suppose the price of food in the international market is P_2 before and P_3 after food policy liberalization in all industrial countries and all developing economies other than the one depicted. Suppose also that this small economy traditionally has chosen to depress the domestic price of food to P_0 by, say, offering a subsidy on food imports and banning food exports. The effects on welfare of the international price rising from P_2 to P_3 in this economy depends on the extent to which the domestic price is allowed to increase above P_0. If this country chose to transmit none of the international price rise it would be worse off, because the international price rise would increase the per unit food import subsidy required to

Figure 4.8: Partial equilibrium effects on a small distorted economy of a higher international price of food

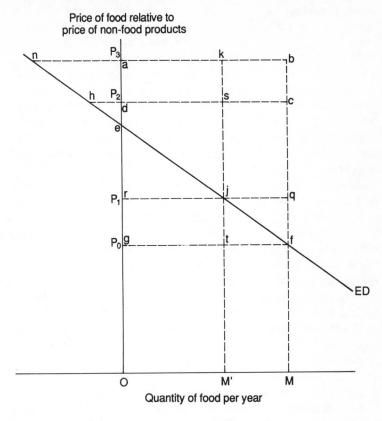

purchase abroad the OM units of food needed at domestic price P_0. This welfare loss is represented by area abcd in Figure 4.8.

If instead this country kept the per unit equivalent of its food import subsidy constant, its domestic price would rise to P_1 (where $P_1P_0=P_3P_2$). In that case the country's net economic welfare would increase, even though it remains an importer of food and thereby faces a worsening in its terms of trade. This can be seen by considering relevant areas in Figure 4.8. The import subsidy had reduced net economic welfare by area cfh. This is made up of the import subsidy payment to foreigners, area cfgd, plus the net loss in producer and consumer surplus, area fge less area deh. With the increase in the domestic price equal to the international price rise, the deadweight net economic welfare loss associated with the country's import subsidy remains unchanged: areas cfh and kjn are identical (given the assumption of a linear excess demand curve). However, the rise in the international food price itself adds to the country's economic welfare, because food is an item in which this country had a comparative advantage at price P_2 and hence P_3. If the market was undistorted, this country would have benefitted by area adhn from the price rise, which is the producer gain net of the consumer loss. In the presence of the import subsidy/export ban on food, the producer gain net of the consumer loss from the price rise is a negative value, area fgrj. However, offsetting that is the reduction in the treasury outlay for the import subsidy to foreigners which is a saving of area bqjk (equal to area cfts). The sum of these is equivalent to area adhn.[7] That is, if the increase in the international food price is fully transmitted to the domestic market, the net welfare effect is equal to the terms of trade effect on welfare that would occur in the absence of this country's import subsidy, *even if the country were to remain a net food importer.*

Thus, a food import-subsidizing developing country would be worse off if the international price of food rose and none of the increase was transmitted domestically, but it would be better off if it were a net food exporter which did not subsidize imports, and if it were to fully transmit the international price change to its domestic market.[8] Clearly, there is a threshold degree of partial price transmission which is just sufficient to ensure that this country is no worse off. The existence of food policies that allow less than full transmission of international price fluctuations to the domestic markets of developing countries is another reason why the effects of international food price increases on developing country welfare should be treated as an empirical question. It requires a model of world food markets which can capture the insulating characteristic of food policies.

The developing country depicted in Figure 4.8 would, of course, gain even more if it not only transmitted the full international price change but also reduced its per unit import subsidy. Removing it entirely would provide the economy with the additional welfare area cfh, and turn the country into a net food exporter. Even a developing country which remains a net importer of food following the removal of food price distortions abroad may, nevertheless, be better off following a rise in the international price of food *if it were to reduce its own food policy distortions sufficiently*. This would occur when the welfare gain from reducing its own distortions more than offsets the welfare loss associated with the worsening terms of trade. Again, whether this would hold for any particular country is a question that can only be resolved empirically.

The net change in national economic welfare also depends importantly on whether prices in other sectors are distorted and whether the *net* distortion in the domestic price of food relative to other products is increased or decreased following liberalization. The World Bank/IFPRI study led by Krueger, Schiff and Valdes (1988) shows clearly that agricultural production is effectively taxed and food consumption subsidized in developing countries, particularly via manufacturing protection policies and overvalued official exchange rates. According to the estimates of Krueger *et al.* these indirect ways of lowering the relative price of food much more than offset the positive effect on the food sector of export taxation of non-food primary products. Removing these non-food distortions may well boost food output in developing countries sufficiently to turn many food-importing poor countries into food exporters.

In the absence of these policy distortions in non-food sectors, such a developing country (i.e. one with a natural comparative advantage in food production) would gain unequivocally from the international price change that would accompany agricultural trade liberalization by industrial countries. However, even in the presence of price distortions in its non-food sectors, such a country may still gain from an increase in international food prices provided a sufficient proportion of that increase is transmitted to its domestic market—again, even it if remains a net importer of food. The reason for this follows from the discussion of Figure 4.8 by recognizing that distortions which raise the domestic price of non-food products have the same effect on the relative price of food (shown on the vertical axis of that diagram) as policies that lower the domestic price of food. The previously mentioned corollary also therefore follows, namely, that if its non-food policies were to be liberalized at the same time as protectionist food policies abroad, this country might enjoy an increase in net economic welfare even if it remains a net importer. Again, this requires that the welfare gain from the country's own liberalization would more than offset the loss due to the deterioration in its terms of trade.

4.5   Liberalization and world welfare

The fact that some countries are distorting their economies' domestic prices away from international price levels, raises the need to qualify another generalization, namely, that global welfare improves when one or more countries liberalize their markets. That exceptions to this rule must exist is clear from the global application of the general theory of the second best (see, for example, Bhagwati 1971).

To see why liberalization in one large country or country group can worsen global welfare, consider Figure 4.9 in which the world is divided into two country groups, A and B. Under free trade, their excess demand-supply curves intersect at b where A sells OX units to B at the equilibrium international price of OP_w. If A imposes an export subsidy of $P_wP'_w$ and B imposes an import tariff of the same amount, the two curves effectively shift down to intersect at d. Trade is unaltered but the international price is now P'_w. This crudely characterizes the world market for dairy products, where producers are protected in almost all countries. Together, these distortions redistribute welfare from exporting countries A to importing countries B, the amount of the transfer being area bdfe; but they do not impose deadweight efficiency losses (apart from the usual costs of administering the policies).

Now suppose the exporting countries remove the subsidy on their exports but the importing countries retain a specific wedge of $P_wP'_w$ between the domestic and international price. This would be like having a subsidizing net exporter of dairy products, such as the EC, remove its subsidies unilaterally (say, under international pressure on the grounds that export subsidies are more offensive to GATT principles than are instruments which protect import-competing industries). The new equilibrium is at c with the international price rising to P''_w and the direction of trade reversing, with B selling OM units to A. Ironically, for this to occur, the former importing countries, B, would now need to offer an export subsidy to maintain their

Figure 4.9: Global welfare effects of unilateral liberalization of a large economy in a distortion-ridden world

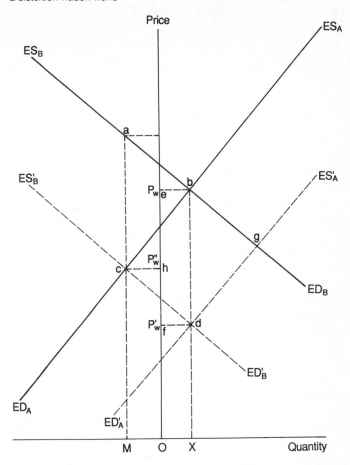

domestic-to-border price gap. This distortion would involve a global deadweight welfare loss equal to area abc, whereas, when both groups distort equally there is no such deadweight loss.

The general lesson to draw from this example is that, whenever some countries continue to maintain distortions, there is the possibility that the removal of distortions by other countries will worsen global welfare, even though it improves national welfare in the liberalizing countries. In practice, this global welfare loss could be larger than the simple characterization indicated in Figure 4.9. If, for example, the countries whose policy regimes are not liberalized (B) fail to transmit the international price change, then other efficiency losses occur similar to those discussed in the previous section. Thus, while global efficiency gains are ensured when multilateral liberalization occurs in all commodity markets, piecemeal reforms can have the opposite effect.

4.6   When is a tax not a tax? The case of producer levies

If a country supports a producer price via an export subsidy and, over time, the excess supply curve moves to the right and/or the international price level falls because of, say, new technologies, the government may come under pressure because the export subsidy payments keep increasing. A common response to this situation (most notably in the European Community) is to propose the imposition of a levy on production to help fund the export subsidy payments. While such a producer tax might reduce the extent of distortion in this market, and hence raise the international price of the product in question, there is the possibility that it could be introduced in such a way as to worsen welfare and to further depress the international price.

To see this, consider Figure 4.10 in which OP_w is the international price and OP is the domestic price which is supported by an export subsidy equal to area abcd (PP_w per unit for the CQ units exported). Now suppose a levy of PP' is imposed on producers but the consumer price is kept at P. Production would fall from Q to Q', consumption would still be OC so exports would fall by Q'Q. The reduced supply from this large economy for the international market would raise the international price to, say, P'_w. As a result, the export subsidy payout is reduced to area efgh of which part (and potentially all) is now funded by the producer levy receipts equal to area jkfv. Consumer welfare in this country would be unchanged, producer welfare would fall by area jbfv and taxpayer welfare would increase by area abcd plus area jkfv less area efgh. Hence, net economic welfare would increase by area abcd less area efgh less area kbf, or the shaded area in Figure 4.10. If other

Figure 4.10: Effects of imposing a producer levy in a large economy distorted by an export subsidy

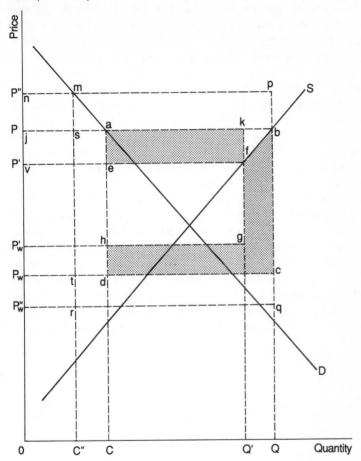

economies are comparatively undistorted, this would also yield a net gain in global welfare.[9]

However, suppose the government is more concerned for the welfare of producers than for consumers-cum-taxpayers, and that it raises the consumer price to P″ at the same time as introducing a producer levy such that the producer price net of the levy is still P. Then production stays at Q but consumption is reduced to C″ so exports expand to C″Q. This depresses the international price to P″w. As a consequence, consumers are worse off by area nmaj, producer welfare is unchanged and the export subsidy payment increases from area abcd to area mpqr. Part of that payment (area npbj) is financed by the producer levy so the net change in the government's revenue outlay is area mpqr less area npbj less area abcd, which is equivalent to area sadcqr less area nmsj and could be positive or negative. Net economic welfare is necessarily lower by the addition of what is effectively an extra tax on consumption. It is reduced by the sum of the changes in producer, consumer and taxpayer welfare, namely, area sadcqr plus area nmsj less area nmaj, or area madcqr. Nonetheless, producers are made no worse off (and would be better off if the domestic price were to rise above P″) and net government revenue outlays may be reduced. Such a policy package would appeal to a government faced with little pressure from food consumers; yet such a package not only worsens welfare in that country but also depresses the international price further. The key point here is that producer levies need not achieve any of the objectives of policy reform. It is clearly possible that net welfare would be reduced domestically and globally (assuming other sectors and other economies are less distorted). Furthermore, it remains an empirical question as to whether this combination of a producer levy with a higher consumer price would reduce government revenue outlays while not reducing producer welfare.[10]

4.7 Distortions with several inter-related commodity markets

So far only a single commodity market has been considered. The effects of distortions on national welfare are somewhat more complicated if there are several interrelated markets, some or all of which may face distortions. One illustration will suffice to demonstrate that, when commodity markets are interconnected, the welfare effects in one economy due to liberalization in another are even more difficult to discern without a quantitative model.

Suppose the international price of grain rises as a consequence of agricultural trade liberalization in a protected market abroad.

In a small open economy that is a net exporter of grain, the welfare of grain producers will increase more than the welfare of grain consumers is reduced and so this economy will be better off as a consequence of this change in the grain market (other things being equal).

But, suppose this grain-exporting country also has a protected import-competing meat industry which also faces a higher international price because of the agricultural trade liberalization abroad. The impact of both price rises is shown in Figure 4.11, which represents the domestic market for meat. The feedgrain price increase is represented by the shift upward in the supply

Figure 4.11: Effects of higher international grain and meat prices on a meat-importing country

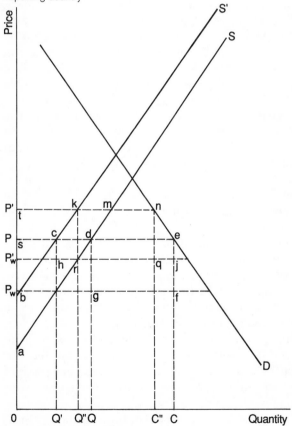

curve from S to S' and the corresponding meat price increase is $P_wP'_w$. The possible meat policy responses range from zero to full transmission of the international price change. On the one hand, if none of the international meat price increase is transmitted to the domestic market, meat production would be reduced from OQ to OQ' because of higher feed costs while meat consumption would stay at OC, requiring imports to increase by Q'Q. Meat consumer welfare is unchanged, meat producer welfare is reduced by area abcd[11] and tariff revenue would change from area defg to area cejh. The net change in welfare of agents in this particular domestic market is therefore area cejh less area defg less area abcd, which need not be negative.

On the other hand, should this country fully transmit the international meat price increase (i.e. raise its domestic meat price from OP to OP') the welfare change is more likely to be negative. This is because consumer welfare will be reduced by more than producer welfare is increased as a consequence of raising the domestic meat market price (the net decrease being area ckne), and that loss is necessarily greater than any possible extra gain in tariff revenue (the difference between area knqr and area cejh) given that PP' equals $P_wP'_w$ by assumption. The net change in welfare for agents in the meat market in this case is the change in producer welfare (area stkc less area abcd) less the loss of consumer welfare (area stne) plus the change in tariff revenue (area rknq less area defg). In general, the smaller the international price rise for meat that is transmitted to the domestic market, the more meat production is reduced and hence the more likely it is that the welfare gain from the increased grain price (the export product) will offset the likely welfare loss from the increased price of meat (the import).

It is already clear that the analysis of domestic welfare impacts is made more complex where international price changes occur in two interacting commodity markets and where some or all of these changes need not be transmitted to the domestic market. The results are not only affected by the directions of price changes and the degrees to which they are transmitted but also by the form of the interaction. In the above case, one product is an intermediate input in the production of the other, but the interaction could take other forms.

Imagine that there is also a price increase in a third

international commodity market, that of sugar, and that our country is also a net sugar importer. The domestic sugar market is affected directly by the international price increase, and it may also be affected insofar as the grain price increase raises the price of the sugar substitute, high-fructose corn syrup. These changes are shown in Figure 4.12 as an increase in the border price of sugar from OP_w to OP'_w and a shift to the right in the sugar demand curve. In the case illustrated, the country is a net importer of sugar and has a tariff on sugar imports. If the tariff is reduced to keep the domestic sugar price at OP, government tariff revenue changes from area efdh to area gfcj.

Figure 4.12: Effects of higher international grain and sugar prices on a sugar-importing country

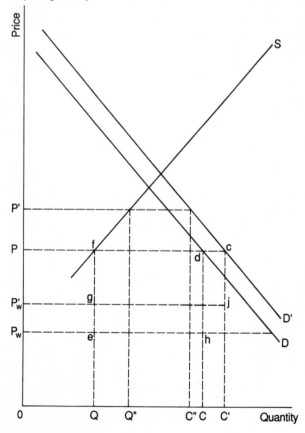

The smaller the shift in the sugar demand curve relative to the increase in the international price of sugar, the more likely it is that government tariff revenue in this market will fall.

In this case, the welfare of sugar consumers is affected only by the price of the substitute and that can be quantified only in the market for corn syrup. To the extent that the international grain price rise is transmitted to the domestic market, consumers of corn syrup must lose. Furthermore, if the sugar price increase were also transmitted, consumer losses would be greater and the shift in the demand curve for sugar could leave D' to the left or the right of D, depending on the relative sizes of the international grain and sugar price increases. This would further reduce the likelihood of any revenue gain from the sugar tariff.

Thus, even though this country gains from an increase in international food prices as an exporter of grain, it may lose as a protecting importer of meat and sugar—and this tendency becomes even greater the more it maintains its protection rates for those import-competing industries. Yet, again, definitive answers on whether such a country would gain or lose from liberalization of food markets in another country can only be obtained by empirical analysis.

4.8   Some important assumptions

The analyses reviewed in this chapter illustrate the fundamental determinants of outcomes from our quantitative assessment of food policies to be discussed later. While they are important in aiding our understanding of those outcomes, they depend upon numerous simplifying assumptions many of which are relaxed in that assessment. First, it is assumed that producer and consumer surplus are appropriate measures of welfare. In poor countries, where the share of income spent on food is comparatively large, this assumption is inaccurate and it is necessary to use equivalent or compensating variations in income (see Chapter 5). Second, the summation of consumer, producer and revenue effects assumes that agents have equal importance from the perspective of governments, that the value to each of income at the margin is the same and that income redistributions can be costlessly achieved by other means. Departures from these assumptions require extensions of the type presented in Tyers (1990a). Third, the analyses exclude any externalities associated with these markets. They also ignore dynamic effects such as the inducement of innovations which shift supply curves (which are included in our assessments in Chapter 6). Nor do the above analyses include other non-price policy instruments such as production quotas and land set-asides. These are incorporated in the model presented in the next chapter.

Worthy of special mention, however, are two other implicit assumptions. One is that agents in these markets, taken as a group, have no power to influence prices elsewhere in the economy. This is probably reasonable in advanced industrial economies where agriculture produces only 2 or 3 per cent of national output and comprises only a small percentage of the nation's international trade. It is less reasonable where food products are a significant proportion of the nation's trade, for then changes in these markets will influence the country's foreign currency exchange rates.[12] It is also unreasonable if agriculture is a large part of the economy, as in many developing countries, because non-food product and primary factor markets will be affected by changes in food prices. The result would be changes in the positions of the food supply and demand curves in the above diagrams (as discussed in Section 3.1 of Chapter 3).

The other important implicit assumption is that there are no distortions in other markets. The welfare analysis in the partial equilibrium models above is weakened if this assumption does not hold. To see this, suppose the economy produces just two goods. Raising the price of food would attract resources from the other sector, resources which would have been in maximum productive use (assuming no externalities). Thus, as predicted in the above partial equilibrium models, a food price rise, induced by domestic policy, reduces welfare. But if, on the other hand, the other sector was already heavily assisted (and so was inefficiently using the nation's resources from society's viewpoint), then an increase in food prices would attract some resources from that sector and thereby raise national output and hence welfare, contrary to the prediction of the partial equilibrium models. Therefore, it must always be kept in mind that the welfare effects predicted by the latter models depend crucially on the assumption that there are no distortions elsewhere in the economy. This point is taken up again in Chapter 6 concerning the effects of agricultural policies on the welfare of developing countries where distortions in non-farm sectors are often very substantial.

4.9   The need for quantitative analyses

This chapter has made it abundantly clear that there are many instances where it is not possible to determine *a priori* even the direction of the effects of some policy or structural changes which alter international prices, let alone their magnitude. This is true in spite of the strong presumption that, in highly distorted markets, changes in the direction of free trade will raise both national and global welfare. If the analysis is to be more precise, the magnitude of the various parameters in these models must first be determined. As the above analyses show, the important parameters are the own-price and cross-price elasticities of demand and supply, the producer and consumer domestic-to-border price ratios, the extent to which countries transmit international price changes to their domestic markets, the country's importance in the world's food markets, and the extent to which the country is self-sufficient in the various food products. Values for these are provided in Appendix 2. Having determined these, the next step is to incorporate them into a computer simulation model of world food markets. The following chapter describes a model that has been built precisely for that purpose.

Notes to Chapter 4

[1] The standard theory to be outlined here is discussed in more detail in Corden (1971, 1974, 1983) and Bhagwati (1971). See also Just *et al.* (1982), McCalla and Josling (1985) and Houck (1986) for some agricultural applications.

[2] If the exporting or importing country is small the transfer to foreigners is zero because the excess demand curves in Figure 4.5 are horizontal. In the case of the large importing country that does not fully transmit the international price decline, the resulting protection that this generates may reduce its own welfare loss through depressing the international price further, and the policy

could even enhance domestic welfare if it moves that country closer to its optimal tariff level.

3 This point is drawn from Tyers and Falvey (1989).

4 Estimates of the extent of the international price rise depend on the range of commodities under discussion, on the time period allowed for adjustment, and on the year(s) chosen to introduce the reform (among other things). This is because protection rates differ across commodities and over time and adjustments will be larger the longer the period of adjustment allowed (Blandford *et al.* 1990; Gardner 1989).

5 This would be expecially so if some of the gains to industrial countries from their trade liberalization were to be redistributed in the form of increased foreign aid to agricultural research programs in, or pertinent to, developing countries.

6 In essence, then, this issue requires an application of the last point from the theory introduced in the previous section.

7 This is established by Tyers and Falvey (1989).

8 This is but another example of one of Bhagwati's (1971) general points, that apparently paradoxical outcomes are possible in a distortion-ridden economy.

9 We are reminded by that, since an import tariff or export subsidy is equivalent to a combination of a consumption tax and a production subsidy, the above is equivalent to reducing the subsidy component.

10 This section draws on a point made in an earlier empirical analysis (Anderson and Tyers 1984), where it is shown that, in the case of the European Community's wheat policy, it is indeed possible that government revenue and producer welfare could both be enhanced if a producer levy were to be combined with an additional consumer tax.

11 This area is equivalent to the change in the area under the meat industry's derived demand curve for grain which is associated with the grain price increase.

12 For a critical discussion of the treatment of exchange rates in agricultural trade models, see for example Chambers and Just (1979).

5

A Model of World Food Market Behaviour

In this chapter a behavioural model of world food markets is introduced which formalizes the relationships between structural changes and food policies on the one hand and their production, consumption, price, trade and welfare consequences on the other. We begin with a non-technical description of the model which is supported by two appendices: Appendix 1 provides a corresponding algebraic description while Appendix 2 lists the values of key model parameters. The chapter then outlines the model's characterization of the protection and market insulation components of food and agricultural policy and provides an illustration of the model's behaviour in response to policy shocks. Finally, the approach adopted for estimating effects on economic welfare is described, again non-technically, with further support from the algebraic description in Appendix 1.

5.1 Model description

Analysts interested in only one food product typically build a single-commodity partial equilibrium model of the world market for that product. For present purposes, in which interest is focused on major traded food staples, a multi-commodity model is needed to capture the interactions in production and consumption between those products. Ideally, this would be a general equilibrium (GE) model of the world economy of the type employed by Whalley (1984). To keep the task manageable, however, such models are typically short on commodity detail and hence represent only crudely, if at all, the commodity interactions within sectors such as agriculture. In the model used by Loo and Tower (1989), for example, agriculture is one undifferentiated sector. The economy-wide model adopted by the OECD (Burniaux *et al.* 1988) had just two sub-sectors for agriculture, plus three processed food sectors within manu-facturing. An earlier GE model by Burniaux and Waelbroeck (1985) also had just two farm sectors. Although each sector produced multiple products, the division of production within sectors was based, crudely, on the assumption that elasticities of transformation are constant across all pairs of products.

There are, however, several partial equilibrium models of world food markets which do incorporate considerable commodity detail. These include models developed by Zietz and Valdes (1985) at the International Food Policy Research Institute, by the United States Department of Agriculture (Roningen 1986), by the International Institute for Applied Systems Analysis (Parikh *et al.* 1988), and by the Agricultural Directorate of the OECD Secretariat (OECD 1987).

We have sought to improve on the latter group of models in a number of ways. The first is in our representation of government intervention. To measure the effects of intervention by any one government it is not sufficient to be able to predict the response of all other private agents in the market. If prices and quantities change when one government distorts the market, we cannot assume that other governments will not intervene or retain constant distortions. We need to understand the reasons for government intervention and to incorporate the responsiveness of governments to international market shocks.

Since, as we saw in the previous two chapters, agricultural protection is intimately tied to the insulation of domestic markets from changes in international prices, it is essential to represent the dynamics of food market behaviour in the short run. The model must therefore incorporate the production uncertainty characteristic of agricultural markets, risk-spreading agents such as stockholders should be represented in it, and it should differentiate the short-run from the long-run respons-iveness of agents such as farmers. In addition, the responsiveness of necessarily endogenous government intervention should be similarly differentiated. Finally, for relevance in the policy debate, it is important that a welfare analysis, by which income equivalents of the effects of food market distortions can be measured and compared, is associated with the model.

To keep the model manageable, attention is restricted to the major traded food staples, namely wheat, coarse grain, rice, meat of ruminants (cattle and sheep), meat of non-ruminants (pigs and poultry), dairy products and sugar. As we saw in Chapter 1, these seven commodity groups account for about half of world food trade (edible oils and beverages account for most of the rest) and one-tenth of global trade in all commodities. The model does not extend to general equilibrium, in that markets for other tradable goods, services and physical and financial factors of production, and for non-tradables, are excluded. Hence, currency exchange rates enter as exogenous variables. This drawback is offset, however, by the following special features of the model:

- it is global in coverage, including 30 countries or country groups spanning the world, so that the international as well as the domestic effects of policy changes and other disturbances in one or more countries or commodity markets can be determined endogenously;
- it incorporates the cross effects in both production and consumption between the interdependent markets for grains, livestock products and sugar;
- it has a dynamic mode, in which the effects of policy or structural changes in a particular year can be simulated for every subsequent year, as well as a static equilibrium mode which can simulate the effects of those changes after any desired degree of adjustment;
- it is stochastic in that production uncertainty is included via probability distributions associated with each commodity's production level;
- stockholding behaviour is endogenous, based on empirical analysis of public and private stock level responses to price and quantity changes in each country; and, most importantly from the viewpoint of the present study,
- policy is endogenous to the extent that price transmission equations are used to incorporate the two key features of each country's food price policies: the protection component (which raises the trend level of food prices faced by domestic producers and consumers around which prices fluctuate) and the stabilization or insulating component (which allows trade fluctuations to limit the degree to which domestic prices

change in response to shifts in domestic supply or in international prices).

It is possible to convert partial equilibrium models of this type into general equilibrium models by adding one or more other traded goods sectors and a non-tradables sector.[1] To do so, however, requires making heroic assumptions about behavioural patterns and parameter values, many of which remain the subject of considerable controversy in the economics literature (Thurow 1984:Ch. 4; Shoven and Whalley 1984). The straightforward behavioural assumptions made in our model are generally non-controversial and the key parameters, particularly the elasticities of demand and supply, have been estimated many times. While the magnitudes of some elasticities are still debated, many of the key parameters are standard currency among food policy analysts.

Furthermore, the partial equilibrium assumption is not unreasonable for most countries. In industrial countries, staple traded food production typically contributes no more than one or two per cent of GNP and employment. In developing countries, while agriculture is a more substantial contributor to GNP and employment, the gross value of grain, livestock and sugar transactions at the wholesale level still average no more than 15 per cent of GNP. In the very poor countries and country groups, such as in South Asia and sub-Saharan Africa, distortions in agriculture probably do affect factor prices, production costs and exchange rates in ways which are not captured in the model. Where these effects are expected to affect the results, however, alternative assumptions regarding exchange rates and factor prices can be examined in sensitivity analyses.

In experiments with the model, the sudden introduction of policy changes, such as the removal of protection in one country or country group, frequently stimulates a cyclical response in world markets as simulated by the model. While such cyclical responses are stable and behaviourally reasonable, the simulated world prices would be stationary only after expensively long simulation intervals. This makes it difficult to estimate the long-run impacts of the removal of protection. To provide a short cut to the estimation of long-run policy impacts that have assembled the static equilibrium version of the model, in which the parameters chosen are appropriate only to long-run closure.

The welfare analysis in Chapter 6 depends both on the dynamic model and on this static equilibrium version.

Behavioural assumptions

Production behaviour is represented by a 'partial adjustment' model which is linear in the logs of production (current or lagged) and producer prices (equations A1.1 and A1.2). Allowance is made for the effect on production of land set-aside policies such as those presently active in the United States (equation A1.3). In the dynamic version of the model, production in each country and country group is subject to random disturbances, such as the effects of weather and pest infestations. These are multiplicative and log-normally distributed, and are based on the distribution of residuals to the reduced-form production equations derived from time-series analysis. Although these disturbances cause markets to fluctuate and farmers to face price and income risks, the choice of a planned level of production is assumed, in this model, to be unaffected by such risks.

Direct human consumption is assumed to be characterized by income and price elasticities of demand which are set to decline slightly over time (equations A1.8 and A1.9). The demand for livestock feeds is based on input-output coefficients for each livestock product which again are assumed to change over time as the proportion of livestock output that is feed-based changes (equation A.10). In the static equilibrium version of the model, this coefficient is applied directly to livestock production. It is not appropriate to do so in the dynamic version, however, where short-run changes in livestock production do not generally follow the corresponding changes in the livestock populations to be fed. In this case, a steady-state level of livestock output is identified which corresponds more closely in the short run to animal feed requirements. This steady-state output is based on a moving average of past production levels (equation A1.11). The average is adjusted so as to take account of short-run changes in animal populations and hence feed demand, which are associated with short-run supply responses (equation A1.12). Since, for most countries, sufficient data are not available for the direct estimation of short-run responses of feed demand to changes in prices and livestock output, we have approximated these responses based on the estimated short-run relationship between livestock output and feed prices.

For example, in the very short run, the response of the beef sector to a price increase in industrial countries is generally to reduce the slaughter rate and to build up herds. Meat output temporarily declines but feed demand increases in both the short and long runs. Conversely, a current year meat price decline would lead to meat output (temporarily) above trend and therefore a steady-state output (and corresponding feed demand) below the moving average. Sustained increases in meat output, on the other hand, suggest above trend steady-state output and feed demand. Similarly, an increase in the price of feed results in a temporary increase in output as the slaughter rate is raised to reduce the cost of carrying stock. In this case, feed demand declines in the short run, as production rises. For all livestock products, then, the direction of the response of feed demand to feed price changes in the short run is opposite to that of the corresponding response of output. Furthermore, for a particular livestock industry, the responses of production and feed demand (though opposite in direction) can be assumed to be similarly distributed through time.[2]

The behaviour of stocks in rice, wheat, coarse grains, sugar and dairy products is based on an empirical adaptation by Tyers and Chisholm (1982) of the model for risk-neutral competitive speculators, first developed by Muth (1961) and later expanded by Turnovsky (1979) and Aiyagari *et al.* (1980). As in the treatment by Aiyagari *et al.*, negative stocks are prohibited. Speculators are assumed to expect the price one year hence to be a four-year moving average of past prices (equation A1.19). The model permits speculative stocks to respond to either international trading prices or (usually insulated) domestic prices, depending on which provided the best fit in our econometric analysis of stock time series (based on equation A1.16).

The adaptation incorporates a term in quantities only, to explain stock changes in countries where government-held stocks dominate and where closing stocks do not depend significantly on either stabilized domestic prices or international prices. The term is the surplus of total domestic supply (production plus carry-in) over its long-run trend. Its estimated coefficient is uniformly positive, confirming that, even in insulated markets, bumper harvests raise the level of stocks carried into subsequent years.

Target levels of closing stocks are set for each commodity at a fixed proportion of trend consumption in importing countries and of trend production in exporting countries (equation A1.17). In the static version of the model, stocks are fixed at these target levels (equation A1.22), while in the dynamic version it is intertemporal deviations from these target levels which are driven by expected speculative profits and departures of domestic supply from the long-run trend.

Government policy is made endogenous through price transmission equations for each country and commodity, based on the formulation introduced in Chapter 2. These equations cover both the protection and the market insulation components of food price and trade policies. They express domestic producer and consumer prices in each country in terms of border prices, which are in turn functions of 'world indicator prices' (equations A1.24–A1.27). The latter relationship depends on the exogenous real exchange rate and a factor reflecting differences between countries in the quality of the commodities they trade and the different costs of freight and insurance associated with shipment to or from major trading partners. These factors are assumed to remain constant, even where changes of trade direction take place (equation A1.28).

In the dynamic version, the price transmission equations are reduced-form Nerlovian lagged adjustment models, with short-run and long-run elasticities of price transmission distinguished. Note that producer prices are based on parameters which generally differ from those determining consumer prices. In this model, the long-run elasticity of price transmission is generally less than unity, reflecting the prevalence of non-tariff protection instruments in food markets. Unless markets are specified as completely insulated (i.e. both the short-run and long-run elasticities of price transmission are zero), governments facing volatile international commodity markets limit both the extent to which the trend of domestic prices can follow that of international prices and, in the interests of domestic price stability, the short-run movements in domestic prices which would otherwise occur as world prices fluctuate. The smaller the short-run elasticity of price transmission in relation to its long-run counterpart, the greater the degree of market insulation and the more sluggish is the eventual transmission of any sustained change in the international price.

Solution

Structurally, the model is simply a set of expressions for quantities consumed, produced and stored, each of which is a function of known past prices and endogenous current prices. It is solved iteratively by starting from the 1980–82 base period and beginning each subsequent year with the assumption that all prices are the same as those in the preceding year and calculating new production, consumption and stock levels in each country. The resulting excess demands are then totalled and international prices adjusted to move world markets towards clearance. The procedure is then repeated until a satisfactory degree of market clearance has been achieved for each commodity. Thus, the model selects that series of international and domestic prices, and the production, consumption and closing stock levels which simultaneously clear all markets in each successive year, from 1983 to the year 2000.

The dynamic version of the model may be run in either stochastic or deterministic mode, the former requiring at least 100 repetitions each using a different set of generated random disturbances from the distributions of production equation error terms. From these many simulations, forecast means and standard deviations are calculated for all key variables in the model for each year of the simulation period. They can also be calculated for the base period (1980–82) simply by replacing the values of all time-dependent parameters with their base period values. The solution algorithm is conventional, depending on endogenous approximations to the global excess demand elasticities, but it is not based on any standard software package. A detailed account of the solution algorithm is provided in Appendix 1.

Parameters

In deriving parameters for the model, the strategy adopted was first to assemble consistent data sets for each country and country group. These include, where available, time series of production, imports, closing stocks, trade values and domestic producer, wholesale and retail prices for each commodity. These data were originally assembled with the assistance of the East-West Center and the United States Department of Agriculture, and subsequently extended through support from the World Bank and the International Economic Data Bank at the Australian National University. The data on which the most recent estimates of model parameters depend is in annual time series for the period 1961 to 1982. More information on this data set is provided in Appendix 2 together with tabulations listing all the key parameters of the model.

Econometric analysis which uses national aggregate data and annual averages of domestic and border prices has its limitations, particularly for the estimation of production and consumption parameters. The professional economics literature abounds with country-specific and commodity-specific studies of consumption and production behaviour. Many of those studies use more sophisticated behavioural models and commit more resources to ensuring that the data used are consistent and accurate than has been possible in preparing this study. Where such studies have been available, and where there is evidence that their results are superior to ours, the resulting parameter estimates have been inserted directly into our model. In the case of protection parameters, for example, we have borrowed in part from the survey of results from Nerlovian supply response models by Askari and Cummings (1977) and from the more general survey by Rojko *et al.* (1978). The exceptions to this general rule are the parameters of the price transmission and storage equations, however. Since few of these alternative estimates are available, these parameters used here are all based on our own econometric analysis (see Tyers 1984).

As for the consumption parameters, the conditions of demand theory are met only within the constraints of a partial equilibrium model which here includes only seven commodity groups. Excluded are not only non-food commodities, but also some close substitutes for the included commodities such as soybeans, tubers, eggs and fish. The degree to which the 'homogeneity' and the 'adding up' conditions are not met, however, is consistent with the exclusion of substitutes in each case. Furthermore, the Slutsky condition linking opposite cross-elasticities of demand is met as a matter of necessity. The reliability of econometric estimates on one side of the matrix is invariably greater than that of their opposite counterparts. Conformity is therefore forced on the weaker estimates.

In the case of the production parameters, even though these are not derived from single production or profit functions, some discipline is imposed on the cross-elasticities of supply. In particular, the corresponding linear response of the net supply of product i to change in the price of j is rendered roughly equal to the response of the supply of j to an identical change in the price of i. This condition parallels the symmetry of the Slutsky matrix on the demand side and is a sufficient condition for path independence in the measurement of producer surplus in the welfare analysis presented below. As with the demand parameters, this condition is imposed by adjusting the comparatively unrobust cross-elasticity estimates.

The appropriateness of parameter estimates can often be judged on what they imply about behaviour at more aggregated levels. For example, whether estimated matrices of own-price and cross-price supply elasticities are reasonable is often evident from their implied total or sectoral supply behaviour. Similarly, the parameters in the model imply excess demand and excess supply elasticities in international trade for individual countries and groups of countries. These values are compared with estimates from other recent studies in Tyers and Anderson (1988, 1989). No amount of such supporting evidence can completely remove controversy regarding key parameter values, however. Where these values are not robust, the ultimate recourse is to sensitivity analysis. Examples of such analysis, as applied to parameters in our model, are provided in Tyers (1985) and Tyers and Anderson (1989).

5.2   The model's characterization of policy

The model has several policy or control parameters. Principal among these are the price transmission parameters, which include target producer-to-border and consumer-to-border price ratios, ρ^P and ρ^C, and the corresponding short-run and long-run price transmission elasticities, ϕ^{PSR}, ϕ^{CSR}, ϕ^{PLR} and ϕ^{CLR}. Other parameters useful in policy analysis include the shifters, μ^P and μ^S, which are the proportional changes in production due to land set-asides and in trend stock levels due to government-held stocks in the United States.

With these basic instruments it is possible to represent a range of quite complex government interventions. To illustrate this, Table 5.1 lists some stylized policy components along with their representation in terms of the above parameters. The first is a simple partial insulation of the domestic market, in which the domestic price is stabilized around the trend of the border price. Since the short-run price transmission elasticity is less than one, changes in border prices are not fully transmitted in the same year. But the long-run price transmission elasticity is unity and therefore the trend of the average domestic price does not deviate from that of the border price. Hence, the distortions which result have no permanent protection component.

The second case is that of a total insulation of the domestic market. In this case the domestic price is fixed permanently at the level of the base period border price. Although the domestic market is undistorted in the base period, it may well become distorted subsequently as the international price departs from its base period value. Following this are four types of *ad valorem* tariffs, taxes and subsidies which distort the average domestic price away from that at the border but which pass through proportional border price changes. These instruments all provide protection but, in and of themselves, they add no comparative stability to the domestic market.

Finally, we include stylized grain policies for the European Community and the United States in the late 1980s. The first of these is a perfectly insulating system of variable levies and export restitutions with a target domestic price 50 per cent higher than the base period border price. All the price transmission elasticities are set to zero and the domestic price remains constant at its target level irrespective of movements in the international price. In the case of US policy, the distortion applies only to the producer side of the domestic market. For simplicity of illustration, we assume all producers are compensated up to a fixed target price by deficiency payments. Their price is therefore held constant while the domestic consumer price is free to follow that in the international market.

Of course, in reality the policies of the EC and the United States are more complex than this. For these and other countries we rely heavily on econometric estimates of base-period

Table 5.1: The characterization of stylized policy components in the world food model

	Producer Price Policy			Consumer Price Policy		
	Base period nominal protection coefficient (ρ^P)	Price transmission		Base period consumer-to-border price ratio (ρ^C)	Price transmission	
		Short run (ϕ^{PSR})	Long run (ϕ^{PLR})		Short run (ϕ^{CSR})	Long run (ϕ^{CLR})
1. Partial stabilization of domestic price around trend of border price	1.0	0.5	1.0	1.0	0.5	1.0
2. Total insulation of domestic market at the base period border price	1.0	0.0	0.0	1.0	0.0	0.0
3. 20% import tariff or export subsidy[a]	1.2	1.0	1.0	1.2	1.0	1.0
4. 20% import subsidy or export tax[a]	0.8	1.0	1.0	0.8	1.0	1.0
5. 20% production subsidy[a]	1.2	1.0	1.0	1.0	1.0	1.0
6. 20% consumption subsidy[a]	1.0	1.0	1.0	0.8	1.0	1.0
7. Stylized EC grain policy: Perfectly insulating variable levy/export restitution with target price 50% above base period border price	1.5	0.0	0.0	1.5	0.0	0.0

(continued)

Table 5.1: *(continued)*

	Producer Price Policy			Consumer Price Policy		
	Base period nominal protection coefficient (ρ^P)	Price transmission		Base period consumer-to-border price ratio (ρ^C)	Price transmission	
		Short run (ϕ^{PSR})	Long run (ϕ^{PLR})		Short run (ϕ^{CSR})	Long run (ϕ^{CLR})
8. Stylized US (post-1985) grain price policy: Production deficiency payment to fixed target price 50% above base period border price, with 100% program participation	1.5	0.0	0.0	1.0	1.0	1.0

[a]Given the constant elasticity formulation of the price transmission equations, tariffs, taxes and subsidies which are applied at *ad valorem* rates are more readily represented than their specific counterparts.

[b]Overall United States grain policy is, of course, much more complex. Its more complete representation in the model, including land set-asides, is discussed in Chapter 7.

distortions and price transmission elasticities, the values of which are listed in Table A1 in Appendix 2. In the important case of the United States, however, a substantial change of policy occurred with the 1985 Food Security Act. Since our model simulates from a base period of 1980–82, it is necessary to permit the values of the policy parameters to change suddenly or gradually (depending on the policy prescription), after 1985. Such changes allow us to represent the large increase in participation in farmer subsidy programs which took place after the Act was implemented and the sudden reductions in prices paid for output committed to public grain stocks. These changes were accompanied by increases in the amount of agricultural land set aside, which are introduced into the model on an annual basis through the parameter μ^P, and reductions in the rate at which government stocks were accumulating, introduced similarly via μ^S. Further details of the representation of US policy are provided in Chapter 7.

All the policies represented so far act primarily on prices. Land set-asides and above-commercial public stocks are indirect measures of price control. But these are introduced into the model with the assumption that they do not change the elasticity of price response of producers or stockholders at the margin. More difficult to represent, however, are binding quotas on production and trade. Such policies require that specific production, import or export targets be met. Since these variables are not readily made exogenous in our model, our approach to their simulation is therefore indirect. We locate, by trial and error, the corresponding price distortion which achieves the quantity target, and represent the quota as a combination of this price distortion with an income transfer, or quota rent.

For example, consider the case of a large country which exports from an undistorted domestic market, as illustrated in Figure 5.1. The imposition of a quota limiting domestic output to Q shifts the country's excess supply curve from ES to ES_Q and raises the international price from P_0 to P_1. The domestic producer price which would ensure domestic output remained at Q if the quota were to be removed is p_1^P. Thus, the price distortion which would have exactly the equivalent effect would be a producer-to-border price ratio of $\rho^P = p_1^P/P_1$. Since the excess demand behaviour of the rest of the world is not readily observed

Figure 5.1: Domestic and international market effects of a large economy imposing a production quota

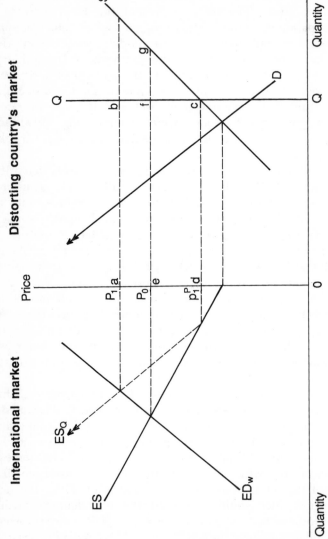

in the model prior to simulation, the value of p_1^P is most readily located by trial and error. The combination of this distortion with the transfer to producers of income equivalent to area abcd then provides an accurate representation of the quota policy.

5.3   Illustrations of the model's behaviour

In the presentation of the results later in the book, there are repeated references to some key behavioural characteristics of the model. To simplify that discussion, we illustrate two aspects of the model's results here. The first relates to the response of policy to external price shocks and the second to the distinctions between the results from the static and dynamic versions of the model.

The transmission of external price shocks

An important feature of the model is its representation of government policy as endogenous. The nature of intervention by the government in one country changes in response to an external shock due to changes in intervention by other countries' governments. Such shocks are transmitted between countries as changes in international prices of commodities and hence as shifts in the terms of trade.[3]

These shocks always result in changes in border prices which are then passed through to the domestic market either imperfectly or not at all, depending on the values of the price transmission elasticities. The net result of this process is frequently that a change of policy (say a trade liberalization) in a foreign country causes a shift in the home country's terms of trade and, because this shift is imperfectly transmitted to the domestic market, a change in the degree to which the home country's domestic market is distorted.

This case is illustrated in Figure 5.2, which plots the domestic against the border price in the home country. The degree to which the domestic market is distorted is then measured by the angle of the ray from the origin on which the point corresponding to the two prices lies. If it lies on the 45 degree line, the market is undistorted. Prior to the international price

Figure 5.2: Relationship between domestic and border prices in response to an external shock

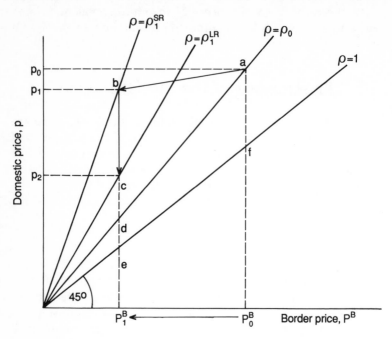

shock, the home country is at point a, where domestic producers are protected at a nominal rate of $\rho_0 = p_0/P_0^B$. The external shock (which might also be due to a real revaluation of the domestic currency) then reduces the border price to P_1^B. In the first year, only a small part of this change in price is passed through to the domestic market and the recipient country moves to point b, where the nominal protection rate is markedly higher, at $\rho_1^{SR} = p_1/P_1^B$. With time, however, more but not all of the change is passed through and the country moves to point c. The ultimate result of the process is an increase in the nominal rate of protection from ρ_0 to $\rho_1^{LR} = p_2/P_1^B$ (providing, of course, that the domestic adjustment has not changed net trade sufficiently to cause a further shift in the border price). In our model results this increase always occurs following either a decline in the international price or a real revaluation of the domestic currency whenever the long-run elasticity of price transmission is less than unity; that is, whenever the country's policy instruments include measures other than *ad valorem* tariffs, taxes and subsidies, or their equivalents.

The way in which this process is modelled has two other important implications. First, border price shocks are transmitted proportionally. This means that, had the long-run elasticity of price transmission been unity, the process just described would have ended up at point d, at which the nominal protection rate is the same as at point a, before the shock. But the absolute size of the price distortion (measured as the difference between the prices) will have decreased from af to de, which is in proportion to the decline in the border price. Thus, even though the same nominal protection coefficient is retained, the change improves economic welfare in the recipient country. Similarly, had the shock been an increase in the border price, the retention of the same nominal protection rate would have led to an expansion in the absolute gap between the prices and hence in the national economic welfare cost of the country's policy.

The second effect depends on the assumption that price transmission elasticities have the same values for both upward and downward changes in border prices. In the example of Figure 5.2, had the shock been an increase in the border price, the net result would have been a lower nominal protection rate, but one which is higher than the rate which would have resulted had the domestic market been perfectly insulated. It is conceivable that the political and other processes by which the domestic price is adjusted in response to an external shock (reviewed in Chapter 3) are not symmetrical. For example, in industrial countries, where farm interests tend to have a strong influence over the process of price determination, upward movements in border prices might be more fully transmitted than downward ones. For the analysis presented in this book, we retain the symmetry assumption, leaving its validation as a matter for further research.

Static and dynamic solutions

The principal difference between the static and the dynamic versions of the model is that the static version calculates equilibrium solutions ignoring all transient effects in the production, stockholding and price transmission equations and setting all behavioural parameters at their long-run values. However, it retains exogenous time trends as they apply to income, population, real exchange rates and the effects of extensification and technical change on production. By using these, it is possible to generate a series of long-run equilibrium solutions along a time path. This time path is then the trend about which the corresponding projection of the dynamic model fluctuates, the deviations from it being short-run responses to sudden changes in the exogenous time trends (in real exchange rates, for example) and to random production shocks.

These characteristics of the static version, combined with its comparative simplicity and ease of interpretation, make it particularly useful in measuring the effects of government interventions. For example, the global food economy can be depicted in equilibrium with or without any chosen group of distortions, as in Chapter 6 below. The dynamic version, on the other hand, is more appropriate for measuring the short-run and medium-run effects of feasible changes in policy and, thereby, for determining the path of adjustment through time towards a new long-run equilibrium, as in Chapter 8 below. The eventual long-run equilibrium effects of the complete removal of whole policy regimes cannot easily be determined using the dynamic version, however, because of the dominance of transient effects.

To illustrate this, consider the impact of the protection afforded producers in one large economy depicted in Figure 5.3. With the parameters characterizing this policy and those of all other countries held constant, the reference projection of the model traces out time paths such as ABC (shown for two endogenous variables: production in the large country and the international price). This would be traced out both by a sequence of static equilibrium solutions using the static version of the model and (approximately) by a single solution of the dynamic version. Parallel to this path is another, DEF (projected by the static version of the model), which corresponds to the case in which the policy of the large country is liberalized. Along this path, domestic production is substantially lower, imports are therefore larger or exports less, and thus the international price is slightly higher. To measure the effects of the protection thus removed, the model compares the two static equilibrium solutions calculated for corresponding periods: for the base

Figure 5.3: Time paths of endogenous variables in reference and liberalization projections by the static and dynamic versions of the world food model

(a) Production in large country

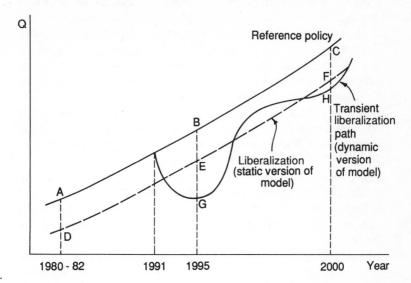

(b) International price

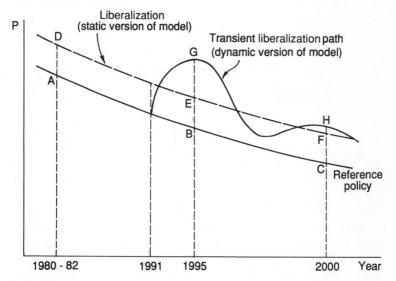

period D with A, for 1993 B with E, or for 2000 C with F. These static equilibrium effects of liberalization are thus calculated assuming there has been time for full adjustment by all agents.

Where measurement of the transient effects of a policy liberalization by the large country is of special interest, this can be readily achieved with the dynamic version of the model. The results commonly obtained from solutions of this type are also illustrated in Figure 5.3 for the case where protection is removed in 1991. They show damped oscillations coverging on the liberal policy path DEF. The effects measured with the dynamic version of the model are substantially larger in the first few years than those based on comparisons of equilibria derived from the static version of the model (GB rather than EB in 1993, for example). Even after ten years, these dynamic results might not be sufficiently close to long-run equilibrium results (HC compared with FC in the year 2000) to be reliable for measuring the full effect of policy changes, even though they are very useful in assessing the transition following the shock.

Thus, while the static version of the model is appropriate for measuring who is assisted and who is hurt by existing policies, and what the effects of change would be after full adjustment, the dynamic version is more appropriate for examining the path of adjustment.

5.4   How the model measures economic welfare effects of policy changes

In measuring the welfare effects of food market distortions, it is helpful to be able to express the resulting quantity, price and income changes facing each group of agents in terms of a standard money metric. This permits the model to calculate, for each group of agents, the income equivalents of simulated departures from existing food policies. With this information it is possible to make normative assessments of the policies and to quantify the extent to which they are effective in transferring income from one group to another. Our emphasis here is on the normal transfer components of welfare impacts, as distinct from the welfare effects of changes in price and income risk of the type accounted for in our simple model with market insulation (presented in Chapter 3 and Appendix 4). The welfare results derived using the multi-commodity trade model, as presented in Chapters 6 and 7, ignore aversion to risk. Technical support for the description which follows is provided in Appendix 1; Section D.

The welfare measures in the model cover four principal groups of agents: consumers, producers (which can be divided into commodity-specific groups), tax-payers (or the government treasury) and stockholders. These groups are not mutually exclusive. Many farmers, for example, are members of all four groups. All are members of at least the first two. Our measures therefore provide only indirect information about the effects of agricultural policy on personal income distribution. They measure the degree to which changes to existing policies assist the activities of consumption, production, tax collection and stockholding. Individuals gain or lose depending on the distribution of their activities among these four.

Before moving to separate presentations of the measures adopted for each group of agents, it is useful to clarify two general characteristics of the approach we adopt. The first is concerned with the measurement of welfare impacts by direct comparison of prices and quantities in alternative model simulations. This is a clumsy process in dynamic stochastic models of this type. It is made simpler by evaluating separately the welfare impacts of price changes projected in each model simulation against the hypothetical case in which prices remain at their common base period (1980–82) values. Thus, a reference simulation is first made in which policy regimes (and hence the policy parameters discussed in Section 5.2) are assumed to remain constant. Changes in welfare projected by the reference simulation are then evaluated relative to the hypothetical case in which all prices remain fixed at base period levels. When a change in policy regime is subsequently introduced, a new simulation is made in which projected welfare changes are again compared with the hypothetical constant-price case. The welfare impact of the change in policy regime is then the difference between the measured changes in the reference and the non-reference cases.

The second general characteristic of our approach is that the welfare measures adopted require that changes in prices be examined in a fixed sequence, with producer and consumer welfare impacts estimated for each commodity at the stage in which its price is changed. The net effects are obtained, once this process is complete, by summing the welfare impacts across all commodities. To do this we must use the model to calculate the levels of production and consumption which would prevail when only some prices deviate from their base-period values. For each country and each year simulated, this process yields matrices with rows listing consumption and production levels for each commodity and columns indicating the number of consumer or producer prices that are distorted. These, combined with the primary results from model projections, are sufficient to calculate the consumer and producer welfare measures.

Consumer welfare

The formulation of a money metric for consumer welfare in strict conformity with economic theory requires that we specify indirect utility functions and use them to derive the income change equivalent to changes in price. This is impractical for a number of reasons. First, it is improper to make the common assumption that proportional changes in prices are small, because total liberalization will involve domestic price changes of more than 50 per cent for some commodities and countries. Second, the uniqueness of a money measure of consumer utility change requires a number of restrictive conditions on the indirect utility function (Silberberg 1978: Ch. 11), including that it be homothetic and therefore that the income elasticities of demand for the commodities whose prices change are unity. For food commodities, especially in industrial countries, income elasticities of demand are generally less than one and often less than zero (see Table A4 in Appendix 2). Finally, the information we have to indicate the pattern of preferences does not extend beyond existing consumption patterns and estimated price and income elasticities of demand. It is appropriate, then, to turn to a standard measure of willingness to pay, such as the equivalent variation in income (Hicks 1943). This measure, while not having a direct correspondence with utility change, is unique and has a simple and plausible interpretation. For any single change in price, it is the area swept out beneath the compensated demand curve, measured at the utility level applying after the price change. When prices change simultaneously in more than one market, it is measured by adding all the changes in the areas to the left of the appropriate compensated demand curves where each is successively conditioned on all previously considered price changes (Just *et al.* 1982: Appendix B).

This is illustrated in Figure 5.4 for the case of an increase in the consumer price of commodity i from its base period level, $\bar{P}^C_i$, to its projected value in year t, P^C_{it}. Changes in the prices of the first i–1 commodities have been accounted for in deriving the Marshallian demand curve D^Y. The level of consumption before the change in the price of i is c^{DC}_{ii-1t}, or that at point A. After the price change, consumption declines to c^{DC}_{iit} at point B. The equivalent variation in income associated with this change is then the area to the left of the compensated demand curve through point B. It is labelled D^U in Figure 5.4—it passes beneath D^Y so long as commodity i has positive income elasticity of demand. This is the area BEGF.

The prices at points A and B emerge as endogenous variables from the model solution and the quantities are readily drawn from the matrix of consumption levels described previously.

Figure 5.4: Uncompensated and compensated demand curves used for measuring changes in consumer welfare

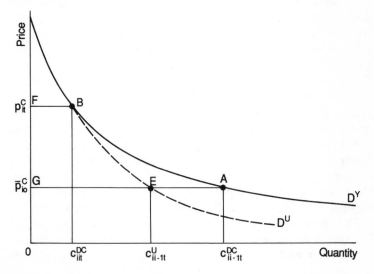

Drawing the compensated demand curve through B to E presents no difficulty since the compensated price elasticity is a function of the known uncompensated elasticity, the income elasticity and the expenditure share. It remains only to integrate under the curve for the area BEGF (see Appendix 1: Section D for details). The total benefit to consumers from the departures of all consumer prices from base period values, V^C, is then the sum over all commodities of the areas thus calculated.

Producer welfare

The changes in prices and quantities simulated by the model can affect the welfare of farmers in four ways. First, there are the effects on their net income of changes in ex-farm product prices. Second, farmers are consumers of intermediate inputs, particularly grain to feed livestock, and are therefore affected when the price of feedgrain changes. Third, the effect of land set-aside policies is to raise the cost of producing a specified level of output and thus to shift food supply curves. Finally, farmers are affected by weather and other sources of randomness in farm output and therefore receive windfall profits in some years and losses in others.

Our approach to the welfare of farmers as producers and as consumers of intermediate inputs relies heavily on Marshallian producer surplus. This is the excess of gross producer receipts over total variable costs, or the sum of profits with total fixed costs. Unlike its consumer counterpart, producer surplus has survived as an exact measure of the income (profit) equivalent of a change in price despite modern extensions to the theory of the competitive firm. Further, if the price change is in the market for an intermediate input, then it can be accurately measured either as the change in consumer surplus under the derived demand curve or as the area swept out by the resulting shift in the supply curve. When multiple price changes occur, the change in producer welfare must be measured by calculating the change in surplus over all markets in sequence, where supply or derived demand curves at each stage are conditioned on all previously considered changes.

The four components of producer welfare change are illustrated in Figure 5.5. The cases considered are a reduction in land set aside, a decline in the price of one intermediate

Figure 5.5: Components of changes in producer welfare

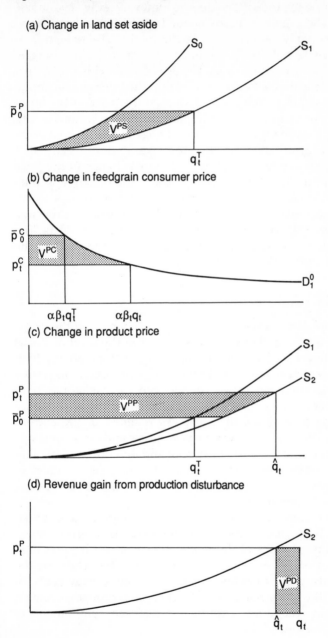

(a) Change in land set aside

(b) Change in feedgrain consumer price

(c) Change in product price

(d) Revenue gain from production disturbance

input, an increase in the price of one product and an increment over planned production due to unexpectedly favourable weather. The supply curve for planned production at base period prices is initially S_0 in part (a) of Figure 5.5. The reduction in land set aside reduces costs and moves it to S_1, resulting in a gain to farmers of the area V^{PS}. Associated with the supply curve S_1 is the derived demand curve for the intermediate input, D_1 in part (b) of Figure 5.5. A decline in the price of the input provides the farmer with additional consumer surplus worth V^{PC}. Next is added the effect of the change in the product price. Before doing so, however, we must take account of any shift in the supply curve, from S_1 to S_2, due to a change in the price of the intermediate input. The product price change is then measured along S_2 as an increase in producer surplus worth V^{PP}. Finally, the unexpectedly good weather results in a revenue gain worth V^{PD} without any associated increase in costs. The total producer welfare effect of these four changes is then the sum of V^{PS}, V^{PC}, V^{PP} and V^{PD}.

Stockholder welfare

The welfare of stockholders is affected by changes in the prices at which stocks are bought and sold and in the level of stocks held. If the price of a stored commodity is comparatively high in the current year, stocks will generally be released. This results in revenue from net sales. To calculate the welfare gain to stockholders, V^S, we must offset against these the opportunity cost of the asset value of the stocks retained in the current year, measured at the current-year price and an exogenous interest rate, and the costs of storage and deterioration of these retained stocks. The marginal cost of storage is assumed to increase linearly with departures from a moving average of stock levels (see Appendix 1: Section A).

All these components of stockholder welfare are accounted for when the dynamic version of the model is in use. In static equilibrium solutions of the model, however, V^S includes only the non-transient components of these measures, which are the opportunity cost of holding stocks and their storage costs. In this case the marginal cost of storage is assumed to remain constant in real terms. Expressions for each component are provided in Appendix 1.

Effects on government revenue

All price distortions characterized in the model are assumed to result from government intervention. Marketing margins other than those due to policy are excluded from the data on which the parameters determining levels are based. The revenue consequences of these distortions are calculated as if they took the form of annually adjusted tariffs, taxes and subsidies which are collected or distributed at zero cost and which introduce no by-product distortions (Corden 1974). The government is therefore envisaged as purchasing domestic output at producer prices, purchasing net imports at border prices, selling for domestic consumption at consumer prices and selling to stockholders at the prices at which stocks are traded (which could be domestic or border prices). Changes in the net revenue position from these transactions, V^G, are calculated based on departures of quantities and prices simulated by the model from base-period values.

Aggregate welfare

The net impact of quantity and price changes on national welfare for any one country is the sum over commodities of the consumer, producer and stockholder welfare impacts combined with the effect on government revenue. Since each is an income equivalent, the measures are comparable and can be added readily in this way. Indeed, when they are converted to a common currency (in this case 1985 US dollars) they can also be added across countries.

It is useful to note, however, that such summations imply a particular social welfare function—one which weights equally the income equivalents of benefits accruing to farming, the consumption of farm products, stockholding and the collection of tax revenue for expenditure on public goods. In practice, however, political systems do not weight these activities equally. Some groups—particularly farmers in industrial countries—have disproportionate influence over policies affecting them. The policy formulation process might therefore be seen as behaving as if it were maximizing a welfare function which gives greater weight to some groups or activities than to others. This insight, which has been used formally in quantitative policy analysis by Sarris and Freebairn (1983, 1984) and Tyers (1990a), is useful in the assessment of proposed policy reforms.[4]

5.5   Model validation

It is appropriate to test the predictive performance of any structural model, even where the primary objective in constructing the model is policy analysis rather than forecasting. One standard approach is to simulate the model over the estimation interval and measure its errors. In this case, the relevant interval is 1962–82. But the approach is not particularly enlightening since the character of the movements in international food markets in that period is dominated by random shocks, principally to food production. Model simulations do little more than follow the observed trend.

An alternative approach is to use *ex post* simulation, where the performance of the model is examined outside the estimation interval. This can readily be done for the period 1983-89, since international price data are available (at the time of writing) for most of the commodities in the model. Although the exogenous variables in the model (particularly national incomes and exchange rates) have a greater influence on the character of international food price movements in this period than during the estimation interval, random production disturbances continue to dominate. A proper test of the model's performance, then, necessitates the estimation and incorporation of those disturbances as exogenous variables. These we have crudely estimated as departures from exponential production trends. To carry out the test, we then included them in the model as exogenous production shifters, applying only to the interval 1983–89.[5]

The results obtained from this *ex post* simulation are illustrated in Figure 5.6 for an index of all international food prices and for prices in the three grain markets depicted in the model. The simulations reflect the pattern of international price movements reasonably accurately. Their predictive performance is quantified in Table 5.2, which compares the coefficient of variation of the actual international price series over the interval with the root mean square per cent simulation error. The errors are comparatively modest in all cases except that of sugar.

Figure 5.6: Actual and simulated indices of real international food prices

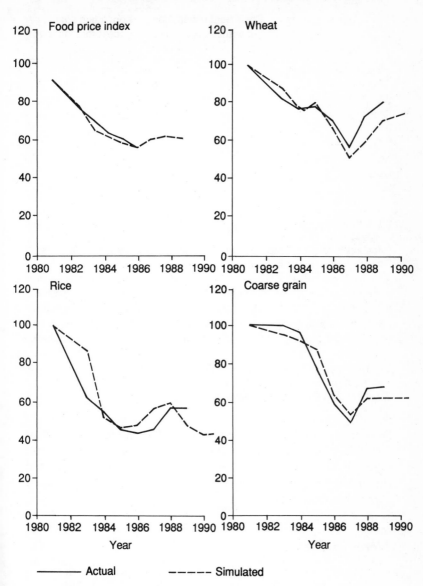

Sources: As for Table 5.2 and authors' model simulations.

Table 5.2: Model validation: *ex post* forecast, 1982–89

	Coefficient of variation of actual price series, per cent	Root mean square per cent forecast error[a]
Index of international food prices[b]	19	6
Wheat	16	7
Coarse grain	26	14
Rice	35	17
Ruminant meat	14	9
Non-ruminant meat	15	10
Dairy products	24	14
Sugar	29	25

[a] The expression used is $[\frac{1}{T} \sum_{1}^{T} (\frac{P-P_a}{P_a})^2]^{1/2}$ where P_a and P are the actual and simulated prices.

[b] The index covers grains, meats, dairy products and sugar and uses shares of international trade values as weights.

Sources: The actual price series are sourced as follows: wheat, rice, coarse grain, ruminant meat and sugar prices are drawn from World Bank (1988c); the prices for maize and beef are used as proxies for coarse grain and ruminant meat; the dairy product price is the export unit value of dried cow's milk from New Zealand (in liquid milk equivalents) and the non-ruminant meat price is a weighted average of the export unit values of pigmeat and poultry meat from the United States, using world trade volume shares as weights; the unit value series are from Food and Agriculture Organisation trade data tapes, supplied by the International Economic Data Bank of the Australian National University.

Despite its good performance overall, the model is clearly at its weakest in simulating the international sugar market, a result which is not surprising when one considers how fragmented that market is and how little of the commodity is actually traded at international spot prices.

Notes to Chapter 5

[1] This has been done by the US Department of Agriculture in adapting its SWOPSIM model, for example (see Krissoff and Ballenger 1989). Note that the IIASA model (Parikh *et al.* 1988) is not a true general equilibrium model in that it has just one non-agricultural sector which is assumed to produce traded goods.

Thus, real exchange rates (the price of tradables relative to non-tradables) cannot be determined endogenously in that model.

2   Notice the negative sign in equation A1.12. Since the denominator is always positive, the sign of the coefficient, τ, is therefore always opposite to that of the supply response. This is particularly appropriate in the case of cattlemeat, where empirical evidence has demonstrated that the short-term supply response is opposite in direction to its long-term counterpart.

3   Shocks with similar effects can also originate from the exogenous time path of real exchange rates.

4   Also implicit in the model's measure of aggregate welfare is the assumption that there are no externalities associated with these food markets. In fact, we know agricultural production does have effects on the environment that could be quantified in terms of welfare (see, for example, Young (1988) and Just and Antle (1990)), but to do so is beyond the scope of the present model.

5   The behaviour of US grain stocks in the late 1980s was so greatly affected by the Food Security Act of 1985 as to render non-representative the empirical estimates of stock parameters, listed in Appendix 2: Table A11, which are based on the period 1960-79. After 1985, therefore, US grain stock parameters are tuned slightly to allow for the greater responsiveness to international price movements which characterized that period.

6

Effects of Existing Policies

The resources are now at our disposal to examine the domestic and international effects of distortionary food policies. To do so, we draw particularly on the estimates of the distortions to food prices in industrial and other countries summarized in Chapter 2, on the theory of distortions and welfare described in Chapter 4, and on the simulation model of world food markets presented in Chapter 5 and Appendices 1 and 2. In this chapter, attention is focused mainly on the policies of industrial countries, but their effects in combination with the policies of developing countries are also considered.

The dynamic nature of world food markets, which was emphasized in Chapters 2 and 3, ensures that the effects of a given set of food policies vary from year to year about a long-run trend. To examine the trend component of these policies, we take advantage of the fact that the base period of the model, 1980-82, saw average international prices (and hence protection levels) in the vicinity of the long-run trend illustrated in Figure 1.1. The effects of policies on prices, on quantities produced, consumed and traded, and on economic welfare are therefore first estimated for this period. But, current interest demands estimates of distortions and their effects in the 1990s and beyond, when food policies will have been influenced by the Uruguay Round of international trade negotiations. For useful counterfactual analysis, it is therefore necessary to use the model to simulate the behaviour of world food markets beyond its base period with and without substantial reforms, in the latter case taking advantage of the endogeneity of protection levels in our model, as discussed in the previous chapter. Our approach to this is detailed in Section

6.1, while our actual estimates of effects in both periods are presented in Section 6.2.

Two key points re-emerge in this analysis. First, sluggish transmission to domestic markets of international food price fluctuations causes the extent to which food policies are distortionary to fluctuate inversely with international prices; and second, because the declining trend of international food prices is also imperfectly transmitted to domestic markets, even in the long run, there exists an underlying trend towards greater protection of food production. Consequently, the trend of protection rates is projected to be considerably above the levels experienced in 1980-82, even in years when simulated international prices rise.

Moreover, since food production is being encouraged and consumption discouraged more in countries with high rates of agricultural protection than in those with lightly assisted agricultures, the trade and welfare effects of even a constant pattern of unequal protection levels tends to increase over time, as shown in the empirical results reported in Section 6.2.

6.1 The extent of food price distortions

What has been the protection trend since 1980-82? During the mid-1980s (i.e. 1983-1987) real international food prices declined steeply to an all-time low (Figure 1.1 above) before rising somewhat in the late 1980s. Since domestic food prices in most countries are allowed by policy to respond only sluggishly and often incompletely to international price changes, the mid-1980s was a period of rapidly increasing domestic-to-border food price ratios, or nominal protection coefficients, for food agriculture. This is reflected in the OECD's estimates of producer subsidy equivalents, reported in Table 2.4 above. As international prices recovered a little in the late 1980s, this growth in protection slowed and even reversed for some countries and commodities. However, if present insulation policies and the long-term decline in real international food prices continue, protection rates will grow even further in the 1990s.

To forecast these protection levels, assuming no changes to past policy trends, projections must be made of world food markets for the years ahead. This is carried out to the year

2000 using the dynamic version of the model described in Chapter 5. The base period for dynamic simulations is 1980-82. For the interval 1983–89, where sufficient data were available, we included shocks to production due to climate as exogenous variables (see the discussion of the model's *ex post* performance in Section 5.5). Thereafter, in deterministic simulations, climatic production shocks are set to zero. In stochastic simulations beyond 1989, they enter the model as synthetic random disturbances and multiple simulations are made. Other exogenous variables enter deterministically throughout, as detailed in Appendix 2. Since the character of the price transmission equations in the model makes actual protection rates endogenous, the resulting projections of market-clearing domestic and international prices yield a matrix of projected nominal protection coefficients.[1]

To support the analysis of current policies presented in the following section, we have made a single deterministic simulation over the period 1983–2000 using the dynamic version of the model. Of course, the analysis of price risk requires corresponding stochastic simulations. These are discussed in Section 6.3.

The resulting projections of relative international food prices are summarized in Figure 6.1, which shows the path of a composite index of real prices for grain, livestock products and sugar through to the year 2000. After bottoming out in 1987, at barely 60 per cent of the 1980–82 level, this index rises in the late 1980s before declining again during the 1990s. It falls to just over 50 per cent of the 1980–82 level by mid-decade before recovering slightly towards the year 2000. This price movement is similar to the World Bank's projection for grains, although the latter is a little lower throughout the 1990s because livestock prices, which are important in the index shown in Figure 6.1, have not fallen as much as grain prices.[2]

For the main industrial market economies, the associated protection coefficients are shown in Table 6.1 for 1987, 1990, 1995 and 2000 for the main industrial market economies, together with the 1980-82 estimates from Table 2.6.

The large fall in international food prices to 1987, together with the sluggish adjustment of domestic prices to that fall, ensured that the protection rates for 1987, and to a lesser extent for 1990, were very much higher than those for the early 1980s.

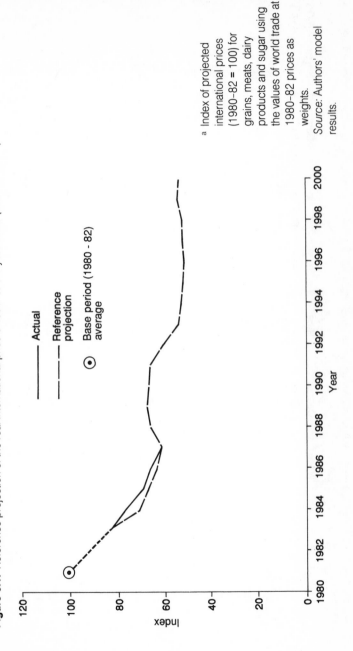

Figure 6.1: Reference projection of the real international price of food[a] to the year 2000 (1980–82=100)

a Index of projected international prices (1980–82 = 100) for grains, meats, dairy products and sugar using the values of world trade at 1980–82 prices as weights.

Source: Authors' model results.

Table 6.1: Nominal protection coefficients (producer-to-border price ratios), various commodities and industrial countries, estimated 1980-82 and projected to the year 2000[a]

	Wheat	Coarse grain	Rice	Ruminant meat	Non-ruminant meat	Dairy products	Sugar	WEIGHTED AVERAGE
EC-12								
1980-82	1.40	1.40	1.35	1.95	1.25	1.75	1.50	1.55
1987	2.55	2.20	2.10	2.65	1.50	2.70	2.15	2.15
1990	1.75	1.75	2.50	2.70	1.40	2.60	2.40	2.00
1995	2.55	1.90	2.55	2.85	1.35	2.85	2.70	2.15
2000	2.10	1.85	2.50	2.90	1.35	3.05	3.00	2.15
EFTA-5								
1980-82	1.65	1.55	1.00	2.30	1.40	2.45	1.55	1.90
1987	3.20	2.85	1.00	3.55	1.80	4.10	2.40	2.95
1990	2.20	2.20	1.00	4.25	1.85	4.60	3.05	3.10
1995	2.90	2.05	1.00	4.60	1.80	5.25	3.65	3.50
2000	1.80	1.55	1.00	3.65	1.50	4.60	3.10	2.90
Japan								
1980-82	3.90	4.30	3.35	2.80	1.50	2.90	3.00	2.35
1987	7.55	10.60	7.45	4.80	1.85	6.15	5.50	3.80
1990	4.70	9.80	10.50	5.30	1.90	6.95	6.75	4.25
1995	5.35	11.20	11.65	5.45	1.95	7.85	7.40	4.05
2000	3.85	11.20	12.00	5.55	1.95	8.70	7.80	3.75

United States							
1980–82	1.15	1.00	1.30	1.10	1.00	2.00	1.40	1.20
1987	1.35	1.15	2.00	1.30	1.00	2.45	1.90	1.30
1990	1.05	1.15	2.10	1.30	1.00	2.30	1.85	1.30
1995	1.35	1.15	2.00	1.30	1.00	2.45	1.90	1.30
2000	1.00	1.00	1.70	1.35	1.00	2.40	2.10	1.20
All industrial countries							
1980–82	1.25	1.15	2.50	1.50	1.20	1.90	1.50	1.40
1987	2.05	1.75	5.55	2.00	1.40	2.80	2.00	1.90
1990	1.35	1.30	7.60	2.05	1.35	2.80	2.30	1.80
1995	1.85	1.30	8.20	2.15	1.30	3.05	2.60	1.90
2000	1.55	1.20	8.30	2.15	1.30	3.20	2.80	1.85

a The projected ratios are taken from the reference projection described in the text. The weighted averages are calculated using production valued at border prices as weights. Ratios have been rounded to the nearest 5 per cent.

Source: Table 2.6 and authors' model results.

For the industrial market economies as a group the average nominal rate of protection for 1990 is double that for the early 1980s (80 per cent compared with 40 per cent). The increase is even larger for Japan, but it is somewhat smaller for the United States. The protection rates are projected to fall a little in the early 1990s as international food prices remain above their 1987 low, but, by 1995, the gap between domestic and border prices will increase again because of the fall in international prices. Then, between 1995 and the turn of the century, the gap is forecast to shrink slightly on average as projected international food prices turn upwards once more.

The protection coefficients in Table 6.1 thus illustrate three important points. First, protection rates fluctuate because insulating policies ensure that domestic food prices are not as volatile as international prices. Second, notwithstanding these fluctuations, the average projected level of protection in these countries in the 1990s is very much above that of the early 1980s, owing to the lower average level of international food prices and the imperfect price transmission by industrial market economies even in the long run. Third, the upward drift in projected rates of protection is higher for some food products (sugar and dairy products, for example) than for others (such as grain and non-ruminant meat).[3]

6.2   Effects of existing policies on trade and welfare: the comparative statics

We have outlined above our use of the world food model to generate a corresponding reference scenario for the period 1980–2000 and the reference nominal protection coefficients for each of the seven commodity groups and 30 countries/country groups. It is now possible to estimate the effects of those protection levels by comparing that reference scenario with scenarios in which one or more countries remove their protection policy. For the most part, this is done using the static long-run equilibrium version of the model, which employs only the model's long-run elasticities of supply, demand and border price transmission.

Thus, our counterfactual analysis compares a reference

scenario, derived using a deterministic yet fully dynamic simulation over the period 1983–2000, with static solutions of the equilibrium versions of the model for 1987, 1990, 1995 and 2000. These latter solutions embody liberalizations of various types. They are intended to show what the world food economy might look like in the years chosen had policy regimes *always* been more liberal in some countries.

The cases considered are the protection policies of:
- the 12 member countries of the European Community,
- the five member countries of the European Free Trade Association,
- Japan,
- all Western Europe and East Asia (the above 18 countries plus Korea and Taiwan),
- the United States, and
- all advanced industrial market economies (the above other than Korea and Taiwan, plus Australia, Canada and New Zealand).

Two sets of effects are examined in this section, namely, the effects on international prices and world food trade volumes, and the effects on economic welfare in both the protectionist countries and other countries. These are presented for the base period 1980-82 as well as for the years 1990 and 2000. The latter two years are appropriate periods for the comparison of scenarios, not only because they bound the current decade, but also because they both lie approximately on a geometric trend fitted to the projected prices shown in Figure 6.1.

An important assumption in the present section is that policies have had no effect on rates of farm technological change. Insofar as sustained high (low) domestic prices encourage (discourage) productivity growth, the results would be somewhat distorted. Thus, in Section 6.3, the key results of this section are compared with results in which it is assumed that productivity growth is positively correlated with the long-run level of domestic producer prices.

Effects on international prices and trade[4]

It is apparent from part I of Table 6.2 that the European Community was the major contributor to the international price-depressing effects of industrial countries' food policies in the

Table 6.2: International price and trade effects of agricultural protection in industrial market economies (IMEs), 1980–82

	Wheat	Coarse grain	Rice	Ruminant meat	Non-ruminant meat	Dairy products	Sugar	WEIGHTED AVERAGE
I International price level % difference due to policies in:								
EC–12	-6	-5	-3	-18	-4	-25	-7	-10
EFTA–5	-1	-1	-1	-3	-1	-6	-0	-1
Japan	-1	-1	-6	-5	-4	-10	-2	-3
All WE & EA[a]	-7	-7	-12	-25	-9	-31	-10	-12
United States	-1	4	-1	-3	1	-22	-3	-4
All IMEs[b]	-9	-3	-10	-23	-7	-38	-10	-14
II World trade volume % difference due to policies in:								
EC–12	4	0	0	-58	6	-17	1	
EFTA–5	-0	-1	1	-10	-1	-12	1	
Japan	0	4	-18	-40	-46	-29	-1	
All WE & EA[a]	3	2	-22	-67	-54	-27	-2	
United States	2	-10	3	-17	-8	-46	-3	
All IMEs[b]	6	-8	-15	-67	-44	-40	-3	

III Net export volume[c] Million tonne difference due to all IME policies for:

All WE & EA[a]	4.3	-4.1	3.8	6.3	1.7	14.0	2.3
Australasia and North America	3.6	-8.1	0.2	-2.5	-0.9	14.4	0.7
Centrally planned Europe	-2.7	1.9	0.0	-0.3	-0.2	-6.2	-0.0
Other developing countries	-5.2	2.0	-4.0	-3.5	-0.8	-22.2	-3.0

[a] All WE & EA refers to the Western European countries in EC-12 and EFTA-5 plus the East Asian protectionist economies of Japan, Korea and Taiwan. The 12 members of the EC are Belgium, Denmark, France, Germany FR, Greece, Ireland, Italy, Luxembourg, Netherlands, Portugal, Spain and the United Kingdom. The 5 included members of the European Free Trade Association are Austria, Finland, Norway, Sweden and Switzerland.

[b] All IMEs refers to Western Europe and Japan (but not Korea and Taiwan) plus Australia, Canada, New Zealand and the United States.

[c] The extent to which exports are greater or imports are smaller as a result of agricultural protection in Western Europe and East Asia. A negative sign signifies that those policies have reduced exports or increased imports for that group of countries.

Source: Authors' model results.

base period. Except for rice, where East Asian policies are also important, the EC's policies have had more impact on international price levels than the combined effect of *all* other industrial countries' policies. Even though protection levels are higher in EFTA and East Asia, those countries are smaller participants in world food markets and hence their policies have only minor influences on international prices. By contrast, Canada and Australasia *are* large participants but, since their protection levels in 1980–82 were relatively low, their impact on prices is too small to be worth including in Table 6.2. The United States, however, does influence international prices through its policies but, at least in 1980–82, in the opposite way to Western Europe and East Asia. If the US had unrestricted food markets in 1980–82, its net exports of coarse grain, pork and poultry would have been greater and so world prices of those products would have been lower. This is because US wheat (and rice) protection was positive in 1980–82 whereas coarse grain protection was virtually zero. Liberalization would therefore have caused US farmers to switch to producing more coarse grain and less wheat.[5]

World trade volumes for all these products except wheat have been reduced by industrial country agricultural policies. In the case of meat and dairy products, the reduction is very substantial (more than 40 per cent) and it is considerable (15 per cent) for rice. Notice that EC policies expand the volume of world wheat and sugar trade, because of the EC practice of disposing of its surpluses via export subsidies. US policies expand world wheat and rice exports but, because of the substitution in production mentioned earlier, the positive assistance to US wheat production in 1980–82 discourages US coarse grain consumption and thereby reduces world trade in coarse grain.

Part III of Table 6.2 shows that without the industrial countries' policies, Western Europe's and East Asia's annual demands for imports in 1980–82 would have been greater (or supply of exports smaller) by 12 million tonnes for grain, 8 million tonnes for meat, 14 million tonnes for milk (in milk equivalent) and 2 million tonnes for sugar. In the absence of these protectionist policies, the traditional food exporters of Australasia and North America would be exporting 4.3 million tonnes more grain and 3.4 million tonnes more meat. The net importing regions of centrally planned Europe and 'other developing countries', on

Table 6.3: Effects of agricultural protection in various industrial market economies on international food price levels, 1980–82, 1990 and 2000 (per cent change)

	Wheat	Coarse grain	Rice	Ruminant meat	Non-ruminant meat	Dairy products	Sugar	WEIGHTED AVERAGE
Per cent change due to protection policies in:								
EC–12								
1980–82	–6	–5	–3	–18	–4	–25	–7	–10
1990	–11	–6	–6	–25	–3	–39	–14	–15
2000	–13	–8	–8	–25	–3	–42	–13	–16
Japan								
1980–82	–1	–1	–6	–5	–4	–10	–2	–3
1990	–1	–1	–9	–13	–5	–23	–3	–6
2000	–1	–1	–9	–14	–6	–25	–2	–6
United States								
1980–82	–1	4	–1	–3	1	–22	–3	–4
1990	3	7	2	–6	2	–26	–3	–1
2000	3	5	1	–7	1	–23	–3	–1

(continued)

Table 6.3 *(continued)*

	Wheat	Coarse grain	Rice	Ruminant meat	Non-ruminant meat	Dairy products	Sugar	WEIGHTED AVERAGE
All industrial market economies[a]								
1980–82	-9	-3	-10	-23	-7	-38	-10	-14
1990	-11	-2	-14	-33	-8	-51	-18	-20
2000	-14	-6	-15	-34	-9	-54	-18	-22

[a] Western Europe and Japan plus Australia, Canada, New Zealand and the United States. Western Europe includes countries in EC-12 and EFTA-5. The 12 members of the EC are Belgium, Denmark, France, Germany FR, Greece, Ireland, Italy, Luxembourg, Netherlands, Portugal, Spain and the United Kingdom. The 5 included members of the European Free Trade Association are Austria, Finland, Norway, Sweden and Switzerland.

Source: Table 6.2 and additional model results.

the other hand, import more of all these products (apart from feedgrains) because of the effect of these protectionist policies in lowering the prices of their food imports. Individual exporting countries within the latter group, however, have suffered in the same way as Australasia or North America. In the case of Argentina, for example, food export earnings were reduced by around US$2 billion per year by the policies of Western Europe and East Asia. This was more than Argentina's total interest payment on its external public debt in the mid-1980s.

How do these effects for 1980–82 compare with those for a decade or two later? Table 6.3 summarizes the model's projections of the effects on international price levels of those policies in 1990 and 2000, as well as in 1980–82. The final column shows that their depressing effects on international prices are increasing over time. In 1980–82, the effect of all industrial countries' policies was to depress food prices in the international market by 14 per cent. But, by 1990, that reduction is estimated to be 20 per cent and, by 2000, 22 per cent. Again, the European Community is the main source of price depression although, by this time, the United States Export Enhancement Program was also contributing (see Section 7.1). The effects on international trade (not shown) are also commensurately larger in the 1990s than in 1980–82.

Before turning to the welfare effects, an important additional point concerns the effects of these policies on domestic producer prices. If all industrial countries were to liberalize their food markets simultaneously, international prices would rise by a greater extent than if only one or a subset of countries were to liberalize. As a consequence, the required fall in domestic prices in a liberalizing country is less the larger the extent of simultaneous liberalizations in other countries. Table 6.4 shows that the difference in price changes can be very considerable. A particularly striking commodity group is dairy products. For example, the US producer price of milk in 1980–82 was 56 per cent higher than it would have been in the absence of US food policy distortions. However, the distortions in other industrial countries had, together with US policies, depressed the international price for dairy products (by 38 per cent, according to Table 6.3). Hence the presence of all these policies meant the producer price for milk in the United States was only 23 per cent above what it would have been in the absence of

Table 6.4: Domestic producer price effects of agricultural protection in all (and individual) industrial market economies, 1980–82 and 1995[a]

	Wheat		Coarse grain		Rice		Ruminant meat		Non-ruminant meat		Dairy products		Sugar	
EC-10														
1980–82	28	(32)	35	(33)	27	(35)	50	(59)	16	(20)	8	(32)	35	(39)
1995	81	(85)	62	(60)	95	(105)	92	(110)	26	(28)	28	(60)	125	(120)
EFTA-5														
1980–82	50	(64)	50	(54)	–	(–)[b]	75	(120)	30	(39)	52	(135)	39	(56)
1995	95	(91)	75	(54)	–	(–)	200	(330)	58	(63)	135	(335)	200	(233)
Japan														
1980–82	255	(285)	315	(320)	200	(210)	215	(255)	39	(45)	85	(160)	170	(195)
1995	260	(285)	950	(950)	750	(810)	255	(365)	72	(80)	250	(460)	505	(635)
United States														
1980–82	4	(14)	–4	(4)	14	(25)	–15	(8)	–7	(1)	23	(56)	25	(37)
1995	–9	(5)	–5	(5)	45	(75)	–9	(21)	–9	(1)	25	(100)	49	(77)

[a] Numbers in parentheses show the percentage by which producer prices are increased by each economy's own food policies alone, after allowing for those policies' effects on international prices. These are presented for comparison with the adjacent numbers which are the effects of distortions to all industrial market economies' food markets on domestic prices in the countries shown.

[b] Not produced.

Source: Authors' model results.

industrial country policies in 1980–82. To put it another way, liberalizing US policies alone would have caused US producer milk prices to fall by more than one-third whereas, if all industrial countries liberalized simultaneously, the US price of milk would have fallen by less than one-fifth. In the 1990s this difference is even larger, highlighting a major domestic political advantage of multilateral as distinct from unilateral liberalization of markets which are highly protected in many countries.

Effects on welfare in industrial countries

From the results of the model simulations it is possible to derive estimates of the annual economic welfare effects of food policies in distorting and other countries, as explained in Chapters 4 and 5. It should be kept in mind that these are partial equilibrium measures. For industrial countries in which agriculture is a small part of the total economy and in which other sectors are relatively undistorted, this is a reasonable approach. It is less reasonable in the case of agrarian developing countries, the implications for which we examine later. The estimated annual domestic benefits and costs of liberalizing the food policies of individual industrial economies are shown in Table 6.5, while some of the international effects are summarized in Table 6.6 below.

Even in 1980–82, the domestic costs of these countries' policies were very large. They were costly not so much to taxpayers (indeed, in Japan's case, these commodities are net earners of government revenue because of import tariffs and their equivalents, such as state trading), but rather, they were costly to consumers.[6] Non-farm households in Western Europe and Japan each had to pay between $800 and $1,700 per year in the form of higher prices for farm products and higher taxes (measured in 1985 US dollars).

The benefits of the protection policies to producers represent a large proportion of gross producer receipts, ranging from one-quarter of gross farm income in the EC to one-third in EFTA and almost two-thirds in Japan (column 4 of Table 6.5). They represent much smaller shares (well below one-fifth) of farm household income, however, because only a small proportion of farm household income comes from farming in those countries (less than 15 per cent in the case of Japan). Moreover, this benefit to producers is considerably less than the cost to non-farm

Table 6.5: Domestic costs and benefits of food policies of various industrial countries, 1980–82, 1990 and 2000 (1985 US$ billion per year)

	Domestic consumer cost	Govern- ment revenue cost	Domestic producer benefit		Net domestic cost		Transfers from consumers/taxpayers:	
			Total	As a % of gross farm receipts[a]	Total[b]	Per capita ($)	Per non- farm household ($)[c]	Per dollar gained by producers[d]
	(1)	(2)	(3)	(4)	(5)	(6)	(7)	(8)
1980–82								
EC-12	55.0	1.2	47.3	23	8.9	25	800	1.19
EFTA-5	11.7	0.6	9.6	35	2.7	85	1710	1.28
Japan	35.6	−6.0	20.6	63	9.0	75	1120	1.44
United States	17.5	2.6	16.9	11	3.2	14	370	1.19
Sub-total	**119.8**	**−1.6**	**94.4**	**25**	**23.8**	**33**	**750**	**1.25**
1990								
EC-12	86.3	−3.7	66.3	33	17.1	55	1130	1.25
EFTA-5	20.9	0.6	18.4	75	3.1	100	2800	1.17
Japan	82.4	−17.4	37.2	89	27.9	230	2290	1.74
United States	26.5	−2.8	18.8	18	5.2	21	400	1.26
Sub-total	**216.1**	**−23.3**	**140.7**	**38**	**53.3**	**75**	**1150**	**1.37**

2000								
EC-12	106.0	7.5	93.3	36	20.6	60	1530	1.22
EFTA-5	17.1	4.9	18.8	58	3.2	100	2840	1.17
Japan	101.7	-20.6	46.0	87	35.1	270	2820	1.76
United States	25.1	-2.8	18.4	14	4.1	16	380	1.21
Sub-total	**249.9**	**-11.0**	**176.5**	**37**	**63.0**	**83**	**1420**	**1.35**

[a] Column (3) divided by the total value of domestic production of grain, livestock products and sugar measured at the protected domestic producer prices received by farmers.

[b] Column (1) plus column (2) minus column (3); that is, it does not include costs of raising and dispersing government tax revenue and of lobbying by farm groups, nor does it include the costs to the rest of the world.

[c] Column (1) plus column (2) divided by the number of non-farm households, obtained assuming four people per household and the following percentages of the population in non-farm households in 1980–82, 1990 and 2000: EC–12, 89, 91, 93; EFTA 92, 93, 94; Japan 90, 91, 92; and United States 96, 97, 97.

[d] Column (1) plus column (2) divided by column (3).

Source: Authors' model results.

households in these protectionist countries. For both the EC and Japan, the estimated net losses in 1980–82 amounted to $9 billion per year, and for the EFTA countries of Western Europe, it amounted to $2.7 billion (column 5). On a per capita basis, this net loss is equivalent to $25 per year for the EC and approximately $80 for EFTA and Japan (column 6).

Moreover, the losses associated with those policies have been growing steadily over time. According to the model's projections, protecting agricultural markets in the 1990s will cost non-farm households in Japan and in the most protected countries in Europe between $2000 and $3000 per year (column 7). And since the producer benefits of protection have grown more slowly than the levels of protection, the net economic cost to these economies in the 1990s is likely to be two to three times greater than in the early 1980s if present policies continue (columns 5 and 6).

The only country for which the estimated losses are not growing during the 1990s (although they are higher than in the early 1980s) is the United States. This result is based on the explicit assumption that agricultural support in the US will be phased down from the high levels of the late 1980s (target prices will not increase in nominal terms). Should it eventuate that the 1990 Farm Bill delivers a policy for the 1991–95 period that is no less protectionist than the 1985 Food Security Act for the period 1986–90, these results will need to be revised upwards.

The growth in the inefficiency of these policies as a means of transferring welfare to farmers can be seen from column 8 of Table 6.5. For each dollar gained by producers in the United States and Western Europe as a consequence of protection in the early 1980s, consumers-cum-taxpayers in those countries paid around $1.20 on average. The corresponding figure for Japan is more than $1.40. By the 1990s, however, these costs per dollar transferred to farmers are projected to rise and be closer to $1.25 for the US and Europe and $1.75 for Japan. In other words, these high-cost policies are not only becoming more costly to the consumers and taxpayers of these protectionist countries but they are also becoming more inefficient over time as a means of transferring welfare to producers.

These may not *seem* very large losses if one assumes that the aim of these policies is to boost farm incomes, because any form of taxation to raise government revenue for the purpose of transferring it to a particular group is costly.[7] But, in fact, they *are* cause for concern, for three reasons. First, the cost to consumers is measured here at the farm-gate level. Insofar as any of the processing and marketing costs in getting food from the farm gate to the consumer are set, in part, as a proportion of the farm-gate price, we have underestimated the cost to consumers. Second, some of each dollar transferred to producers will be spent on socially unproductive lobbying—and consumers, taxpayers, supermarkets and producers of other tradable products will also spend resources countering the demands of protectionists. Thus the cost to the non-farm sector of transferring a dollar (net) to producers in Western Europe or Japan may well be substantially larger than the $1.25 or $1.75 mentioned above. Third, and perhaps most important, is the fact that, if the aim of these policies is to boost the welfare of low income farm households, say the poorest 30 per cent of farmers, then existing policies are extremely inefficient as transfer devices. This is because the poorest 30 per cent of commercial farmers in industrial countries produce only about one tenth of all output, so perhaps 90 per cent of the above transfer from consumers and taxpayers is unnecessary. In other words, from the viewpoint of boosting welfare of poor farmers, existing policies are costing consumers in industrial countries not $1.25 but perhaps more than $10 per dollar received by target farm households.

These domestic costs of the agricultural policies of major industrial countries represent only part of the welfare effects of such policies. Another important part involves the effects on other countries of the reduction in international food prices caused by any one country's or group of countries' policies. Other countries which are net food exporters would tend to lose, while countries which are net food importers would tend to gain, from lower international prices. Just as in the protectionist countries themselves, however, the net welfare effect for other countries is minor compared with the transfer of welfare within those countries, from food consumers (who would gain) to farmers who would lose from lower international food prices. Moreover, insofar as other countries prefer more stable prices to less stable prices, welfare in both food-importing and food-exporting countries is harmed by the greater instability of international food prices that follows from the insulating component of industrial country policies (to be quantified in the following section). As we saw in Chapter 3, it is difficult to estimate the values placed on stability by different groups. For present purposes, we refer to a deterministic analysis, deferring further discussion of price risk until Section 6.3. Our estimates of the welfare effects of the reductions in mean international prices and in net food imports by protected countries are detailed in Table 6.6.

Clearly, the agricultural policies of industrial countries have had very substantial effects on economic welfare in other countries. In 1990, for example, the estimated benefit to producers in Western Europe and Japan of food policies of industrial countries in aggregate, amounts to $104 billion ($137 billion by the year 2000), but the loss to producers elsewhere in the world, because of those policies, is $45 billion (or $60 billion by the year 2000). Farmers in the highly protected countries clearly benefit at the expense not only of non-farm households in those countries but also at the expense of farmers in the rest of the world. The estimated global *net* welfare loss due to these policies amounts to between $50 billion and $57 billion per year in the 1990s. This is more than three times the estimated global loss due to these policies as of the early 1980s. Japan's policies are the main contributor (around $30 billion) and most of the rest is due to EC policies, as shown in Table 6.7. Notice, though, that US policies have almost no net effect on global welfare. This is because its land set-asides and conservation reserves take out of production about the same amount of resources as US price supports encourage into production in the United States.[8]

The countries most hurt by these policies are, of course, the lightly subsidized agricultural exporting nations. In per capita terms, New Zealand loses most (a little over $300 per year in the 1990s) followed by Argentina and Australia (just over $100 each). Thailand's loss amounts to around $5 which, while small in absolute terms, is just as large as Australia's loss relative to national income.[9] It is not surprising that these nations joined forces with ten other agricultural exporters to form the so-called Cairns Group to lobby in the Uruguay Round of multilateral trade negotiations for liberalization of agricultural markets in protected industrial countries.

Table 6.6: Global welfare effects of food policies of all industrial market economies, 1980-82, 1990 and 2000 (1985 US $ billion per year)

	Consumer/ taxpayer welfare	Producer welfare	Net economic welfare
Effects in 1980-82 on:			
EC-12	-42.8	35.3	-7.5
EFTA-5	-8.7	7.0	-1.7
Japan	-24.8	19.3	-5.5
United States	-2.5	-0.2	-2.7
Canada, Australia & NZ	-0.5	3.4	2.9
All industrial economies	-78.3	58.0	-16.2
All developing economies	28.6	-26.3	2.3
Centrally planned Europe	8.8	-7.0	1.8
Global total	**-40.9**	**24.7**	**-16.2**
Effects in 1990 on:			
EC-12	-64.5	53.1	-11.4
EFTA-5	-16.7	14.5	-2.2
Japan	-55.7	36.1	-19.6
United States	0.4	-3.2	-2.8
Canada, Australia & NZ	1.0	-4.4	-3.4
All industrial economies	-135.6	96.1	-39.5
All developing economies	15.3	-26.5	-11.2
Centrally planned Europe	11.2	-10.6	0.6
Global total	**-109.1**	**59.0**	**-50.1**
Effects in 2000 on:			
EC-12	-93.7	78.6	-15.1
EFTA-5	-17.5	14.2	-3.3
Japan	-69.5	44.4	-25.1
United States	3.0	-7.5	-4.5
Canada, Australia & NZ	-0.9	-3.1	-4.0
All industrial economies	-178.6	126.6	-52.0
All developing economies	33.4	-34.9	-1.5
Centrally planned Europe	11.1	-14.6	-3.5
Global total	**-134.1**	**77.1**	**-57.0**

Source: Authors' model results.

Table 6.7: Global net economic welfare effects of food policies of industrial market economies, 1990 and 2000 (1985 US $ billion per year)

	EC-12 policies	United States' policies	Japan's policies	Policies of all industrial market economies
Effects in 1990 on:				
Industrial market economies	-15.4	-1.7	-25.3	-39.5
Developing economies	1.5	0.4	0.6	-11.2
Centrally planned Europe	-3.2	-0.0	-1.9	0.6
Global total	**-17.1**	**-1.3**	**-26.6**	**-50.1**
Effects in 2000 on:				
Industrial market economies	-22.1	0.0	-32.4	-52.0
Developing economies	-0.9	0.1	-0.7	-1.5
Centrally planned Europe	4.9	1.9	1.2	-3.5
Global total	**-18.8**	**2.0**	**-31.9**	**-57.0**

Source: Authors' model projections.

In addition to looking at the international effects of the food policies of all industrial countries, it is revealing also to examine the effects of the policies of the large players on each other's producers. As Table 6.8 shows, there are some important size differences in these effects. The results show that EC policies hurt US producers much more (twice as much per farm) than US policies hurt EC farmers. Hence the vehemence of the US producer demands for reform in the EC on the one hand, and the indifference of the EC to the offer by the US to liberalize its own policies if the EC agrees to reform. The results also show that US producers would gain little, and Canada's may even lose, if all industrial countries (including the US and Canada) were to liberalize, whereas the gain per producer in Australia and New Zealand would be of the order of $25,000 per farm (last row of Table 6.8). This helps explain why the US is not a member of the Cairns Group and why Canada's commitment to the Group's cause is half-hearted. Finally, recognition of the smaller adverse effects of Japan's policies (and EFTA's, not shown) on export producers helps to explain why the producers focus their attention on the EC even though EC

Table 6.8: Producer and net economic welfare effects of food policies of individual and of all industrial market economies, 1990 (1985 US dollars per year)

	EC-12 policies	United States' policies	Japan's policies	Policies of all industrial market economies
Effects on aggregate welfare ($ million) in:				
EC-12				
- producer welfare	66,300	-4,900	-8,700	53,100
- net economic welfare	-17,100	-2,900	2,800	-11,400
United States				
- producer welfare	-7,870	18,780	-4,150	-3,200
- net economic welfare	-760	5,200	60	-2,800
Canada				
- producer welfare	-2,300	-210	-830	610
- net economic welfare	-260	480	100	670
Australia and NZ				
- producer welfare	-3,190	-660	-1,300	-4,990
- net economic welfare	-1,720	-220	-630	-2,800
Effects on producer income[a]				
EC-12				
- $ per farm holding	11,100	-800	-1,500	8,900
- as % of gross receipts	(47)	(-3)	(-6)	(37)
United States				
- $ per farm holding	-3,400	8,100	-1,800	-1,400
- as % of gross receipts	(-6)	(14)	(-3)	(-2)
Canada				
- $ per farm holding	-9,800	-900	-3,500	2,600
- as % of gross receipts	(-9)	(-1)	(-3)	(3)
Australia and NZ				
- $ per farm holding	-16,800	-3,500	-6,800	-26,300
- as % of gross receipts	(-10)	(-2)	(-4)	(-16)

[a] The total number of commercial farms producing grains, meat, milk and sugar is very difficult to determine. The following numbers which have been used should be considered as only approximate: EC-12 6,000,000 (two-thirds of the total number of farm holdings); United States 2,330,000; Canada 235,000; Australia and New Zealand 190,000.

Source: Authors' model results.

policies involve lower levels of protection than those of EFTA and Japan.

Another feature worth noting from Table 6.8 is that the producer welfare loss that would be associated with liberalizing markets of industrial countries would be less where the liberalization involves other countries than if it were unilateral. The larger the degree of involvement of other countries, the more international food prices will rise and hence the smaller the cut in domestic prices to lower them to border prices. For example, EC producers would have lost $66 billion in the year 1990 if their protection had been removed unilaterally but only $53 billion if other industrial countries had also liberalized their food markets. The difference is even more marked for the US: producers there would lose $19 billion in a unilateral liberalization but they would *gain* $3 billion if all industrial countries participated.

A final point to be made from Table 6.8 is that US *net* economic welfare is affected very little by EC policies, in contrast to its effect on Australasian welfare (bearing in mind the twelve-fold difference in population). The small effect on the United States is an example of one of the paradoxes mentioned previously in Chapter 4. In the absence of its own policy distortions, the United States would be a net importer of ruminant meat, sugar and dairy products. Since the EC's policies lower the international prices of these products, the US economy experiences an improvement in its terms of trade. Evidently this is enough to offset the negative effect on the United States of depressed prices for grains resulting from EC policies (see Tyers and Falvey 1988).

Effects on welfare in developing countries

How is welfare in developing countries affected by these (and other) distortionary policies? Officials in the European Community often argue that even though EC agricultural policies harm agricultural exporting countries, they help the consumers in, and governments of, most developing countries by lowering their per unit cost of food imports. While this is true, as demonstrated by the results presented in Table 6.2, any beneficial changes to the terms of trade of developing countries will depend on a number of factors (see Chapter 4: Section 4.4).

Among these are, first and foremost, the degree to which the economies of the developing countries are presently distorted by their own policies and, second, the extent of any acceleration in technological change in developing countries should food prices there rise following liberalization in industrial countries.

Early partial equilibrium modelling work, including studies by the present authors (Tyers and Anderson 1986 and 1988; and Tyers 1989), has suggested that developing countries as a group might be net losers from food trade liberalization by industrial countries. Even ignoring the possible effects of changes in productivity growth, general equilibrium modellers such as Burniaux *et al.* (1985, 1988, 1990) and Loo and Tower (1989, 1990), report results suggesting that developing countries as a group might gain from that reform.

We seek to reconcile these two conflicting sets of findings by including, in the estimates of developing countries' price distortions used in our model, the depressing effects on the relative prices of food products that result from the non-food policies of those countries. The recent study by Krueger, Schiff and Valdes (1988), the key results of which we have summarized already (Chapter 2: Table 2.8), provides a substantial empirical basis for compiling a set of adjustments for such non-food policy distortions. Using the results from that study, we have adjusted downward most of the domestic-to-border price ratios used in the model (listed, for 1980–82, in Chapter 2:Table 2.9), these being estimates based originally on direct comparisons of food prices alone.[10]

These adjusted measures of price distortions effectively lower the levels of relative domestic food prices, compared with relative international prices, thereby allowing the model to approximate the effects of non-food price distortions. While they have no effect on simulated changes in quantities and prices due to reforms by industrial countries, they substantially change the welfare implications of such reforms for developing countries. This is because such reforms raise international food prices and hence, when at least some part of the price changes are transmitted to domestic markets in developing countries, they improve the terms of trade of farmers and lead to some expansion of the food sector. Thus, the greater the extent to which the food sector is discriminated against by domestic policies, the more net welfare is improved.

The results presented in Table 6.6 showed that food is indeed made cheaper in developing countries by the existing policies of the industrial countries and that consumer and taxpayer welfare is between $15 billion and $33 billion per year higher as a result. But, the other side of the story is the loss inflicted on farmers in developing countries, which, from Table 6.6, amounts to between $26 billion and $35 billion per year in aggregate. Thus, the net effect on developing country welfare was small in the early 1980s and became substantially negative as industrial country protection rose in the late 1980s.

Indeed, if East Asia's newly industrialized economies are excluded from the group, the welfare of other developing countries is seen to be even more adversely affected; slightly so in 1990 and more substantially (by an estimated $6 billion) in 2000. This illustrates one of the apparent paradoxes that can arise in international trade when the direction of trade is reversed by changes in the terms of trade due to policies abroad. Even though developing countries as a group are net importers in the presence of protection policies abroad, industrial country reform would reverse their net trade pattern sufficiently to allow them to benefit as net exporters from the higher international prices which result.

To address the second of the factors examined analytically in Chapter 4, namely the price responsiveness of the rate of technical progress in the food sector, we have carried out a second set of liberalization experiments in which it is assumed that permanent price changes due to reform yield larger production responses in the long run. In particular, long-run supply elasticities are made larger in all commodity markets in all countries by the addition of 0.5 to their respective values. We refer to these alternative results as having 'price-responsive productivity growth'.

Under these conditions, the effects of industrial country liberalization during the 1990s are most appropriately examined for the year 2000. They are summarized in Table 6.12, which suggests that such reform would boost international prices slightly more than in our reference case, in which productivity growth rates are unaffected by reforms (26 per cent as compared with 22 per cent). This reflects the fact that productivity growth in countries where domestic prices would rise is slightly more than offset by slower productivity growth in countries where domestic prices fall. Not surprisingly, since food prices rise in all developing countries, they gain more in this scenario than in the previous scenario in which exogenous growth is assumed: $6 billion as compared with $2 billion per year. But, industrial countries as a group also enjoy a larger benefit in this scenario, despite falls in some domestic food prices. Evidently, the price rises in the traditional food-exporting countries of Australasia and North America, together with the adjustments of farm resources away from the most protected to the least protected farm enterprises within what were highly protected economies, is sufficient to ensure an improved outcome for rich countries also. In aggregate, industrial country liberalization raises world economic welfare by almost a quarter more when productivity growth is price responsive than otherwise.

Moreover, if a broader definition of welfare is used which incorporates equity, risk and food security concerns, then the harm done to people in poor countries by continuing with agricultural protectionism in rich countries is seen to be even greater. Consider first the issue of equity. In developing countries the majority of people—especially poorer folk—are members of farm households and are net sellers of staple foods, while the net buyers of food are mainly relatively affluent urban consumers (World Bank 1990). The price-decreasing effect of agricultural protection in industrial countries, therefore, almost certainly worsens the inequality of spending power within poor countries.

Second, the price-depressing effects of protection policies abroad tend to reduce food self-sufficiency and thereby the perceived food security of poor countries. As noted in Chapter 1, the growth of agricultural protection in industrial countries in recent decades has reduced the competitiveness of developing country producers and raised their net import dependence despite their substantial productivity growth in agriculture. If industrial countries were to remove their agricultural protection, however, the developing countries as a group would, after full adjustment, become net *exporters* of food: self-sufficiency would average 102 per cent by the year 2000, instead of only 93 per cent as in the reference projection. This means developing countries would have a food trade surplus of $9 billion in that year, a difference of $38 billion over the reference projection deficit of $29 billion. Moreover, higher international food prices may well encourage Eastern Europe to raise its producer prices also and use food exports as a means of obtaining much needed hard currency.

Thirdly, as quantified in the next section, the insulating component of agricultural protection policies increases substantially the volatility of international food prices. Given the importance of food in poor agrarian economies, both producers and consumers of food in such countries are likely to prefer food prices to be more rather than less stable through time. Thus, welfare of all people in poor countries is reduced by the greater market instability resulting from protection policies of rich countries.

Effects of developing countries' own policies

The tendency for the policies of developing countries to reduce the domestic relative price of food increases consumption and discourages production, causing their self-sufficiency levels to be lower than otherwise. Overall welfare is also reduced, both domestically and globally, by these distortions. So too is equity, to the extent that poorer people in these countries are net sellers of food. Given the importance of developing countries in the world food economy, international food prices are raised by the larger volume of net imports of food thus induced. As Table 6.9 shows, this roughly offsets the overall price-depressing effect (across all seven commodity groups) in international markets of protection in industrial countries.[11] It is worth noting that, by contrast, the domestic market-insulating component of developing countries' policies does not offset the corresponding industrial countries' policies. As we see in the next section, it adds very substantially to the instability of international food markets.

World trade in these foods is reduced by one-quarter because of industrial country policies, and by an even greater amount because of developing country policies. The former policies limit imports of food (a limitation that is only partly offset by export subsidies), while the latter restrict farm exports. Together, these policies more than halve world food trade, though again it varies by commodity: the effect is even more severe for the meat and dairy product trade but minor for wheat and coarse grain (last row of Table 6.9).

Table 6.9 International price and trade effects of policy distortions of food markets in industrial market economies and developing economies, 1990

	Wheat	Coarse grain	Rice	Ruminant meat	Non-ruminant meat	Dairy products	Sugar	WEIGHTED AVERAGE
International price level % difference due to policies in:								
All industrial market economies	-11	-2	-14	-33	-8	-51	-18	-20
All IMEs and developing economies	1	14	6	-10	26	-55	16	-1
World trade volume % difference due to policies in:								
All industrial market economies	10	-7	-26	-52	-13	-53	-22	-25
All IMEs and developing economies	5	-13	-61	-68	-75	-66	-46	-56

Source: Authors' model results.

In the absence of these policies, what would food self-sufficiency in industrial and developing countries be in, say, the year 2000, compared with the situation if current policies were to continue? Should policies remain unchanged, the pattern of self-sufficiency would be much the same as in the 1980s: developing countries would be only 93 per cent self-sufficient in these foods while industrial countries' production would exceed consumption by 4 per cent. In the absence of food market distortions in industrial countries, the latter would be only 85 per cent self-sufficient, with developing countries and centrally planned Europe supplying the other 15 per cent of their consumption. Self-sufficiency in developing countries would then average 102 per cent. Moreover, if developing countries also removed their own distortionary policies, their export surplus would be even greater (production exceeding consumption by 19 per cent) and industrial market economies would be only three-quarters self-sufficient in food, according to our model's results (Table 6.10). The effect of these policies on foreign exchange earnings is therefore very substantial: developing country net foreign exchange earnings from food trade would be $39 billion greater in the year 2000 in the absence of industrial country food policies, and $81 billion greater if developing country policy distortions also were removed.

Food self-sufficiency would not increase in *all* developing countries after liberalization, of course. Because international prices would be higher for some foods and lower for others

Table 6.10: Food self-sufficiency in industrial and developing economies with and without current policies, year 2000 (per cent)

	Reference case	Without industrial market economies' food policies	Without IMEs' and developing economies' policies
Self-sufficiency in food in:			
Industrial market economies	104	85	74
Centrally planned Europe	107	112	109
Developing economies	93	102	119
Total	**100**	**100**	**100**

Source: Authors' model results.

(see row 2 of Table 6.9), and because there is a wide range of domestic-to-border price ratios for different foods in the various countries, the terms of trade and domestic food prices would be higher in some cases and lower in others. Other things being equal, Latin America and all but the northern part of Africa would enjoy substantial increases in exports and food self-sufficiency, as would Indo-China, the People's Republic of China and parts of South Asia.

The welfare effects of developing countries' policies are apparent from Table 6.11. While global welfare is lowered by about $50 billion per year because of industrial country food policies, the effect of developing country policies on the world food economy is of a similar order of magnitude. That is, in the absence of both sets of policies, global welfare would be between $90 billion and $105 billion per year greater, according to these estimates. Net economic welfare in developing countries would be considerably greater without their own policy distortions: even though consumers currently benefit by about $30 billion per year from those policies, farmer welfare is reduced by more than twice that. The net loss annually is therefore of the order of $30 billion.

Once again, however, the assumption that productivity growth would remain unchanged following reforms is subject to question. Again we might ask how different these results would be in the 'price-responsive productivity growth' scenario. As can be seen from Table 6.12, altering the productivity assumption in this way strengthens the conclusions that can be drawn from the above results. First, the tendency of food policies in industrial market economies to increase domestic production and depress world prices is estimated to be enhanced with price-responsive productivity. But so too is the opposite tendency of developing country policies, which means that the combined effect of industrial and developing countries' policies is roughly neutral as far as average international food prices are concerned.

Secondly, developing countries are harmed even more by industrial country policies with this change of assumption (by $5.7 billion instead of $1.5 billion in the year 2000), and the estimated loss in global economic welfare is 30 per cent greater at $74 billion instead of $57 billion per year.[12] Likewise, the combined effect of developing and industrial country policies on global welfare is greater with price-responsive productivity

Table 6.11: Annual effects on global economic welfare of industrial and developing countries' distortions to their domestic food markets, 1990 and 2000 (1985 US $ billion)

	Effects of industrial market economies' food policies on net economic welfare	Effects of policies in industrial and developing economies on:			
		Consumer welfare	Taxpayer welfare	Producer welfare	Net economic welfare
1990					
Industrial market economies	-39.5	-245.9	21.0	162.8	-62.1
Centrally planned Europe	0.6	3.4	0.4	-3.7	0.1
Developing economies	-11.2	32.8	3.9	-64.4	-27.7
Global total	**-50.1**	**-209.7**	**25.3**	**94.7**	**-89.7**
2000					
Industrial market economies	-52.0	-271.9	9.7	189.8	-72.4
Centrally planned Europe	-3.5	7.1	0.3	-8.0	-0.6
Developing economies	-1.5	27.8	11.9	-71.5	-31.8
Global total	**-57.0**	**-237.0**	**21.9**	**110.3**	**-104.8**

Source: Table 6.6 and additional model results.

Table 6.12: Difference in results for the year 2000 when price-responsive instead of exogenous productivity growth is assumed[a]

	Effect of industrial market economies' policies with:		Effect of industrial and developing economies' policies with:	
	exogenous productivity growth	price-independent productivity growth	exogenous productivity growth	price-independent productivity growth
International food price level (% difference)	−22	−26	−9	−10
Global net economic welfare (1985 US $ billion)				
Industrial market economies	−52.0	−64.8	−72.4	−88.6
Centrally planned Europe	−3.5	−3.7	−0.6	−0.7
Developing economies	−1.5	−5.7	−31.8	−37.7
Global total	**−57.0**	**−74.2**	**−104.8**	**−127.0**
Food self-sufficiency (production as % of consumption)				
Industrial market economies	85	83	74	67
Centrally planned Europe	112	115	109	114
Developing economies	102	108	119	125

[a] The alternative assumption, that productivity growth is not exogenous but rather price responsive, is introduced by raising the long-run price elasticities of supply by 0.5 in non-reference runs.
Source: Tables 6.10 and 6.11 above and additional model results.

growth, by 21 per cent or an extra $22 billion per year.

Lastly, developing countries would enjoy a greater degree of food security because food self-sufficiency would be 6 per cent higher than that obtained under the assumption of exogenous productivity growth. On the other hand, industrial countries would be more dependent on food imports (see final 3 rows of Table 6.12).

Thus, the evidence that developing countries as a group could benefit from agricultural trade reform is substantial. But how widespread are those gains to developing countries? Table 6.13 presents the results only for the scenarios assuming price-responsive productivity growth (because the directions of effects are virtually the same as for the scenarios assuming exogenous productivity growth). These results suggest that the gains are extremely widespread: welfare in almost all of the larger individual developing economies and sub-groups of smaller developing economies improves with liberalization of food policies in industrial countries. Moreover, apart from Bangladesh and Egypt, the exceptions are to be found among the wealthiest developing economies: Korea, South Africa, Taiwan and the Middle East. They are exceptions because, being highly specialized in exports of manufactures or petroleum, they are relatively heavily dependent on food imports (as are Bangladesh and Egypt). Virtually all other food-importing developing economies are close enough to being self-sufficient in food (or would be in the absence of their own distortionary policies) that industrial country liberalization serves to make them better off. Moreover, no developing country is projected to face an increased food import bill: domestic food production and food self-sufficiency increase enough so that the decline in the volume of imports more than offsets the increase in the price of food. Indeed, China, India and Pakistan all switch from being net importers to net exporters of these foods in this scenario.

When developing countries also liberalize their policies, columns 4–6 in Table 6.13 show that even fewer developing countries lose: Korea and Taiwan would enjoy a large increase in economic welfare as they remove their agricultural protection policies and purchase food imports at a slightly lower price. The only other developing countries that would not increase their net foreign exchange earnings from food exports or reduce their spending on food imports in this scenario (in which

Table 6.13: Effects of completely liberalizing food markets on foreign exchange earnings and economic welfare in individual developing countries assuming price-responsive productivity growth, 1990 (1985 US$ billion per year)

	Reform in industrial economies only			Reform in industrial and developing economies		
	Change in net foreign exchange earnings from food trade	Change in farmers' welfare	Change in net economic welfare[a]	Change in net foreign exchange earnings from food trade	Change in farmers' welfare	Change in net economic welfare[a]
Bangladesh	0.2	0.7	-0.2	0.1	0.5	0.1
China	6.3	6.1	2.9	37.0	29.4	12.9
India	5.8	5.7	1.3	3.3	1.6	1.1
Indonesia	1.8	1.3	0.4	-1.3	-1.1	0.9
Korea, Rep.	0.0	0.4	-0.9	-6.8	-6.8	6.5
Pakistan	1.9	1.1	0.3	3.9	3.5	0.4
Philippines	0.1	0.1	0.0	0.3	-0.2	-0.1
Taiwan	0.1	0.4	-0.2	-1.7	-1.8	0.4
Thailand	1.0	0.6	0.5	-0.5	0.3	-0.2
Other Asia	1.8	1.4	0.5	15.3	7.5	1.7
Sub-total, Asia	**20.0**	**17.8**	**4.6**	**49.0**	**32.9**	**23.7**
Argentina	7.7	1.9	5.4	13.8	11.3	5.1
Brazil	7.9	3.8	2.9	7.8	5.8	0.8
Mexico	2.8	1.0	1.2	5.1	3.1	0.9
Other Latin America	6.4	2.3	3.2	8.6	7.4	0.8
Sub-total, Latin America	**24.8**	**9.0**	**12.7**	**35.3**	**27.6**	**7.6**

(continued)

Table 6.13 (continued)

	Reform in industrial economies only			Reform in industrial and developing economies		
	Change in net foreign exchange earnings from food trade	Change in farmers' welfare	Change in net economic welfare[a]	Change in net foreign exchange earnings from food trade	Change in farmers' welfare	Change in net economic welfare[a]
Egypt	0.0	0.2	-0.3	0.1	0.3	0.4
Nigeria	1.2	0.4	0.6	1.3	0.8	0.2
South Africa	1.1	1.3	-0.7	-1.2	-0.5	-0.2
Other sub-Saharan Africa	3.9	1.3	2.0	12.2	7.5	2.3
Other North Africa & Middle East	0.0	1.5	-2.3	0.8	1.3	-0.6
Sub-total, Africa & Middle East	**6.2**	**4.7**	**-0.7**	**13.2**	**9.4**	**2.1**
TOTAL, developing economies	**51.0**	**31.5**	**16.6**	**97.5**	**69.9**	**33.4**
TOTAL, industrial economies	**-78.5**	**-87.0**	**46.5**	**-134.2**	**-160.9**	**73.3**
WORLD TOTAL[b]	**-20.8**	**-44.4**	**62.2**	**-35.2**	**-87.5**	**106.4**

a Net welfare includes the effects on food consumers, taxpayers and food stockholders as well as food producers. Effects on expenditures to administer and to lobby for and against food policies, not included above, would add to the net welfare gains from reform.
b The world total includes effects on Eastern Europe and the USSR.
Source: Authors' model results.

international food prices do not rise) are Indonesia, the Philippines, South Africa and Thailand. As a group, the developing countries' net foreign exchange earnings from food trade are projected to be almost $100 billion per year higher when both developing and industrial countries reform (equal to about one-quarter of total exports by developing countries measured in constant 1985 dollars).

6.3   The effects of existing policies on food price risk

To examine the effects of market insulation by individual economies on international price stability, we use the dynamic version of the world food model in stochastic mode, as described in Chapter 5. The results for existing policies are retrospective in that both the protection and the insulation policies are removed at the base period of the model, which is 1980–82. For any particular set of 200 simulations, roughly constant levels of forecast price uncertainty are observed after a few years and it is these which are compared in Table 6.14. The index used is the coefficient of variation of the simulated international price, which is the per cent deviation above and below the mean within which that price can be found about two-thirds of the time. Thus, as the coefficient of variation becomes smaller, price volatility is reduced.

The results in Table 6.14 clearly show that world food markets would be very much less volatile if agricultural trade policies were liberalized, or changed so as to be non-insulating. The latter could be achieved, for example by transforming existing policies so that the only instruments used are *ad valorem* tariffs and export taxes or subsidies. If such a change were conducted only in the industrial market economies, it would reduce food market volatility by a quarter. If it were carried out in the very populous and highly insulated economies of South and East Asia the reduction would be even more dramatic. A commitment by all industrialized and developing countries to use non-insulating policies would reduce global food market volatility by more than two-thirds, to a level smaller than the domestic inflation rates of most countries.

Table 6.14: Effects on international price instability of liberalizing food markets (coefficient of variation around trend levels, per cent)[a]

	Wheat	Coarse grain	Rice	Ruminant meat	Non-ruminant meat	Dairy products	Sugar	WEIGHTED AVERAGE[b]
Reference	58	53	38	24	8	26	36	34
Coefficient in the absence of domestic insulation by:								
EC-12	39	45	32	15	8	13	28	26
Japan	54	51	33	9	7	18	33	28
United States	60	64	36	17	10	27	31	35
All industrial market economies	**33**	**47**	**28**	**7**	**8**	**11**	**25**	**23**
Developing Asia	29	43	16	14	7	13	12	20
All developing economies	**17**	**23**	**10**	**6**	**6**	**8**	**8**	**12**
All industrial and developing economies	**15**	**23**	**9**	**4**	**5**	**6**	**7**	**10**

[a] Liberalization in some developing countries does not mean the removal of *all* market insulation, only of that part estimated to be due to policies which affect domestic prices directly. Crude estimates suggest that in China this is 50% of the insulation, in Indonesia 54%, the Philippines 67%, Thailand 68%, Bangladesh 51%, India 50%, Pakistan 55%, Brazil 55%, Egypt 71%, Nigeria 61% and sub-Saharan Africa 51%. In all other countries all market insulation is removed.

[b] Based on weights derived from the shares of each commodity group's exports in total grain, livestock product and sugar exports.

Source: Authors' model results.

The domestic price implications of such a liberalization are quantified in Table 6.15. To simplify exposition, the table includes only the effects of liberalization on international and domestic rice prices. The first column lists the simulated coefficients of variation of producer and consumer rice prices which stem from current policies in selected industrial and developing countries. All are smaller than those for the international price, with the tendency (consistent with the arguments in Chapter 3) for industrial countries to insulate producer prices more than consumer prices and for most developing countries to do the opposite. The other columns list the corresponding coefficients

Table 6.15: Effects of food policies on coefficients of variation in producer (and consumer) rice prices in various developing economies[a]

| | Coefficients in the presence of current distortionary policies | | Coefficients in the absence of distortionary policies in: | | | |
			all industrial market economies		all IMEs and developing economies	
Bangladesh	26	(5)	21	(4)	8	(6)
China	5	(3)	12	(3)	7	(6)
India	7	(7)	6	(6)	6	(6)
Indonesia	10	(3)	8	(2)	7	(6)
Korea, Rep.	3	(3)	3	(3)	9	(9)
Pakistan	14	(4)	11	(3)	7	(6)
Philippines	3	(2)	3	(2)	7	(6)
Taiwan	13	(12)	10	(10)	9	(9)
Thailand	21	(4)	16	(11)	8	(8)
Argentina	20	(20)	16	(16)	9	(9)
Brazil	8	(10)	6	(8)	7	(7)
Mexico	15	(15)	11	(11)	9	(9)
Egypt	6	(6)	5	(5)	7	(7)
Nigeria	10	(10)	8	(8)	7	(7)
South Africa	29	(29)	23	(23)	9	(9)
Other sub-Saharan Africa	10	(10)	8	(8)	6	(6)

[a] The coefficient of variation is the standard deviation divided by the mean value for 200 repeated simulations with random weather shocks. Consumer price coefficients are in parentheses.
Source: Authors' model results.

of variation after liberalization. The most striking result seen from the table is that liberalization by all industrial and developing countries would reduce international price volatility to a level almost as low as, and in many cases lower than that currently enjoyed in insulated domestic markets. This demonstrates strongly the collective gain from a switch to non-insulating policies by as many countries as possible. Furthermore, the gain (in terms of reduced international food market volatility) is more than twice as great if developing countries also adopt non-insulating policies than if they do not.

Further insight into the consequences of such a multilateral reform can be gleaned from examining the changes which would occur in government expenditure risk and in balance of payments risk. Consider, first, the effect of liberalization by the industrial market economies (IMEs) on government expenditure risk in those developing countries identified in the model, summarized in Table 6.16.[13] The index used is the ratio of the standard deviation of simulated net food intervention costs to total government expenditure in 1986. Where food market interventions make up a large proportion of net government expenditures, as in China, Bangladesh, Egypt and other sub-Saharan Africa, government expenditure risk due to food price volatility is also large.[14] Irrespective of its present magnitude, however, the model simulations confirm that the reductions in border price volatility, which would stem from the IME reforms, would reduce expenditure risk in all cases. Thus, if governments are averse to such risk on behalf of taxpayers, none should oppose multilateral reforms on those grounds.

The effect of such reforms on balance of payments risk in developing countries is not as clear cut. International price volatility contributes to balance of payments risk through fluctuations in the value of food exports or imports. These fluctuations are affected directly by the price volatility and indirectly by associated fluctuations in food trade volumes; the latter, of course, requiring some transmission of food price changes to domestic agents. One suitable index of the contribution of trade volatility to balance of payments risk is the coefficient of variation of gross export earnings net of any food import costs, $r = S/E$, where S is the standard deviation and E the mean. Thus, a country's balance of payments risk is increased if the only change is an increase in the volatility of

Table 6.16: Food price volatility and government expenditure risk[a]

	Standard deviation of simulated net food intervention cost as a per cent of 1986 government expenditure		
	Reference	**IME liberalization**	
Korea, Rep.	10	9	(−1)
Taiwan	4	3	(−1)
China	27	22	(−5)
Indonesia	8	6	(−2)
Philippines	8	8	
Thailand	7	7	
Bangladesh	115	113	(−2)
India	10	6	(−4)
Pakistan	10	7	(−3)
Argentina	18	17	(−1)
Brazil	3	3	
Mexico	3	3	
Egypt	16	13	(−3)
Nigeria	12	12	
South Africa	3	3	
Other sub-Saharan Africa	22	17	(−5)

[a] Shown in parentheses are the differences, where they exceed half a per cent.
Source: Authors' model results and World Bank (1990).

the net foreign exchange cost of food trade (because this would raise S). It is also increased if the only change is an increase in the average net food import bill or a decrease in the net value of food exports (because these would reduce E). The latter follows because such a change makes the impact of trade value fluctuations larger relative to average export earnings.[15]

The effects of multilateral liberalization on this index are indicated in Table 6.17, which lists proportional changes in r, expressed in per cent. Where these are positive, the analysis suggests that food trade reform would increase balance of payments risk.

Consider, first, the case where only the industrial market economies liberalize. In all but two developing countries, Bangladesh and Egypt, this reform would reduce balance of payments risk. The reason why it raises the risk in these two

Table 6.17: Food price volatility and balance of payments risk[a]

	Proportional change (per cent) in the coefficient of variation of total export earnings net of any food import costs, after liberalization by	
	All industrial economies	**All industrial and developing economies**
Australia	-18	-22
Canada	-2	-4
United States	-6	-7
EC-12	8	6
Japan	26	28
Korea, Rep.	–	15
Taiwan	–	2
China	-10	-81
Indonesia	-2	-3
Philippines	-2	-1
Thailand	-12	-25
Bangladesh	141	208
India	-6	43
Pakistan	-10	-56
Argentina	-6	-91
Brazil	-26	-55
Mexico	-6	-14
Egypt	12	161
Nigeria	-3	72
South Africa	-9	-1
Other sub-Saharan Africa	-9	38

[a] See chapter endnote 15 for the expression from which the above results are derived.

Source: The mean and standard deviation of the food component of net exports are from simulations using the Tyers-Anderson model of world trade in staple foods. The mean of gross total export earnings is an average for 1984–87, while the corresponding standard deviation is that around a fitted geometric trend over the interval 1975–87. Gross export statistics were drawn from the IMF, *International Financial Statistics*, Washington, D.C., various issues.

countries is that average international prices rise following the industrial country reforms. Since these increases are only partially transmitted to their domestic markets, their net food import volumes decline only slightly and hence the net cost of food imports rises in both cases, shrinking the denominator of the index. This effect dominates the decline in the numerator due to the reduced volatility of international food prices.

In all the other developing countries included in the sample, however, exactly the opposite is true. Less insulation than in the case of Egypt yields greater short- and long-run adjustment by their domestic agents to international price changes. The higher yet more stable international prices, which would prevail after the industrial country reforms, actually accompany an increase in the volatility of the simulated net foreign exchange cost of food trade in some of these countries but this increase is insufficient to offset the associated beneficial effects on the mean.

Thus, with the exceptions of Bangladesh and Egypt, these results suggest that balance of payments risk in developing countries would be reduced by the liberalization of agricultural distortions in the industrial countries. Such multilateral reform would therefore be expected to reduce the overall pressure on balance of payments stabilizing systems such as the IMF's Compensatory Financing Facilities. Their application would instead be more highly focused on a few poor countries, particularly those whose food import costs are high in relation to their gross export earnings.

The second column of Table 6.17 examines the effects of a multilateral liberalization in which the developing countries participate. The removal of their insulating policies exposes their agents to all international price changes. Such reform, undertaken unilaterally by any one developing country, would increase its balance of payments risk. But, as Table 6.14 showed, coordinated multilateral reform would drastically reduce international price volatility. The results suggest that the net effect of the more comprehensive reform on balance of payments risk, as indicated in Table 6.17, is adverse in only seven out of the 16 developing countries in the sample; and two of those (Korea and Taiwan) are comparatively wealthy. Even then, the change is very large only in Bangladesh and Egypt. Nevertheless, although agricultural trade liberalization would greatly stabilize

international food prices, yielding substantial risk benefits where
domestic agents are exposed to international market volatility
(of the type reviewed in Chapter 3), a few more countries might
be expected to require assistance from the IMF's balance of
payments stabilizing facilities.

6.4   Some qualifications

It should be remembered that the results reported here refer
only to a subset of foods and feeds. Soybean and other feedgrain
substitutes (manioc, corn gluten, citrus pellets) are obvious
omissions. Since these items enter most feed-importing
countries (including the EC) virtually free of duty, and are
subject to relatively few distortions in feed-exporting countries
(except Brazil), their inclusion would not change the results
substantially. The fact that coarse grain prices in the
international market would be higher in the absence of industrial
country policies suggests that freer trade would increase the
demand for feedgrain substitutes. But the lower domestic prices
for coarse grain in liberalizing countries would induce a
production expansion of soybean (except perhaps in the
European Community where, since 1980, there has been a
producer subsidy for soybean), and this could more or less offset
the demand expansion.

It should also be kept in mind that these results are derived
from a partial equilibrium model and are of course dependent
on the various parameter values used. A general equilibrium
model would probably generate similar effects for agricultural
markets, but would also provide insights into the effects of
agricultural distortions on other sectors and on factor markets.
The most obvious intersectoral effect of agricultural protection
in industrial countries is that their exports of manufactures are
lower than they would be without barriers to food imports
(Burniaux and Waelbroeck 1985). On the other hand, freer
markets in developing countries would encourage more labour
intensive manufacturing as well as more farm production, and
the former would shift the food supply and demand curves
in those countries—a factor that could not be incorporated in
the above analysis.[16]

Changes in the parameter values used in the model would

of course change the magnitude of the estimates presented above, but, within feasible ranges, they would be unlikely to change the basic thrust of the results. This belief is based on the results of sensitivity analysis of the earlier grain/meat version of the model reported in Tyers (1985), as well as on the robustness of the various preliminary results which were generated for the present study. In general we have tried to err on the conservative side. For example, we have assumed the supply elasticities are constant during the forecast period (1980 to 2000) even though, in practice, those elasticities are increasing with the increasing importance of purchased inputs in farm production (see chapter endnote 3).

As already noted, it should be remembered that there are some important costs of policy not included in the above estimates of welfare effects. One is the cost of raising government revenue for distributing as subsidies. This involves not only the obvious administrative costs but also the costs to society associated with greater tax evasion and with greater trading-off of leisure for work as marginal tax rates increase (Browning 1987). Moreover, the more society observes its government capitulating to pressure-group demands for favoured treatment, the more it will engage in costly rent-seeking activities instead of using resources to expand national product.

Two particular parameter assumptions are worth focusing on, however, because the magnitude of their effect on the results may be substantial. One is the assumption that all products are homogeneous, regardless of source of production. It may be that consumers in rich countries have health concerns about consuming livestock products from poor countries, for example. In that case, livestock producer prices in developing countries would be affected less by industrial country policies than the above results suggest, and international prices for livestock products would be affected more. To obtain an upper-bound estimate of the effect of any such consumer prejudice, the above simulation of the effect of industrial country policies was re-run assuming producer prices of livestock in developing countries are unaffected by any changes in the international price of such products. The effects are as one would expect: the policies of industrial countries under this alternative extreme assumption depress international prices for livestock products more than suggested above (substantially in the case of pork and poultry), reduce developing countries' food self-sufficiency less (by 3 per cent), and reduce net economic welfare by less (up to $5 billion per year less in the case of industrial countries, up to $10 billion less in the case of developing economies). Presumably, if such prejudice did exist, it could be in the interests of developing country exporters to invest in improving their image in rich countries to reduce the extent of loss of potential market sales.[17]

As for the analytical structure of the model, it has not been adapted to account properly for types of preferential trade arrangements which the United States, the Soviet Union and the European Community practice with respect to their sugar imports from developing countries. For this reason, the effects of industrial country sugar policies on the level and instability of international sugar prices are grossly understated and should be treated only as lower bound estimates.

6.5   Conclusions

While it is of course unrealistic to expect all countries to liberalize their food price and trade policies totally, these results are useful in providing an estimate of the high (and rising) costs and distributional consequences of current food policies. Since these costs are prompting governments in industrial countries to consider reforming their policies, it is useful to try to estimate the magnitude of the adjustments that might be made through the 1990s if there were to be a phased partial liberalization of OECD food markets. To that end, Chapter 7 presents some results from the dynamic version of our model and Chapter 8 addresses the important question of what might happen to world food markets as a consequence of possible changes in centrally planned economies during the next decade.

Notes to Chapter 6

[1] While it is not our primary objective that these projections should provide accurate forecasts, their accuracy does affect the associated policy analysis. Because protection rates are endogenous in the model, if low (high) international prices are projected, protection rates in countries with insulating policies rise (fall). The accuracy of

our estimates of the effects of policies in the late 1990s is therefore sensitive to the underlying price projections. A recent exploration of this point finds this sensitivity to be comparatively slight, at least as far as estimates of the welfare consequences of policies are concerned (Tyers 1990c).

2 The World Bank's international price index for grain, when converted to a base of 1980–82 = 100, takes values of 50, 55, 51 and 53 for the years 1987, 1990, 1995 and 2000 respectively. See the World Bank's revision of its constant US dollar Weighted Index of Commodity Prices dated 21 November 1989. Similar forecasts are presented by the US Department of Agriculture and by Iowa State University's Food and Agricultural Policy Research Institute (see Roningen, Dixit and Seeley 1990; and Johnson, Meyers, Westhoff and Womack 1989).

3 A fourth point might also be made about increasing protection levels, although it does not follow directly from Table 6.1. It concerns the increasing importance of intermediate inputs in the value of agricultural production, shown in Table 2.5 above. This phenomenon, associated with the modernization of agriculture in industrializing economies, ensures that the output price elasticity of supply of agricultural products is increasing over time. Were that phenomenon to be reflected in the parameter set for our model of world food markets, the model would measure larger effects of policies over time even if nominal protection rates did not grow. However, since reliable estimates of the rates at which those supply elasticities are increasing for all the commodities and country groups in our model are not available, and since we prefer to err on the conservative side rather than be accused of exaggerating the effects of policies, the world food model's supply elasticities are assumed to remain constant during the two decade period being analysed in what follows.

4 The estimated effects presented in this and the next chapter differ, although not in any major ways, from those from the authors' earlier work presented in Chapter 6 of the World Bank's *World Development Report 1986*. The differences result from the following changes: (i) present results relate to the years 1980-82 and the 1990s rather than 1985, (ii) the European Community results now include Spain and Portugal, (iii) all values are expressed in 1985 rather than 1980 US dollars, and (iv) there have been slight revisions to a number of parameters in the model, particularly the long-run price-transmission elasticities which were previously assumed to be unity but have since been replaced by econometric estimates which are typically less than unity. Compatible results have also

been published in Anderson and Tyers (1986, 1992) and Tyers and Anderson (1988b).

[5] In addition, the United States had acreage set-aside and diversion-payment policies and Commodity Credit Corporation (CCC) loan programs which, in effect, shifted the US grain supply curves to the left and shifted the US public stock demand curves to the right. Set asides had only a minor effect in 1982 and no effect in 1980 and 1981, however, so they contribute little to explaining the positive effect in 1980–82 of US policy on international prices for coarse grain.

[6] The EC government revenue benefit of $1.2 billion in 1980-82 may appear low for the Common Agricultural Policy. However, it is important to remember that this refers only to grain, meat, milk products and sugar, and is net of all government revenue from import tariffs and levies on these products. The actual expenditure during 1980-82 by the EC on all agricultural commodity programs net of receipts from levies, etc., averaged $3.7 billion per year in current US dollars (calculated from the Australian Bureau of Agricultural Economics (1985:14)).

[7] The costs of raising government revenue to distribute as subsidies can be very substantial, because in addition to obvious administrative costs there are costs associated with evading taxes, with trading-off leisure for work as marginal tax rates increase, and so on. Recent estimates suggest such costs may be 20 per cent or more of the total revenue raised (Browning 1987). See also Alston and Hurd (1990).

[8] This is an important issue in agricultural trade policy which has been the subject of a substantial literature in the United States. See, for example, Dvoskin (1987) and Rutherford *et al.* (1990).

[9] The loss in Thailand, due to industrial country policies affecting grain, sugar and livestock markets, excludes the effect of the EC's voluntary export restraint agreement with Thailand on cassava. An extension of the model to incorporate the cassava market yields very small net effects when all industrial country policies are accounted for. See Setboonsarng and Tyers (1988).

[10] The adjustments required are for the indirect effect of overvaluation and of direct distortions to other tradable sectors' prices (most notably through industrial protection policies). Based on estimates published by Krueger, Schiff and Valdes (1988) and others, the adjustments to the domestic-to-border price ratios for food involved reducing them by 0.15 for Bangladesh, Brazil, China, Egypt, India, Indonesia, other North Africa and Middle East, South

Africa and Thailand, and by 0.30 for all other developing countries (except Korea and Taiwan for which, as with advanced industrial countries, no adjustments were made). No adjustment is made to the positions of the food demand and supply curves in developing countries, however: even though we are aware that non-food policies have affected them, we have no basis for determining the extent of that effect. Analyses incorporating this adjustment to developing country price distortions are not included in any of our previously published work except the preliminary results in Anderson and Tyers (1990). Those presented in the latter are superseded in this section.

11 The price effects vary between individual food items, however. Beef and especially dairy product prices are substantially depressed by the combination of these two groups of countries' policies while sugar, non-ruminant meat and coarse grain are raised by them. Hence the impact on any one country will depend on which food items it imports and exports.

12 This assumes the global cost of agricultural research and extension is unchanged. In fact, that cost would be less in protective industrial countries and more in developing countries if domestic prices were lower in the former and higher in the latter; thus, the estimated welfare effects in columns 2 and 4 of Table 6.12 are, to some extent, underestimates for industrial countries but overestimates for developing countries.

13 Since the Tyers–Anderson model represents all policies as equivalent tariffs or export taxes or subsidies, it does not always yield accurate estimates of the implications of change for government expenditures.

14 The particularly large value for Bangladesh is unrealistic only in that the food intervention bill in that country is paid partly in the form of concessional food imports and other forms of aid not included in government expenditure.

15 The index of balance of payments risk is the coefficient of variation, r, of gross export earnings (inclusive of *net* earnings from food trade). Thus, $r = S/E$, where E is the mean and S the corresponding standard deviation. The components of E are: $E = E_m + E_f$, where E_m is average gross non-food export earnings and E_f is net export earnings from food trade (which is negative for net food importing countries). Assuming fluctuations in E_m are independent of those in E_f, and labelling the standard deviations of E_m and E_f as S_m and S_f, respectively, the proportional change in r (dr/r) following small changes in S_f and E_f is approximately $dr/r = (S^2_f/S^2) (dS_f/S_f) - dE_f/E$.

[16] For some general equilibrium analyses that incorporate this factor, see Loo and Tower (1989) and OECD (1990b).

[17] A recent study by Dries and Unnevehr (1990) suggests that the extent to which the international beef market is segmented into countries trading beef from areas infected with foot-and-mouth disease and those trading beef from areas free of that disease is much less than previously imagined.

THREE

FOOD POLICY REFORM

7

Effects of Gradual Liberalization of OECD Food Markets

Total liberalization of world food markets is not likely to happen in the foreseeable future. However, gradual and partial liberalizations are not out of the question, especially as international pressure for such reform intensifies and thereby offsets the growth in the political power of domestic producer interests. In the late 1980s, we have seen commitments to expand beef import quotas in Japan and Korea, for example, as well as the reduction in milk and butter surpluses in the European Community. Gradual liberalizations have the political advantage of merely slowing the growth of domestic production in a liberalizing country, rather than requiring the volume of production to be cut back in absolute terms.

To gain an idea of the likelihood of such politically desirable effects occurring in industrial countries, we again make use of the dynamic version of the simulation model of world food markets introduced in Chapter 5. The reference simulation discussed in Chapter 6 projects how these markets would fare through the 1990s if present policy regimes continue. This reference scenario is then compared with two alternatives (this time fully dynamic simulations), both involving a concept which was introduced into the Uruguay Round of multilateral trade negotiations, known as 'tariffication'.

The conversion of food import barriers to tariffs was first proposed by the United States in February 1985 to the GATT Committee on Trade in Agriculture. The idea is that, as a first step towards reducing levels of protection provided to farmers in industrial countries, all of the various non-tariff import barriers should be replaced by equally protective tariffs. This would make explicit the extent of protection afforded by each country's import policies, and thereby facilitate the negotiation, implementation and monitoring of reductions in those trade barriers. It would also reduce the extent of domestic market insulation, thereby enhancing the risk-spreading role of international food markets. While the idea received little support in 1985, it was revived in 1989 following the United States' submission to the Uruguay Round's agricultural negotiating group in November 1988 (Bredahl *et al.* 1989).

For the purposes of this study it is helpful to think of tariffication as a slightly broader concept than as defined by Bredahl *et al.*, in two respects. First, export subsidies can only operate if an import restriction is in place to prevent the re-importation of subsidized exports. Hence, if all import barriers are to be lowered, it is necessary to also lower any export subsidies. Secondly, since any gap between consumer and producer prices (other than because of marketing costs) is the result of a consumer tax-cum-subsidy, it is reasonable to reduce that price gap as well in order to maintain relativity between those two prices.

Given this concept of tariffication, the two alternative scenarios to be considered in this chapter are as follows:

- the conversion of all forms of price supports in 1991 to equivalent *ad valorem* tariffs and/or export subsidies followed by the gradual reduction of these through the 1990s until they are halved by the year 2000; and
- the same conversion of all forms of price support in 1991 to equivalent *ad valorem* border price distortions but followed by a gradual phasing down of any 1991 tariff/export subsidy that is above the 1980–82 average nominal rate of agricultural (producer) protection for industrial countries to 40 per cent by the year 2000, while other tariff rates are held constant through the 1990s.

Thus, the remainder of this chapter compares the results from dynamic simulations representing these two scenarios with the reference projection introduced in Chapter 6. Section 7.1 provides a reminder of the nature and content of the reference projection, and contains some further details not discussed in previous chapters but which are particularly relevant here. Sections 7.2 and 7.3 take distinctly different approaches to the comparison of the scenarios. The analysis discussed in Section 7.2 is deterministic, ignoring risk considerations and employing single dynamic simulations of the model in which all synthetic

production shocks are set to zero. The results presented therefore approximate the mean effects of the changes in policy.[1]
In Section 7.3 we examine price risk explicitly, in the context
of the first of the two partial reform proposals, incorporating
climatic production disturbances and using stochastic
simulation.

7.1   The reference scenario

The pattern of changes in international prices and trade which
would emerge in the 1990s if policy regimes were to remain
unchanged everywhere is referred to as the reference scenario.
Its derivation, using the world food trade model (presented in
Chapter 5), has been described in Section 6.1, where the
emphasis is on projected price distortions. For our present
purpose, it is important to remember that the formulation of
such a scenario requires, among other things, projecting growth
in populations, per capita incomes and agricultural productivity,
trends in supply and demand elasticities, trends in exchange
rates and, most importantly, trends in the policies affecting food
prices, trade and stockholding. The latter amounts to projecting
the domestic food price levels which governments will choose.
The reference projection assumes that each country adjusts its
domestic producer and consumer food prices each year from
1983 to 2000 by some fraction of the change in international
prices (net of exchange rate changes), given by the estimated
price transmission elasticities.

The one exception is the United States where, as described
in Chapter 5, price policies changed after the implementation
of the 1985 Food Security Act. According to that Act, real target
grain prices were set to fall gradually through 1990, while the
corresponding domestic consumer prices were set slightly above
international levels, as a consequence of the export subsidies
implicit in the Act's Export Enhancement Program. In particular,
we have assumed US producer grain prices will continue to
fall at the same rates in real terms (4 per cent per year) even
after 1990 (i.e. that they remain roughly constant in nominal
terms), as long as they are above border prices. In the dairy
sector, the Act imposed price penalties on production in excess
of domestic demand. These have been incorporated in the model

in different ways: first, in the form of the same declining trend of real prices (constant nominal prices) as for target grain prices; and second, with the application of an additional four per cent price penalty if the national surplus should exceed four per cent of domestic demand, with surpluses of intermediate sizes incurring proportionally smaller penalties. The Act also provides for a dairy herd 'buy-back' scheme which we assume (other things being equal) will reduce production after 1985 by 5.5 per cent.

The treatment of US policy in the reference scenario differs from that of other economies in two further respects. First, the various programs which result in the setting aside of agricultural land are represented by reductions in production, as described in Chapter 5. Although the effects on production are of complex origin, depending on the level of voluntary participation by farmers in the various programs, they are exogenous in the reference projection. Their values are based on more detailed studies of US policy, including that by Johnson *et al.* (1986). The associated percentage changes in production (shifts in supply curves) are listed in Appendix 2, Table A6. Second, the behaviour of US grain stocks in the late 1980s and 1990s is so greatly affected by the Act as to render non-representative the empirical estimates of US stock parameters presented in Appendix 2, Table A11, which were estimated for the period 1962-79. Accordingly, the coefficients in the equations for US grain stocks are tuned so as to better represent the greater responsiveness of US grain stocks to international price movements which characterized the post-1985 period.

Finally, climatic production shocks in all markets and all countries are exogenous in the *ex post* simulation interval (generally 1983-89, depending on data availability), as explained in Chapter 5. This made possible our *ex post* validation test on the model (Section 5.5) and it ensures that the reference simulation tracks actual behaviour in international food markets through most of the period prior to the introduction of multi-lateral reforms. Of course, other exogenous variables, such as population and real income levels and exchange rates, follow independently projected paths as detailed in Appendix 2, Tables A7 and A10. For single simulations, exogenous production shocks are no longer introduced after 1989. Random production shocks are introduced after 1990, however, if the stochastic simulation capacity of the model is used to measure the uncertainty associated with projected prices and quantities in each food market.

As we saw in Chapter 6, in the reference scenario, the index of international food prices bottoms out in 1987 at less than two-thirds the level of 1980–82 prices in real terms before rising to about 70 per cent of the 1980–82 level by 1990, then dipping again in the mid-1990s (see Figure 6.1). Having established the reference projection, we compared projected domestic prices with border prices for the various countries and commodities to see what the model suggests would be the nominal protection coefficients in future years under the assumptions built into that reference projection. The resulting nominal protection coefficients are shown in Table 6.1 for the main industrial market economies, together with our 1980–82 estimates.

Agricultural protection is projected to rise in the 1990s just as it did in the 1980s. The reason is the same as for the 1980s, namely, that existing policies do not allow the full transmission to domestic markets of the continued declining trend in international food prices—a decline which is exacerbated by those protectionist policies to the extent that they slow the growth in the industrial countries' excess demand for food products. By the year 2000, domestic food prices in industrial countries would be almost twice international food price levels on average, compared with slightly less than 50 per cent above in the early 1980s.

7.2   The effects of 'tariffication' and partial liberalization: deterministic simulations

How different would the world food economy appear if, instead of the continuation of present policies as represented in the base (reference) scenario, industrial market economies converted all policies which drive a wedge between domestic and border prices to their equivalent *ad valorem* import tariffs or export subsidies? The major effect, if these tariffs remained unchanged in the 1990s, would be, on the one hand, a substantial reduction in the instability of international food prices and of domestic food prices in relatively open economies and, on the other, a slight increase in the instability of domestic food prices in countries which currently insulate their domestic markets via variable levies or variable import quotas.[2] This is because the use of tariffs would ensure complete transmission of international price changes to currently insulated markets of industrial countries, so they share in adjustments to market fluctuations.

The extent of the reductions in international price risk which stem from the conversion to tariffs is addressed in Section 7.3. Here we focus on the changes in quantities and prices in the context of the additional reforms designed to lower average levels of protection. These are approximated using fully dynamic single simulations which are deterministic in that all synthetic (post-1989) production disturbances are set to zero.

The aim of the US proposal for tariffication was that it should become a means of facilitating multilateral negotiations for the liberalization of world food markets. Specifically, the proposal involved a liberalization of food markets beginning in 1991, at the conclusion of the Uruguay Round, and phased in over the decade to the year 2000. We consider two possible scenarios involving liberalizations of industrial market economies in which agricultural protection instruments are replaced by equivalent tariffs in 1991. These tariffs are steadily reduced over the next ten years so that, by the turn of the century, *either* all tariffs are half their 1990 level in those countries (and the extent of land set-asides in the United States is also gradually halved during this period), *or* all tariffs above 40 per cent are phased down to 40 per cent during the 1990s while other tariff rates are fixed.

Tariffication in 1991 with a phased 50 per cent reduction in protection

Partial liberalization would cause the international prices of most grains, livestock products and sugar to be higher than would otherwise be the case. Figure 7.1 shows that, in the first of these partial liberalizations the average of those prices would be higher than in the base scenario by 8 per cent in the year 2000 and by even more in the mid-1990s when the reference international food prices are at the bottom of a cycle.

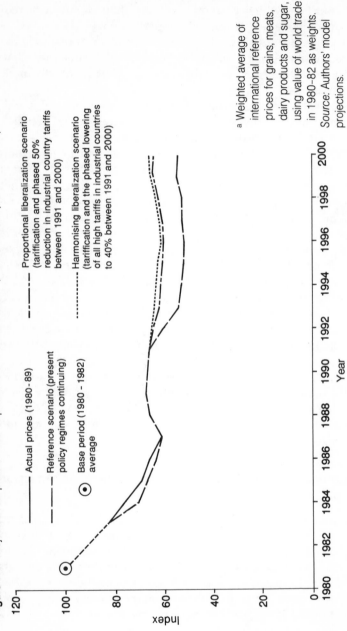

Figure 7.1: Projected real price of food staples in international markets[a], 1983 to 2000 (1980–82 = 100)

Legend:
— Actual prices (1980-89)
–– Reference scenario (present policy regimes continuing)
⊙ Base period (1980 - 1982) average

–·– Proportional liberalization scenario (tariffication and phased 50% reduction in industrial country tariffs between 1991 and 2000)

······ Harmonising liberalization scenario (tariffication and the phased lowering of all high tariffs in industrial countries to 40% between 1991 and 2000)

[a] Weighted average of international reference prices for grains, meats, dairy products and sugar, using value of world trade in 1980–82 as weights.
Source: Authors' model projections.

A breakdown of these price effects is shown in Table 7.1 for individual commodity groups. Notice that the effect of gradual liberalization on prices for meat, dairy products and sugar steadily increases throughout this period. For grains, however, the effect on prices weakens after 1996. The latter has two causes. First, in the base scenario, where current policy regimes are assumed to continue, the grain price cycle turns upwards from 1996 so there is a slowdown in the decline in domestic grain prices required to meet the tariff liberalization target. Second, we have assumed that there will be a simultaneous release of land for grain production that had been previously set aside in the United States (in this tariff liberalization scenario the area set aside is gradually halved between 1991 and 2000).

The estimated effect of liberalization on domestic food production is far less dramatic than is often feared in protectionist countries. As Table 7.2 shows, production in Western Europe, even by the year 2000, is estimated for each commodity to be less than one-eighth below what it would otherwise have been. Furthermore, on average, Europe's production would be no more than 3 per cent below the reference scenario level, because output in some industries (notably intensive livestock) would actually be considerably higher with liberalization, due to lower feedgrain prices. For Japan, the production differences would be somewhat larger, but even there the average decline is only one-eighth below the reference scenario's production level.

Moreover, because farm output in all these economies is expanding over time as a result of productivity growth, the absolute levels of production do not contract in this partial liberalization scenario. On the contrary, they expand considerably despite the steady lowering of protection. By the year 2000, the EC's output of these products would be one-fifth larger than in 1990 and EFTA's output would be more than one-quarter larger. Indeed, Table 7.3 suggests that none of the seven commodity groups would experience a decline in production in the EC during the 1990s despite this gradual liberalization. Perhaps even more surprising is that, on average, Japan's aggregate farm output would also not decline in the 1990s in this liberalization scenario: the reduction in grain output would be more than offset by the expansion in intensive livestock production which is made relatively more profitably by the fall in grain prices.

Table 7.1: Estimated effect of a phased 50 per cent reduction in agricultural protection in industrial countries between 1991 and 2000 on international prices of various foods[a] (per cent difference between liberalization and reference scenarios)

	Wheat	Coarse grain	Rice	Ruminant meat	Non-ruminant meat	Dairy products	Sugar	WEIGHTED AVERAGE
1991	0.7	-1.5	0.0	-0.2	0.3	4.8	4.7	1.5
1992	6.6	-6.4	-0.3	5.2	-0.2	7.0	7.9	5.1
1993	15.6	-7.0	1.8	7.6	0.3	9.6	8.8	9.5
1994	17.6	-5.1	4.1	4.9	0.5	14.6	7.8	10.2
1995	19.1	-0.7	5.9	8.0	1.0	17.5	6.2	11.3
1996	19.3	3.0	6.9	14.0	1.6	23.1	5.4	12.5
1997	18.7	-0.4	6.4	14.5	2.2	27.8	6.4	12.8
1998	13.8	-6.9	5.2	15.9	2.2	30.4	8.4	11.3
1999	3.7	-2.5	4.2	15.7	2.9	34.9	10.8	8.1
2000	2.6	-4.3	4.1	18.3	3.2	39.7	12.3	8.3

[a] All industrial country policies are assumed to be converted to *ad valorem* tariffs and export subsidies as of 1991.
Source: Authors' model projections.

Table 7.2: Estimated effects on food production in industrial market economies in 1995 and 2000 of a phased 50 per cent liberalization during the 1990s[a] (percentage by which the level in the liberalization scenario exceeds that in the reference scenario)

	Wheat	Coarse grain	Rice	Ruminant meat	Non-ruminant meat	Dairy products	Sugar	WEIGHTED AVERAGE[b]
EC-12								
1995	-5	-2	1	0	0	0	-4	-1
2000	-12	-7	-7	-12	8	-2	-8	-3

EFTA-5								
1995	-8	-1	0	-5	4	-3	-8	-2
2000	-5	5	0	-9	13	-3	-6	0
Japan								
1995	-9	1	-2	-4	-5	-5	-7	-4
2000	8	-25	-9	-17	-15	-18	-15	-13
Australia								
1995	6	-5	-1	2	2	0	-1	2
2000	7	-5	-3	4	2	1	-1	3
Canada								
1995	4	-6	0	2	-1	-1	-5	0
2000	3	-3	0	-1	-8	-7	-10	-2
New Zealand								
1995	-6	-2	0	0	-1	6	0	2
2000	-4	-5	0	-1	-2	16	0	4
United States								
1995	-4	4	12	3	2	-2	-3	1
2000	0	6	14	3	5	-4	-4	2

[a] All industrial country policies are assumed to be converted to *ad valorem* tariffs and export subsidies as of 1991.
[b] Weights based on the base scenario's projected domestic production, valued at border prices.
Source: Authors' model projections.

Table 7.3: Estimated levels of food production in 1995 and 2000 in industrial countries following a phased 50 per cent reduction in agricultural protection compared with production in 1990[a] (percentage by which projected output in the year shown exceeds the 1990 level)

	Wheat	Coarse grain	Rice	Ruminant meat	Non-ruminant meat	Dairy products	Sugar	WEIGHTED AVERAGE[b]
EC-12								
1995	9	1	4	6	14	8	8	10
2000	13	2	0	6	31	14	17	19
EFTA-5								
1995	-3	-13	0	15	0	15	9	8
2000	0	-8	0	30	26	40	33	27
Japan								
1995	-3	-16	1[c]	7	17	8	1	8
2000	-27	-9	-11[c]	6	48	6	0	15
Australia								
1995	13	13	6	11	29	1	6	13
2000	16	30	11	24	64	2	16	25
Canada								
1995	7	21	0	10	17	5	-6	12
2000	13	39	0	25	30	7	-24	22
New Zealand								
1995	-3	15	0	12	21	2	0	9
2000	0	33	0	28	41	6	0	21

United States

| 1995 | 8 | 21 | 17 | 8 | 14 | 3 | 6 | 12 |
| 2000 | 28 | 38 | 23 | 20 | 28 | 7 | 14 | 25 |

a All industrial country policies are assumed to be converted to *ad valorem* tariffs and export subsidies as of 1991.

b Weights based on the base scenario's projected domestic production valued at border prices.

c Assumes no change to amount of diversion of Japan's rice land (which averaged around one-fifth of all rice land during 1980–86).

Source: Authors' model projections.

These moderate effects of a phased 50 per cent liberalization on production are matched by moderate effects on consumption, the net effect of which is only minor impacts on self-sufficiency ratios. For the European Community, self-sufficiency would decline only for beef, dairy products and rice during the 1990s, while in EFTA, only grain self-sufficiency would decrease over that decade of liberalization (Table 7.4). Japan's food self-sufficiency would of course fall somewhat more, given its higher initial protection rates. The main concern in Japan would be rice self-sufficiency, which is shown in Table 7.5 to fall from 100 to 81 per cent in this liberalization scenario. This scenario, however, involves no change to the incentives Japan has in place to divert paddy land from rice production. During the period 1980–86, that diversion policy reduced the area sown to rice by between 20 and 23 per cent, and also appears to have reduced rice production by about one-fifth.[3] If those incentives to reduce rice acreage were gradually eliminated through trade liberalization in the 1990s, Japan's rice production would, according to these results, be almost exactly sufficient to satisfy consumption throughout the decade.

Just as the effects of liberalization on food production, consumption and hence trade, of the highly protected industrial economies are modest in relative terms, also modest are the effects of that gradual reform on traditional food exporters. Table 7.2 shows that the volume of food production by the traditional food-exporting countries of Australasia and North America would be only 2 to 4 per cent above what it would otherwise be in the year 2000 following a 50 per cent liberalization.

The value of food production would be affected not only by output changes but also by the rise in export prices. Their combined impact on exporting countries is reported in Table 7.5. For Australia, a major effect of the reforms is the boosting of the value of ruminant meat production in the year 2000 by a quarter and of wheat production by one-twelfth, with the overall value of food production rising by 9 per cent. For New Zealand, the boost is even larger, totalling 14 per cent and amounting to more than 60 per cent for dairy products. The increase is somewhat smaller for the United States because the boost to the value of grain production of more than 10 per cent is almost fully offset by the decline in the value of (what has been highly protected) milk and sugar production. Canada

Table 7.4: Estimated levels of food self-sufficiency in selected industrial countries without and with a 50 per cent phased reduction in agricultural protection, 1990 to 2000[a] (production as a percentage of consumption)

		Wheat	Coarse grain	Rice	Ruminant meat	Non-ruminant meat	Dairy products	Sugar
EC-12								
1990		128	85	79	101	96	108	97
1995	ref.	144	97	77	104	95	108	103
	(lib.)	(125)	(93)	(75)	(94)	(97)	(105)	(95)
2000	ref.	162	113	75	109	97	109	112
	(lib.)	(128)	(100)	(60)	(84)	(102)	(99)	(98)
EFTA-5								
1990		130	81	0	105	90	120	81
1995	ref.	128	64	0	122	80	139	95
	(lib.)	(110)	(63)	(0)	(106)	(77)	(130)	(83)
2000	ref.	129	54	0	136	89	166	111
	(lib.)	(120)	(55)	(0)	(116)	(96)	(155)	(100)
Japan								
1990		11	2	101	47	42	83	32
1995	ref.	9	1	100	46	43	86	32
	(lib.)	(8)	(1)	(95)[b]	(38)	(38)	(70)	(30)
2000	ref.	8	1	99	46	48	88	32
	(lib.)	(8)	(1)	(81)[b]	(28)	(35)	(50)	(27)

(continued)

Table 7.4 (continued)

		Wheat	Coarse grain	Rice	Ruminant meat	Non-ruminant meat	Dairy products	Sugar
United States								
1990		204	160	192	93	83	101	75
1995	ref.	217	171	198	94	85	101	80
	(lib.)	(213)	(177)	(222)	(97)	(87)	(97)	(76)
2000	ref.	251	176	194	101	84	102	88
	(lib.)	(253)	(183)	(224)	(103)	(90)	(95)	(80)

[a] Both scenarios assume 'tariffication' in 1991. The reference scenario ('ref') assumes a continuation of current policy regimes; the liberalization scenario ('lib.') involves a phased 50 per cent liberalization.

[b] Assumes no change to amount of diversion of Japan's rice land (which averaged close to one-fifth of all rice land during 1980–86).

Source: Authors' model projections.

Table 7.5: Estimated effects on value of food production by traditional food exporters in 1995 and 2000 of a 50 per cent phased liberalization during the 1990s of agricultural protection in industrial market economies[a] (percentage by which the value in the liberalization scenario exceeds that in the reference scenario)

	Wheat	Coarse grain	Rice	Ruminant meat	Non-ruminant meat	Dairy products	Sugar	TOTAL
Australia								
1995	21	-10	-2	8	3	3	-3	6
2000	8	-11	-10	23	6	5	-4	9
Canada								
1995	14	-7	0	0	-7	-11	-18	-1
2000	0	-7	0	-5	-21	-28	-27	-13
New Zealand								
1995	-17	-14	0	5	-4	24	0	6
2000	-16	-21	0	12	-9	61	0	14
United States								
1995	-10	6	14	3	3	-9	-14	0
2000	3	12	23	5	8	-12	-26	3

[a] All industrial country policies are assumed to be converted to *ad valorem* tariffs and export subsidies as of 1991.
Source: Authors' model projections.

benefits less from grain expansion than the United States (the latter being helped by the assumed 50 per cent reduction in set-aside land), suffers more of a decline in milk and sugar receipts and, in addition, encounters lower meat receipts. Thus, the overall value of output of these foods in Canada is forecast to be one-eighth less in the liberalization scenario than in the base scenario.[4]

The main effects of liberalization on the trade volumes and foreign exchange earnings of traditional food exporters are summarized in Table 7.6. From the final column it can be seen that, by the year 2000, this partial liberalization is estimated to boost annual net foreign exchange earnings from food by 16 per cent for Australia, 10 per cent for Thailand, 20 per cent for the United States, 25 per cent for New Zealand and 29 per cent for Argentina. Clearly these are non-trivial magnitudes, and vindicate the interest of the United States and the so-called Cairns Group in ensuring an outcome of agricultural liberalization from the Uruguay Round of multilateral trade negotiations.

The economic welfare effects that would be associated with this liberalization further support the placing of agriculture high on the agenda of the Uruguay Round talks. These effects, summarized in Table 7.7, show that the gains from trade liberalization increase roughly in proportion to the extent of liberalization, with the annual net welfare gains to industrial market economies and the world as a whole being roughly twice as large in the year 2000 as in 1995 (when only half the liberalization will have been implemented). The countries which gain most, on a per capita basis, are of course the most protected economies of EFTA and Japan, followed by the European Community. But, the traditional food exporters among the industrial countries also gain substantially because of the higher prices for their exports in the liberalization scenario. By the year 2000, this benefit amounts to almost $100 per person (in 1985 US dollars) in New Zealand and $30 in both Australia and Canada per year.[5] Industrial countries as a group would be more than $35 billion per year better off by the turn of the century with this partial liberalization, or $45 per capita.

Table 7.6: Estimated effects in 1995 and 2000 of a 50 per cent phased reduction in agricultural protection in industrial market economies on the volumes of net exports of food products from and foreign exchange earnings of traditional food exporters[a,b]

	Change in volume of net exports (thousand metric tons, per cent in brackets)							Effect on foreign exchange earnings in 1985 US $million (and per cent of food exports)
	Wheat	Coarse grain	Rice	Ruminant meat	Non-ruminant meat	Dairy products	Sugar	
Australia								
1995	752	−473		116			71	686
	(5)	(−19)		(11)			(3)	(13)
2000	1469	−652		273		31	−119	965
	(11)	(−29)		(23)		(11)	(−4)	(16)
Canada								
1995	1412	−1097		21	−56	−451		662
	(4)			(280)	(−11)	(−220)		(14)
2000	1579	388		−58	−255	−1834		−654
	(5)	(49)		(−45)	(−38)	(−420)		(−10)
New Zealand								
1995						422		181
						(38)		(11)
2000		−63				1097		442
		(−11)				(190)		(25)

(continued)

Table 7.6 (continued)

	Change in volume of net exports (thousand metric tons, per cent in brackets)							Effect on foreign exchange earnings in 1985 US $million (and per cent of food exports)
	Wheat	Coarse grain	Rice	Ruminant meat	Non-ruminant meat	Dairy products	Sugar	
United States								
1995	-1390 (-4)	12590 (11)	431 (23)	250 (36)	453 (15)	-2648 (340)	-341 (-20)	2255 (28)
2000	-511 (-1)	16420 (11)	573 (29)	296 (270)	1356 (40)	-5296 (-410)	-760 (-70)	2755 (20)
Argentina								
1995	1330 (16)	-1098 (-20)		104 (9)		363		678 (16)
2000	1561 (22)	-1200 (-22)		337 (31)		948		1241 (29)
Thailand								
1995	25 (6)	-185 (-8)	85 (1)	10 (9)	8 (2)		25 (1)	101 (5)
2000		-138 (-9)	296 (4)	37 (20)	28 (5)		56 (4)	220 (10)

a All industrial country policies are assumed to be converted to *ad valorem* tariffs and export subsidies as of 1991.
b The thousands of metric tons (or percentage) by which net exports in the partial liberalization scenario exceed those in the reference scenario. Only changes exceeding 20,000 tons or 5 per cent are shown. Percentage changes are shown in parentheses.
Source: Authors' model projections.

Table 7.7: Estimated effects on economic welfare of a phased 50 per cent reduction in agricultural protection in industrial market economies, 1995 and 2000 (1985 U.S. $ billions, p.a.)

	1995				2000			
	Producer welfare	Consumer welfare	Net economic welfare[a]		Producer welfare	Consumer welfare	Net economic welfare[a]	
			Total	Per capita ($)			Total	Per capita ($)
EC-12	-22.95	25.18	7.46	26	-47.02	48.34	14.10	48
EFTA-5	-4.99	5.21	1.76	55	-3.56	3.31	1.68	53
Japan	-12.08	16.90	6.97	55	-24.87	37.78	17.89	139
Australia	0.54	0.03	0.45	27	0.78	-0.19	0.53	30
Canada	-0.31	0.48	0.76	28	-2.57	1.77	0.69	24
New Zealand	0.18	-0.08	0.14	38	0.46	-0.19	0.34	91
United States	-1.37	1.86	0.99	4	2.84	2.06	0.38	2
All industrial countries			**18.52**	**24**			**35.60**	**45**

[a] The sum of the effects on producer welfare, consumer welfare, government revenue and stock profits or losses. It does not include differences in costs of raising and dispersing government tax revenue nor of lobbying by farm groups and others.

Source: Authors' model projections.

Tariffication in 1991 with a phased reduction of all protection rates above 40 per cent by the year 2000

An alternative to reducing all protection rates by the same proportion is to gradually reduce only the high rates of protection and thereby reduce the dispersion in protection rates across commodities (the 'harmonization' option). To see how the effects of such a strategy might differ from the previous partial liberalization case, consider the following scenario in which all individual commodity protection rates in industrial countries that are above 40 per cent in 1990 are gradually phased down to 40 per cent by the year 2000, while other protection rates are left unchanged. In 1990, the average nominal rate of agricultural protection in industrial countries is projected by our model to be about 80 per cent, twice the rate in 1980–82. This is therefore an alternative approach to reducing the overall level of protection in industrial countries by half.

The resulting protection coefficients in the year 2000 are shown in Table 7.8, together with those for the reference scenario and for the previous proportional liberalization. Clearly, such harmonization involves a greater (slightly smaller) degree of liberalization for the currently more (less) protected countries than is the case in the proportional liberalization scenario. That is why international food prices are raised more in this scenario than in the previous one (see Figure 7.1 above). By the year 2000, they are 15 per cent higher than the reference scenario, compared with 8 per cent higher in the proportional liberalization case.

The value of production and exports of the traditional food-exporting countries is thus boosted considerably more in this scenario than in the previous liberalization case. As shown in Table 7.9, such harmonization would boost the value of Australia's food production by twice as much (an increase of 20 per cent instead of 9 per cent) over the reference scenario level, and it would increase the value of food production in New Zealand and the United States by almost three times as much. Also, Canada's production value would fall by much less in this than in the previous scenario. For Australia and New Zealand, the increase in export earnings would also be twice as great. By the year 2000, Australia's food exports are worth an extra $1.6 billion per year (or 27 per cent) more in this

Table 7.8: Projected producer-to-border price ratios in the year 2000 for the reference scenario, the proportional liberalization scenario and the harmonizing liberalization scenario[a]

	Wheat	Coarse grain	Rice	Ruminant meat	Non-ruminant meat	Dairy products	Sugar	WEIGHTED AVERAGE
EC-12								
Ref.	2.05	1.87	2.50	2.88	1.36	3.08	2.83	2.10
Prop.	1.37	1.38	1.75	1.86	1.21	1.81	1.62	1.50
Harm.	1.40	1.40	1.40	1.40	1.40	1.40	1.40	1.40
EFTA-5								
Ref.	1.73	1.62	1.00	3.62	1.49	4.59	2.92	2.90
Prop.	1.60	1.63	1.00	2.62	1.44	2.81	1.91	2.15
Harm.	1.40	1.40	1.00	1.40	1.40	1.40	1.40	1.40
Japan								
Ref.	3.79	11.27	12.03	5.52	1.94	8.70	7.48	3.73
Prop.	2.87	5.40	5.88	3.16	1.46	3.97	3.67	2.29
Harm.	1.40	1.40	1.40	1.40	1.40	1.40	1.40	1.40
United States								
Ref.	1.00	1.00	1.72	1.32	1.00	2.42	2.03	1.22
Prop.	1.00	1.10	1.66	1.14	1.00	1.60	1.39	1.14
Harm.	1.00	1.00	1.40	1.29	1.00	1.40	1.40	1.14
Canada								
Ref.	1.13	1.00	1.00	1.42	1.33	3.32	2.05	1.38
Prop.	1.06	1.00	1.00	1.15	1.10	1.82	1.28	1.15
Harm.	1.12	1.00	1.00	1.30	1.20	1.40	1.40	1.19

(continued)

Table 7.8 (continued)

	Wheat	Coarse grain	Rice	Ruminant meat	Non-ruminant meat	Dairy products	Sugar	WEIGHTED AVERAGE
All industrial market economies								
Ref.	1.48	1.19	8.30	2.13	1.32	3.20	2.64	1.83
Prop.	1.17	1.16	4.15	1.49	1.17	1.89	1.58	1.39
Harm.	1.18	1.08	1.40	1.30	1.26	1.39	1.36	1.267

[a] 'Ref.', 'Prop.' and 'Harm.' refer respectively to the reference scenario, the proportional liberalization scenario and the harmonizing liberalization scenario.

Source: Authors' model projections.

Table 7.9: Estimated effects on the value of food production and exports by traditional food exporters in the year 2000 of the proportional and harmonizing liberalizations during the 1990s[a] (percentage by which the value in the liberalization scenario exceeds that in the reference scenario)

		Value of production								Value of foreign earnings in 1985 US million dollars (and per cent of food exports)
		Wheat	Coarse grain	Rice	Ruminant meat	Non-ruminant meat	Dairy products	Sugar	TOTAL	
Australia	Prop.	8	-11	-10	23	6	5	-4	9	965 (16)
	Harm.	14	-3	20	42	-7	69	5	20	1,610 (27)
Canada	Prop.	0	-7	0	-5	-21	-28	-27	-13	-654 (-10)
	Harm.	10	1	0	28	-19	-30	-26	-4	-250 (-4)
New Zealand	Prop.	-16	-21	0	12	-9	61	0	14	442 (25)
	Harm.	-12	-1	0	32	-11	125	0	38	929 (52)
United States	Prop.	3	12	23	5	8	-12	-26	3	2,755 (20)
	Harm.	9	3	-4	44	-6	0	-23	9	3,205 (24)

[a] The results for the proportional liberalization scenario (Prop.) are from Tables 7.5 and 7.6.
Source: Authors' model projections.

simulation compared with the reference scenario where current policies continue through the 1990s.

Similarly, the welfare gains to Australia and New Zealand are about twice as great from this harmonizing liberalization as from the proportional liberalization, as a comparison of Tables 7.7 and 7.10 shows. The much higher gains to EFTA and Japan compared with the EC are due to the fact that the extent of the price reduction to bring tariffs down to 40 per cent would not have to be as great for the EC as in the proportional liberalization scenario (see Table 7.8).

7.3 The effects of partial reform on price risk

In this section we compare once again the reference scenario with the proportional liberalization scenario but, this time, we introduce synthetic climatic shocks to production in all countries and commodity markets and present the results from multiple stochastic simulations. Our main interest is in the degree to which international and domestic price volatility are affected by the conversion of all industrial country food policies to *ad valorem* tariffs and export subsidies as of 1991, and the proportional reduction in these to half their 1990 levels by the year 2000.

The effects on international food price volatility are broadly summarized in Figure 7.2, which presents bands wherein projected prices might be expected to be found with about a two-thirds probability.[6] Synthetic production shocks, and hence stochastic simulation, only begin in the 1990s. (As discussed in the last two chapters, *ex post* data permit the use of exogenous production shocks for most commodity markets in earlier years.) Two important points about the effects of tariffication and partial liberalization on price risk emerge from Figure 7.2. First, the effect of tariffication is to reduce price volatility substantially in the 1990s, as evidenced by the reduction in band width. Second, the path of the mean price index is smoother than before, reflecting the improved information content of the prices on which farmers base their expectations and the wider

Table 7.10: Estimated effects on economic welfare in 1995 and 2000 of a harmonizing liberalization which gradually lowers all protection levels in industrial countries to 40 per cent during the 1990s (1985 US $ billions p.a)

	1995				2000			
	Producer welfare	Consumer welfare	Net economic welfare[a] Total	Per capita($)	Producer welfare	Consumer welfare	Net economic welfare[a] Total	Per capita($)
EC-12	-24.17	28.37	9.49	34	-47.30	52.83	15.20	53
EFTA-5	-7.76	7.85	2.58	81	-10.51	9.60	3.54	111
Japan	-19.62	27.71	12.55	100	-39.05	71.38	29.62	230
Australia	0.93	-0.22	0.52	31	2.14	-0.97	0.92	52
Canada	0.37	0.07	0.77	28	-0.56	0.59	0.69	24
New Zealand	0.39	-0.17	0.21	59	1.22	-0.50	0.69	185
United States	0.58	-1.09	1.62	6	11.04	-8.02	1.30	5
All industrial countries			**33.38**	**43**			**51.97**	**67**

[a] The sum of the effects on producer welfare, consumer welfare, government revenue and stock profits or losses. It does not include differences in costs of raising and dispersing government tax revenue nor of lobbying by farm groups and others.

Source: Authors' model projections.

Figure 7.2: Projected real price of food staples[a]: reference vs 1991 tariffication in industrial countries with a phased 50 per cent tariff reduction by the year 2000 (Bands are means ± one standard deviation)

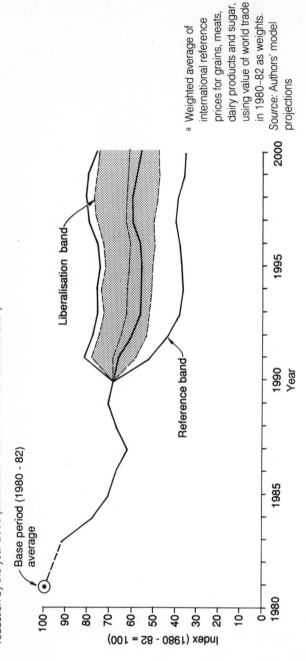

[a] Weighted average of international reference prices for grains, meats, dairy products and sugar, using value of world trade in 1980–82 as weights.

Source: Authors' model projections

spreading of shocks occurring in years when global production is particularly good or particularly bad.

The extent to which prices are less volatile in each international commodity market is quantified in Table 7.11. As in Chapter 6, the index of volatility used is the projected coefficient of variation of real international food prices. Table 7.11 shows that the international food price index is reduced by almost half and that the greatest commodity-specific reductions occur in the wheat, ruminant meat and dairy product markets. The reason why the reductions in other markets are smaller is suggested by the discussion of price risk in Chapter 6, where it was seen that the major component of policy-induced price volatility is due to the insulation of markets in developing countries. Clearly, commodities such as rice and sugar, whose volatility is reduced only a little by industrial country reforms, are mainly produced in developing countries.

The corresponding effects on domestic price volatility are summarized in Table 7.12. This table compares coefficients of variation of reference domestic prices with those after industrial country reform. In this case, we use indices of all seven domestic food prices, calculated separately for producer and consumer prices and using production or consumption values as weights.

Table 7.11: Effects on international price instability in the year 2000 of tariffication combined with a phased 50 per cent reduction in industrial country protection rates

	Coefficients of variation of simulated international prices, per cent	
	Reference	**Industrial countries' reforms**
Wheat	68	36
Coarse grain	76	62
Rice	41	32
Ruminant meat	27	12
Non-ruminant meat	9	9
Dairy products	23	10
Sugar	36	24
International food price index	**32**	**18**

Source: Authors' model results.

Table 7.12: Effects on domestic price instability in the year 2000 of tariffication combined with a phased 50 per cent reduction in industrial country protection rates

	Coefficients of variation of simulated international prices, per cent[a]	
	Reference	**Industrial countries' reforms**
International price index[a]	**32**	**18**
Domestic price indices in:		
Australia	17 (10)	12 (19)
Canada	20 (7)	17 (9)
United States	16 (9)	17 (9)
EC–12	3 (2)	11 (8)
EFTA–5	2 (1)	12 (8)
Japan	2 (2)	14 (12)
Korea, Rep.	1 (2)	1 (2)
Taiwan	6 (6)	5 (5)
China	18 (3)	12 (2)
Indonesia	7 (3)	6 (3)
Philippines	4 (3)	3 (2)
Thailand	13 (7)	9 (5)
Bangladesh	22 (6)	17 (4)
India	6 (6)	4 (4)
Pakistan	4 (3)	2 (2)
Other Asia	6 (5)	5 (3)
Argentina	19 (16)	11 (8)
Brazil	9 (8)	7 (5)
Mexico	7 (4)	5 (3)
Other Latin America	7 (9)	4 (5)
Egypt	2 (2)	2 (1)
Other Nth Africa & Middle East	1 (1)	1 (1)
Nigeria	11 (10)	8 (7)
South Africa	18 (14)	13 (9)
Other sub-Saharan Africa	8 (7)	6 (5)

[a] Indices of producer and consumer prices are calculated separately in the model, using domestic values of production and consumption as weights.
Source: Authors' model results.

Reforms in the highly protected and highly insulated agricultural economies of Western Europe and Japan clearly increase their domestic price volatility (to levels of the order of 10 per cent). This is only about one-third the level of price volatility against which market insulating policies in these countries are currently directed, namely that of international prices in the reference case. Furthermore, on the consumer side, the commodities included are mostly processed commercially before entering final demand in those economies and hence the effects of such volatility on consumer food prices is substantially overestimated in the table.

In the industrialized food-exporting countries, domestic price volatility also tends to decline as the effects of more stable border prices outweigh the removal of any domestic insulation. All other countries enjoy less volatile domestic food prices as improved international market stability is transmitted to domestic markets. Nevertheless, the gains from reform which might be expected in terms of reduced price risk continue to depend most on those countries making up the bulk of the world's food production and consumption, namely the developing countries. As the results in Chapter 6 showed, reforms by both industrial and developing countries would yield such dramatic reductions in price risk as to eliminate the need for market insulation in virtually all countries.

Finally, it is useful to reflect on results summarized in Figure 7.2 in the context of the deterministic analysis of the previous section. That analysis emphasized the projected changes in mean international prices which would stem from reform and their direct and indirect welfare implications. From the width of the bands in the figure, it is clear that those price changes are small compared with the range of possible outcomes. Although the mean price is projected to be higher in the year 2000 after partial reform than otherwise, there is nevertheless a projected decline in mean international food prices, even with reform. On the other hand, there remains about a one-third chance that international food prices will rise by the end of the century to levels above those prevailing in 1990, even if reference policy regimes are retained, and that this rise would be larger with reform.

This substantial uncertainty about the actual path of international food prices is important in the GATT negotiations.

For example, the case being made by a group of food-importing developing countries that food trade reforms should be accompanied by compensation for higher prices, ignores the very substantial likelihood that their terms of trade will continue to improve even with reforms in industrial countries[7]

7.4   Some qualifications

Any modelling exercise is subject to important qualifications about the extent to which the model simulates the real world and the scenarios match the proposed policy changes. It is helpful to qualify the present results in both of these respects.

The main limitations of the model have been outlined above in Chapters 5 and 6. A key point to bear in mind is that, while it is a multi-commodity model, it is limited to seven food commodity groups. It is not a general equilibrium model and so is unable to describe, or account for, effects on other sectors. Nor does it include the edible oils or feedgrain substitutes, such as cassava. Productivity growth rates are set exogenously in the scenarios in this chapter, whereas in practice there is probably a positive correlation between changes in protection levels and changes in the rate of productivity growth, as examined in the comparative statics of Chapter 6. As well, different assumed values for the elasticities and the initial protection levels in the model can lead to different outcomes. However, we believe that, providing parameters are varied within feasible ranges, they would be unlikely to change the basic thrust of the results. This is based on the robustness of various preliminary results which were generated for this and earlier studies using the model.

With respect to the representation of policies, several points need to be made. First, it was not feasible for all known instruments of food policy to be included in the model. For example, there is no explicit representation of quotas on milk production in the EC and Canada, and so the model may be overstating the negative milk supply response to liberalizations in those economies. Second, the size of the price and quantity effects are roughly proportional to the extent of any liberalization (given the assumption of constant price elasticities). Thus, it is possible to get a crude idea of the effects of, say, half as much liberalization as assumed here by halving the changes shown in the tables. The effects of liberalizing in more or fewer countries, or of liberalizing only a subset of commodities, cannot be easily anticipated from the above results, however, because of the global and multi-commodity nature of the model. It should be noted that the price and trade policies of industrial market economies alone are liberalized in this model, with the assumption that the policies of the 1980s in developing countries and in centrally planned Europe continue through the 1990s (discussed in the Chapter 8). Finally, the above results assume stock policies remain unchanged. If the United States or the EC were also to alter their policies concerning the public holding of stocks (particularly grain), the adjustment path and trade effects of policy changes would differ.

There has been a distinction made in the Uruguay Round of agricultural trade negotiations between import barriers on the one hand and production and export subsidies on the other (see, for example, Bredahl *et al.* 1989 and 1990). In terms of this model, all three interventions have effects on domestic prices and it is their aggregate effect on commodity prices which is captured in estimates of domestic-to-border price ratios. It would not be possible to maintain a given level of export subsidy while continuing to reduce the corresponding import barrier (now a tariff) because subsidized exported produce would immediately be re-imported for resale at the high domestic consumer price. Hence, it makes sense to lower export subsidies while also lowering import barriers, as is done in the above simulations. However, the above simulations also lower any difference between producer and consumer prices. To the extent that a real-world tariffication/liberalization would not include such a change to domestic price distortions, the above results slightly exaggerate the estimated effects of the policy changes proposed for the Uruguay Round.

Finally, the harmonization of protection rates (or rebalancing approach as it is sometimes called) is envisaged by the European Community to include not only the lowering of high protection rates but also the raising of some low (or zero) protection rates. The latter has not been incorporated in the scenario reported above because the items in that category of main interest to the EC, namely oilseeds and feedgrain substitutes such as cassava and citrus pellets, are not included in our model. If they were, such a liberalization would benefit exporters of the latter products (the United States and Thailand) less and may benefit exporters of livestock products (Australia and New Zealand) more than the above tables suggest.[8]

7.5   Conclusions

Clearly, even partial liberalizations of the type considered in this chapter can be expected to bestow major benefits not only on the liberalizing countries but also on the traditional food-exporting countries. Of course, the benefits will be larger the greater the extent of any liberalization. Moreover, there would also be considerable benefits from tariffication at the outset of any liberalization program. These are discussed in detail (along with some complications) in Bredahl *et al.* (1989), but two points are worth reiterating by way of conclusion. First, tariffs would yield less insulation of domestic markets from international markets, so international price fluctuations would be lowered, as would domestic price fluctuations in currently less-insulated countries. Second, it would be much easier to negotiate, implement and monitor liberalizations of agricultural trade if distortions were only in the form of *ad valorem* tariffs and export subsidies.

Notes to Chapter 7

[1]   Deterministic projections are chosen for this purpose to simplify the analysis and its interpretation by eliminating shifts in means due to the volatility of prices and quantities. Such mean shifts stem from the various non-linearities in the model. (It has not been practical to subject the selection of these non-linearities to rigorous econometric testing.) We have taken the view that the deterministic, or certainty equivalent, approach offers results which are no less valuable but which are easier to interpret than the use of projected means from stochastic simulations.

[2]   While this is the major effect of relevance here, a thorough economic analysis can demonstrate several other effects which, in sum, show the inferiority of non-tariff import barriers compared with tariffs. See, for example, J.E. Anderson (1988).

3 That is, the yield per hectare of the land diverted was apparently not much lower than that remaining in production. Data relating to these programs is provided in, for example, Roberts *et al.* (1989: Appendix 3.1).

4 Because the effect of milk production quotas in Canada is not explicitly represented in the model, the results for Canada may overstate the adjustment that would in fact take place in dairying.

5 The absolute size of the net welfare gain to countries such as Australia is less than the gain in foreign exchange earnings because of both the costs of producing extra output and the losses to domestic consumers who have to pay higher prices for food.

6 These bands are drawn symmetrically, even though there is substantial upward skewness in the distribution of prices. The exact form of the distribution has not been quantified.

7 Such claims by developing countries are examined by Hertel (1990) and Knudsen (1990).

8 See, for example, the analyses by Andrews *et al.* (1990) and Setboonsarng and Tyers (1988).

8

Economic Reform in the Centrally Planned Economies: The Great Enigma

No study of distortions in world food markets would be complete without mentioning the centrally planned economies. Traditionally, these economies have discriminated heavily against their agricultural sectors, particularly through setting producer and consumer prices of food relative to industrial products well below international levels when measured at shadow exchange rates. Because these countries play such an important role in the world food economy, accounting in the mid-1980s for more than one-third of world food production and consumption and one-quarter of world food imports (see Figure 8.1 and Figure 1.2 above), even small changes in their policies can have large effects on international markets for farm products.

Unfortunately, it is not possible to estimate even roughly the effects of the policy distortions in centrally planned economies, for several reasons. First, numerous prices often operate simultaneously (for example, quota, above-quota and residual free-market producer prices; the subsidized ration price; and the free-market price for consumers) with restrictions on inter-regional trade enabling prices to differ also across regions within a country. Even if reliable quantitative data were available to obtain a weighted average price for producers or consumers (and typically such data are not available), these would not be good indicators of the *marginal* price facing agents in multi-price markets. Second, quantitative restrictions affect producer and consumer activities much more in these than in other economies for example. Queues at food shops are a clear manifestation of rationing on the consumer side. Third, the currencies of these economies are typically not convertible, and the official prices for foreign exchange are usually grossly overvalued, sometimes by several orders of magnitude. In the

Figure 8.1: Shares of world food[a] production and consumption held by centrally planned, developing and industrial market economies, 1975 to 1986 (per cent)

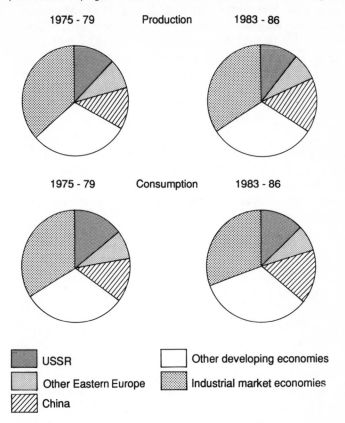

[a] Grains, meat, milk products and sugar, each valued at their average price in international markets.
Source: See Appendix 2.

absence of estimates of shadow exchange rates, it is a hazardous exercise to try to convert foreign currency border prices into local currency prices for the purpose of comparing them with domestic producer or consumer prices. Finally, there are also gross distortions to prices and quantities in markets for non-food products in these economies, so the extent to which agriculture is discriminated against (or favoured) is even more difficult to ascertain than in developing countries. Thus, to say the very least, modelling the responses of agents to price or policy changes in these countries is somewhat problematic.

Even so, this does not mean that the countries of centrally planned Europe and Asia cannot be placed in scenarios of policy reform in a bid to project their transitions to more market-driven economies. The bulk of this chapter addresses the case of China. It draws on the theory presented in Section 1.3 of Chapter 1, as well as on projections from our world food model, to address the question: what is likely to happen to food production, consumption and trade in China during the 1990s as that economy grows, given the reform experience of China itself in the 1980s and the historical experiences of its rapidly growing neighbours in earlier decades? A more brief but similar analysis is then presented concerning other centrally planned Asian economies, the Soviet Union and other East European economies.

8.1   The case of China[1]

Recent growth and structural change

China has provided the world with a fascinating case study of what is possible when a centrally planned economy begins to decentralize and move towards a more market-driven economic system. Prior to the first announcement of major policy reforms in December 1978, per capita income growth in the People's Republic of China had averaged 4.0 per cent per year in real terms, a growth rate which was only a little above the average for developing countries and which had started from a very low base in the early 1950s. By contrast, economic growth in the decade following the 1978 reforms was almost twice as fast, averaging 7.7 per cent per capita for the 1978–87 period according to official Chinese data—or 9.3 per cent during 1980–86 according to World Bank data (Anderson 1990:33–4).

According to the theory presented above in Section 1.3 of Chapter 1, one might expect the relative importance of agriculture in the densely populated Chinese economy to have declined throughout the post-war period (and especially during the 1980s), and its comparative advantage to have moved away from agriculture and towards labour-intensive manufactures such as textiles and clothing. (China's 22 per cent of the world's population is squeezed onto just 7 per cent of the world's land area.) This is indeed what has happened. Agriculture's share of exports (including processed food) fell from above 50 per cent in the 1950s to 30 per cent by the end of the 1970s and to less than 20 per cent by 1987. Agriculture's contribution to employment fell more slowly, however, from 85 per cent in the early 1950s to 70 per cent in the late 1970s and 60 per cent by 1987. In addition, agriculture's share of net material product fell from two-thirds to one-third between 1949 and 1978, while the industrial sector almost quadrupled its share of national product from only one-eighth in 1949. (Anderson 1990:36–9).

A striking feature of the 1980s, though, was the initial rise in agriculture's share of net material product, from 33 per cent in 1978 to 40 per cent in 1984, before it fell back to 34 per cent in 1987 (at current domestic prices). This reflects the fact that China's reforms have been implemented to a much greater degree in rural than in urban areas. In particular, farm product prices rose much more substantially than the general level of producer prices during that decade, and the introduction of the household responsibility system improved the opportunity for farmers to take advantage of these much improved incentives. Agricultural output by 1988 was 83 per cent above the 1978 level, a quite remarkable achievement for such a large country. This increase in volume, together with the increases in real prices of farm products, were sufficient to reverse the long-run decline in agriculture's share of national product in the early 1980s. However, with the freeing-up of non-farm markets in rural areas as well, opportunities gradually emerged for farm families to seek nearby off-farm work and so agriculture resumed its relative decline from the mid-1980s onwards. Indeed, total grain production each year during the 1985–89 period was below the 1984 record level of 407 million metric tons (Table 8.1).

A rough indication of changes in China's comparative advantage is gained by examining the share of agricultural goods in China's exports relative to the share of those goods in world trade. Table 8.2 shows that, prior to the reforms begun in 1978, agricultural goods were more than twice as important to China's exports as to world exports (index greater than 2), whereas, since the reforms began, that ratio has been falling steadily and

Table 8.1: Grain production in China, 1931 to 1989[a]

	Annual production (million metric tons)	Annual rate of production growth (%)
1931–37	160	
1950–54	152	6.5
1955–59	183	3.6
1960–64	158	-2.9
1965–69	209	5.8
1970–74	254	4.0
1975–79	298	3.2
1980–84	359	3.8
1984–89	394	-0.2
1952–77	210	2.2
1977–89	360	2.8
1978	305	7.8
1979	321	9.0
1980	321	-3.3
1981	325	1.2
1982	355	9.2
1983	387	9.0
1984	407	5.2
1985	379	-6.9
1986	392	3.4
1987	403	2.8
1988	394	-2.2
1989	407	3.3

[a] Grain in China refers to cereals, potatoes and soybeans, with potatoes being converted to grain equivalents by dividing their weight by 5.
Source: U.S. Department of Agriculture, *Agricultural Statistics of the People's Republic of China, 1949–86*, Washington, D.C., April 1988:p.19 and official updates.

was only 1.3 in 1987. Labour-intensive manufactures, on the other hand, have increased their importance in China's exports dramatically: for textiles and clothing, for example, the index of 'revealed' comparative advantage is shown in Table 8.2 to have risen from 3.4 in the early 1970s to 5.5 in 1987.

However, this index says nothing about changes in the pattern of imports.[2] During the first few years of reform, the growth in farm output—which was much faster for livestock, fishing

Table 8.2: Index of 'revealed' comparative advantage in agriculture, other primary products, textiles and clothing, and other manufactures,[a] China, 1955 to 1987

	Agriculture	Fuels, minerals and metals	Textiles and clothing	Other manufactures
1955–59	n.a.	n.a.	2.1	n.a.
1965–69	2.1	0.3	3.3	0.4
1970–74	2.3	0.3	3.4	0.5
1975–77	2.2	0.7	3.9	0.5
1978–80	1.9	0.8	4.6	0.5
1981–83	1.6	1.0	5.0	0.5
1984–86	1.4	1.1	5.1	0.5
1987[p]	1.3	0.7	5.5	0.5

[a] Share of an economy's exports due to these commodities relative to those commodities' shares in total world exports, following Balassa (1965). Agriculture is defined as SITC sections 0, 1, 2 (excluding 27, 28) and 4; fuels, minerals and metals as SITC section 3 and divisions 27, 28 and 68; textiles and clothing as SITC divisions 65 and 84; and other manufactures as SITC sections 5 to 9 (excluding 65, 68 and 84).

[p] Preliminary.

Source: Anderson (1990:Table 3.8).

and sideline activities than for crops (Table 8.3)—roughly matched the growth in consumption. Between 1978 and 1984, the value of China's exports net of imports of agricultural products remained close to zero. Immediately following the bumper grain and cotton crops of 1984 there was a sharp reduction in imports of both goods for two years, causing China to record a substantial trade surplus in agricultural goods (Table 8.3). This put considerable downward pressure on world grain (and cotton) prices and prompted concern in traditional agricultural-exporting countries, which had hoped that China would become another major net importer of farm products in East Asia. That concern eased only a little as China's net export surplus fell in the late 1980s, accompanied by a subsequent slowdown of the Chinese economy and the return of the rhetoric of food self-sufficiency in the speeches of Chinese policy makers. The important question now facing those food exporting countries—not to mention China itself—is: to what extent is China's food and feed production growth likely to diverge from consumption growth in the 1990s, and what will be the consequences for world food markets?[3]

Table 8.3: China's agricultural output and trade, 1980 to 1989

	1980	1981	1982	1983	1984	1985	1986	1987	1988	1989
Index of agricultural output (1978 = 100):										
Crops	107	113	124	135	148	145	147	154	154	...
Livestock	123	130	147	153	173	203	214	221	244	...
Forestry	...	...	129	142	169	176	170	169	176	...
Fisheries	...	...	122	132	156	185	223	264	295	...
Sidelines[a]	...	...	153	170	230	277	333	384	424	...
TOTAL	**109**	**116**	**133**	**146**	**156**	**162**	**167**	**177**	**183**	...
(% increase p.a.)	(5)	(6)	(15)	(10)	(7)	(3)	(3)	(6)	(3)	...
Value of agricultural trade (US$ billion):										
Exports	4.2	4.6	4.3	4.6	5.2	6.3	7.1	8.0	9.5	9.7
(% of total exports)	(22)	(21)	(19)	(20)	(21)	(23)	(22)	(19)	(20)	(18)
Imports	5.2	5.1	4.9	3.9	2.8	2.4	2.7	3.9	5.8	6.7
(% of total imports)	(27)	(28)	(29)	(19)	(11)	(5)	(6)	(9)	(10)	(11)
Net exports	-1.0	-0.5	-0.6	0.7	2.4	3.9	4.4	4.1	3.7	3.0
(% of total exports)	(-5)	(-2)	(-3)	(3)	(10)	(14)	(14)	(10)	(8)	(6)

[a] Handicrafts and processing of farm products.

Source: Anderson (1990) and US Department of Agriculture, *China: Agriculture and Trade Report*, July 1986 and *CPE Agriculture Report*, March/April 1990, Washington, D.C.

To begin to answer that question, it is necessary first to assess the likely rate of China's overall output (and hence income) growth, and the associated changes in the intersectoral structure of the economy. This is followed by an assessment of likely changes within the agricultural sector, including those projected by our world food model under various assumptions. The section concludes by summarizing the analysis and drawing out the policy implications for both China and its trading partners.

China's prospective growth and intersectoral changes in the 1990s

The dramatic economic growth during the first decade of China's post-1978 reforms ceased at the end of the 1980s with the events leading up to the massacre in Beijing on 4 June 1989. This return to heavy-handed central control of the economy, with its dampening effect on economic growth, may last only two or three years but could well continue into the next century. In the latter event, the best one might expect in terms of aggregate output growth is that which occurred prior to the 1978 reforms, namely 6 per cent per year. A similarly conservative population growth rate is also projected at 1.7 per cent per year (lower than the late 1980s but higher than the early 1980s before the strict controls and incentives for small families were eased somewhat), and per capita incomes would be growing at 4.3 per cent. In what follows, this will be assumed to be the reference scenario.

An alternative, more optimistic scenario would see China returning to the reform agenda and repeating the remarkable growth performance of its first decade of reforms. In that scenario, output would grow 50 per cent faster at 9 per cent per year and the population growth rate would again drop, say to 1.3 per cent. This would yield a per capita income growth of 7.7 per cent or a doubling in ten years, the same as China officially recorded during the 1978–87 period.

Optimists such as Garnaut (1988) believe a repeated doubling of incomes would be possible in the 1990s if the political leadership returned to its earlier commitment to economic reform and was able to maintain political stability. Several reasons are given to support that view. One is that China's greatest problem in rapidly catching up with its neighbouring

East Asian market economies has already been overcome, namely, the problem of actually beginning the process and of proving that it is possible. The material gains from that first decade of reform were not only very large but were also widely distributed. There is thus a widespread desire to continue with the reform process, especially in rural areas where most Chinese people live. A second reason is that China has the experiences of its highly successful neighbours to look to and learn from. Japan (some decades ago) and, more recently, the four newly industrialized economies of Hong Kong, Singapore, South Korea and Taiwan, all enjoyed a doubling in output per capita during their first decade of practising a more outward-looking, export-oriented development strategy—and none of them failed to double their output per capita again in the following decade. Moreover, they have continued to grow rapidly ever since and only now is Japan beginning to show signs of decelerating its economic growth. The mainland Chinese people, if they so wish, have the powerful examples of ethnically similar Hong Kong and Taiwan to emulate, providing, of course, that they are given the opportunity by their government.[4]

How might agriculture's share of the Chinese economy change by the year 2000 under these two different growth scenarios? To answer that question, use can be made of the regression equations in Section 1.3 of Chapter 1. The equations for agriculture's shares of employment and GDP predict almost exactly China's 1986 shares of 61 per cent for employment and 31 per cent for GDP, assuming China's per capita income in 1986 was US$540 (following Perkins 1988). Should real incomes per capita grow at the conservative rate of 4.3 per cent per year between 1986 and the end of the century, the regression equations project agriculture's shares of employment and GDP to fall to 50 per cent and 25 per cent, respectively. However, should rapid income per capita growth of 7.7 per cent be maintained, these equations suggest that agriculture's shares would be as low as 43 per cent of employment and 20 per cent of GDP. These results imply that real agricultural GDP would grow at 2.8 per cent in the conservative scenario and at 4.4 per cent (about 50 per cent faster) in the optimistic scenario (Table 8.4).

Table 8.4: Agriculture's share of employment and GDP, China, actual 1986 and projected for the year 2000 (per cent)

	Assumed real growth (1986 to 2000)			Employment share		GDP share		Growth in real agricultural GDP (% p.a.)		
	Total GDP	Population	GDP per capita	1986 actual	2000 projected	1986 actual	2000 projected	1965-80 actual	1980-86 actual	1986-2000 projected
Conservative scenario	6.0	1.7	4.3	61	50	31	25	3.0	7.9	2.8
Optimistic scenario	9.0	1.3	7.7	61	43	31	20	3.0	7.9	4.4

Source: Actual GDP data are from the World Bank (1988). Projections are based on equations (1) and (2) of Section 1.3 of Chapter 1 above.

Projected changes in China's food and feed markets

What difference would it make to the food economies of China
and of the world if China were to continue growing rapidly
through to the turn of the century, as in the above optimistic
scenario, instead of at the rates assumed in the conservative
(reference) scenario? The latter is the reference case in our world
food model, so it is possible to establish the nature of this difference by comparing the model's reference or base scenario with
that generated under the alternative high-growth assumptions.

The specific assumptions in the optimistic scenario for the
1990s which differ from the conservative base scenario are as
follows:

- national output and hence income grow 50 per cent faster;
- food productivity growth is also 50 per cent faster (except
  for rice, which is assumed to be unable to grow faster because
  of constraints on available water);
- population grows at a somewhat slower rate (1.3 instead of
  1.7 per cent per year); and
- the proportion of livestock that need to be grainfed is
  somewhat higher because it is assumed that all the extra
  livestock produced in this scenario, over and above those
  produced in the base scenario, have to be grainfed.

The proportions of livestock grainfed by the year 2000 under
the two assumptions are shown in Table 8.5, along with the
assumed income elasticities of direct demand and the assumed
price-independent rates of growth in output due to productivity
growth in the 1990s. In both scenarios, real domestic food prices
in the 1990s are assumed to remain unchanged from their 1990
level.

The impact made by faster growth on China's food economy
would be quite considerable. Per capita consumption of food
is of course higher in the optimistic scenario. As Table 8.6 shows,
by the year 2000, polished grain consumption (not including
potatoes, soybean, etc., which are included in China's official
definition of grain) is projected to be almost 85 kg (or 22 per
cent) greater under the optimistic scenario compared with the
base scenario. This is largely because of the greater demand
for feedgrains, given the assumed faster rate of growth of the
livestock sector, a point subjected to more detailed analysis by
Yang and Tyers (1989). The consumption of livestock products

Table 8.5: Food model parameter assumptions for China in the 1990s

	Wheat	Coarse grain	Rice	Ruminant meat	Non-ruminant meat	Dairy products	Sugar
Income elasticity of direct demand	0.5	0.1	0.1	1.1	1.0	1.2	1.0
Price-independent productivity growth rate (% p.a.)							
–base scenario	3.5	2.5	2.0	5.0	5.0	5.0	5.0
–optimistic scenario	5.2	3.7	2.0	7.5	7.5	7.5	7.5
(Historical production growth rates, % p.a.							
1952–77	3.2	1.6	2.5	..	3.3	..	5.5
1977–88	6.9	2.7	2.5	10.1	9.8	15.8	10.7)
Proportion of livestock grainfed by year 2000							
–base scenario	n.a.	n.a.	n.a.	0.26	0.50	0.34	n.a.
–optimistic scenario	n.a.	n.a.	n.a.	0.42	0.61	0.43	n.a.
(Assumed grain use per unit of grainfed output	n.a.	n.a.	n.a.	6.0	5.0	0.4	n.a.)

Source: See Appendix 2.

Table 8.6: Food consumption per capita, China and East Asian market economies, 1961 to 2000 (kg per year)

	Wheat	Coarse grain	Rice	Sub-total, grain	Ruminant meat	Non-ruminant meat	Sub-total, meat	Dairy products	Sugar	Eggs
China ($500)[a]										
1965-69	41	64	84	189	0.4	8	8	3	3	2
1975-79	56	77	95	228	0.6	10	11	3	4	3
1985-86	97	84	117	298	1.0	18	19	5	7	6
1990	106	93	112	311	1.3	20	21	6	7	:
2000 – conservative										
($1,000)	132	130	119	381	2.1	31	33	9	11	:
– optimistic										
($1,500)	159	184	123	466	3.1	41	44	13	16	:
South Korea ($2,180)										
1965-69	38	59	130	227	1	4	5	2	4	3
1975-79	50	95	154	299	3	7	10	8	12	6
1985-86	85	118	141	344	5	14	19	25	23	8
Taiwan ($3,100)										
1965-69	33	108	159	300	1	25	26	3	27	3
1975-79	38	134	122	294	4	38	42	12	28	6
1985-86	41	254	96	391	6	54	60	18	28	10
Hong Kong ($6,200)										
1965-69	37	30	94	161	13	43	56	23	11	10
1975-79	31	49	71	151	18	57	75	30	n.a.	14
1985-86	47	65	67	179	18	73	91	40	n.a.	12

Singapore ($7,400)									
1965-69	87	n.a.	86	n.a.	11	29	40	45	24	8
1975-79	63	74	81	218	12	61	73	55	50	12
1985-86	58	137	76	271	11	68	79	66	43	14
Japan ($11,330)									
1965-69	50	87	113	250	4	9	13	41	23	13
1975-79	52	145	91	288	7	20	27	58	28	17
1985-86	51	177	82	310	9	27	36	69	24	18

a Per capita incomes for 1985 are shown in parentheses for each economy in 1985 US dollars, except in the final two rows under China which refer to real (in 1985 dollars) per capita income in the year 2000 in those different scenarios.

b Wheat, coarse grain and polished rice only. (China's official definition of 'grain' also includes unpolished rice and potatoes, soybean, etc.) Note that this includes the indirect consumption of grain via animal products.

Source: Appendix 2 and authors' model projections.

in China by the year 2000 in the optimistic scenario is similar to consumption in Hong Kong and Singapore in the 1960s and in Taiwan in the 1970s. (Japan and Korea, by contrast, have had lower levels of meat consumption because of very high domestic prices maintained by import barriers.)

The projected trade and self-sufficiency levels in the two scenarios for the year 2000 are summarized in Table 8.7, together with historical levels for the 1970s and 1980s. Overall, self-sufficiency in these seven food groups is projected to continue its decline of the 1970s and 1980s, to 90 per cent by the year 2000 in both scenarios. Despite the much larger volume of coarse grain imports to feed animals, self-sufficiency in livestock products in the optimistic scenario is still well below 100 per cent. In this respect, China would be following the pattern of self-sufficiency decline already followed by Korea, Taiwan and Japan—although in the latter economies, the downward trend would have been much faster had it not been for the rapid growth of agricultural protectionism (see final column of Table 8.8).

The projected effects of faster economic growth in China on international prices and world trade in food are summarized in Table 8.9. International food prices would be higher in the optimistic scenario (by an average of 3 per cent in the year 2000) as a consequence of China's greater food and feed import demand. The volume of world trade in coarse grain would be substantially greater, with China displacing Japan as the world's largest importer of coarse grain. Yet, despite the much faster increase in China's grain imports in the optimistic scenario, such that the total volume of its imports is 50 per cent higher by the year 2000 (140 instead of 90 million metric tons), international grain prices are only about 4 or 5 per cent higher in this scenario compared with the reference scenario. This is a testament to the flexibility of world food markets to adjust both production and consumption to changes in import demand by a large country.

Needless to say, these projections are only illustrative because they depend heavily on the assumptions made, particularly those summarized in Table 8.5 (plus the assumption of constant real domestic food prices in China). Nonetheless, the explicitness of the assumptions makes the results useful because they highlight the policy changes needed to bring about a different outcome, a point to which we now turn.

Table 8.7: Net imports of and self-sufficiency in various foods, China, 1970–86 actual and 1990 and 2000 projected (million metric tons and per cent)

	Wheat	Coarse grain	Rice	Sub-total, grain[a]	Ruminant meat	Non-ruminant meat	Dairy products	Sugar	WEIGHTED AVERAGE[b]
Self sufficiency (%)									
1970–74	93	104	105	98	101	102	100	79	102
1975–79	96	103	104	97	101	101	99	72	101
1980–84	86	100	101	96	103	101	99	76	98
1985–86	87	96	100	99	104	101	98	80	96
Projected									
2000 – reference	75	73	101	82	97	94	92	91	90
2000 – optimistic	78	62	102	78	89	96	87	87	90
Imports net of exports (mmt)									
1970–74	4.7	0.6	-1.8	3.5	0.0	-0.2	0.0	0.6	
1975–79	6.2	0.9	-1.9	5.2	0.0	-0.1	0.0	1.0	
1980–84	11.4	-0.1	-0.6	10.7	-0.0	-0.2	0.0	1.3	
1985–86	7.6	-3.6	-0.7	3.3	-0.0	-0.2	0.1	1.5	
Projected									
2000 – reference	45.5	47.7	-1.3	91.9	0.1	2.6	1.0	1.3	
2000 – optimistic	46.2	94.0	-2.3	137.9	0.4	2.0	2.3	2.9	

[a] Volume based.
[b] Weights based on domestic production of the individual products valued at international prices.
Source: Appendix 2 and authors' model projections.

Table 8.8: Food self-sufficiency and agricultural protection in Japan, Korea and Taiwan, 1961 to 1986 (production as a percentage of apparent consumption)

	Wheat	Coarse grain	Soybean	Rice	Ruminant meat	Non-ruminant meat	Dairy products	Sugar	Food weighted average[a]	Average nominal[b] rate of protection
Japan										
1961–64	30	36	20	97	66	99	92	24	78	68
1965–69	20	19	8	109	51	97	90	27	77	87
1970–74	6	5	4	94	51	95	90	20	67	110
1975–79	5	3	4	110	45	92	87	20	67	147
1980–84	11	2	4	92	51	91	86	31	64	151
1985–86	14	2	4	107	52	90	88	34	67	..
Korea, Rep.										
1961–64	20	87	89	100	100	100	26	0	92	3
1965–69	18	98	94	94	99	100	54	0	86	18
1970–74	7	68	81	91	89	102	85	0	77	75
1975–79	3	40	66	96	69	100	97	0	75	146
1980–84	3	22	58	93	69	100	96	0	69	195
1985–86	0	13	50	98	96	100	99	0	69	239

Taiwan

1961–64	9	25	29	103	100	100	38	253	120	2
1965–69	5	16	20	105	100	100	33	254	115	2
1970–74	0	6	9	100	70	103	28	252	97	17
1975–79	0	4	5	111	16	103	23	187	85	36
1980–84	0	4	4	119	5	103	22	147	77	57
1985–86	0	7	1	104	5	107	29	125	77	..

[a] Weights based on value of domestic production at border prices.

[b] The percentage by which the domestic producer price for grain and meat exceeds the international price at the country's border. The final period shown for Japan and Taiwan is 1980–82, and that for Korea is 1985. These estimates are from Anderson, Hayami and others (1986:22) and Anderson (1989).

Source: See Appendix 2.

Table 8.9: Projected effects of faster economic growth in China on international food prices and trade volumes and on China's share of world food trade, year 2000 (per cent)

	Wheat	Coarse grain	Rice	Ruminant meat	Non-ruminant meat	Dairy products	Sugar
International price (% difference between optimistic and reference scenarios)	4	5	1	2	-1	2	6
World trade volume[a] (% difference between optimistic and reference scenarios)	-1	14	1	1	2	-0	3
China's share of world imports (%)							
1970-74	9	1	-26	-0	-7	0	4
1975-79	9	1	-12	-0	-4	0	6
1980-84	12	-0	-7	-1	-11	0	7
1985-86	9	-6	-7	-1	-11	1	8
2000 – reference case[b]	31	21	-6	1	17	2	5
2000 – optimistic case[b]	32	35	-10	5	12	4	10

[a] 'World' trade volumes excludes trade within the various country groups specified as aggregate 'countries' in the model, most notably the European Community.

[b] China's shares are inflated, especially (by a factor of 3 or 4) for dairy products and non-ruminant meat which are heavily traded between EC countries (see note a).

Source: Authors' model projections.

Policy implications for China and its trading partners

Many Chinese policy makers would be horrified by the prospect of their country's food import dependence increasing to ten per cent of domestic consumption. To avoid this, a number of options are available. One is simply to restrict food imports and ration consumption quantitatively so that it grows less rapidly than in the above scenarios. A second is to raise the real level of domestic food prices facing producers and/or consumers. One other option is to foster even faster productivity growth than has been assumed in the above scenarios. The first option of food rationing has been commonly used in Eastern Europe, but it is highly unpopular and breeds corruption. It would also be contrary to the spirit of moving towards a more market-oriented economy. The second option would happen automatically in a more open Chinese economy, because domestic prices for many foods are well below international food prices when converted at the shadow rate of foreign exchange (see Anderson and Tyers 1987b and Sicular 1989, 1990). This is especially true of urban consumer prices which are often lower than the price received by farmers. Already, the budgetary cost of subsidizing this difference has become a great burden to China's central government, but raising consumer prices of such basic necessities has proved to be extremely difficult politically. That dilemma in turn makes it difficult for the government to raise domestic producer prices.

The third option, of fostering faster productivity growth on farms, also seems to be proving difficult. As Table 8.1 shows, grain production in China declined between 1984 and 1989, and growth in output of other farm products has also been slow in recent years once the increases in product prices in the late 1970s/early 1980s, and the phasing in of the household responsibility system, had had their effect (Sicular 1990). Indeed, it is possible that agricultural productivity growth may be substantially slower than non-farm productivity growth as industrialization in China proceeds (judging by the experiences of China's neighbours to the east), in which case food import dependence would be even greater than the above optimistic growth scenario suggests.

One possible avenue for reducing the growing import dependence on coarse grain (and soybean) for animal feed is to make better use of available pasture land. How much scope there is for doing this is a vexed question, because the environmental risks of over-grazing in China may be high. Another avenue is to boost grain yields through investing more in research, including the adaptation of technologies imported from abroad.[5] Since China's grain yields per hectare are already 50 per cent above the world average, however, any such boost to agricultural research expenditure is more likely to raise the productivity of labour and capital than of land. Furthermore, the land available for grain production continues to diminish as urban areas expand and the demand for cropland for fruit and vegetables grows with income and population growth (Anderson 1990:Ch. 4).[6]

In short, the development of the Chinese economy is almost certain to lead to an increasing demand for food (and especially feed) imports, during the next decade and beyond. These demands will become even more pressing as industrialization proceeds rapidly and the government lags behind in allowing domestic food prices to rise towards international levels. The food and feed imports could be paid for by exporting other goods, especially light manufactures such as textiles and clothing (Anderson 1990:Ch. 6).

The decision facing the Chinese government as to where to set the intersectoral terms of trade is likely to be determined not by domestic economic and political pressures alone but also by perceptions of the rest of the world's preparedness to do business with China. The Chinese leadership will need clear signals from food-exporting countries, particularly the United States, that relying on food imports will not leave China vulnerable to political pressure from outside. It will need similar assurances from advanced economies that their markets for imports of textiles, clothing and other labour-intensive manufactures will remain open, so that China has the foreign exchange earnings necessary to import farm products. This underlines the importance of ensuring that both agriculture and textiles and clothing are brought under the full discipline and spirit of the General Agreement on Tariffs and Trade in the 1990s.

8.2 Possible impacts of reforms in other socialist economies

Just as changes in China's income and food production growth have caused short-run shocks to international food markets in recent years, so too might the economic reforms in other socialist economies which began in the late 1980s. In virtually all socialist economies, food is low in price but rationed to consumers (as demonstrated by the queues at food stores). How production and consumption will respond as these economies reform is very difficult to predict, however, because many other goods and services are also in short supply at current prices in these economies.

If markets were freed up and producers were permitted to specialize in production according to their comparative advantage, what might the pattern of trade specialization of these economies look like after initial adjustment to the new equilibrium situation? The theory and empirical evidence in Chapter 1 suggests that agriculture's share of exports is likely to be higher the lower a country's per capita income and population density. Theory also suggests that the greater the country's population densities, the more likely it is that the share of agricultural exports will fall (and the share of manufactured goods in exports rise) as per capita income increase (with the rise in importance of manufactured goods in exports beginning earlier and initially involving more labour-intensive manufactures).

The populations of the centrally planned economies (CPEs) of Asia and Europe, and their population densities, are shown in Table 8.10. Vietnam and North Korea are the two large Asian CPEs in addition to China, and both are extremely poorly endowed with agricultural land per capita (less than one-eighth the global average). Vietnam is one of the world's poorest economies, so a freeing-up of its markets, particularly if reform were to begin in the countryside, would probably cause rice and other agricultural products to dominate exports initially. But, as human and other capital stocks begin to accumulate and as industrial reforms also start to take effect, one would expect agriculture's export share to decline rapidly as exports of unskilled labour-intensive manufactures emerge. In this

Table 8.10: Population (total and per unit of agricultural land), centrally planned and other economies, 1987

	Population total (millions)	Population per square kilometre of agricultural land
Asian centrally planned		
China	1,086	261
Korea, DPR	21	876
Kampuchea	8	80
Laos	4	222
Vietnam	63	925
USSR	283	47
Other centrally planned Europe		
Albania	3	277
Bulgaria	9	145
Czechoslovakia	16	230
Germany, DPR	17	269
Hungary	11	163
Poland	38	200
Romania	23	152
Yugoslavia	23	166
Sub-total	**139**	**186**
For comparison:		
European Community (EC12)	324	241
European Free Trade Association	32	252
Sub-total (Western Europe)	**356**	**242**
United States	246	57
Japan	122	2,290
Korea, Rep.	43	1,910
Thailand	54	256
World	**5,026**	**107**

Source: Food and Agriculture Organisation, *Production Yearbook*, Rome, 1988.

respect it would be following the development path of its rice-exporting neighbour Thailand.[7] However, it is less likely to be able to follow Thailand in terms of remaining a net agricultural exporter and increasing its food self-sufficiency. This is because Vietnam has more than three times as many people per hectare of agricultural land as Thailand. Thus, while a rapidly growing, open Vietnamese economy may initially expand its net exports of food, it is likely to become a net food importer as it industrializes and approaches middle-income status next century.

North Korea is almost as poorly endowed as Vietnam in terms of agricultural land, has a poorer climate for growing food, and has a much greater stock of human and industrial capital per worker than Vietnam. If its economy were to be freed up and opened to international competition, it undoubtedly would develop a strong export specialization in light (and perhaps some heavy) manufactured goods while importing much of its food needs, or at least feedgrains. It may even become more dependent on imported food than present-day South Korea (even though its per capita income is probably less than two-thirds that of South Korea and the latter has even less farmland per capita) because South Korea's food import dependence is kept artificially low by very high agricultural protection.

Neither of these Asian CPEs will have a major impact on world food markets on their own, however, simply because of their relatively small populations and national incomes. Even in combination with the other CPEs of Indo-China, this group of economies is not large, although it may have some impact on the international rice market. Of potentially much greater significance, in terms of both their impact on world food markets and the probability of their economies being reformed substantially during the 1990s, are the USSR and the other East European countries. How might their patterns of food trade specialization change as their markets are freed up?

Per capita incomes in these CPEs in 1990 probably ranged between one-quarter and one-half the average of those for Western Europe, as perhaps did industrial capital stocks. Agricultural land per capita in the USSR is close to that of the United States and well above that of Western Europe. However, the climate there is closer to the harshness of Canada than to that of the United States or the European Community. That factor, together with the poor incentives offered to agricultural producers and the preparedness to devote increasing amounts of foreign exchange to buying imported food, have contributed to the steady decline in Soviet self-sufficiency in grain. The USSR has also imported increasing volumes of livestock products from

Table 8.11: Food self-sufficiency in the USSR and other centrally planned Europe, 1961 to 1986

	Wheat	Coarse grain	Rice	Sub-total, grain	Ruminant meat	Non-ruminant meat	Sub-total, meat	Dairy products	Sugar	WEIGHTED AVERAGE
USSR										
1961–64	107	108	45	107	101	100	100	101	79	101
1965–69	103	100	65	101	100	100	100	100	82	99
1970–74	99	97	90	98	98	99	99	100	80	97
1975–79	92	88	80	90	96	98	97	100	69	92
1980–84	82	85	79	83	94	96	95	98	61	88
1985–86	88	91	96	90	94	96	95	98	64	91
Other centrally planned Europe										
1961–64	74	96	25	88	97	103	101	100	97	95
1965–69	89	99	28	95	108	104	105	101	96	100
1970–74	88	93	33	91	103	104	103	101	92	98
1975–79	90	90	28	90	105	106	106	102	93	99
1980–84	94	95	30	95	105	106	106	102	90	100
1985–86	98	97	42	97	108	108	108	101	86	102
All centrally planned Europe/USSR										
1961–64	98	103	37	100	100	101	101	100	85	99
1965–69	99	99	54	99	102	102	102	101	86	99
1970–74	96	95	75	96	99	101	100	100	84	97
1975–79	92	89	70	90	98	103	101	100	76	95
1980–84	85	89	70	87	96	101	99	99	71	93
1985–86	91	93	84	92	97	102	100	99	71	95

Source: See Appendix 2.

its East European allies, so overall food self-sufficiency has fallen from 100 per cent in the 1960s to 90 per cent since the late 1970s (Table 8.11).

All the smaller East European economies have below-average endowments of agricultural land per capita. On average they are almost twice as densely populated as the world as a whole, and almost as badly off in this respect as Western Europe (Table 8.10). As in the USSR, their food prices have been low but queues have been long. Hence it is unclear whether, in a freer market, they would move above or below their current level of close to 100 per cent food self-sufficiency (see Table 8.11).

As shown in Table 8.12, crop yields are low in Eastern Europe compared with those in adjacent West European countries, and

Table 8.12: Annual crop yields per hectare, centrally planned Europe and other industrial economies, 1985 to 1987 (kg per hectare)

	Wheat	Coarse grain	Soybean
Centrally planned Europe			
USSR	1,810	1,770	930
Albania	3,030	2,760	n.a.
Bulgaria	3,880	3,720	910
Czechoslavakia	4,920	4,290	n.a.
Germany, DPR	5,280	4,050	n.a.
Hungary	4,730	5,290	1,890
Poland	3,640	2,810	n.a.
Romania	3,580	5,940	1,520
Yugoslavia	3,770	3,900	2,080
Western Europe			
Austria	4,480	5,120	1,790
France	5,720	5,660	2,440
Germany, FR	6.360	4,810	n.a.
Sweden	5,350	3,480	n.a.
North America			
Canada	1,780	3,030	2,480
United States	2,380	5,580	2,100
World	**2,330**	**2,390**	**1,810**

Source: Food and Agriculture Organisation, *Production Yearbook*, Rome, 1988.

those in the USSR are low compared with North America. If producer incentives such as the grain/fertilizer price ratio were to rise, if fertilizers and weedicides were to become readily available for farmers to buy, and if individual farm households were given more scope to retain the rewards from their labour, food production could probably expand substantially in these countries.

But such reforms would also raise real incomes, especially if they were extended to non-farm activities. If the latter were to be liberalized simultaneously, there may even be a net flow of resources out of agriculture if income-earning prospects off the farms improved faster than those in farming. With higher incomes and less rationing of food, consumption per capita would rise substantially at current prices. This is especially so for livestock products which, as Table 8.13 shows, are consumed much less in Eastern than Western Europe.

It is unlikely that the governments of these countries would continue to hold down consumer prices of food in this new environment, however. Even though there would be strong political resistance to consumer price rises initially, this would tend to weaken as real wages rise in the course of the new economic growth. But whether such consumer price increases reduce the growth in food consumption to less or more than the growth in food production during the 1990s is something that only time will tell.

The eventual pattern of trade specialization of the East European and USSR economies, should they open up substantially, is thus very difficult to assess. It is made more difficult partly because they do not have the extreme factor endowment ratios of East Asia's economies, partly because their economies have been so grossly distorted for so long that present production and trade patterns provide little guide to their natural comparative advantages, and partly because their trade may well be affected by preferential access to markets in the West. The East German economy, for example, was fully integrated into the European Community in late 1990 and its agriculture became immediately subject to the EC's Common Agricultural Policy, while other East European economies may eventually become associate members of the EC. About all that can be said with reasonable certainty, therefore, is that in the short run the initial impact of any substantial reforms will be

Table 8.13: Food consumption per capita in Europe and the USSR, 1965 to 1986 (kg per year)

	Wheat	Coarse grain	Rice	Ruminant meat	Non-Ruminant meat	Dairy products	Sugar	Eggs
USSR								
1965–69	170	280	2	12	11	166	23	4
1975–79	196	417	3	15	13	179	23	7
1985–86	173	407	3	16	16	183	24	8
Other centrally planned Europe								
1965–69	110	411	2	7	20	141	19	5
1975–79	136	537	2	9	28	163	22	7
1985–86	140	504	2	9	30	168	23	8
European Community (10)								
1965–69	158	234	3	28	36	365	42	13
1975–79	155	249	4	29	47	375	51	15
1985–86	191	196	4	29	54	390	55	15
EFTA-5								
1965–69	112	327	3	22	33	485	31	11
1975–79	104	395	3	25	43	452	37	13
1985–86	109	370	6	23	47	471	36	14

Source: See Appendix 2.

a struggle towards new domestic market equilibria which will tend to destabilize international food markets to some extent— as indeed occurred in the EC when the barrier to trade between East and West Germany was lifted in July 1990. This adds yet another element of urgency to the need for agricultural policy reforms in advanced industrial economies, for the latter will improve the capacity of formerly centrally planned economics to make the transition towards market economies.

Notes to Chapter 8

[1] This section draws heavily on Anderson (1990) and the references therein. See also our earlier quantitative analysis (Anderson and Tyers 1987b) and the paper by Sicular (1990).

[2] This ratio is a crude indicator of comparative advantage for another reason as well, namely, that it does not exclude the influence of policy distortions on the pattern of trade specialization.

[3] The consequences of China's economic growth and its policies on natural fibre trade (and on world markets for textiles and clothing) are addressed in Anderson (1990, 1991a and 1991b).

[4] For further discussion of the growth-enhancing features which China shares with its neighbours to the east, see Perkins (1986), Garnaut (1988) and Anderson (1990:55-9).

[5] China appears to have been grossly under-investing in agricultural research. In 1980, for example, its expenditure represented only 0.6 per cent of the value of its agricultural output compared with 0.8 per cent in all middle-income countries and 1.5 per cent in advanced industrial countries, according to Judd, Boyce and Evenson (1986:Table 3).

[6] Prospects for boosting output via increased irrigation are also slim. In the mid-1980s China already irrigated 46 per cent of its cropland, compared with a world average of only 15 per cent and less than 30 per cent elsewhere in Asia.

[7] In the early 1970s, Thailand earned more than 90 per cent of its exports from primary products and less than 5 per cent from textiles and clothing, but by 1987 only 48 per cent of its exports were primary products and 18 per cent were textiles and clothing (see Suphachalasai 1991). Nevertheless, Thailand's self-sufficiency in staple food products rose from 121 per cent in 1970-74 to 150 per cent by 1983-86 (see Appendix 2).

9

Policy Implications and Prospects for Reform

Economically desirable policy changes are not always politically feasible. The final section is therefore devoted to examining various prospects for reforming food policies in the light of the political economy discussion of Chapter 3. It suggests that, while progress will not be easy, there are nonetheless some developments that may lead to reductions in the current state of disarray in world food markets. Following a summary of the main findings of this study, the key implications for the policies of industrial market economies are presented, and the implications of their reform for developing and (formerly) centrally planned economies are discussed.

9.1 Summary of findings

As a basis for drawing out some important policy implications from the study, a reminder of some of the key findings is helpful. Among the main findings are the following broad themes.

- The long-run downward trend in the real prices of food in international markets accelerated in the 1970s and 1980s, and the year-to-year fluctuations in those prices around their trend increased.
- Industrial market economies have, since the 1960s, gradually switched from being slight net importers to being large net exporters of food staples while developing economies have made the opposite switch, despite large increases in food consumption in industrial countries and relatively rapid food output growth in developing countries (Chapter 1).
- Although low and declining price and income elasticities of demand for food help to explain the decline in real inter-

national food prices, and seasonal factors help to explain why food prices fluctuate around trend, the acceleration in this decline and the increase in price variance since the early 1970s (together with the large change in the pattern of food trade between industrial and developing countries), suggest there has been an increase in distortions due to government policy intervention.

- An empirical examination indeed reveals that there has been an acceleration in the long-run growth of nominal and effective rates of agricultural protection in industrial countries. It also reveals that such protection has spread to numerous middle-income and rapidly industrializing economies, that there has been an increased use of trade volume fluctuations (including by the USSR) to help stabilize domestic markets, and that the use of variable export subsidies is expanding as countries retaliate against the adoption by the EC of this method of disposing of its surpluses (Chapter 2).

- Reasons for this growth in protectionism in industrialized and newly industrializing economies, for the effective taxation of agriculture in many developing countries, and for the increasing use of non-tariff trade barriers by rich and poor countries alike (to help insulate their domestic markets from fluctuations in international food prices), can be found by identifying those who gain and those who lose from these policies and the relative costs faced by these groups of becoming informed and of influencing policy makers (Chapter 3).

- The costs and distributional consequences at home and abroad of the myriad food policy instruments used by government depend on a large number of parameters. The direction of effects (and the time path of adjustment to policy and structural changes) cannot be easily determined, if at all, without recourse to empirical study (Chapter 4); hence the need for a dynamic, stochastic, multi-commodity simulation model of world food markets of the type described in Chapter 5.

- The model results in Chapter 6 present us with a number of useful findings: (i) if the food policies of the 1980s remain in place in the 1990s, their annual cost to industrial market economies and globally will be more than double what it was in the early 1980s; (ii) industrial country policies are becoming increasingly inefficient at transferring welfare to low income farmers in those countries; (iii) the policies of the early 1980s were depressing the average level of food prices in international markets by about one-seventh and increasing their year-to-year fluctuations by about 50 per cent; (iv) should the same policy regimes remain in place through the 1990s, the effects are projected to be half as large again, reducing enormously the average value and stability of export earnings of traditional food-exporting countries, including many debt ridden Latin American ones; (v) even though developing economies as a group are net importers of food, their economic welfare (narrowly defined) is reduced by the current policies of advanced industrial economies, partly because, in the absence of these policies, the developing world would be a net exporter of food, but also because other developing country policies already discriminate against agriculture; (vi) economic welfare is reduced even more when it is defined more broadly so as to include equity, risk and food security concerns; and (vii) were the industrial countries to reduce the protection and insulation of their food markets, the higher and more stable international prices that would result may well stimulate developing countries to reduce the taxation and insulation of their farmers, the combined effect of which would be to leave the average international price of food roughly unchanged but subject to only about one-third as much year-to-year instability (or less than that which currently still prevails in most countries despite the insulation component of their policies).

- All of the above has prompted industrial and developing countries alike to negotiate multilaterally to reduce agricultural protection and insulation. One proposal seeks to convert all import barriers to tariffs and then to phase them down through the 1990s. The potential welfare improving effects of such a move are shown to be very substantial even if reforms only occur in industrial countries (Chapter 7).
- Because of their partial and phased nature, such reforms would allow production of most foods in virtually all industrial countries to continue to expand in the 1990s, albeit at a slower rate than if policies continued unreformed. The reforms would also ensure that any declines in food self-sufficiency are modest.

• Finally, the reforms that began in China in the late 1970s and in Eastern Europe and the USSR in the late 1980s are, at least initially, introducing further instability to world food markets. This adds urgency to the need for reduced agricultural protection and insulation elsewhere, not only as an offsetting influence in the international marketplace but also to facilitate the process of adjustment by former centrally planned economies towards greater reliance on market forces.

9.2 Policy implications for industrial countries

The industrial countries' farm policies are thus contributing substantially to the very problem they are meant to alleviate, namely declining and fluctuating prices for farm products. This situation illustrates a classic free-rider problem of the sort discussed by Kindleberger (1978, 1986): each country would like to see higher and more stable international food prices, but is unprepared to reform its own policies to contribute to that end unless other countries are prepared to make a similar commitment and thereby lower the political cost and perhaps raise the economic benefit of contributing. The standard solution to the problem of underprovision of a public good (in this case an international one) is to get together the parties who will benefit and have them agree jointly to act. As is clear from the protracted debate during the Uruguay Round of multilateral trade negotiations, however, the willingness of the different parties to participate varies enormously—which is understandable, since the domestic economic and political benefits and costs of reform also vary enormously. For example, unilateral liberalization of US food policies in 1990 would have reduced US producer welfare by $19 billion (in 1985 dollars), whereas if all industrial countries liberalized simultaneously, US producers would have *gained* $3 billion. By contrast, EC farmers lose substantially from multilateral as well as unilateral liberalization (even though the loss from the latter is more, being $66 billion, compared with $53 billion when all industrial countries liberalize—see Table 6.8).

Nevertheless, the cost to domestic food consumers and

taxpayers of maintaining protectionist policies is continuing to rise while their inefficiency and inequity in transferring welfare to low-income farmers becomes ever more evident. The bulk of the benefits go to large farmers and are incorporated into the value of farm assets. The extent of such capitalization can be enormous, as is apparent from the escalation in the value of paddy land in Japan as rice price supports have risen (Table 9.1). Moreover, since poor people spend a larger share of their income on food, the implicit taxation of food consumption in protected countries is regressive also.

Clearly, even an agreement to halt protection growth would be an achievement, since it would prevent the disarray in world food markets from worsening. Perhaps some aggregate measure of support index could be adopted to monitor whether countries are abiding by such an agreement (although no single index will be without problems—see Hertel 1989 and Ballinger *et al.* 1990). It would certainly help if import restrictions were converted to tariffs, not only because they are more transparent than the myriad non-tariff barriers currently used, but also because that would reduce the degree of insulation of domestic from international food markets, thereby contributing to the stabilization of international food prices. Furthermore, as discussed in Chapter 3, any lessening of the policy imperative to make domestic prices more stable will reduce the extent to which the process of formulating stabilized domestic prices is captured by vested interests whose primary interest is in raising or lowering those prices. Were a conversion to *ad valorem* tariffs and export subsidies achieved, the results in Chapter 7 make clear that even a partial lowering of protection rates would reap substantial economic benefits—benefits that could then be used to supplement the incomes of farmers more directly and more equitably. These results also show that, providing the liberalization is gradual enough, farm output need not decline. It would simply expand less rapidly than otherwise. Even self-sufficiency in key staple foods would not fall dramatically under such a phased program.

Simple support policies such as tariffs have much to commend themselves over more complex production control schemes associated with higher price supports. Set-aside programs of the sort used in the United States are socially wasteful not only because land resources are wasted and administrative costs are

Table 9.1: Nominal rate of rice protection and paddy land price, Japan, 1955 to 1980

	Nominal rate of rice protection (%)[a]	Price of paddy land (million yen per hectare)	
		Current yen	1980 yen[b]
1955	<20[c]	1.2	4.5
1960	50	2.0	6.4
1965	72	3.4	9.0
1970	99	10.2	20.4
1975	160	28.2	35.0
1980	263	38.3	38.3

[a] For the five years prior to the year shown.

[b] Deflated by the GNP deflator.

[c] The rate for 1955 is difficult to estimate accurately given that the price controls at the time were undermined by a black market. Saxon and Anderson (1982:Table 4) show that the government procurement price averaged 14% above the Thai export price and that the black market price (for an unknown share of consumption) averaged 30% above the government procurement price.

Sources: Anderson, Hayami *et al.* (1986:Table A1.1) and Hayami (1988:Table 4.6).

high but also because deciding whether and when to participate absorbs large amounts of farm managerial time and energy (Perry *et al.* 1989). Several other complex programs, such as producer levy schemes to fund export subsidies can, as we saw in Section 4.4 above, simply be another covert means by which producers extract larger transfers at the expense of domestic consumers and producers in other countries (see also Anderson and Tyers 1984).

An additional advantage to industrial countries of liberalizing their agricultural policies is that it encourages developing and centrally planned economies to reform their policies also. This is partly because international food prices would gyrate less, with less protection and insulation of industrial country markets, thereby reducing the risks associated with trade in food.[1] This would be especially helpful in the 1990s for countries such as China and the USSR which may become more dependent on food imports as they open their economies. For those developing economies with a natural comparative advantage in farm products, there would be the additional advantage that they may be better able to export their way out of poverty if protectionism in industrial countries were to decline. For example, Vietnam's initial export earning prospects would be enhanced considerably if Japan were to open its rice market.

9.3 Policy implications for developing and centrally planned economies

During the Uruguay Round, developing countries were not always strong advocates of reforms to agricultural protection and insulation policies. Yet the empirical results presented above suggest that, as a group, they would benefit economically from such reforms: international food prices would fluctuate less, and many developing countries would have opportunities to expand net foreign exchange earnings. Such opportunities would be even greater if those countries spent more on agricultural research, since investments in such research currently have a very high payoff (a payoff which would be enhanced by higher international food prices.)[2] Developing countries would then have even more reason to join the so-called Cairns Group of countries seeking the progressive lowering of agricultural protection in industrial countries.

All but the most insulating developing countries would also benefit if developing countries as a group agreed to join with industrial countries in reducing their degree of insulation. Fluctuations in international food prices would thereby be lowered even more—indeed to less than is currently the extent of fluctuations of domestic food prices in most developing countries. Of course, if those countries also lowered the effective taxation of their farm sectors, the economic benefits to their economies and to the world would be even greater.

Even those developing countries which would remain as net food importers, if world food markets were liberalized, have reason to support the agricultural liberalization cause. This is because, by participating in multilateral negotiations, they would have a legitimate claim to trade concessions in other areas in return for supporting reforms which raise the cost of their food imports. Such concessions could include lower barriers to industrial country markets for tropical and other primary and processed primary products, and for textiles and clothing. The latter markets are especially important for densely populated, newly or imminently industrializing economies because their comparative advantage is likely to be strongest in light manufactures as they open their economies.

Similarly, formerly centrally planned economies have much to gain from opening up and relying more on markets rather than planning. Even if they were to become large importers of food as a result, as in the optimistic scenario for China (Chapter 8), the impact on international food prices and hence on the per unit price of their imports need not be very large—a testament to the very considerable flexibility of the world food market even in the presence of current insulation policies.[3] Nevertheless, two sets of assurances might be sought by such countries as they embark on their economic reforms. One is that food exporting countries agree not to use food export embargos as a political or economic weapon, otherwise the future use of such instruments could undermine support for the whole reform process in the socialist economies. The other assurance they might seek is that industrial country markets be open to the exports of these reforming economies. Without that, they would simply not have the hard currency to purchase food imports from the West.

For China and the densely populated countries of Eastern Europe, the alternatives to becoming more dependent on food imports are not very attractive. Continuing to restrict imports and rationing consumers, with the ever-longer queues at grocery stores, is simply not sustainable politically. There is the possibility of steadily raising producer prices to encourage greater domestic production and farm productivity growth so that output can keep pace with increases in domestic consumption, as Japan, South Korea and Taiwan have tried to do. But, as China has found, that can lead to excessive strain on treasury revenue if it is not accompanied by increases in consumer prices of food; and urban consumers in poor countries typically are intolerant of such price increases. It is therefore in the interests of industrial countries, who expect to benefit from reforms in socialist economies to provide an international economic environment, including one for farm products, which is conducive to those economies embarking on their historic reforms.

9.4 Prospects for reducing the disarray

Is it likely that industrial countries will commit themselves to, and deliver, major agricultural policy reforms, given the presence of the political forces discussed in Chapter 3? Or is it inevitable that protection for the declining agricultural sector will continue to grow in currently protected economies and to spread to less developed economies as they industrialize? Consider first the factors affecting the distribution of gains and losses from a policy bias towards agriculture. In the course of economic growth at home and abroad, the *per capita* benefits to farmers will continue to grow relative to the per capita losses to other groups. This is because economic growth is likely to continue to be characterized by declines in agriculture's shares of GDP and employment, and in the share of farm products in household expenditure, and by the more rapid decline in the value-added share of output in agriculture than in other sectors. The costs of collective action by farmers relative to these costs for other groups are also likely to keep falling as the numbers of farmers decline and as farmer associations become firmly established. Moreover, unless most countries simultaneously adopt reforms to insulation policies, the real price of agricultural products in international markets is likely to continue to gyrate around a declining long-run trend.

In this environment, politicians are understandably reluctant to deregulate and thereby reduce producer returns and increase the variability of food prices. Such action can always be taken 'after the next election' when the inefficiency of present policies will be even more obvious! As the costs of protection become more evident, as with the emergence of surplus farm products in the EC during the past decade, the inclination of politicians and bureaucrats is to 'do something' rather than to 'undo something' (Winters 1987). So, rather than reduce domestic-to-border price ratios, the tendency is to introduce a quantitative limit on production which maintains existing farmers' incomes and ensures more bureaucrats are needed but reduces the visibility of the policy and prevents potential newcomers from enjoying the benefits of protection (Tyers 1990a).

There is, however, the possibility that, with the decline in the proportion of employment (and hence votes) and of GDP from farming and agro-industrial firms, the rightward shift in the *aggregate* demand in the political marketplace for farm support policies will slow down (Hillman 1982; Cassing and Hillman 1986). In addition, the downward movement of the supply curve in Figure 3.1, which represents the declining marginal political costs of providing such policies, could eventually be reversed.

There are at least three reasons for expecting such a reversal. One is that, where the continuation of high domestic food prices eventually generates an exportable surplus of agricultural products (which can be disposed of in international markets only with the help of explicit subsidies, as in the European Community), there tends to be much more opposition to continued farm support than where the support is in the more covert form of import restrictions alone. A second and related reason is that, once export subsidies are used, the food security justification for further assistance to agriculture looks hollow and has prompted traditional agricultural exporting countries to intensify their commercial diplomatic pressure for reform by such countries, using the threat of retaliatory trade restrictions. A third reason is that the high food prices themselves encourage farmers in protected countries to use greater volumes of chemical fertilizers, pesticides and water than would otherwise be the case (see Table 9.2, Anderson (in press) and Young (1988)). The consequent adverse effect on the environment, especially in densely populated countries, reduces the preparedness of urban people to continue to tolerate agricultural price supports.[4]

The prospects for reform of agricultural protection policies have been further enhanced by the publication of numerous empirical studies of the changing extent of agricultural protection (see, for example, Mabbs–Zeno *et al.* 1988 and OECD 1990a). The hidden costs and adverse distributional implications of agricultural policies have been the focus of a number of other studies. Apart from the present volume, the latter includes a number of studies by the US Department of Agriculture which use the SWOPSIM model (Roningen 1986), a study by the International Institute for Applied Systems Analysis (Parikh *et al.* 1988), and the studies based on the OECD's trade mandate model (OECD 1987). These and other quantitative studies are increasing the transparency of current policies, which lowers the cost of information for domestic consumers, domestic producers of non-agricultural tradable products, and for food

Table 9.2: Agricultural producer subsidy equivalent and use of fertilizer per hectare, various industrial countries, 1979-85

	Producer subsidy equivalent (%) 1979-85	Fertilizer use (kg per hectare of arable land and permanent crops, 1985)
Australia	11	24
New Zealand	20	31
United States	30	94
Canada	35	50
Austria	36	255
European Community-10	39	303
Sweden	46	141
Finland	62	210
Japan	68	430
Switzerland	71	436
Norway	73	276

Source: OECD (1990a); and Food and Agriculture Organisation, *Fertiliser Yearbook 1986*, Rome.

exporters abroad in whose interest it is to oppose such policies (Spriggs 1990). The so-called Cairns Group of 14 lightly subsidizing, agricultural exporting countries have, in particular benefitted from this information in their efforts to obtain a reformist outcome for agriculture from the Uruguay Round of multilateral trade negotiations.

Finally, the increasing globalization of firms in the manufacturing and services sectors is ensuring that there is a growing lobby in industrial countries for outward-oriented trade policies and a declining tolerance of protectionist policies. This trend is being encouraged by the '301' provisions in the trade policy of the United States, whereby countries that restrict entry for some US export items run the risk of having US imports of other products from that country curtailed in retaliation. While we do not favour bilateral actions in general, that type of threat was instrumental in opening the Japanese market for beef and citrus in the late 1980s, and for ensuring that agriculture remained high on the agenda of the Uruguay Round.

9.5   Areas for further research

Among the many fruitful areas for further research, two in particular are worth mentioning by way of conclusion. One is to improve our understanding of the way the political market for agricultural (and other) policies works. The more we understand the policy-making process, the better we will be at including policy endogenously in empirical models of food and other markets and the better equipped we will be to suggest politically feasible but economically superior policy instruments for achieving society's objectives. A start has been made by researchers using policy preference functions to explore the political attractiveness of various farm policy instruments for the EC (see, for example, Rausser and de Gorter 1989; Tyers 1990a), but there is scope for a great deal more work in this area. There is also much to be gained from developing general equilibrium approaches to political economy, building on the work of Magee, Brock and Young (1989), as well as from exploring at a finer level of analysis such questions as why the dairy industry is so highly protected in both rich and poor countries.

Secondly, there is a great deal of scope for improving current models of world food markets. Our model, for example, could be enhanced by adding more sectors (other agriculture, other tradables, and non-tradables). It would then be able to capture basic intersectoral effects of policy and structural changes as well as allowing the real exchange rate for each country (the price of tradables relative to non-tradables) to be determined endogenously. And, like all models, it would benefit from further econometric work aimed at providing better estimates of its underlying parameters. In addition, the new generations of computable general equilibrium models, which can incorporate the realities of economies of scale and imperfect competition, now provide the potential for even more sophisticated analysis of agricultural and other policies.

But that is all for another day.

Notes to Chapter 9

[1] The industrial countries could form the 'critical mass' necessary to attract other countries to agricultural reforms along the lines suggested in Chapter 3 (Section 3.3), and by Runge *et al.* (1989).

2 For evidence on the high rate of return from agricultural research investments in developing countries, see, for example, Ruttan (1982).

3 That flexibility is reflected in the comparatively high price elasticities in international food trade. For estimates of those elasticities, see for example Carter (1988). The elasticities implicit in our model of world food markets are reported in our chapter in the Carter volume as well as in Tyers and Anderson (1989), which includes estimates for country groups, such as Western Europe and the Cairns Group.

4 An offsetting effect of increasing environmental awareness among consumers is the heightened concern in industrial countries about food safety. Uncertainty about chemical residues in food, as well as hygiene in food processing operations, is being used by farm lobby groups to scare consumers away from purchasing foreign food, particularly from Eastern Europe and developing countries. While information on the safety of different foods remains costly to obtain, this factor may even lead to import prohibitions on certain foods.

APPENDICES

Appendix 1   Algebra of the World Food Model and its Solution Algorithm

Quantity and price equations of the model

The equations are given for the dynamic version of the model described in Chapter 5 but, where the static version uses a different (generally simpler) formulation, the latter is presented at the end of each subsection.

The production equations are an exponential version of the Nerlovian partial adjustment model, expressed in structural form. q^T is the exogenous trend in production, due to extensification and cost-reducing technical change. The target output level of commodity i in country k is

$$q^*_{ikt} = q^T_{ikt} \prod_j \left\{ \left(\frac{P_{jkt}}{\bar{P}_{jk0}}\right)^{b_{0ijk}} \left(\frac{P_{jkt-1}}{\bar{P}_{jk0}}\right)^{b_{1ijk}} \left(\frac{P_{jkt-2}}{\bar{P}_{jk0}}\right)^{b_{2ijk}} \right\} \qquad (A1.1)$$

Partial adjustment to target output level is given by

$$q_{ikt} = q^T_{ikt} \left(\frac{q_{ikt-1}}{q^T_{ikt}}\right) \left(\frac{q^*_{ikt}}{q^T_{ikt}} \frac{q_{ikt-1}}{q^T_{ikt-1}}\right)^{\delta_{ik}} e^{\epsilon_{ikt}} \qquad (A1.2)$$

The production trend is

$$q^T_{ikt} = q^T_{ik0} (1-\mu^P_{ikt}) e^{g_{ik}t}, \qquad (A1.3)$$

where μ^P_{ikt} is the fraction by which output is reduced by set-aside policy and g_{ik} is the growth rate due to extensification and cost-reducing technical change. Random production disturbances are distributed normally

$$\epsilon_{kt} \sim N(0, U_k). \qquad (A1.4)$$

Prices faced by producers are

$$P_{jkt} = \begin{cases} p_{jkt}^P & \text{where j is a production substitute.} \\ p_{jkt}^C & \text{where i is a livestock product and} \\ & \text{j is an animal feed.} \end{cases} \tag{A1.5}$$

In the static version of the model, equation (A1.2) becomes

$$q_{ikt} = q_{ikt}^* \quad (\delta_{ik} = 1.0, \epsilon_{kt} = 0). \tag{A1.6}$$

Consumption

Direct consumption and consumption as animal feed are accounted for by

$$c_{ikt} = c_{ikt}^D + c_{ikt}^F \tag{A1.7}$$

Where direct consumption is given by

$$c_{ikt}^D = c_{ikt}^{TD} \prod_j \left(\frac{p_{jkt}^C}{\overline{P}_{jk0}^C} \right)^{a_{ijk}} \tag{A1.8}$$

and population and income effects are accounted for by the following direct consumption shifter:

$$c_{ikt}^{TD} = c_{ik0}^{TD} \left(\frac{N_{kt}}{N_{k0}} \right) \left(\frac{y_{kt}}{y_{k0}} \right)^{\eta_{ik}}. \tag{A1.9}$$

Consumption of commodity j as animal feed is related to the output of livestock product i via a fixed input-output coefficient, α_{ij}, and an exogenous time-dependent feed intensity, β_{ikt}, as follows:

$$c_{jkt}^F = \sum_i \alpha_{ji} \beta_{ikt} q_{ikt}^S \tag{A1.10}$$

where q^S is the steady-state livestock output given the animal population in year t. This is formulated in the dynamic version as follows. Over-trend production is assumed to run down livestock populations in the short run. Under-trend production builds them up. Thus, q^S is approximated by a moving average of production levels which is adjusted for short-run deviations from trend in the following way

$$q_{ikt}^S = \bar{q}_{ikt} [1 + \tau_{0ik} (\frac{q_{ikt}}{\bar{q}_{ikt}} - 1) + \tau_{1ik} (\frac{q_{ikt-1}}{\bar{q}_{ikt-1}} - 1)$$

$$+ \tau_{2ik}(\frac{q_{ikt-2}}{\bar{q}_{ikt-2}} - 1)]. \tag{A1.11}$$

Adjustments depend on short-run livestock population changes. Their direction and phasing are related to the livestock output response to a change in the price of feed j. The fraction of this total response in the vth year

$$\tau_{vik} = - \left(\frac{b_{vijk}}{b_{0ijk} + b_{1ijk} + b_{2ijk}}\right) \tag{A1.12}$$

The moving average spans three years and is adjusted for exogenous production shifters as follows

$$\bar{q}_{ikt} = \frac{1}{3}(q_{ikt} + q_{ikt-1} \frac{q_{ikt}^T}{q_{ikt-1}^T} + q_{ikt-2} \frac{q_{ikt}^T}{q_{ikt-2}^T}) \tag{A1.13}$$

In the static version

$$q_{ikt}^S = q_{ikt}. \tag{A1.14}$$

The total consumption shifter is then given by

$$c_{jkt}^T = c_{jkt}^{TD} + \sum_i \alpha_{ji} \beta_{ikt} q_{ikt}^T \tag{A1.15}$$

Closing stocks

Closing stocks each year are determined by

$$\frac{S_{ikt}}{z_{ikt}} = \pi_{ik} [p_{ikt+1}^S - (1 + r_k)p_{ikt}^S - \theta_{ik} \frac{S_{ikt}}{\bar{S}_{ikt}}]$$

$$+ \psi_{ik} \frac{q_{ikt} + S_{ikt-1} - \bar{q}_{ikt} - \bar{S}_{ikt}}{z_{ikt}} + \omega_{ik} (1 + \mu_{ikt}^s) \tag{A1.16}$$

where the first term is expected profits from stockholding, the second is the quantity trigger and the third is a constant term subject to exogenous manipulation through μ^s to reflect changes in the average level of public stocks.

The quantity shifter is

$$z_{ikt} = \begin{cases} \bar{q}_{ikt'} & \bar{q}_{ikt} > \bar{c}_{ikt} \\ \bar{c}_{ikt'} & \bar{q}_{ikt} < \bar{c}_{ikt} \end{cases} \tag{A1.17}$$

The consumption moving average, adjusted for exogenous trends by the total consumption shifter (equation A1.15) is

$$\bar{c}_{ikt} = \frac{1}{3}\left(c_{ikt} + c_{ikt-1}\frac{c_{ikt}^T}{c_{ikt-1}^T} + c_{ikt-2}\frac{c_{ikt}^T}{c_{ikt-2}^T}\right). \tag{A1.18}$$

The expected stockholder price in year $t + 1$ is

$$p_{ikt+1}^S = \frac{1}{4}\left(p_{ikt}^S + p_{ikt-1}^S + p_{ikt-2}^S + p_{ikt-3}^S\right). \tag{A1.19}$$

The actual stockholder price in year t is

$$p_{ikt}^S = \begin{cases} p_{ikt}^C \text{ where stocks are traded domestically.} \\ p_{ikt}^B \text{ where stocks are traded at the border.} \end{cases} \tag{A1.20}$$

The stock-level moving average, adjusted for changes in quantity shifter z, is given by

$$\bar{s}_{ikt} = \frac{1}{3}\left(s_{ikt} + s_{ikt-1}\frac{z_{ikt}}{z_{ikt-1}} + s_{ikt-2}\frac{z_{ikt}}{z_{ikt-2}}\right). \tag{A1.21}$$

In the static version of the model,

$$s_{ikt} = w_{ik}\,z_{ikt} \tag{A1.22}$$

and the static quantity shifter is

$$z_{ikt} = \begin{matrix} q_{ikt}\,, & q_{ikt} > c_{ikt}\,, \\ c_{ikt}\,, & q_{ikt} < c_{ikt}\,. \end{matrix} \tag{A1.23}$$

Price transmission

The dynamic price transmission equations relate the domestic producer and consumer prices to the corresponding border prices. They are, like the production equations, based on an exponential lagged adjustment model. When expressed in reduced form, domestic consumer prices are as follows

$$p_{ikt}^C = \rho_{ikt}^C\,\bar{P}_{ik0}^B \left(\frac{p_{ikt-1}^C}{p_{ikt-1}^C\bar{P}_{ik0}^B}\right)^{(1-\frac{\phi_{ikt}^{CSR}}{\phi_{ikt}^{CLR}})} \left(\frac{P_{it}}{\bar{P}_{i0}}\right)^{\phi_{ikt}^{CSR}}. \tag{A1.24}$$

In the static version they take the form

$$p_{ikt}^C = \rho_{ikt}^C\,\bar{P}_{ik0}^B \left(\frac{P_{it}}{\bar{P}_{i0}}\right)^{\phi_{ikt}^{CLR}} \tag{A1.25}$$

Domestic producer prices are given in the dynamic version by

$$P^P_{ikt} = \rho^P_{ikt}\, \bar{P}^B_{ik0} \left(\frac{P^P_{ikt-1}}{P^P_{ikt-1}\bar{P}^B_{ik0}}\right)^{(1-\frac{\phi^{PSR}_{ikt}}{\phi^{PLR}_{ikt}})} \left(\frac{P_{it}}{\bar{P}_{i0}}\right)^{\phi^{PSR}_{ikt}}, \tag{A1.26}$$

while in the static version they take the form

$$P^P_{ikt} = \rho^P_{ikt}\, \bar{P}^B_{ik0} \left(\frac{P_{it}}{\bar{P}_{i0}}\right)^{\phi^{PLR}_{ikt}}, \tag{A1.27}$$

where the border prices, P^B, are functions of the international indicator prices, P, and exogenous real exchange rates and trade cost factors:

$$P^B_{ikt} = h_{ik}\, P_{it}/x_{kt} \tag{A1.28}$$

The base period border price is

$$\bar{P}^B_{ik0} = h_{ik}\, \bar{P}_{i0}/\bar{x}_{k0}. \tag{A1.29}$$

Excess demand

At the level of country k, excess demand for commodity i is

$$m_{ikt} = c_{ikt} + s_{ikt} - q_{ikt} - s_{ikt-1}. \tag{A1.30}$$

Global market clearing condition

The condition for all markets to clear is then simply Walra's Law: that there be no global excess demands

$$\sum_{k}^{n} m_{ikt} = 0. \tag{A1.31}$$

Nomenclature

Indices

i,j	Commodity counters.
k	Counter for countries and country groups.
v	Counter for years of lag in production response.
t	Time.

Quantities

q_{ikt}	Production of commodity i in country k and year t.
q_{ikt}^T	Production trend. This would be the path of production in the absence of producer price changes.
q_{ikt}^S	Livestock output which would take place in a steady state with the livestock numbers actually prevailing in year t.
c_{ikt}	Consumption of commodity i in country k and year t.
c_{ikt}^D	Direct consumption.
c_{ikt}^F	Consumption as animal feed.
c_{ikt}^{TD}	Direct consumption shifter. This would be the trend of direct consumption in the absence of consumer price changes.
c_{ikt}^T	Total consumption shifter.
m_{ikt}	Excess demand for commodity i in country k and year t.
s_{ikt}	Closing stock of commodity i in country k and year t.
ϵ_{ikt}	Proportional random production disturbance.
U_k	Variance-covariance matrix of random production disturbances across commodities in country k.

Prices

p_{ikt}	Domestic price of commodity i in country k and year t. This price is used in equation (A1.1). Equation (A1.5) indicates where a producer or consumer price is implied.
$\bar{p}_{ik0}$	Average domestic price in the base period, 1980–82, to correspond with p_{ikt}.
p_{ikt}^S	Price at which stocks are traded. Equation (A1.20) indicates where this is the domestic consumer price and where it is the border price.
P_{ikt}^B	The border price of i in country k.
P_{it}	International indicator price—standard trading price of commodity i in year t.
$\bar{P}_{i0}$	Base period (1980–82) international indicator price. Based on f.o.b. export prices at the major ports in Thailand (rice), Canada (wheat), USA (maize, pork and poultry), Australia (beef), New Zealand (milk) and the Caribbean (sugar).

Parameters (constants)

b_{vijk} The elasticity of *target* production of commodity i with respect to the price of j in country k. The subscript v indicates the length of response lag; v=0: less than one year; v=1: one year; v=2: two years.

δ_{ik} The partial adjustment elasticity for the production of commodity i in country k.

g_{ik} The growth rate in the trend of production of commodity i in country k which would be sustained with constant real producer prices.

a_{ijk} The elasticity of direct demand for commodity i with respect to the consumer price of j.

η_{ik} The income elasticity of demand for commodity i in country k.

α_{ij} Input-output coefficient: the quantity of commodity i used in the production of one unit of commodity j. This is assumed to be invariant across countries in the grainfed components of livestock sectors.

β_{ikt} The fraction of the production of livestock product i which is grainfed in country k and year t.

τ_{vik} For livestock products, this parameter measures the fraction of the total *target* supply response which occurs v years after the price change.

r_k The real rate of interest in country k.

θ_{ik} Steady-state marginal cost of storage of commodity i in country k.

π_{ik} The response of closing stocks of commodity i to expected speculative storage profits in country k.

ψ_{ik} The response of closing stocks to the carry-in level of commodity i in country k.

ω_{ik} The steady-state level of working stocks of commodity i, as a proportion of trend consumption in importers and of production in exporters.

h_{ik} The base-period ratio of the border price of commodity i in country k, $\bar{P}^B_{ik0}$ to the standard or indicator international price, $\bar{P}_{i0}$. These divergences reflect quality differences, freight costs and the pattern of concessional sales, all of which are assumed to remain constant.

Exogenously projected variables

N_{kt} The population of country k in year t.

y_{kt} National income per capita in country k in year t.

x_{kt} The real exchange rate in US dollars per unit of local currency.

Policy parameters

ρ_{ikt}^{P} The target nominal protection coefficient for producers of commodity i in country k. This can be changed through time exogenously.

ρ_{ikt}^{C} The corresponding ratio indicating the degree to which consumer prices are distorted by government policy.

ϕ_{ikt}^{PSR} The short-run elasticity of price transmission for the producer price of i in country k. This parameter may also be adjusted along some exogenous time-path.

ϕ_{ikt}^{PLR} The corresponding long-run elasticity of price transmission for producer prices of i in country k.

ϕ_{ikt}^{CSR} The short-run elasticity of price transmission for the consumer price of i in country k.

ϕ_{ikt}^{CLR} The corresponding long-run elasticity of price transmission for consumer prices of commodity i in country k.

μ_{ikt}^{P} The fraction by which set-aside policies shift the supply curve of commodity i in country k to the left.

μ_{ikt}^{S} The fraction by which the mean level of stocks departs from its base period value as a consequence of changes in government-held stocks.

The solution algorithm

The objective is to derive a set of world indicator prices at which all domestic markets and world markets for each commodity will clear to within an acceptable tolerance. That is, global excess demand should be acceptably near to zero (equations A1.30 and A1.31). This is achieved using iterative Walrasian adjustment. In any year, world indicator prices are first set at their values in the previous period. From equations (A1.1) through (A1.30) global excess demands are calculated:

$$dm_{it} = \sum_k m_{ikt}.$$ (A1.32)

These global excess demands are acceptable if all meet the following criteria:

$$dm_{it} \leq 0.0001 \, Q_{it} \qquad \text{for all } i, t$$ (A1.33)

where

$$Q_{it} = \sum_k q^T_{ikt}.$$ (A1.34)

If, however, any one or more markets have unacceptably large excess demands, world indicator prices are adjusted as follows:

$$P^{New}_t = P^{Old}_t (1 - E^{-1}u)$$ (A1.35)

where

$$u = (\frac{dm_{it}}{Q_{it}}, \ldots, \frac{dm_{nt}}{Q_{nt}})$$ (A1.36)

and $E = [e_{ij}]$ is a matrix of global excess demand elasticities. The negative sign in equation (A1.35) is required to offset the behavioural tendency of excess demand to increase as prices decline. Here, positive excess demand must induce higher market prices to bring the market into clearance.

Approximate values for the global excess demand elasticities, $[e_{ij}]$, can be derived from the parameters of the model. Since they depend on policy parameters, and most especially on the price transmission elasticities, the efficiency of the algorithm is greatly improved if they are newly calculated for each solution in which these parameters deviate from their reference values.

From the new set of world indicator prices, new domestic prices can be calculated using the price transmission equations (A.24) through (A.29). With these known, excess demands for each country and commodity are then derived and new estimates made of global excess demands. This procedure is repeated until excess demands are acceptably small. The model rarely takes more than four iterations to clear all world markets to within 0.0001 of global supply, even where random production disturbances are large.

Derivation of the global excess demand elasticities

These elasticities must embody all quantity adjustments to price changes. They are formulated with total global production as a common quantity base.

$$e_{ij} = \frac{dm_i}{Q_i} \Big/ \frac{dP_j}{P_j} \tag{A1.37}$$

where dP_j is $P_j^{Old} - P_j^{New}$ (dropping the time subscript for simplicity of exposition) and Q_i is global production of commodity i. Note that $e_{ij} < 0$ where i=j.

We present here a reliable analytical approximation to the elements of the matrix $[e_{ij}]$, based on the structural equations and parameters of the model. First, we seek an expression for the adjustment in global excess demand dm_i, in terms of changes in prices. This adjustment is simply the sum of the adjustments made in the countries, k:

$$dm_i = \sum_k \{dc_{ik}^D + dc_{ik}^F - dq_{ik} + ds_{ik}\} \tag{A1.38}$$

The first term is the adjustment in direct demand, the second is that in feed demand, the third is that in production and the final term is the adjustment in stock levels. It is convenient to express each of these terms as functions of domestic prices in country k. The direct consumption adjustment is readily derived from the differentiation of equation (A.8) as

$$dc_{ik}^D = c_{ik}^D \sum_j a_{ijk} \frac{dp_{jk}^C}{p_{jk}^C} \tag{A1.39}$$

The corresponding adjustments in feed demand, production and stock levels depend on the length of run. Here we consider three extreme cases: adjustment in the same year, after one year, and in the long run.

(i) Adjustment in the same year

The relationship between feed demand and livestock production is based in the model on fixed input-output coefficients which link that demand to steady-state livestock output, as is specified in equations (A1.10) and (A1.11). Taking derivatives of the terms in these equations and in (A1.1) and (A1.2), which depend on prices in the current year, and summing over the feed consuming sectors, n, we obtain the following expression:

$$dc_{ik}^F = \sum_n \alpha_{in} \, \beta_{nk} \, \tau_{0nk} \, q_{nk} \, \delta_{nk} \sum_j b_{0njk} \frac{dp_{jk}}{p_{jk}} \tag{A1.40}$$

The prices in this equation are consumer prices where commodity j is a livestock feed and producer prices where it is a livestock product (see equation A1.5).

The corresponding production adjustment is derived in the same way, from equations (A1.1) and (A1.2):

$$dq_{ik} = q_{ik} \, \delta_{ik} \sum_j b_{0ijk} \frac{dp_{ik}}{p_{jk}} \tag{A1.41}$$

where the same rule applies regarding the prices in the final term (equation A1.5).

The stock level adjustment requires some manipulation. The quantity held in storage is given by equation (A1.16). This equation has the level of stocks on both sides, however, since this level affects the physical cost of storage and hence the profitability of holding stocks. We first correct this

$$s_{ikt} \left(1 + \frac{\pi_{ik}\theta_{ik}z_{ikt}}{\bar{s}_{ikt}}\right) = \pi_{ik} \, z_{ikt} \, [p_{ikt+1}^S - (1 + r_k) \, p_{ikt}^S]$$

$$+ \, \psi_{ik} \, [q_{ikt} + s_{ikt-1} - \bar{q}_{ikt} - \bar{s}_{ikt}] + w_{ik} \, z_{ikt}. \tag{A1.42}$$

In practice, the prices facing stockholders, p_{ikt}^S, are in some instances domestic consumer prices and in others border prices. To simplify exposition, we consider only the case where $p_{ikt}^S = p_{ikt}^C$. Since our aim is to approximate the global excess demand elasticities, it is convenient to ignore the indirect dependence of z_{ikt}, $\bar{q}_{ikt}$ and $\bar{s}_{ikt}$ on current period prices. Thus, noting equation (A1.19) and again dropping the time subscript, we have the approximate total derivative:

$$ds_{ik} \approx \left(\frac{\bar{s}_{ik}}{\bar{s}_{ik} + \pi_{ik} \, \theta_{ik} \, z_{ik}}\right) [\psi_{ik} \, dq_{ik} - \pi_{ik} \, z_{ik} \, (\tfrac{3}{4} + r_k) \, dp_{ik}^C]. \tag{A1.43}$$

Replacing dp_{ik}^C with $\bar{p}_{ik0} \frac{dp_{ik}^C}{p_{ik}^C}$, and substituting for dq_{ik} from equation (A1.41), equation (A1.43) is reduced to an expression in the proportional changes in producer and consumer prices.

If we then set c_{ik}^D, q_{ik}, z_{ik} equal to the appropriate quantity shifters ($\bar{c}_{ik}$ or $\bar{q}_{ik}$) and $\bar{s}_{ik}$ to $w_{ik} z_{ik}$ (the steady-state storage level), equations (A1.39), (A1.40), (A1.41) and (A1.43) can be combined in equation (A1.37) to yield the following expression for the adjustment in the overall excess demand of country k in terms of price changes:

$$dm_{ik} \approx \sum_j [A_{jk} \frac{dp_{jk}^C}{p_{jk}^C} + B_{jk} \frac{dp_{jk}^P}{p_{jk}^P}] \tag{A1.44}$$

where A_{jk} and B_{jk} are constants in any given year.

An expression in international prices is needed, however. This is achieved by noting, from equations (A1.24) and (A1.26)

$$\frac{dp_{jk}^C}{p_{jk}^C} = \phi_{jk}^{CSR} \frac{dP_j}{P_j}, \quad \frac{dp_{jk}^P}{p_{jk}^P} = \phi_{jk}^{PSR} \frac{dP_j}{P_j} \tag{A1.45}$$

where ϕ_{jk}^{CSR} and ϕ_{jk}^{PSR} are the same-year price transmission elasticities. The adjustment in global excess demand is then:

$$dm_i = \sum_j \frac{dP_j}{P_j} \sum_k (\phi_{jk}^{CSR} A_{jk} + \phi_{jk}^{PSR} B_{jk}). \tag{A1.46}$$

From equation (A.37), the global excess demand elasticity is then:

$$e_{ij} = \frac{\sum_k (\phi_{jk}^{CSR} A_{jk} + \phi_{jk}^{PSR} B_{jk})}{Q_i}. \tag{A1.47}$$

(ii) Adjustment after one year

In this case the terms in equation (A1.38) depend on the sum of other same-year and the one-year lagged adjustments in consumption, production and stocks. It is convenient to begin with the production adjustment. For equations (A1.1) and (A1.2) it is possible to eliminate target production and assemble a reduced form expression for q_{ik} in terms of lagged production and prices. From repeated applications of this reduced form it is evident that the one-year production response is:

$$dq_{ik}^1 = q_{ik} \delta_{ik} \sum_j [(2 - \delta_i) b_{0ijk} + b_{1ijk}] \frac{dp_{jk}}{p_{jk}} \tag{A1.48}$$

where the prices are again those determined in equation (A1.5).

The response of feed demand after one year then depends on the adjustment of steady-state livestock production to changes in price. In this case, two terms in equation (A1.11) are active and the feed consumption adjustment is:

$$dc_{ik}^F = \sum_n \alpha_{in} \, \beta_{nk} \, (\tau_{0nk} \, dq_{nk}^0 + \tau_{1nk} \, dq_{nk}^1) \tag{A1.49}$$

where dq_{nk}^0 is the same-year production adjustment, given in equation (A1.41), and dq_{nk}^1 is the one-year adjustment, given in equation (A1.48).

The one-year storage adjustment can be derived from the application of a price change to equation (A1.42) in successive time periods. Similar approximations to those underlying equation (A1.43) are required. The result is:

$$ds_{ik} \approx \lambda_{ik} \, \psi_{ik} \, dq_{ik}^1 - \lambda_{ik} \, \pi_{ik} \, z_{ik} \, [r_k + \frac{1}{2} + \lambda_{ik} \, \psi_{ik} \, (r_k + \frac{3}{4})] \bar{p}_{ik0} \frac{dp_{ik}}{p_{ik}} \tag{A1.50}$$

where, again, the price variable is either a domestic consumer price or a border price, depending which performed best in the econometric analysis. As before, we assume for expository purposes that the domestic consumer price is appropriate.

The adjustment in global overall excess demand can then be formulated in terms of changes in domestic producer and consumer prices, as in equation (A1.44). It remains to link these domestic price changes to changes in international prices. This is readily achieved by applying changes in international prices to equations (A1.24) and (A1.26) in successive years. The result is the formulation of the one-year price transmission elasticity in terms of the corresponding same-year and long-run elasticities, which are both parameters in the model. Since the expression is identical for domestic consumer and producer prices, we drop the P and C superscripts:

$$\frac{dp_{jk}}{p_{jk}} = \phi_{jk}^{SR} \, (2 - \frac{\phi_{jk}^{SR}}{\phi_{jk}^{LR}}) \, \frac{dP_j}{P_j} \tag{A1.51}$$

(iii) Adjustment in the long run

In this case, the global excess demand elasticities embody all long-run quantity adjustments to price changes. Again, equations (A1.37) and (A1.38) apply, except that changes in stock levels in the long run do not effect annual excess demand. Accordingly, the third term in (A1.37) is dropped.

The changes in direct and feed consumption are now:

$$dc_{ik}^D = c_{ik}^D \sum_j a_{ijk} \frac{dp_{jk}^C}{p_{jk}^C} \qquad (A1.52)$$

$$dc_{ik}^F = \sum_n \alpha_{in} \beta_{nk} q_{nk} \sum_j (b_{0njk} + b_{1njk} + b_{2njk}) \frac{dp_{jk}}{p_{jk}}. \qquad (A1.53)$$

Note that long-run supply elasticities are used in the second term—the sum of the lagged supply response elasticities of equation (A1.1). These same elasticities are the basis for the change in production:

$$dq_{ik} = q_{ik} \sum_j (b_{0ijk} + b_{1ijk} + b_{2ijk}) \frac{dp_{jk}}{p_{jk}}. \qquad (A1.54)$$

Substituting (A1.52), (A1.53) and (A1.54) into (A1.38), and setting ds_{ik} to zero, we derive an expression as equation (A1.44). The expression for the long-run demand elasticity then differs from equation (A1.47) only in that the constants A_{jk} and B_{jk} differ and the price transmission elasticities which appear are the long run values, ϕ_{jk}^{CLR} and ϕ_{jk}^{PLR}.

Welfare equations of the model

Consumption and production with sequential price changes

In the case where only the first j consumer prices change and the remaining consumer and all producer prices hold their base period values, the level of direct consumption of commodity i in year t is:

$$c_{ijt}^{DC} = c_i^D (p_{1t}^C, \ldots, p_{jt}^C, \bar{p}_{j+1}^C, \ldots, \bar{p}_n^C) \qquad (A1.55)$$

where $\bar{p}^C$ is the base period average consumer price.

The corresponding long-run level of production is

$$q_{ijt}^C = q_i (q_{1t}^C, \ldots, p_{jt}^C, \bar{p}_{j+1}^C, \ldots, \bar{p}_n^C, \bar{p}_1^P, \ldots, \bar{p}_n^P) \qquad (A1.56)$$

where $\bar{p}^P$ is the base period average producer price.

Then, when all consumer prices and the first j producer prices change, the level of production is:

$$q^P_{ijt} = q_i(p^C_{1t}, \ldots, p^C_{nt}, p^P_{it}, \ldots, p^P_{jt}, \bar{p}^P_{j+1}, \ldots, \bar{p}^P_n).$$ (A1.57)

Equations (A1.56) and (A1.57) are based on the substitution of equations (A1.1) into equation (A1.6). That is, the long-run static supply relationship is used to simplify the calculation. This does cause some error in the welfare analysis associated with results from the dynamic version of the model, when supply has only partially adjusted to price shocks. The error is small, however. In any case, the bulk of the welfare analysis reported is based on the static version of the model and hence is unaffected by this assumption.

The consumer welfare measure

From Figure 5.4 in the text, the appropriate measure of consumer welfare is the area BEGF. The prices at points A and B emerge as endogenous variables from the model solution and the quantities are readily derived from equation (A1.55). To derive the welfare change it is necessary, in addition, to calculate consumption at point E, $c^U_{ii\text{-}lt}$. This is done by drawing the compensated demand curve through B as follows:

$$c^U_{ii\text{-}lt} = c^{DC}_{iit} (\bar{p}^C_i / p^C_{it})^{a^U_{ii}}$$ (A1.58)

where the compensated own-price elasticity of demand (defined as negative) is $a^U_{ii} = a_{ii} + \zeta_i \, \eta_i$, with ζ_i the expenditure share and η_i the income elasticity of demand. The equivalent variation in income is then obtained by integration as:

$$V^C_{it} = \begin{cases} K \, [\, (p^C_{it})^{a^U_{ii}+1} - (\bar{p}^C_i)^{a^U_{ii}+1}] \, / \, (a^U_{ii} + 1) & a^U_{ii} \neq -1 \\[2ex] K \, [\, \log(p^C_{it}) - \log(\bar{p}^C_i)] & a^U_{ii} = -1 \end{cases}$$ (A1.59)

where $K = c^U_{ii\text{-}lt}(\bar{p}^C_i)^{-a^U_{ii}}$.

The total benefit, V^C_t, to consumers from the departures of all consumer prices from base period values is then the sum over all commodities i of V^C_{it}. Where welfare impacts are based on multiple stochastic simulations of the dynamic version of the model, V^C_{it} refers to the expected value of the right hand side of equation (A1.59).

The producer welfare measures

While the sequence in which the changes of prices are introduced in the estimation of producer welfare effects is the same as that for the consumer effects, two quantity shifts are also involved. We begin with the effects of changes to land set-aside restrictions, applying them to supply curves unaffected by deviations of prices from base period values. The effect on producer welfare due to random disturbances in output is added last. A corresponding schematic is provided as Figure 5.5 of the main text.

A land set-aside policy in the market for commodity i is assumed to affect the supply curve which would apply in year t so as to reduce the output of i by the fraction μ_i^P along the length of the supply curve. The effect on producer surplus of relaxing this set-aside restriction is:

$$V_i^{PS} = \frac{1}{2}\,\bar{p}_i^P\,\mu_i^P\,q_{it}^T. \tag{A1.60}$$

Next the effects of consumer price changes are evaluated. Consider the change in the consumer price of commodity j, which may be both directly consumed and fed to animals. The equivalent variation in income in this case is the area under the ordinary derived demand curve, shown in Figure 5.5 (b). As in the case of the consumer welfare measure, this area is obtained by integration as:

$$V_{it}^{PC} = \begin{cases} K\,[\,(p_{jt}^C)^{b_{ij}+1} - (\bar{p}_j^C)^{b_{ij}+1}\,]\,/\,(b_{ij}+1) & b_{ij} \neq -1 \\[2mm] K\,[\,\log(p_{jt}^C) - \log\,(\bar{p}_j^C)\,] & b_{ij} = -1 \end{cases} \tag{A1.61}$$

where $K = \alpha_{ji}\,\beta_{it}\,q_{ij\text{-}1t}^C\,(\bar{p}_i^C)^{-b_{ij}}$. Note the dependence of K on the input-output coefficient α_{ji} and the feed intensity β_{it}. The term b_{ij} is the long-run elasticity of the supply of i to a change in the price of j ($=b_{0ij} + b_{1ij} + b_{2ij}$), and $q_{ij\text{-}1t}^C$ is from equation (A1.56).

The welfare effect of a change in an output price is illustrated in Figure 5.5 (c). Since price changes are introduced in a fixed sequence, the effect of a change in the price of i can be measured in terms of the area shown, assuming that changes in all consumer prices and the first i-1 producer prices have already been accounted for in deriving the supply curve S_2 in the figure. The result is then obtained from integration as:

$$V_{it}^{PP} = K \, [\, (p_{it}^P)^{b_{ii}+1} - (\bar{p}_j^P)^{b_{ii}+1} \,] \, / \, (b_{ii}+1) \tag{A1.62}$$

where $K = q_{ii-1t}^P \, (\bar{p}_i^P)^{-b_{ii}}$, b_{ii} is the long-run elasticity of the supply of i to a change in its own price ($= b_{0ii} + b_{1ii} + b_{2ii}$), and q_{ii-1t}^P is from equation (A1.57).

Finally, we turn to the effect of random production disturbances on producer welfare. These disturbances apply only to the dynamic version of the model. For most commodities, production in year t is assumed to be planned in t–1, based on relative prices in t–1 and previously. Planned production, $\hat{q}_{it}$, is derived directly from equations (A1.1) through (A1.2) of the model, omitting only the effect of the production disturbance ($\epsilon_t = 0$). In large countries, this disturbance affects not only the ultimate level of output but also the output price. The price effect has already been accounted for, however, in the derivation of $V^{PP}{}_i$. It remains only to add the effect of the quantity disturbance on sales revenue, all of which accrues to the producer, since production disturbances are assumed not to alter costs:

$$V_i^{PD} = p_{it}^P \, (q_{it} - \hat{q}_{it}). \tag{A1.63}$$

The total benefit to the producer of commodity i is then:

$$V_{it}^P = V_i^{PS} + V_i^{PC} + V_i^{PP} + V_i^{PD}. \tag{A1.64}$$

As for the consumer welfare measure, where welfare impacts are based on multiple stochastic simulations of the dynamic version of the model, $V^P{}_{it}$ refers to the expected value of the right hand side of equation (A1.64).

Stockholder welfare

The effect on stockholders of a policy change is measured as the average change in profits from holding stocks. These profits have three components: transient income from net sales in year t; the opportunity cost of the asset value of stocks held through year t; and the cost of storing them. In year t of a particular simulation, stock profits are given by:

$$\Gamma_{it}^S = p_{it}^S \, (s_{it-1} - s_{it}) - r \, p_{it}^S \, s_{it} - \frac{1}{2} \, \theta_i \, s_{it}^2 \, / \bar{s}_{it} \tag{A1.65}$$

where r is the real rate of interest and θ_i is the steady state marginal cost of storage. The change in welfare derived from the holding of stocks in commodity i is then the difference in mean profits between a reference and any non-reference simulation, $V_{it}^S = \Delta E\{\Gamma_{it}^S\}$. The welfare analysis supporting static equilibrium solutions omits the transient first term in equation (A1.65).

Effects on government revenue

As indicated in the text, the government is envisaged as the purchaser of domestic output at domestic prices and of net imports at border prices. Its income derives from differences in the prices at which the domestic product and imports are acquired and then sold to consumers or for storage. The net revenue position from these exchanges of commodity i is

$$G_{it} = c_{it}\,p_{it}^C + (s_{it} - s_{it-1})\,p_{it}^S - q_{it}\,p_{it}^P - m_{it}\,P_{it}^B \qquad (A1.66)$$

The change in welfare derived through revenue generation associated with distortions in the market for commodity i is then the difference in the mean revenue derived in year t between a reference and any non-reference simulation, $V_{it}^G = \Delta E\{G_{it}\}$. The welfare analysis supporting static equilibrium solutions omits the transient second term in equation (A1.66).

Aggregate welfare

Net national welfare impacts are all measured as equivalent variations in income associated with departures from a reference model simulation. They can therefore be converted to a common currency and added across groups of agents within and between countries. For a particular country, the net welfare impact is simply the sum over commodities of the measures formulated above, that is,

$$W_t = \sum_i (V_{it}^C + V_{it}^P + V_{it}^S + V_{it}^G) \qquad (A1.67)$$

Appendix 2   Parameters Used in the World Food Model

Central to the effectiveness of the model are the data on quantities produced, consumed, traded and stored and the data on domestic and international prices from which its parameters are estimated. The particular datasets used in our study are available through the International Economic Data Bank at the Australian National University. They are described in full in International Economic Data Bank (1990), which up-dates Tyers and Phillips (1986) and Saxon, Anderson and Tyers (1986) beyond the period covered by our study. Both the quantity and price datasets are hybrids, combining statistics provided on tape by the United Nations Food and Agriculture Organisation and the United States Department of Agriculture with extracts from the publications of numerous government agencies. Our approach to the estimation of parameters from these data and the selection of some parameter values from other studies follows that detailed in Tyers (1984).

The results presented in this volume depend primarily on four sets of parameters based originally on the above data. Values for the parameters are presented in the following tables. They are the price policy parameters (Table A1), the own-price and cross-price elasticities of supply (Tables A2 and A3) and of demand (Tables A4 and A5), the assumed effects of set-aside policies on output in the United States (Table A6) and the projected changes in real exchange rates through the year 2000 (Table A7). Table A10 lists the exogenous projections of population and national income which are used in the model and Table A11 lists the parameters of the stockholding equations. This appendix also includes indices of each country's importance in world food markets (Table A8) and of each country's self-sufficiency in staple food (Table A9).

Table A1: Price policy parameters

	Producer prices			Consumer prices		
	Base period domestic-to-border price ratio, 1980–82	Price transmission elasticity		Base period domestic-to-border price ratio, 1980–82	Price transmission elasticity	
		Short run	Long run		Short run	Long run
Australia						
Rice	1.15	0.62	0.84	1.70	0.23	1.00
Wheat	1.05	0.78	1.00	1.05	0.11	0.63
Coarse grain	1.00	0.69	0.96	1.00	0.69	0.96
Sugar	1.05	0.49	0.54	1.40	0.00	0.00
Dairy	1.30	0.40	0.45	1.40	0.13	0.39
Ruminant meat	1.00	0.73	1.00	1.00	1.00	1.00
Non-ruminant meat	1.00	0.46	0.52	1.00	0.25	0.34
Canada						
Rice	1.00	1.00	1.00	1.00	0.90	0.90
Wheat	1.15	0.68	1.00	1.15	0.68	1.00
Coarse grain	1.00	1.00	1.00	1.00	1.00	1.00
Sugar	1.25	0.07	0.25	1.25	0.12	0.60
Dairy	1.95	0.06	0.40	1.95	0.06	0.40
Ruminant meat	1.10	0.27	0.46	1.10	0.08	0.40
Non-ruminant meat	1.10	0.08	0.40	1.10	0.83	0.85

(continued)

Table A1 *(continued)*

	Producer prices			Consumer prices		
	Base period domestic-to-border price ratio, 1980–82	Price transmission elasticity		Base period domestic-to-border price ratio, 1980–82	Price transmission elasticity	
		Short run	Long run		Short run	Long run
EC-10						
Rice	1.40	0.11	0.46	1.40	0.11	0.22
Wheat	1.40	0.09	0.20	1.45	0.08	0.11
Coarse grain	1.40	0.24	0.58	1.40	0.13	0.26
Sugar	1.50	0.00	0.00	1.50	0.00	0.00
Dairy	1.75	0.08	0.30	1.80	0.08	0.30
Ruminant meat	1.95	0.09	0.14	1.95	0.02	0.04
Non-ruminant meat	1.25	0.12	0.76	1.25	0.62	0.76
EFTA-5						
Rice	1.00	1.00	1.00	1.00	0.30	0.30
Wheat	1.65	0.11	0.79	1.65	0.11	0.79
Coarse grain	1.55	0.15	1.00	1.55	0.15	1.00
Sugar	1.55	0.00	0.00	1.55	0.00	0.00
Dairy	2.45	0.06	0.19	2.45	0.06	0.19
Ruminant meat	2.30	0.01	0.04	2.30	0.01	0.04
Non-ruminant meat	1.40	0.13	0.68	1.40	0.16	0.16

Japan						
Rice	3.35	0.04	0.15	2.90	0.03	0.12
Wheat	3.90	0.20	1.00	1.25	0.06	0.25
Coarse grain	4.30	0.02	0.12	1.25	0.20	1.00
Sugar	3.00	0.01	0.01	2.60	0.01	0.01
Dairy	2.90	0.03	0.08	2.90	0.03	0.08
Ruminant meat	2.80	0.10	0.24	2.80	0.10	0.24
Non-ruminant meat	1.50	0.49	0.63	1.50	0.47	0.86
New Zealand						
Rice	1.00	1.00	1.00	1.00	0.90	0.90
Wheat	1.00	0.20	0.49	1.00	0.20	0.49
Coarse grain	1.00	0.20	0.60	1.00	0.36	0.60
Sugar	1.00	0.60	0.70	1.00	0.50	0.70
Dairy	1.00	1.00	1.00	1.00	1.00	1.00
Ruminant meat	1.00	0.77	0.78	1.00	0.51	0.63
Non-ruminant meat	1.00	0.10	0.20	1.00	0.10	0.20
Spain and Portugal						
Rice	1.15	0.25	0.71	1.15	0.25	0.71
Wheat	1.35	0.18	1.00	1.35	0.18	1.00
Coarse grain	1.30	0.35	0.49	1.30	0.35	0.49
Sugar	1.65	0.06	0.90	1.65	0.07	1.00
Dairy	1.75	0.14	0.41	1.75	0.14	0.41
Ruminant meat	1.65	0.24	0.69	1.65	0.24	0.69
Non-ruminant meat	1.10	0.32	1.00	1.10	0.50	0.50

(continued)

Table A1 *(continued)*

	Producer prices			Consumer prices		
	Base period domestic-to-border price ratio, 1980–82	Price transmission elasticity		Base period domestic-to-border price ratio, 1980–82	Price transmission elasticity	
		Short run	Long run		Short run	Long run
United States						
Rice	1.25	0.30	0.55	1.00	0.71	1.00
Wheat	1.15	1.00	1.00	1.00	1.00	1.00
Coarse grain	1.00	1.00	1.00	1.00	1.00	1.00
Sugar	1.40	0.10	0.48	1.40	0.10	0.48
Dairy	2.00	0.07	0.36	2.00	0.06	0.18
Ruminant meat	1.10	0.60	0.61	1.10	0.21	0.53
Non-ruminant meat	1.00	1.00	1.00	1.00	1.00	1.00
USSR						
Rice	1.05	0.06	0.30	1.05	0.06	0.30
Wheat	0.90	0.05	0.45	0.90	0.05	0.45
Coarse grain	0.95	0.02	0.17	0.95	0.02	0.17
Sugar	1.40	0.02	0.04	1.40	0.02	0.04
Dairy	1.70	0.05	0.13	1.70	0.05	0.13
Ruminant meat	1.10	0.05	0.20	1.10	0.05	0.20
Non-ruminant meat	0.90	0.05	0.20	0.90	0.05	0.20

Other centrally planned Europe						
Rice	1.05	0.06	0.30	1.05	0.06	0.30
Wheat	0.90	0.05	0.45	0.90	0.05	0.45
Coarse grain	0.95	0.02	0.17	0.95	0.02	0.17
Sugar	1.40	0.02	0.04	1.40	0.02	0.04
Dairy	1.70	0.05	0.13	1.70	0.05	0.13
Ruminant meat	1.10	0.05	0.20	1.10	0.05	0.21
Non-ruminant meat	0.90	0.05	0.20	0.90	0.05	0.20
Egypt						
Rice	0.50	0.10	0.50	0.50	0.10	0.50
Wheat	0.60	0.00	0.00	0.60	0.00	0.00
Coarse grain	0.70	0.13	0.20	0.70	0.13	0.20
Sugar	0.65	0.15	0.47	0.65	0.15	0.47
Dairy	1.60	0.09	0.11	1.60	0.09	0.11
Ruminant meat	1.50	0.10	0.17	1.50	0.10	0.17
Non-ruminant meat	1.50	0.01	0.20	1.50	0.01	0.20
Nigeria						
Rice	1.70	0.22	0.52	1.70	0.22	0.52
Wheat	1.95	0.23	0.64	1.95	0.23	0.64
Coarse grain	2.05	0.31	0.53	2.05	0.31	0.53
Sugar	1.50	0.05	0.30	1.50	0.05	0.30
Dairy	2.30	0.34	0.40	2.30	0.34	0.40
Ruminant meat	1.95	0.18	0.42	1.95	0.18	0.42
Non-ruminant meat	1.70	0.40	0.60	1.70	0.40	0.60

(continued)

Table A1 *(continued)*

	Producer prices			Consumer prices		
	Base period domestic-to-border price ratio, 1980–82	Price transmission elasticity		Base period domestic-to-border price ratio, 1980–82	Price transmission elasticity	
		Short run	Long run		Short run	Long run
South Africa						
Rice	1.00	0.70	1.00	1.00	0.70	1.00
Wheat	1.60	0.50	1.00	1.60	0.50	1.00
Coarse grain	1.15	0.90	1.00	1.15	0.90	1.00
Sugar	0.90	0.30	0.50	0.90	0.30	0.50
Dairy	2.05	0.30	0.50	2.05	0.30	0.50
Ruminant meat	1.10	0.80	0.90	1.10	0.80	0.90
Non-ruminant meat	1.00	0.90	0.90	1.00	0.90	0.90
Other sub-Saharan Africa						
Rice	1.00	0.20	0.50	1.00	0.20	0.50
Wheat	1.05	0.20	0.60	1.05	0.20	0.60
Coarse grain	0.95	0.30	0.50	0.95	0.20	0.50
Sugar	0.55	0.15	0.17	0.55	0.15	0.17
Dairy	1.20	0.34	0.40	1.20	0.34	0.40
Ruminant meat	0.75	0.18	0.42	0.75	0.18	0.42
Non-ruminant meat	0.75	0.40	0.60	0.75	0.40	0.60

Other North Africa and Middle East						
Rice	1.20	0.10	0.50	1.20	0.10	0.50
Wheat	1.20	0.00	0.00	1.20	0.00	0.00
Coarse grain	1.20	0.00	0.00	1.20	0.00	0.00
Sugar	1.00	0.15	0.50	1.00	0.15	0.50
Dairy	1.80	0.10	0.25	1.80	0.10	0.25
Ruminant meat	1.00	0.10	0.20	1.00	0.10	0.20
Non-ruminant meat	1.00	0.02	0.20	1.00	0.50	0.50
Bangladesh						
Rice	0.95	0.71	0.74	0.90	0.13	0.19
Wheat	1.00	0.24	1.00	0.90	0.24	1.00
Coarse grain	1.00	0.60	0.85	1.00	0.60	0.85
Sugar	0.60	0.00	0.00	0.60	0.00	0.00
Dairy	1.30	0.13	0.23	1.30	0.08	0.23
Ruminant meat	0.90	0.38	0.60	0.90	0.38	0.60
Non-ruminant meat	0.90	0.30	0.60	0.90	0.50	0.60
China						
Rice	0.85	0.35	0.58	0.80	0.05	0.40
Wheat	1.45	0.44	0.60	1.30	0.05	0.60
Coarse grain	1.15	0.54	0.87	1.10	0.05	0.70
Sugar	1.15	0.19	0.23	1.60	0.05	0.20
Dairy	2.35	0.10	0.16	2.35	0.05	0.12
Ruminant meat	0.70	0.48	0.66	0.70	0.05	0.50
Non-ruminant meat	0.65	0.17	0.25	0.65	0.05	0.22

(continued)

Table A1 *(continued)*

	Producer prices			Consumer prices		
	Base period domestic-to-border price ratio, 1980–82	Price transmission elasticity		Base period domestic-to-border price ratio, 1980–82	Price transmission elasticity	
		Short run	Long run		Short run	Long run
India						
Rice	0.90	0.17	0.26	0.85	0.17	0.26
Wheat	1.00	0.15	0.90	0.95	0.15	0.90
Coarse grain	1.00	0.14	0.80	1.00	0.14	0.80
Sugar	0.80	0.09	0.20	0.80	0.09	0.20
Dairy	1.50	0.15	0.25	1.50	0.15	0.25
Ruminant meat	1.00	0.15	0.40	1.00	0.15	0.40
Non-ruminant meat	1.00	0.15	0.60	1.00	0.15	0.60
Indonesia						
Rice	1.10	0.20	0.60	0.85	0.05	0.40
Wheat	1.00	1.00	1.00	1.50	0.09	1.00
Coarse grain	1.30	0.47	0.94	1.30	0.46	1.00
Sugar	2.65	0.02	0.20	2.65	0.02	0.20
Dairy	1.60	0.05	0.20	1.60	0.05	0.20
Ruminant meat	1.80	0.05	0.40	1.80	0.05	0.40
Non-ruminant meat	2.00	0.05	0.40	2.00	0.20	0.40

Korea						
Rice	2.50	0.00	0.00	2.40	0.00	0.00
Wheat	2.45	0.17	0.35	1.45	0.50	0.10
Coarse grain	2.30	0.14	0.38	1.30	0.14	0.39
Sugar	1.00	1.00	1.00	2.90	0.02	0.20
Dairy	2.95	0.02	0.06	2.95	0.02	0.06
Ruminant meat	3.75	0.07	0.29	3.75	0.07	0.29
Non-ruminant meat	2.50	0.34	0.76	2.50	0.32	1.00
Pakistan						
Rice	0.75	0.31	0.58	0.75	0.11	0.13
Wheat	0.90	0.05	0.07	0.90	0.05	0.07
Coarse grain	0.90	0.52	0.70	0.90	0.40	0.60
Sugar	0.70	0.20	0.40	0.70	0.35	0.39
Dairy	1.65	0.15	0.23	1.65	0.15	0.23
Ruminant meat	1.00	0.13	0.60	1.00	0.13	0.60
Non-ruminant meat	1.00	0.13	0.60	1.00	0.13	0.60
Philippines						
Rice	1.00	0.07	0.15	1.00	0.06	0.08
Wheat	1.00	1.00	1.00	1.00	0.53	0.60
Coarse grain	1.15	0.33	0.69	1.15	0.37	0.50
Sugar	0.80	0.31	0.41	0.80	0.31	0.41
Dairy	1.70	0.01	0.20	1.70	0.01	0.10
Ruminant meat	1.60	0.05	0.20	1.60	0.05	0.14
Non-ruminant meat	1.40	0.08	0.16	1.40	0.08	0.16

(continued)

Table A1 (continued)

	Producer prices			Consumer prices		
	Base period domestic-to-border price ratio, 1980–82	Price transmission elasticity		Base period domestic-to-border price ratio, 1980–82	Price transmission elasticity	
		Short run	Long run		Short run	Long run
Taiwan						
Rice	2.65	0.24	1.00	2.65	0.22	1.00
Wheat	2.10	0.09	0.60	1.00	0.42	1.00
Coarse grain	2.10	0.40	0.43	1.00	0.91	1.00
Sugar	1.00	0.51	0.73	1.00	0.51	0.73
Dairy	2.80	0.01	0.20	2.80	0.01	0.20
Ruminant meat	2.50	0.54	0.93	2.50	0.08	0.62
Non-ruminant meat	1.15	0.43	0.53	1.15	0.20	0.32
Thailand						
Rice	0.90	0.49	0.74	0.90	0.31	0.58
Wheat	1.00	0.10	1.00	1.00	0.40	0.60
Coarse grain	1.00	0.85	1.00	1.00	0.75	0.84
Sugar	1.00	0.02	0.20	1.50	0.02	0.80
Dairy	1.60	0.01	0.20	1.60	0.01	0.20
Ruminant meat	0.95	0.17	0.30	0.95	0.17	0.31
Non-ruminant meat	0.90	0.18	0.50	0.90	0.18	0.50

Other Asia						
Rice	0.75	0.20	0.80	0.75	0.15	0.50
Wheat	0.85	0.05	0.20	0.85	0.05	0.20
Coarse grain	0.95	0.40	0.80	0.95	0.30	0.50
Sugar	0.75	0.20	0.40	0.75	0.20	0.20
Dairy	1.30	0.00	0.00	1.30	0.20	0.20
Ruminant meat	0.90	0.15	0.60	0.90	0.20	0.20
Non-ruminant meat	0.80	0.32	0.60	0.80	0.20	0.20
Argentina						
Rice	0.80	0.56	0.56	0.80	0.56	0.56
Wheat	0.90	0.80	1.00	0.90	0.80	1.00
Coarse grain	0.85	0.70	0.80	0.85	0.70	0.80
Sugar	0.85	0.00	0.00	0.85	0.00	0.00
Dairy	0.85	0.34	0.35	0.85	0.34	0.35
Ruminant meat	0.85	0.58	0.63	0.85	0.77	0.90
Non-ruminant meat	0.90	0.43	0.46	0.90	0.66	0.80
Brazil						
Rice	0.80	0.16	0.46	0.80	0.26	0.32
Wheat	1.05	0.42	0.79	1.05	0.42	0.79
Coarse grain	0.90	0.57	1.00	0.90	0.35	0.42
Sugar	0.75	0.24	0.90	0.75	0.24	0.90
Dairy	1.25	0.54	0.54	1.25	0.54	0.54
Ruminant meat	0.80	0.44	0.60	0.80	0.44	0.60
Non-ruminant meat	0.90	0.72	0.77	0.90	0.72	0.77

(continued)

Table A1 (continued)

	Producer prices			Consumer prices		
	Base period domestic-to-border price ratio, 1980–82	Price transmission elasticity		Base period domestic-to-border price ratio, 1980–82	Price transmission elasticity	
		Short run	Long run		Short run	Long run
Cuba						
Rice	0.80	0.02	0.20	0.80	0.02	0.20
Wheat	0.70	1.00	1.00	0.70	0.00	0.00
Coarse grain	0.80	0.11	0.30	0.80	0.11	0.30
Sugar	0.50	0.00	0.00	1.00	0.00	0.00
Dairy	0.90	0.00	0.00	0.90	0.00	0.00
Ruminant meat	0.60	0.00	0.00	0.60	0.00	0.00
Non-ruminant meat	0.65	0.24	0.24	0.65	0.24	0.24
Mexico						
Rice	0.90	0.37	0.47	0.90	0.90	0.00
Wheat	1.00	0.25	0.61	1.00	0.25	0.61
Coarse grain	1.40	0.31	1.00	0.95	0.21	0.23
Sugar	0.70	0.00	0.00	0.70	0.00	0.00
Dairy	2.35	0.10	0.20	2.35	0.10	0.20
Ruminant meat	1.00	0.13	0.34	1.00	0.13	0.34
Non-ruminant meat	1.20	0.50	0.50	1.20	0.50	0.50

Other Latin America						
Rice	0.90	0.60	0.80	0.90	0.60	0.80
Wheat	1.00	0.50	0.80	1.00	0.50	0.80
Coarse grain	1.00	0.50	0.80	1.00	0.50	0.80
Sugar	0.85	0.07	0.38	0.85	0.24	0.38
Dairy	1.50	0.02	0.20	1.50	0.20	0.30
Ruminant meat	0.90	0.50	0.80	0.90	0.50	0.80
Non-ruminant meat	1.00	0.50	0.80	1.00	0.60	0.90

Table A2: Short-run supply response parameters

	Rice	Wheat	Coarse grain			Sugar	Dairy			Ruminant meat			Non-ruminant meat		
	t=1	t=1	t=1	t=2	t=3	t=1	t=0	t=1	t=2	t=0	t=1	t=2	t=0	t=1	t=2
Australia															
Rice	0.20	-0.09	0.00	0.00		0.00		0.00			0.00			0.00	
Wheat	0.00	0.31	0.00	-0.03		0.00		0.00			-0.04			0.00	
Coarse grain	0.00	-0.10	0.00	0.20		0.00		0.00			0.00			0.00	
Sugar	0.00	0.00	0.00	0.00		0.10		0.00			0.00			0.00	
Dairy	0.00	0.00	0.00	0.00	0.00	0.00	0.00	0.05	0.08	0.00	-0.07	0.08	0.00	0.00	0.00
Ruminant meat	0.00	-0.05	0.00	0.00	0.00	0.00	-0.10	-0.05	0.09	-0.10	0.09	0.16	0.00	0.00	-0.02
Non-ruminant meat	0.00	0.00	0.00	0.00	0.00	0.00	0.00	0.00	0.00	0.00	-0.02	0.00	0.00	0.20	0.00
Canada															
Rice	0.00	0.00	0.00	0.00		0.00		0.00			0.00			0.00	
Wheat	0.00	0.33	0.00	-0.14		0.00		0.00			-0.04			0.00	
Coarse grain	0.00	-0.26	0.00	0.52		0.00		0.00			0.00			0.00	
Sugar	0.00	0.00	0.00	0.00		0.10		0.00			0.00			0.00	
Dairy	0.00	0.00	0.00	0.00	0.00	0.00	0.00	0.06	0.06	0.00	0.01	-0.01	0.00	0.00	-0.02
Ruminant meat	0.00	0.00	0.00	0.00	0.00	0.00	-0.12	0.00	0.04	-0.12	0.12	0.30	0.00	0.00	-0.09
Non-ruminant meat	0.00	0.00	0.00	0.00	0.00	0.00	0.00	0.00	-0.03	0.00	-0.05	0.00	0.00	0.31	0.00

Short-run elasticity of supply (lag t years) with respect to the price of

EC-10

Rice	0.20	0.00	0.00	0.00	0.00	0.00	0.00	0.00	0.00	0.00	0.00	0.00	0.00
Wheat	0.00	0.30	-0.22	-0.02	0.00	0.00	0.00	0.00	0.00	0.00	0.00	0.00	0.00
Coarse grain	0.00	-0.22	0.40	-0.02	0.00	0.00	0.00	0.00	0.00	0.00	0.00	0.00	0.00
Sugar	0.00	-0.02	-0.02	0.10	0.00	0.00	0.00	0.00	0.00	0.00	0.00	0.00	0.00
Dairy	0.00	0.00	0.00	0.00	0.00	0.07	0.10	0.00	0.02	-0.03	0.00	0.00	0.00
Ruminant meat	0.00	0.00	0.00	0.00	0.00	0.00	0.04	0.00	0.12	0.22	0.00	0.00	-0.16
Non-ruminant meat	0.00	0.00	0.00	0.00	0.00	0.00	0.00	0.00	-0.06	-0.14	0.00	0.76	0.00

EFTA-5

Rice	0.00	0.00	0.00	0.00	0.00	0.00	0.00	0.00	0.00	0.00	0.00	0.00	0.00
Wheat	0.00	0.30	-0.20	0.00	0.00	0.00	0.00	0.00	0.00	0.00	0.00	0.00	0.00
Coarse grain	0.00	-0.09	0.40	0.00	0.00	0.00	0.00	0.00	0.00	0.00	0.00	0.00	0.00
Sugar	0.00	0.00	0.00	0.16	0.00	0.00	0.00	0.00	0.00	0.00	0.00	0.00	0.00
Dairy	0.00	0.00	0.00	0.00	0.00	0.07	0.10	0.00	0.02	-0.03	0.00	0.00	0.00
Ruminant meat	0.00	0.00	0.00	0.00	0.00	0.00	0.04	0.00	0.06	0.17	0.00	0.00	-0.16
Non-ruminant meat	0.00	0.00	0.00	0.00	0.00	0.00	0.00	0.00	-0.32	-0.03	0.00	0.90	0.00

Japan

Rice	0.08	0.00	0.00	0.00	0.00	0.00	0.00	0.00	0.00	0.00	0.00	0.00	0.00
Wheat	0.00	0.30	-0.15	0.00	0.00	0.00	0.00	0.00	0.00	0.00	0.00	0.00	0.00
Coarse grain	0.00	-0.20	0.30	0.00	0.00	0.00	0.00	0.00	0.00	0.00	0.00	0.00	0.00
Sugar	0.00	0.00	0.00	0.10	0.00	0.00	0.00	0.00	0.00	0.00	0.00	0.00	0.00
Dairy	0.00	0.00	0.00	0.00	0.00	0.05	0.30	0.00	-0.02	-0.02	0.00	0.00	0.00
Ruminant meat	0.00	0.00	0.00	0.00	0.00	0.00	0.02	-0.10	0.10	0.40	0.00	0.00	-0.05
Non-ruminant meat	0.00	0.00	0.00	0.00	0.00	0.00	0.00	0.00	-0.02	0.00	0.00	0.33	0.00

(continued)

Table A2 *(continued)*

| | Short-run elasticity of supply (lag t years) with respect to the price of | | | | | | | | | | | | | | |
| | Rice | Wheat | Coarse grain | | | Sugar | Dairy | | | Ruminant meat | | | Non-ruminant meat | | |
	t=1	t=1	t=1	t=2	t=3	t=1	t=0	t=1	t=2	t=0	t=1	t=2	t=0	t=1	t=2
New Zealand															
Rice	0.00	0.00		0.00		0.00		0.00			0.00			0.00	
Wheat	0.00	0.60		-0.32		0.00		0.00			-0.07			0.00	
Coarse grain	0.00	-0.19		0.37		0.00		0.00			0.00			0.00	
Sugar	0.00	0.00		0.00		0.00		0.00			0.00			0.00	
Dairy	0.00	0.00	0.00	0.00	0.00	0.00	0.00	0.21	0.21	0.00	-0.07	-0.06	0.00	0.00	0.00
Ruminant meat	0.00	-0.01	0.00	0.00	0.00	0.00	0.00	-0.02	-0.03	-0.10	0.10	0.10	0.00	0.00	-0.02
Non-ruminant meat	0.00	0.00	0.00	0.00	0.00	0.00	0.00	0.00	0.00	0.00	-0.10	0.00	0.00	0.20	0.00
Spain and Portugal															
Rice	0.24	0.00		0.00		0.00		0.00			0.00			0.00	
Wheat	0.00	0.32		-0.18		0.00		0.00			0.00			0.00	
Coarse grain	0.00	-0.10		0.30		0.00		0.00			0.00			0.00	
Sugar	0.00	0.00		0.00		0.14		0.00			0.00			0.00	
Dairy	0.00	0.00	0.00	0.00	0.00	0.00	-0.02	0.15	0.10	0.00	-0.02	-0.01	0.00	0.00	0.00
Ruminant meat	0.00	0.00	0.00	0.00	0.00	0.00	0.00	0.00	0.02	0.00	0.10	0.25	0.00	0.00	-0.30
Non-ruminant meat	0.00	0.00	0.00	0.00	0.00	0.00	0.00	0.00	0.00	0.00	0.00	-0.12	0.00	0.66	0.00

United States

Rice	0.35	-0.09	0.00	0.00	-0.02	0.07	0.00	0.08	0.03	0.00	-0.10	0.00	0.00
Wheat	-0.02	0.45	-0.30	0.00	0.00	0.00	0.00	0.00	-0.20	0.00	0.32	0.00	-0.08
Coarse grain	0.00	-0.15	0.40	0.00	0.00	0.00	0.00	0.00	0.00	0.00	-0.02	0.00	0.00
Sugar	-0.01	0.00	0.00	0.00	0.07	0.00	0.00	0.03	0.00	0.00	0.00	0.00	0.00
Dairy	0.00	0.00	0.00	0.00	0.02	0.00	0.02	0.00	0.24	0.03	0.00	0.00	0.00
Ruminant meat	0.00	0.00	0.00	0.00	0.01	0.00	0.01	0.00	0.13	-0.05	0.08	0.00	-0.08
Non-ruminant meat	0.00	0.00	0.00	0.00	0.00	0.00	0.00	0.00	0.00	0.00	0.00	0.00	0.61

USSR

Rice	0.04	0.00	0.00	0.00	0.00	0.00	0.00	0.04	0.00	0.00	0.01	0.00	0.00
Wheat	0.00	0.06	-0.04	0.00	0.00	0.00	0.00	0.02	-0.08	0.00	0.08	0.00	-0.08
Coarse grain	0.00	-0.04	0.09	0.00	0.00	0.00	0.00	0.00	0.00	0.00	-0.08	0.00	0.00
Sugar	0.00	0.00	0.00	0.00	0.11	0.00	0.00	0.00	0.00	0.00	0.00	0.00	0.00
Dairy	0.00	0.00	0.00	0.00	0.02	0.00	0.02	0.00	0.13	-0.02	0.00	0.00	0.00
Ruminant meat	0.00	0.00	0.00	0.00	0.00	0.00	0.00	0.00	0.00	0.13	0.08	0.00	-0.08
Non-ruminant meat	0.00	0.00	0.00	0.00	0.00	0.00	0.00	0.00	0.00	0.00	-0.08	0.00	0.28

Other centrally planned Europe

Rice	0.20	0.00	-0.18	0.00	0.00	0.00	0.00	0.02	0.00	0.00	0.00	0.00	0.00
Wheat	0.00	0.06	-0.04	0.00	0.00	0.00	0.00	0.02	-0.08	0.00	0.08	0.00	-0.10
Coarse grain	0.00	-0.02	0.09	0.00	0.00	0.00	0.00	0.00	0.00	0.00	-0.06	0.00	0.00
Sugar	0.00	0.00	0.00	0.00	0.05	0.00	0.00	0.00	0.00	0.00	0.00	0.00	0.00
Dairy	0.00	0.00	0.00	0.00	0.01	0.00	0.01	0.00	0.13	0.00	0.00	0.00	0.00
Ruminant meat	0.00	0.00	0.00	0.00	0.00	0.00	0.00	0.00	0.00	0.13	0.08	0.00	-0.10
Non-ruminant meat	0.00	0.00	0.00	0.00	0.00	0.00	0.00	0.00	0.00	0.00	-0.06	0.00	0.53

(continued)

Table A2 (continued)

Short-run elasticity of supply (lag t years) with respect to the price of

	Rice	Wheat	Coarse grain			Sugar	Dairy			Ruminant meat			Non-ruminant meat		
	t=1	t=1	t=1	t=2	t=3	t=1	t=0	t=1	t=2	t=0	t=1	t=2	t=0	t=1	t=2
Egypt															
Rice	0.12	0.00		0.00		-0.05		0.00			0.00			0.00	
Wheat	0.00	0.36		-0.25		0.00		0.00			0.00			0.00	
Coarse grain	0.00	-0.10		0.21		0.00		0.00			0.00			0.00	
Sugar	-0.04	0.00		0.00		0.10		0.00			0.00			0.00	
Dairy	0.00	0.00	0.00	0.00	0.00	0.00	0.00	0.10	0.10	0.00	0.00	0.00	0.00	0.00	0.00
Ruminant meat	0.00	0.00	0.00	0.00	0.00	0.00	0.00	0.00	0.00	-0.10	0.10	0.18	0.00	0.00	-0.02
Non-ruminant meat	0.00	0.00	0.00	0.00	0.00	0.00	0.00	0.00	0.00	0.00	0.00	-0.06	0.00	0.40	0.00
Nigeria															
Rice	0.12	0.00		-0.03		-0.01		0.00			0.00			0.00	
Wheat	0.00	0.05		0.00		0.00		0.00			0.00			0.00	
Coarse grain	-0.01	0.00		0.13		0.00		0.00			0.00			0.00	
Sugar	-0.09	0.00		0.00		0.17		0.00			0.00			0.00	
Dairy	0.00	0.00	0.00	0.00	0.00	0.00	0.00	0.10	0.05	0.00	0.00	0.05	0.00	0.00	0.00
Ruminant meat	0.00	0.00	0.00	0.00	0.00	0.00	0.00	0.00	0.00	-0.15	0.15	0.22	0.00	0.00	-0.07
Non-ruminant meat	0.00	0.00	0.00	0.00	0.00	0.00	0.00	0.00	0.00	0.00	0.00	-0.10	0.00	0.35	0.00

South Africa

Rice	0.00	0.00	0.00	0.00	0.00	0.00	0.00	0.00	0.10	0.00	0.00	0.00	0.00
Wheat	0.00	0.22	0.00	-0.10	0.00	0.00	0.00	0.00	0.00	0.00	0.00	0.00	0.00
Coarse grain	0.00	-0.08	0.00	0.20	0.00	0.00	0.00	0.00	0.00	0.00	0.00	0.00	0.00
Sugar	0.00	0.00	0.00	0.00	0.00	0.10	0.00	0.00	0.00	0.00	0.00	0.00	0.00
Dairy	0.00	0.00	0.00	0.00	0.00	0.00	0.00	0.10	0.00	0.00	0.05	0.00	0.00
Ruminant meat	0.00	0.00	0.00	0.00	0.00	0.00	0.00	0.00	-0.10	0.10	0.18	0.00	-0.02
Non-ruminant meat	0.00	0.00	0.00	0.00	0.00	0.00	0.00	0.00	0.00	0.00	-0.05	0.37	0.00

Other sub-Saharan Africa

Rice	0.02	0.00	0.00	-0.05	0.00	-0.02	0.00	0.00	0.05	0.00	0.00	0.00	0.00
Wheat	-0.01	0.20	0.00	-0.10	0.00	0.00	0.00	0.00	0.00	0.00	0.00	0.00	0.00
Coarse grain	-0.02	-0.01	0.00	0.20	0.00	0.00	0.00	0.00	0.00	0.00	0.00	0.00	0.00
Sugar	-0.02	0.00	0.00	0.00	0.00	0.17	0.00	0.00	0.00	0.00	0.00	0.00	0.00
Dairy	0.00	0.00	0.00	0.00	0.00	0.00	0.00	0.10	0.00	0.00	0.05	0.00	0.00
Ruminant meat	0.00	0.00	0.00	0.00	0.00	0.00	0.00	0.00	-0.10	0.10	0.15	0.00	-0.04
Non-ruminant meat	0.00	0.00	0.00	0.00	0.00	0.00	0.00	0.00	0.00	-0.10	-0.10	0.30	0.00

Other North Africa and Middle East

Rice	0.21	-0.10	0.00	0.00	0.00	0.00	0.00	0.00	0.05	0.00	0.00	0.00	0.00
Wheat	-0.01	0.31	0.00	-0.03	0.00	0.00	0.00	0.00	0.01	-0.04	0.00	0.00	0.00
Coarse grain	0.00	-0.10	0.00	0.20	0.00	0.00	0.00	0.00	0.00	0.00	0.00	0.00	0.00
Sugar	0.00	0.00	0.00	0.00	0.00	0.10	0.00	0.00	0.00	0.00	0.00	0.00	0.00
Dairy	0.00	0.00	0.00	0.00	0.00	0.00	0.00	0.05	0.00	0.00	-0.02	0.00	0.00
Ruminant meat	0.00	-0.04	0.00	0.00	0.00	0.00	0.00	-0.04	-0.10	0.10	0.18	0.00	-0.02
Non-ruminant meat	0.00	0.00	0.00	0.00	0.00	0.00	0.00	0.00	0.00	-0.05	0.00	0.50	0.00

(continued)

Table A2 *(continued)*

	Rice	Wheat	Coarse grain			Sugar		Dairy			Ruminant meat			Non-ruminant meat		
								Short-run elasticity of supply (lag t years) with respect to the price of								
	t=1	t=1	t=1	t=2	t=3	t=0	t=1	t=0	t=1	t=2	t=0	t=1	t=2	t=0	t=1	t=2
Bangladesh																
Rice	0.13	0.00		0.00			0.00		0.00			0.00			0.00	
Wheat	-0.10	0.10		0.00			0.00		0.00			0.00			0.00	
Coarse grain	-0.10	0.00		0.01			0.00		0.00			0.00			0.00	
Sugar	-0.10	0.00		0.00			0.25		0.00			0.00			0.00	
Dairy	0.00	0.00	0.00	0.00	0.00	0.00	0.00	0.00	0.00	0.05	0.00	0.00	0.00	0.00	0.00	0.00
Ruminant meat	0.00	0.00	0.00	0.00	0.00	0.00	0.00	0.00	0.00	0.00	0.00	0.00	0.09	0.00	0.00	-0.03
Non-ruminant meat	0.00	0.00	0.00	0.00	0.00	0.00	0.00	0.00	0.00	0.00	0.00	-0.05	0.00	0.00	0.18	0.00
China																
Rice	0.08	-0.01		-0.01			-0.01		0.00			0.00			0.00	
Wheat	-0.01	0.06		-0.01			0.00		0.00			0.00			0.00	
Coarse grain	-0.01	-0.01		0.08			0.00		0.00			0.00			0.00	
Sugar	-0.02	0.00		0.00			0.15		0.00			0.00			0.00	
Dairy	0.00	0.00	0.00	0.00	0.00	0.00	0.00	0.00	0.15	0.05	0.00	0.00	-0.02	0.00	0.00	0.00
Ruminant meat	0.00	0.00	0.00	0.00	0.00	0.00	0.00	0.00	0.00	0.03	-0.10	0.20	0.10	0.00	0.00	-0.05
Non-ruminant meat	0.00	0.00	0.00	0.00	0.00	0.00	0.00	0.00	0.00	0.00	0.00	0.00	0.00	0.00	0.30	0.00

India	Rice	Wheat	Coarse grain	Sugar	Dairy	Ruminant meat	Non-ruminant meat
Rice	0.22	-0.06	-0.04	-0.03	0.00	0.00	0.00
Wheat	-0.12	0.31	-0.07	-0.05	0.00	0.00	0.00
Coarse grain	-0.12	-0.10	0.15	-0.04	0.00	0.00	0.00
Sugar	-0.03	-0.02	-0.01	0.12	0.00	0.00	0.00
Dairy	0.00	0.00	0.00	0.00	0.03	0.02	0.00
Ruminant meat	0.00	0.00	0.00	0.00	0.04	0.06	-0.02
Non-ruminant meat	0.00	0.00	0.00	0.00	0.00	0.00	0.25

Indonesia	Rice	Wheat	Coarse grain	Sugar	Dairy	Ruminant meat	Non-ruminant meat
Rice	0.12	0.00	-0.02	-0.01	0.00	0.00	0.00
Wheat	0.00	0.00	0.00	0.00	0.00	0.00	0.00
Coarse grain	-0.20	0.00	0.13	0.00	0.00	0.00	0.00
Sugar	-0.02	0.00	0.00	0.30	0.00	0.00	0.00
Dairy	0.00	0.00	0.00	0.00	0.20	0.00	0.10
Ruminant meat	0.00	0.00	0.00	0.00	0.00	0.90	-0.10
Non-ruminant meat	0.00	0.00	0.00	0.00	0.00	-0.08	0.35

Korea	Rice	Wheat	Coarse grain	Sugar	Dairy	Ruminant meat	Non-ruminant meat
Rice	0.10	0.00	-0.02	0.00	0.00	0.00	0.00
Wheat	-0.01	0.37	-0.30	0.00	0.00	0.00	0.00
Coarse grain	-0.10	-0.02	0.14	0.00	0.00	0.00	0.00
Sugar	0.00	0.00	0.00	0.05	0.00	0.00	0.00
Dairy	0.00	0.00	0.00	0.00	0.30	-0.01	0.01
Ruminant meat	0.00	0.00	0.00	0.00	0.02	0.10	0.25
Non-ruminant meat	0.00	0.00	0.00	0.00	0.00	-0.03	0.57

(continued)

Table A2 *(continued)*

Short-run elasticity of supply (lag t years) with respect to the price of

	Rice	Wheat	Coarse grain			Sugar	Dairy			Ruminant meat			Non-ruminant meat		
	t=1	t=1	t=1	t=2	t=3	t=1	t=0	t=1	t=2	t=0	t=1	t=2	t=0	t=1	t=2
Pakistan															
Rice	0.02	-0.02	0.00			0.00		0.00			0.00			0.00	
Wheat	-0.01	0.06	-0.01			0.00		0.00			0.00			0.00	
Coarse grain	0.00	-0.16	0.15			-0.01		0.00			0.00			0.00	
Sugar	0.00	-0.01	0.00			0.10		0.00			0.00			0.00	
Dairy	0.00	0.00	0.00	0.00	0.00	0.00	0.00	0.10	0.01	0.00	0.00	0.02	0.00	0.00	0.00
Ruminant meat	0.00	0.00	0.00	0.00	0.00	0.00	0.00	0.00	0.05	0.00	0.06	0.06	0.00	0.00	0.00
Non-ruminant meat	0.00	0.00	0.00	0.00	0.00	0.00	0.00	0.00	0.00	0.00	-0.20	0.00	0.00	0.50	0.00
Philippines															
Rice	0.16	0.00	-0.06			-0.01		0.00			0.00			0.00	
Wheat	0.00	0.00	0.00			0.00		0.00			0.00			0.00	
Coarse grain	-0.10	0.00	0.20			0.00		0.00			0.00			0.00	
Sugar	-0.02	0.00	0.00			0.13		0.00			0.00			0.00	
Dairy	0.00	0.00	0.00	0.00	0.00	0.00	0.00	0.10	0.10	0.00	0.00	-0.05	0.00	0.00	0.00
Ruminant meat	0.00	0.00	0.00	0.00	0.00	0.00	0.00	0.00	0.00	-0.05	0.05	0.13	0.00	0.00	-0.04
Non-ruminant meat	0.00	0.00	0.00	0.00	0.00	0.00	0.00	0.00	0.00	0.00	-0.03	0.00	0.00	0.55	0.00

	Rice	Wheat	Coarse grain	Sugar	Dairy	Ruminant meat	Non-ruminant meat
Taiwan							
Rice	0.20	0.00	0.00	0.00	0.00	0.00	0.00
Wheat	-0.50	0.33	0.00	0.00	0.00	0.00	0.00
Coarse grain	-0.30	0.00	0.25	0.00	0.00	0.00	0.00
Sugar	0.00	0.00	0.00	0.20	0.00	0.00	0.00
Dairy	0.00	0.00	0.00	0.00	0.08	0.16	0.00
Ruminant meat	0.00	0.00	0.00	0.00	0.00	0.25	-0.04
Non-ruminant meat	0.00	0.00	0.00	0.00	0.00	-0.05	0.62
Thailand							
Rice	0.20	0.00	-0.01	-0.02	0.00	0.00	0.00
Wheat	0.00	0.00	0.00	0.00	0.00	0.00	0.00
Coarse grain	-0.06	0.00	0.25	-0.10	0.00	0.00	0.00
Sugar	-0.03	0.00	-0.02	0.35	0.00	0.00	0.00
Dairy	0.00	0.00	0.00	0.00	0.14	0.14	0.00
Ruminant meat	0.00	0.00	0.00	0.00	0.00	0.26	-0.02
Non-ruminant meat	0.00	0.00	0.00	0.00	0.00	-0.07	0.34
Other Asia							
Rice	0.05	-0.01	-0.01	0.00	0.00	0.00	0.00
Wheat	-0.08	0.16	-0.11	0.00	0.00	0.00	0.00
Coarse grain	-0.06	-0.08	0.15	0.00	0.00	0.00	0.00
Sugar	-0.04	-0.01	-0.01	0.10	0.00	0.00	0.00
Dairy	0.00	0.00	0.00	0.00	0.08	0.01	0.00
Ruminant meat	0.00	0.00	0.00	0.00	0.07	0.09	0.08
Non-ruminant meat	0.00	0.00	0.00	0.00	0.00	-0.09	0.50

(continued)

Table A2 *(continued)*

	Short-run elasticity of supply (lag t years) with respect to the price of														
	Rice	Wheat	Coarse grain			Sugar	Dairy			Ruminant meat			Non-ruminant meat		
	t=1	t=1	t=1	t=2	t=3	t=1	t=0	t=1	t=2	t=0	t=1	t=2	t=0	t=1	t=2
Argentina															
Rice	0.20	0.00		0.00		0.00		0.00			0.00			0.00	
Wheat	0.00	0.31		-0.10		0.00		0.00			-0.01			0.00	
Coarse grain	0.00	-0.10		0.20		0.00		0.00			0.00			0.00	
Sugar	0.00	0.00				0.39		0.00			0.00			0.00	
Dairy	0.00	0.00	0.00	0.00	0.00	0.00	0.00	0.05	0.05	0.00	0.00	-0.04	0.00	0.00	0.00
Ruminant meat	0.00	0.00	0.00	0.00	0.00	0.00	0.00	0.00	-0.01	-0.10	0.10	0.18	0.00	0.00	-0.02
Non-ruminant meat	0.00	0.00	0.00	0.00	0.00	0.00	0.00	0.00	0.00	0.00	0.00	-0.10	0.00	0.33	0.00
Brazil															
Rice	0.50	-0.01		-0.06		-0.05		0.00			0.00			0.00	
Wheat	-0.03	0.30		-0.09		0.00		0.00			0.00			0.00	
Coarse grain	-0.02	-0.01		0.30		-0.02		0.00			0.00			0.00	
Sugar	-0.04	0.00		-0.03		0.40		0.00			0.00			0.00	
Dairy	0.00	0.00	0.00	0.00	0.00	0.00	0.00	0.28	0.05	0.00	0.01	-0.05	0.00	0.00	0.00
Ruminant meat	0.00	0.00	0.00	0.00	0.00	0.00	0.00	-0.03	0.00	-0.10	0.10	0.20	0.00	0.00	-0.04
Non-ruminant meat	0.00	0.00	0.00	0.00	0.00	0.00	0.00	0.00	0.00	0.00	0.00	-0.06	0.00	0.48	0.00

	Rice	Wheat	Coarse grain	Sugar	Dairy	Ruminant meat	Non-ruminant meat
Cuba							
Rice	0.32	0.00	−0.09	−0.01	0.00	0.00	0.00
Wheat	0.00	0.00	0.00	0.00	0.00	0.00	0.00
Coarse grain	−0.50	0.00	0.20	0.00	0.00	0.00	0.00
Sugar	0.00	0.00	0.00	0.13	0.00	0.00	0.00
Dairy	0.00	0.00	0.00	0.00	0.10	0.05	−0.02
Ruminant meat	0.00	0.00	0.00	0.00	0.10	0.13	−0.04
Non-ruminant meat	0.00	0.00	0.00	0.00	−0.05	−0.09	0.62
Mexico							
Rice	0.56	0.00	0.00	0.00	0.00	0.00	0.00
Wheat	0.00	0.45	−0.30	0.00	0.00	0.00	0.00
Coarse grain	0.00	−0.04	0.20	−0.02	0.00	0.00	0.00
Sugar	0.00	0.00	−0.07	0.15	0.00	0.00	0.00
Dairy	0.00	0.00	0.00	0.00	0.10	0.10	0.00
Ruminant meat	0.00	0.00	0.00	0.00	0.15	0.23	−0.02
Non-ruminant meat	0.00	0.00	0.00	0.00	−0.10	−0.01	0.30
Other Latin America							
Rice	0.40	−0.01	−0.10	0.06	0.00	0.00	0.00
Wheat	−0.03	0.40	−0.22	0.00	0.00	0.00	0.00
Coarse grain	−0.07	−0.05	0.40	−0.01	0.00	0.00	0.00
Sugar	−0.01	0.00	−0.01	0.40	0.00	0.00	0.00
Dairy	0.00	0.00	0.00	0.00	0.05	0.10	0.00
Ruminant meat	0.00	0.00	0.00	0.00	0.10	0.30	−0.04
Non-ruminant meat	0.00	0.00	0.00	0.00	−0.10	−0.04	0.50

Table A3: Long-run supply response parameters

	Trend production 1980–82 (million tonnes)	Long-run elasticity of supply with respect to the price of							Price-independent production growth rate (%p.a.) 1990s
		Rice	Wheat	Coarse grain	Sugar	Dairy	Ruminant meat	Non-ruminant meat	
Australia									
Rice	0.49	0.33	-0.15	0.00	0.00	0.00	0.00	0.00	0.020
Wheat	15.67	-0.01	0.88	-0.09	0.00	0.00	-0.11	0.00	0.025
Coarse grain	6.65	0.00	-0.30	0.60	0.00	0.00	0.00	0.00	0.045
Sugar	3.34	0.00	0.00	0.00	0.50	0.00	0.00	0.00	0.020
Dairy	5.35	0.00	0.00	0.00	0.00	0.58	0.04	0.00	0.005
Ruminant meat	2.19	0.00	-0.09	0.00	0.00	0.07	0.27	-0.04	0.025
Non-ruminant meat	0.54	0.00	0.00	0.00	0.00	0.00	-0.11	1.09	0.040
Canada									
Rice	0.00	0.00	0.00	0.00	0.00	0.00	0.00	0.00	0.000
Wheat	26.04	0.00	0.53	-0.22	0.00	0.00	-0.06	0.00	0.025
Coarse grain	23.13	0.00	-0.34	0.68	0.00	0.00	0.00	0.00	0.030
Sugar	0.13	0.00	0.00	0.00	0.50	0.00	0.00	0.00	0.000
Dairy	7.77	0.00	0.00	0.00	0.00	0.50	0.00	-0.08	0.015
Ruminant meat	1.09	0.00	0.00	0.00	0.00	0.08	0.60	-0.18	0.020
Non-ruminant meat	1.41	0.00	0.00	0.00	0.00	-0.09	-0.14	0.89	0.030

EC-10

Rice	0.70	0.40	0.00	0.00	0.00	0.00	0.00	0.020
Wheat	57.77	0.00	0.90	-0.66	-0.06	0.00	0.00	0.025
Coarse grain	67.30	0.00	-0.51	0.92	-0.05	0.00	0.00	0.030
Sugar	14.16	0.00	-0.10	-0.10	0.50	0.00	0.00	0.036
Dairy	118.76	0.00	0.00	0.00	0.00	0.51	-0.03	0.020
Ruminant meat	7.52	0.00	0.00	0.00	0.00	0.12	1.02	-0.48	0.020
Non-ruminant meat	14.81	0.00	0.00	0.00	0.00	0.00	-0.30	1.14	0.030

EFTA-5

Rice	0.00	0.00	0.00	0.00	0.00	0.00	0.00	0.000
Wheat	3.54	0.00	0.90	-0.60	0.00	0.00	0.00	0.010
Coarse grain	11.87	0.00	-0.20	0.91	0.00	0.00	0.00	0.020
Sugar	1.11	0.00	0.00	0.00	0.32	0.00	0.00	0.035
Dairy	16.23	0.00	0.00	0.00	0.00	0.51	-0.03	0.035
Ruminant meat	0.78	0.00	0.00	0.00	0.00	0.12	0.69	-0.48	0.020
Non-ruminant meat	1.50	0.00	0.00	0.00	0.00	0.00	-0.59	1.50	0.020

Japan

Rice	9.38	0.20	0.00	0.00	0.00	0.00	0.00	0.000
Wheat	0.68	0.00	0.60	-0.30	0.00	0.00	0.00	0.000
Coarse grain	0.40	0.00	-0.40	0.60	0.00	0.00	0.00	0.000
Sugar	0.85	0.00	0.00	0.00	0.50	0.00	0.00	0.020
Dairy	6.80	0.00	0.00	0.00	0.00	0.80	-0.09	0.022
Ruminant meat	0.48	0.00	0.00	0.00	0.00	0.04	0.80	-0.10	0.040
Non-ruminant meat	2.62	0.00	0.00	0.00	0.00	0.00	-0.06	0.99	0.060

(continued)

Table A3 (continued)

| | Trend production 1980–82 (million tonnes) | Long-run elasticity of supply with respect to the price of | | | | | | | Price-independent production growth rate (%p.a.) 1990s |
		Rice	Wheat	Coarse grain	Sugar	Dairy	Ruminant meat	Non-ruminant meat	
New Zealand									
Rice	0.00	0.00	0.00	0.00	0.00	0.00	0.00	0.00	0.000
Wheat	0.32	0.00	0.93	-0.49	0.00	0.00	-0.11	0.00	0.010
Coarse grain	0.73	0.00	-0.31	0.60	0.00	0.00	0.00	0.00	0.040
Sugar	0.00	0.00	0.00	0.00	0.00	0.00	0.00	0.00	0.000
Dairy	6.67	0.00	0.00	0.00	0.00	0.61	-0.19	0.00	0.005
Ruminant meat	1.19	0.00	-0.02	0.00	0.00	-0.10	0.20	-0.04	0.025
Non-ruminant meat	0.07	0.00	0.00	0.00	0.00	0.00	-0.30	0.60	0.030
Spain and Portugal									
Rice	0.33	0.40	0.00	0.00	0.00	0.00	0.00	0.00	0.015
Wheat	4.39	0.00	0.91	-0.51	0.00	0.00	0.00	0.00	0.010
Coarse grain	9.09	0.00	-0.30	0.90	0.00	0.00	0.00	0.00	0.030
Sugar	1.23	0.00	0.00	0.00	0.70	0.00	0.00	0.00	0.035
Dairy	7.62	0.00	0.00	0.00	0.00	0.39	-0.05	0.00	0.025
Ruminant meat	0.70	0.00	0.00	0.00	0.00	0.04	0.70	-0.60	0.025
Non-ruminant meat	2.31	0.00	0.00	0.00	0.00	0.00	-0.18	0.99	0.040

United States

Rice	4.71	0.75	-0.20	0.00	-0.04	0.00	0.00	0.00	0.030
Wheat	72.30	-0.04	0.80	-0.53	0.00	0.00	0.00	0.00	0.030
Coarse grain	211.49	0.00	-0.28	0.75	0.00	0.00	0.00	0.00	0.030
Sugar	5.32	-0.04	0.00	0.00	0.28	0.85	0.00	0.00	0.020
Dairy	61.81	0.00	0.00	0.00	0.00	0.03	-0.20	0.00	0.030
Ruminant meat	10.58	0.00	0.00	0.00	0.00	0.00	0.72	-0.16	0.015
Non-ruminant meat	13.99	0.00	0.00	0.00	0.00	0.00	-0.13	1.12	0.025

USSR

Rice	1.63	0.11	0.00	0.00	0.00	0.00	0.00	0.00	0.020
Wheat	81.67	0.00	0.18	-0.12	0.00	0.00	0.00	0.00	0.015
Coarse grain	85.67	0.00	-0.12	0.27	0.00	0.00	0.00	0.00	0.028
Sugar	7.43	0.00	0.00	0.00	0.21	0.30	0.00	0.00	0.010
Dairy	92.10	0.00	0.00	0.00	0.00	0.08	-0.05	0.00	0.025
Ruminant meat	7.48	0.00	0.00	0.00	0.00	0.00	0.52	-0.32	0.025
Non-ruminant meat	7.78	0.00	0.00	0.00	0.00	0.00	-0.32	1.12	0.030

Other centrally planned Europe

Rice	0.14	0.40	0.00	-0.36	0.00	0.00	0.00	0.00	0.020
Wheat	33.58	0.00	0.08	-0.06	0.00	0.00	0.00	0.00	0.030
Coarse grain	65.28	0.00	-0.03	0.14	0.00	0.00	0.00	0.00	0.030
Sugar	5.70	0.00	0.00	0.00	0.08	0.21	0.00	0.00	0.020
Dairy	44.02	0.00	0.00	0.00	0.00	0.05	-0.01	0.00	0.030
Ruminant meat	2.68	0.00	0.00	0.00	0.00	0.00	0.30	-0.23	0.020
Non-ruminant meat	8.45	0.00	0.00	0.00	0.00	0.00	-0.09	0.77	0.020

(continued)

Table A3 *(continued)*

| | Trend production 1980–82 (million tonnes) | Long-run elasticity of supply with respect to the price of | | | | | | | Price-independent production growth rate (%p.a.) 1990s |
		Rice	Wheat	Coarse grain	Sugar	Dairy	Ruminant meat	Non-ruminant meat	
Egypt									
Rice	1.59	0.20	0.00	0.00	-0.08	0.00	0.00	0.00	0.025
Wheat	1.98	0.00	1.08	-0.75	0.00	0.00	0.00	0.00	0.020
Coarse grain	4.10	0.00	-0.30	0.63	0.00	0.00	0.00	0.00	0.020
Sugar	0.75	-0.13	0.00	0.00	0.32	0.00	0.00	0.00	0.030
Dairy	1.95	0.00	0.00	0.00	0.00	0.80	0.00	0.00	0.030
Ruminant meat	0.28	0.00	0.00	0.00	0.00	0.00	0.72	-0.08	0.020
Non-ruminant meat	0.16	0.00	0.00	0.00	0.00	0.00	-0.18	1.20	0.040
Nigeria									
Rice	0.87	0.31	0.00	-0.08	-0.03	0.00	0.00	0.00	0.050
Wheat	0.03	0.00	0.21	0.00	0.00	0.00	0.00	0.00	0.050
Coarse grain	7.99	-0.02	0.00	0.22	0.00	0.00	0.00	0.00	0.010
Sugar	0.09	-0.27	0.00	0.00	0.51	0.00	0.00	0.00	0.040
Dairy	0.36	0.00	0.00	0.00	0.00	0.60	0.20	0.00	0.020
Ruminant meat	0.38	0.00	0.00	0.00	0.00	0.00	0.60	-0.19	0.020
Non-ruminant meat	0.29	0.00	0.00	0.00	0.00	0.00	-0.30	1.05	0.040

South Africa

Rice	0.00	0.00	0.00	0.00	0.00	0.00	0.00	0.00	0.000
Wheat	2.19	0.00	0.66	-0.30	0.00	0.00	0.00	0.00	0.030
Coarse grain	6.15	0.00	-0.24	0.60	0.00	0.00	0.00	0.00	0.025
Sugar	2.00	0.00	0.00	0.00	0.30	0.00	0.00	0.00	0.020
Dairy	2.59	0.00	0.00	0.00	0.00	0.80	0.20	0.00	0.020
Ruminant meat	0.64	0.00	0.00	0.00	0.00	0.00	0.72	-0.08	0.020
Non-ruminant meat	0.36	0.00	0.00	0.00	0.00	0.00	-0.15	1.11	0.040

Other sub-Saharan

Rice	3.30	0.50	-0.01	-0.13	-0.05	0.00	0.00	0.00	0.030
Wheat	1.62	-0.03	0.50	-0.25	0.00	0.00	0.00	0.00	0.025
Coarse grain	27.70	-0.04	-0.02	0.40	0.00	0.00	0.00	0.00	0.020
Sugar	3.48	-0.05	0.00	0.00	0.51	0.00	0.00	0.00	0.040
Dairy	6.82	0.00	0.00	0.00	0.00	0.60	0.20	0.00	0.010
Ruminant meat	2.64	0.00	0.00	0.00	0.00	0.00	0.60	-0.16	0.020
Non-ruminant meat	0.71	0.00	0.00	0.00	0.00	0.00	-0.60	0.90	0.040

Other North Africa and Middle East

Rice	1.27	0.35	-0.17	0.00	0.00	0.00	0.00	0.00	0.030
Wheat	30.77	-0.01	0.41	-0.04	0.00	0.00	-0.05	0.00	0.030
Coarse grain	15.20	0.00	-0.20	0.40	0.20	0.00	0.00	0.00	0.025
Sugar	2.71	0.00	0.00	0.00	0.00	0.00	0.00	0.00	0.040
Dairy	14.93	0.00	0.00	0.00	0.00	0.40	-0.08	0.00	0.030
Ruminant meat	1.94	0.00	-0.16	0.00	0.00	-0.12	0.72	-0.08	0.030
Non-ruminant meat	1.19	0.00	0.00	0.00	0.00	0.00	-0.10	1.00	0.050

(continued)

Table A3 *(continued)*

	Trend production 1980–82 (million tonnes)	Long-run elasticity of supply with respect to the price of							Price-independent production growth rate (%p.a.) 1990s
		Rice	Wheat	Coarse grain	Sugar	Dairy	Ruminant meat	Non-ruminant meat	
Bangladesh									
Rice	14.12	0.74	-0.02	0.00	-0.01	0.00	0.00	0.00	0.030
Wheat	1.09	-0.67	0.67	0.00	0.00	0.00	0.00	0.00	0.060
Coarse grain	0.03	-0.40	-0.02	0.04	0.00	0.00	0.00	0.00	0.040
Sugar	0.59	-0.20	0.00	0.00	0.51	0.00	0.00	0.00	0.020
Dairy	1.57	0.00	0.00	0.00	0.00	0.50	0.00	0.00	0.025
Ruminant meat	0.25	0.00	0.00	0.00	0.00	0.00	0.20	-0.06	0.021
Non-ruminant meat	0.09	0.00	0.00	0.00	0.00	0.00	-0.36	1.29	0.050
China									
Rice	110.62	0.12	-0.01	-0.01	-0.01	0.00	0.00	0.00	0.010
Wheat	69.82	-0.02	0.10	-0.02	0.00	0.00	0.00	0.00	0.020
Coarse grain	85.29	-0.02	-0.02	0.16	0.00	0.00	0.00	0.00	0.030
Sugar	5.01	-0.12	0.00	0.00	0.88	0.00	0.00	0.00	0.055
Dairy	7.68	0.00	0.00	0.00	0.00	0.80	-0.08	0.00	0.070
Ruminant meat	0.82	0.00	0.00	0.00	0.00	0.10	0.80	-0.20	0.050
Non-ruminant meat	15.00	0.00	0.00	0.00	0.00	0.00	0.00	0.60	0.050

India

Rice	53.38	0.29	-0.08	-0.05	-0.04	0.00	0.00	0.00	0.040
Wheat	38.85	-0.16	0.41	-0.09	-0.07	0.00	0.00	0.00	0.045
Coarse grain	31.11	-0.17	-0.14	0.21	-0.06	0.00	0.00	0.00	0.015
Sugar	16.02	-0.12	-0.08	-0.04	0.46	0.00	0.00	0.00	0.035
Dairy	33.71	0.00	0.00	0.00	0.00	0.15	0.10	0.00	0.040
Ruminant meat	0.62	0.00	0.00	0.00	0.00	0.20	0.40	-0.10	0.025
Non-ruminant meat	0.21	0.00	0.00	0.00	0.00	0.00	-0.40	1.00	0.045

Indonesia

Rice	23.04	0.30	0.00	-0.05	-0.02	0.00	0.00	0.00	0.040
Wheat	0.00	0.00	0.00	0.00	0.00	0.00	0.00	0.00	0.000
Coarse grain	4.28	-0.34	0.00	0.22	0.00	0.00	0.00	0.00	0.013
Sugar	1.82	-0.04	0.00	0.00	0.59	0.00	0.00	0.00	0.042
Dairy	0.11	0.00	0.00	0.00	0.00	1.20	-0.20	0.00	0.040
Ruminant meat	0.22	0.00	0.00	0.00	0.00	0.00	1.76	-0.20	0.010
Non-ruminant meat	0.29	0.00	0.00	0.00	0.00	0.00	-0.23	1.00	0.050

Korea

Rice	5.21	0.14	0.00	-0.03	0.00	0.00	0.00	0.00	0.030
Wheat	0.08	-0.01	0.55	-0.45	0.00	0.00	0.00	0.00	0.000
Coarse grain	0.94	-0.20	-0.04	0.28	0.00	0.00	0.00	0.00	0.020
Sugar	0.00	0.00	0.00	0.00	0.00	0.00	0.00	0.00	0.000
Dairy	0.57	0.00	0.00	0.00	0.00	0.80	0.00	0.00	0.040
Ruminant meat	0.08	0.00	0.00	0.00	0.00	0.04	0.50	-0.10	0.045
Non-ruminant meat	0.38	0.00	0.00	0.00	0.00	0.00	-0.04	0.85	0.060

(continued)

Table A3 (continued)

	Trend production 1980–82 (million tonnes)	Long-run elasticity of supply with respect to the price of							Price-independent production growth rate (%p.a.) 1990s
		Rice	Wheat	Coarse grain	Sugar	Dairy	Ruminant meat	Non-ruminant meat	
Pakistan									
Rice	3.38	0.07	-0.07	0.00	0.00	0.00	0.00	0.00	0.030
Wheat	11.73	-0.04	0.16	-0.03	-0.01	0.00	0.00	0.00	0.045
Coarse grain	1.61	0.00	-0.20	0.19	-0.01	0.00	0.00	0.00	0.010
Sugar	2.85	-0.01	-0.01	0.00	0.13	0.00	0.00	0.00	0.040
Dairy	9.44	0.00	0.00	0.00	0.00	0.34	0.06	0.00	0.040
Ruminant meat	0.80	0.00	0.00	0.00	0.00	0.12	0.29	0.00	0.040
Non-ruminant meat	0.06	0.00	0.00	0.00	0.00	0.00	-0.40	1.00	0.050
Philippines									
Rice	5.13	0.26	0.00	-0.10	-0.02	0.00	0.00	0.00	0.030
Wheat	0.00	0.00	0.00	0.00	0.00	0.00	0.00	0.00	0.000
Coarse grain	3.25	-0.20	0.00	0.40	0.00	0.00	0.00	0.00	0.040
Sugar	2.51	-0.11	0.00	0.00	0.68	0.00	0.00	0.00	0.030
Dairy	0.03	0.00	0.00	0.00	0.00	0.80	-0.20	0.00	0.030
Ruminant meat	0.13	0.00	0.00	0.00	0.00	0.00	0.50	-0.15	0.035
Non-ruminant meat	0.66	0.00	0.00	0.00	0.00	0.00	-0.06	1.04	0.040

Taiwan

Rice	2.45	0.28	0.00	-0.01	0.00	0.00	0.00	0.00	0.020
Wheat	0.00	-0.75	0.49	0.00	0.00	0.00	0.00	0.00	0.000
Coarse grain	0.12	-0.60	0.00	0.50	0.00	0.00	0.00	0.00	0.040
Sugar	0.79	0.00	0.00	0.00	0.40	0.60	0.00	0.00	0.010
Dairy	0.06	0.00	0.00	0.00	0.00	0.00	-0.10	0.00	0.050
Ruminant meat	0.01	0.00	0.00	0.00	0.00	0.00	0.50	-0.10	0.030
Non-ruminant meat	0.78	0.00	0.00	0.00	0.00	0.00	0.00	0.93	0.050

Thailand

Rice	11.93	0.40	0.00	-0.02	-0.04	0.00	0.00	0.00	0.033
Wheat	0.00	0.00	0.00	0.00	0.00	0.00	0.00	0.00	0.000
Coarse grain	4.22	-0.11	0.00	0.46	-0.18	0.00	0.00	0.00	0.050
Sugar	3.13	-0.13	0.00	-0.09	1.50	0.00	0.00	0.00	0.020
Dairy	0.01	0.00	0.00	0.00	0.00	0.62	-0.04	0.00	0.030
Ruminant meat	0.22	0.00	0.00	0.00	0.00	0.00	0.99	-0.21	0.040
Non-ruminant meat	0.53	0.00	0.00	0.00	0.00	0.00	-0.11	0.91	0.080

Other Asia

Rice	28.00	0.08	-0.02	-0.02	0.00	0.00	0.00	0.00	0.030
Wheat	4.76	-0.16	0.32	-0.21	-0.01	0.00	0.00	0.00	0.030
Coarse grain	6.92	-0.12	-0.16	0.31	0.00	0.00	0.00	0.00	0.025
Sugar	1.11	-0.07	-0.02	-0.01	0.20	0.00	0.00	0.00	0.030
Dairy	2.74	0.00	0.00	0.00	0.00	0.36	0.11	0.00	0.025
Ruminant meat	0.81	0.00	0.00	0.00	0.00	0.07	0.44	-0.22	0.020
Non-ruminant meat	1.39	0.00	0.00	0.00	0.00	0.00	-0.12	3.12	0.040

(continued)

Table A3 *(continued)*

	Trend production 1980–82 (million tonnes)	Long-run elasticity of supply with respect to the price of							Price-independent production growth rate (%p.a.) 1990s
		Rice	Wheat	Coarse grain	Sugar	Dairy	Ruminant meat	Non-ruminant meat	
Argentina									
Rice	0.24	0.33	0.00	0.00	0.00	0.00	0.00	0.00	0.030
Wheat	11.87	0.00	0.88	-0.28	0.00	0.00	-0.03	0.00	0.020
Coarse grain	17.86	0.00	-0.30	0.60	0.00	0.00	0.00	0.00	0.035
Sugar	1.63	0.00	0.00	0.00	0.69	0.00	0.00	0.00	0.035
Dairy	5.59	0.00	0.00	0.00	0.00	0.40	-0.16	0.00	0.015
Ruminant meat	2.73	0.00	-0.01	0.00	0.00	-0.04	0.72	-0.08	0.018
Non-ruminant meat	0.74	0.00	0.00	0.00	0.00	0.00	-0.30	0.99	0.040
Brazil									
Rice	5.88	0.75	-0.02	-0.09	-0.07	0.00	0.00	0.00	0.030
Wheat	2.06	-0.09	0.90	-0.27	0.00	0.00	0.00	0.00	0.030
Coarse grain	21.60	-0.06	-0.05	0.90	-0.06	0.00	0.00	0.00	0.035
Sugar	9.26	-0.07	0.00	-0.05	0.80	0.00	0.00	0.00	0.046
Dairy	10.52	0.00	0.00	0.00	0.00	0.60	-0.07	0.00	0.033
Ruminant meat	2.40	0.00	0.00	0.00	0.00	-0.12	0.80	-0.16	0.030
Non-ruminant meat	2.56	0.00	0.00	0.00	0.00	0.00	-0.11	0.91	0.050

Cuba

Rice	0.32	0.52	0.00	-0.15	-0.02	0.00	0.00	0.00	0.040
Wheat	0.00	0.00	0.00	0.00	0.00	0.00	0.00	0.00	0.000
Coarse grain	0.10	-1.00	0.00	0.40	0.00	0.00	0.00	0.00	0.025
Sugar	7.88	0.00	0.00	0.00	0.68	0.80	0.00	0.00	0.030
Dairy	1.21	0.00	0.00	0.00	0.00	0.00	-0.08	0.00	0.040
Ruminant meat	0.15	0.00	0.00	0.00	0.00	0.00	0.50	-0.15	0.010
Non-ruminant meat	0.16	0.00	0.00	0.00	0.00	0.00	-0.12	1.03	0.040

Mexico

Rice	0.34	0.93	0.00	0.00	0.00	0.00	0.00	0.00	0.030
Wheat	3.49	0.00	0.84	-0.56	0.00	0.00	0.00	0.00	0.030
Coarse grain	13.63	0.00	-0.11	0.60	-0.07	0.00	0.00	0.00	0.035
Sugar	2.87	0.00	0.00	-0.21	0.45	0.00	0.00	0.00	0.020
Dairy	7.53	0.00	0.00	0.00	0.00	0.50	0.00	0.00	0.040
Ruminant meat	0.69	0.00	0.00	0.00	0.00	0.00	0.46	-0.04	0.030
Non-ruminant meat	1.02	0.00	0.00	0.00	0.00	0.00	-0.02	0.90	0.040

Other Latin America

Rice	3.88	0.40	-0.01	-0.10	0.06	0.00	0.00	0.00	0.040
Wheat	1.48	-0.05	0.63	-0.35	0.00	0.00	0.00	0.00	0.000
Coarse grain	8.63	-0.10	-0.07	0.59	-0.01	0.00	0.00	0.00	0.030
Sugar	8.09	-0.02	0.00	-0.01	0.59	0.00	0.00	0.00	0.025
Dairy	10.49	0.00	0.00	0.00	0.00	0.30	-0.10	0.00	0.020
Ruminant meat	2.58	0.00	0.00	0.00	0.00	0.00	0.60	-0.08	0.025
Non-ruminant meat	1.74	0.00	0.00	0.00	0.00	0.00	-0.08	1.00	0.050

Table A4: Direct demand parameters

	Trend consumption 1980–82 (million tonnes)	Elasticity of direct demand with respect to the price of:							Income elasticity of demand
		Rice	Wheat	Coarse grain	Sugar	Dairy products	Ruminant meat	Non-ruminant meat	
Australia									
Rice	0.07	-0.40	0.20	0.00	0.00	0.00	0.00	0.00	0.10
Wheat	3.16	0.01	-0.15	0.04	0.00	0.00	0.00	0.00	-0.25
Coarse grain	0.59	0.00	0.20	-0.30	0.00	0.00	0.00	0.00	-0.25
Sugar	0.77	0.00	0.00	0.00	-0.18	0.00	0.00	0.00	0.15
Dairy products	4.46	0.00	0.00	0.00	0.00	-0.20	0.00	0.00	0.10
Ruminant meat	1.43	0.00	0.00	0.00	0.00	0.00	-0.63	0.33	0.20
Non-ruminant meat	0.53	0.00	0.00	0.00	0.00	0.00	0.60	-1.00	0.40
Canada									
Rice	0.11	-0.30	0.10	0.10	0.00	0.00	0.00	0.00	0.15
Wheat	5.50	0.00	-0.18	0.05	0.00	0.00	0.00	0.00	0.05
Coarse grain	2.49	0.00	0.15	-0.20	0.00	0.00	0.00	0.00	0.05
Sugar	0.99	0.00	0.00	0.02	-0.08	0.00	0.00	0.00	0.06
Dairy products	7.00	0.00	0.00	0.00	0.00	-0.40	0.00	0.00	0.20
Ruminant meat	1.10	0.00	0.00	0.00	0.00	0.00	-0.65	0.30	0.30
Non-ruminant meat	1.30	0.00	0.00	0.00	0.00	0.00	0.25	-0.75	0.45

EC-10

Rice	0.90	-0.80	0.25	0.10	0.00	0.00	0.00	0.00	0.11
Wheat	47.90	0.01	-0.30	0.02	0.00	0.00	0.00	0.00	0.10
Coarse grain	7.00	0.00	0.17	-0.20	0.05	0.00	0.00	0.00	0.00
Sugar	11.00	0.00	0.00	0.01	-0.12	0.00	0.00	0.00	0.10
Dairy products	107.20	0.00	0.00	0.00	0.00	-0.40	0.02	0.02	0.30
Ruminant meat	7.60	0.00	0.00	0.00	0.00	0.02	-0.60	0.25	0.30
Non-ruminant meat	14.00	0.00	0.00	0.00	0.00	0.02	0.26	-0.90	0.55

EFTA-5

Rice	0.10	-0.60	0.40	0.10	0.00	0.00	0.00	0.00	0.11
Wheat	3.50	0.02	0.42	0.12	0.00	0.00	0.00	0.00	0.10
Coarse grain	1.20	0.00	0.40	-0.73	0.00	0.10	0.00	0.00	0.00
Sugar	1.50	0.00	0.00	0.00	-0.12	0.00	0.00	0.00	0.10
Dairy products	14.70	0.00	0.00	0.00	0.00	-0.20	0.00	0.00	0.10
Ruminant meat	0.70	0.00	0.00	0.00	0.00	0.00	-0.70	0.32	0.30
Non-ruminant meat	1.50	0.00	0.00	0.00	0.00	0.00	0.22	-0.70	0.55

Japan

Rice	10.5	-0.18	0.03	0.01	0.00	0.00	0.00	0.00	0.18
Wheat	6.30	0.24	-0.60	0.14	0.00	0.00	0.00	0.00	0.00
Coarse grain	3.80	0.16	0.25	-0.50	0.00	0.00	0.00	0.00	0.00
Sugar	2.90	0.01	0.00	0.00	-0.05	0.00	0.00	0.00	0.40
Dairy products	8.10	0.00	0.00	0.00	0.00	-0.80	0.00	0.00	0.44
Ruminant meat	0.70	0.00	0.00	0.00	0.00	0.00	-1.00	0.30	0.70
Non-ruminant meat	2.90	0.00	0.00	0.00	0.00	0.00	0.18	-1.40	1.00

(continued)

Table A4 (continued)

	Trend consumption 1980–82 (million tonnes)	Elasticity of direct demand with respect to the price of:							Income elasticity of demand
		Rice	Wheat	Coarse grain	Sugar	Dairy products	Ruminant meat	Non-ruminant meat	
New Zealand									
Rice	0.80	-0.30	0.01	0.00	0.00	0.00	0.00	0.00	0.10
Wheat	0.40	0.00	-0.15	0.00	0.00	0.00	0.00	0.00	0.25
Coarse grain	0.20	0.00	0.02	-0.15	0.00	0.00	0.00	0.00	0.00
Sugar	0.10	0.00	0.00	0.00	-0.18	0.00	0.00	0.00	0.15
Dairy products	3.00	0.00	0.00	0.00	0.00	-0.20	0.00	0.00	0.10
Ruminant meat	0.40	0.00	0.00	0.00	0.00	0.00	-0.60	0.10	0.20
Non-ruminant meat	0.07	0.00	0.00	0.00	0.00	0.00	0.40	-0.80	0.40
Spain & Portugal									
Rice	0.40	-0.50	0.13	0.10	0.00	0.00	0.00	0.00	0.11
Wheat	5.80	0.02	-0.42	0.15	0.00	0.00	0.00	0.00	0.10
Coarse grain	3.70	0.03	0.25	-0.30	0.01	0.00	0.00	0.00	0.00
Sugar	1.70	0.00	0.00	0.01	-0.24	0.00	0.00	0.00	0.18
Dairy products	8.00	0.00	0.00	0.00	0.00	-0.60	0.02	0.02	0.50
Ruminant meat	0.70	0.00	0.00	0.00	0.00	0.02	-0.90	0.40	0.40
Non-ruminant meat	2.30	0.00	0.00	0.00	0.00	0.01	0.20	-0.70	0.55

United States

Rice	2.00	-0.20	0.08	0.04	0.00	0.00	0.00	0.00	-0.10
Wheat	27.00	0.01	-0.12	0.06	0.00	0.00	0.00	0.00	-0.20
Coarse grain	26.80	0.01	0.08	-0.20	0.07	0.00	0.00	0.00	0.20
Sugar	8.70	0.00	0.00	0.05	-0.20	0.00	0.02	0.00	0.00
Dairy products	60.50	0.00	0.00	0.00	0.00	-0.30	0.02	0.01	-0.10
Ruminant meat	11.20	0.00	0.00	0.00	0.00	0.02	0.50	0.20	0.00
Non-ruminant meat	13.80	0.00	0.00	0.00	0.00	0.01	0.20	-0.80	0.41

USSR

Rice	2.10	-1.00	0.28	0.03	0.00	0.00	0.00	0.00	1.00
Wheat	106.00	0.02	-0.40	0.02	0.00	0.00	0.00	0.00	0.09
Coarse grain	28.40	0.00	0.07	-0.15	0.00	0.00	0.00	0.00	0.00
Sugar	14.00	0.00	0.00	0.00	-0.10	0.00	0.00	0.00	0.09
Dairy products	94.40	0.00	0.00	0.00	0.00	-0.50	0.01	0.00	0.40
Ruminant meat	80.00	0.00	0.00	0.00	0.00	0.02	-0.30	0.01	0.25
Non-ruminant meat	8.20	0.00	0.00	0.00	0.00	0.00	0.01	-0.70	0.50

Other centrally planned Europe

Rice	0.40	-0.70	0.16	0.10	0.00	0.00	0.00	0.00	0.30
Wheat	37.80	0.00	-0.20	0.05	0.00	0.00	0.00	0.00	0.10
Coarse grain	13.50	0.01	0.15	-0.20	0.00	0.00	0.00	0.00	0.00
Sugar	6.20	0.00	0.00	0.00	-0.80	0.00	0.00	0.00	0.80
Dairy products	43.90	0.00	0.00	0.00	0.00	0.00	-0.50	0.00	0.40
Ruminant meat	2.50	0.00	0.00	0.00	0.00	0.00	-0.50	0.20	0.30
Non-ruminant meat	8.10	0.00	0.00	0.00	0.00	0.00	0.07	-0.70	0.30

(continued)

Table A4 *(continued)*

	Trend consumption 1980–82 (million tonnes)	Elasticity of direct demand with respect to the price of:							Income elasticity of demand
		Rice	Wheat	Coarse grain	Sugar	Dairy products	Ruminant meat	Non-ruminant meat	
Egypt									
Rice	1.60	-0.60	0.20	0.00	0.00	0.00	0.00	0.00	0.40
Wheat	8.00	0.07	-0.65	0.10	0.00	0.00	0.00	0.00	0.48
Coarse grain	3.70	0.00	0.20	-0.50	0.00	0.00	0.00	0.00	0.00
Sugar	1.50	0.00	0.00	0.00	-0.80	0.00	0.00	0.00	0.70
Dairy products	2.70	0.00	0.00	0.00	0.00	-0.80	0.00	0.00	1.00
Ruminant meat	0.40	0.00	0.00	0.00	0.00	0.00	-1.30	0.20	1.00
Non-ruminant meat	0.20	0.00	0.00	0.00	0.00	0.00	0.40	-1.20	1.00
Nigeria									
Rice	1.60	-0.61	0.10	0.10	0.00	0.00	0.00	0.00	0.40
Wheat	1.60	0.20	-0.80	0.10	0.00	0.00	0.00	0.00	0.40
Coarse grain	7.80	0.04	0.02	-0.80	0.00	0.00	0.00	0.00	0.20
Sugar	1.10	0.00	0.00	0.00	-0.80	0.00	0.00	0.00	0.50
Dairy products	1.00	0.00	0.00	0.00	0.00	-1.00	0.00	0.00	1.00
Ruminant meat	0.40	0.00	0.00	0.00	0.00	0.00	-1.40	0.20	1.00
Non-ruminant meat	0.30	0.00	0.00	0.00	0.00	0.00	0.37	-1.40	1.00

South Africa

Rice	0.10	-0.50	0.05	0.10	0.00	0.00	0.00	0.00	0.40
Wheat	2.20	0.01	-0.30	0.05	0.00	0.00	0.00	0.00	0.25
Coarse grain	4.00	0.01	0.05	-0.30	0.00	0.00	0.00	0.00	0.20
Sugar	1.30	0.00	0.00	0.00	-0.60	0.00	0.00	0.00	0.57
Dairy products	2.60	0.00	0.00	0.00	0.00	-0.80	0.00	0.00	0.70
Ruminant meat	0.60	0.00	0.00	0.00	0.00	0.00	-1.00	0.28	0.70
Non-ruminant meat	0.40	0.00	0.00	0.00	0.00	0.00	0.40	-1.20	0.70

Other sub-Saharan Africa

Rice	5.30	-0.90	0.08	0.10	0.00	0.00	0.00	0.00	0.70
Wheat	3.40	0.20	-1.20	0.40	0.00	0.00	0.00	0.00	0.90
Coarse grain	27.40	0.05	0.10	-0.85	0.00	0.00	0.00	0.00	0.60
Sugar	2.80	0.00	0.00	0.00	-0.80	0.00	0.00	0.00	0.70
Dairy products	8.00	0.00	0.00	0.00	0.00	-0.80	0.00	0.00	0.80
Ruminant meat	2.70	0.00	0.00	0.00	0.00	0.00	-1.20	0.10	1.00
Non-ruminant meat	0.70	0.00	0.00	0.00	0.00	0.00	0.40	-1.40	0.70

Other North Africa and Middle East

Rice	3.20	-1.20	0.20	0.00	0.00	0.00	0.00	0.00	1.00
Wheat	43.10	0.03	-0.46	0.03	0.00	0.00	0.00	0.00	0.40
Coarse grain	9.30	0.00	0.27	-0.30	0.00	0.00	0.00	0.00	0.00
Sugar	6.00	0.00	0.00	0.00	-0.50	0.00	0.00	0.00	0.45
Dairy products	21.30	0.00	0.00	0.00	0.00	-1.00	0.00	0.00	1.00
Ruminant meat	2.50	0.00	0.00	0.00	0.00	0.00	-0.63	0.20	0.40
Non-ruminant meat	1.70	0.00	0.00	0.00	0.00	0.00	0.30	-1.00	0.70

(continued)

Table A4 *(continued)*

	Trend consumption 1980–82 (million tonnes)	Elasticity of direct demand with respect to the price of:							Income elasticity of demand
		Rice	Wheat	Coarse grain	Sugar	Dairy products	Ruminant meat	Non-ruminant meat	
Bangladesh									
Rice	14.40	-0.30	0.04	0.00	0.00	0.00	0.00	0.00	0.20
Wheat	2.60	0.50	-0.40	0.00	0.00	0.00	0.00	0.00	1.00
Coarse grain	0.30	0.80	0.15	-0.50	0.00	0.00	0.00	0.00	-1.50
Sugar	0.60	0.00	0.00	0.00	-1.00	0.00	0.00	0.00	1.00
Dairy products	1.70	0.00	0.00	0.00	0.00	-0.80	0.00	0.00	0.70
Ruminant meat	0.20	0.00	0.00	0.00	0.00	0.00	-1.20	0.20	0.75
Non-ruminant meat	0.80	0.00	0.00	0.00	0.00	0.00	0.80	-1.70	1.10
China									
Rice	109.80	-0.20	0.13	0.05	0.00	0.00	0.00	0.00	0.00
Wheat	85.80	0.14	-0.30	0.06	0.00	0.00	0.00	0.00	0.25
Coarse grain	64.10	0.10	0.10	-0.30	0.00	0.00	0.00	0.00	0.10
Sugar	6.60	0.00	0.00	0.00	-1.50	0.00	0.00	0.00	1.00
Dairy products	8.00	0.00	0.00	0.00	0.00	-2.00	0.00	0.00	1.00
Ruminant meat	0.70	0.00	0.00	0.00	0.00	0.00	-1.50	0.40	1.00
Non-ruminant meat	15.00	0.00	0.00	0.00	0.00	0.00	0.04	-1.00	0.90

India									
Rice	53.3	-0.40	0.10	0.02	0.00	0.00	0.00	0.00	0.40
Wheat	40.20	0.24	-0.40	0.06	0.00	0.00	0.00	0.00	0.90
Coarse grain	30.60	0.07	0.10	-0.35	0.00	0.00	0.00	0.00	-0.11
Sugar	15.10	0.00	0.00	0.00	-0.80	0.00	0.00	0.00	0.70
Dairy products	43.30	0.00	0.00	0.00	0.00	-1.00	-0.10	0.00	0.70
Ruminant meat	0.60	0.00	0.00	0.00	0.00	0.01	0.00	0.20	0.05
Non-ruminant meat	0.20	0.00	0.00	0.00	0.00	0.00	0.00	-1.40	1.10
Indonesia									
Rice	23.70	-0.51	0.03	0.02	0.01	0.00	0.00	0.00	0.40
Wheat	1.60	0.50	-1.20	0.02	0.00	0.00	0.00	0.00	0.55
Coarse grain	3.40	0.25	0.02	-0.35	0.00	0.00	0.00	0.00	-0.10
Sugar	2.40	0.02	0.00	0.00	-1.20	0.00	0.00	0.00	1.20
Dairy products	0.50	0.00	0.00	0.00	0.00	-1.00	0.00	0.00	1.00
Ruminant meat	0.20	0.00	0.00	0.00	0.00	0.00	-1.40	0.20	1.00
Non-ruminant meat	0.30	0.00	0.00	0.00	0.00	0.00	0.25	-1.40	1.10
Korea									
Rice	5.40	-1.18	0.02	0.01	0.00	0.00	0.00	0.00	0.05
Wheat	2.20	0.20	-0.36	0.08	0.00	0.00	0.00	0.00	0.10
Coarse grain	2.90	0.10	0.10	-0.22	0.00	0.00	0.00	0.00	0.00
Sugar	0.40	0.01	0.00	0.00	-0.80	0.00	0.00	0.00	0.60
Dairy products	0.50	0.00	0.00	0.00	0.00	-0.80	0.00	0.00	0.70
Ruminant meat	0.10	0.00	0.00	0.00	0.00	0.00	-1.20	0.40	0.77
Non-ruminant meat	0.30	0.00	0.00	0.00	0.00	0.00	0.26	-1.50	1.20

(continued)

Table A4 *(continued)*

	Trend consumption 1980–82 (million tonnes)	Elasticity of direct demand with respect to the price of:							Income elasticity of demand
		Rice	Wheat	Coarse grain	Sugar	Dairy products	Ruminant meat	Non-ruminant meat	
Pakistan									
Rice	2.20	-0.35	0.15	0.01	0.00	0.00	0.00	0.00	1.20
Wheat	12.00	0.05	-0.40	0.01	0.00	0.00	0.00	0.00	0.51
Coarse grain	1.50	0.03	0.12	-0.35	0.00	0.00	0.00	0.00	-1.40
Sugar	2.80	0.00	0.00	0.00	-1.00	0.00	0.00	0.00	1.00
Dairy products	9.60	0.00	0.00	0.00	0.00	-1.00	0.00	0.00	1.00
Ruminant meat	0.70	0.00	0.00	0.00	0.00	0.00	-1.30	0.05	1.10
Non-ruminant meat	0.60	0.00	0.00	0.00	0.00	0.00	1.00	-1.40	1.10
Philippines									
Rice	5.40	-0.42	0.02	0.05	0.02	0.00	0.00	0.00	0.29
Wheat	0.90	0.15	-0.20	0.04	0.00	0.00	0.00	0.00	0.03
Coarse grain	1.60	0.25	0.02	-0.25	0.00	0.00	0.00	0.00	-0.10
Sugar	1.50	0.05	0.00	0.00	-1.40	0.00	0.00	0.00	1.40
Dairy products	0.50	0.00	0.00	0.00	0.00	-1.00	0.00	0.07	1.00
Ruminant meat	0.10	0.00	0.00	0.00	0.00	0.00	-0.80	0.13	0.66
Non-ruminant meat	0.60	0.00	0.00	0.00	0.00	0.01	0.06	-0.50	0.42

Taiwan

Rice	1.80	-0.20	0.02	0.01	0.00	0.00	0.00	0.00	-0.10
Wheat	0.70	0.20	-0.36	0.04	0.00	0.00	0.00	0.00	0.20
Coarse grain	0.30	0.20	0.08	-0.30	0.00	0.00	0.00	0.00	0.00
Sugar	0.50	0.01	0.00	0.00	-0.80	0.00	0.00	0.00	0.60
Dairy products	0.60	0.00	0.00	0.00	0.00	-1.00	0.00	0.00	0.70
Ruminant meat	0.20	0.00	0.00	0.00	0.00	0.00	-1.50	0.50	0.90
Non-ruminant meat	0.70	0.00	0.00	0.00	0.00	0.00	0.05	-0.80	0.50

Thailand

Rice	8.00	-0.05	0.00	0.00	0.00	0.00	0.00	0.00	0.04
Wheat	0.20	0.20	-0.66	0.03	0.00	0.00	0.00	0.00	0.87
Coarse grain	0.30	0.07	0.20	-0.40	0.00	0.00	0.00	0.00	0.00
Sugar	1.50	0.01	0.00	0.00	-0.70	0.00	0.00	0.00	0.60
Dairy products	0.20	0.00	0.00	0.00	0.00	-0.80	0.00	0.10	0.80
Ruminant meat	0.20	0.00	0.00	0.00	0.00	0.00	-1.20	0.25	0.70
Non-ruminant meat	0.50	0.00	0.00	0.00	0.00	0.01	0.09	-1.40	0.60

Other Asia

Rice	28.40	-0.20	0.03	0.02	0.00	0.00	0.00	0.00	0.12
Wheat	7.20	0.18	-0.60	0.13	0.00	0.00	0.00	0.00	0.23
Coarse grain	7.20	0.20	0.15	-0.35	0.00	0.00	0.00	0.00	0.00
Sugar	1.80	0.00	0.00	0.00	-1.00	0.00	0.00	0.00	1.00
Dairy products	3.90	0.00	0.00	0.00	0.00	-1.00	0.00	0.00	0.80
Ruminant meat	0.90	0.00	0.00	0.00	0.00	0.00	-1.40	0.50	0.90
Non-ruminant meat	1.60	0.00	0.00	0.00	0.00	0.00	0.30	-1.40	1.00

(continued)

Table A4 *(continued)*

	Trend consumption 1980–82 (million tonnes)	Elasticity of direct demand with respect to the price of:							Income elasticity of demand
		Rice	Wheat	Coarse grain	Sugar	Dairy products	Ruminant meat	Non-ruminant meat	
Argentina									
Rice	0.10	-1.00	0.30	0.07	0.00	0.00	0.00	0.00	0.50
Wheat	4.80	0.02	-0.30	0.06	0.00	0.00	0.00	0.00	0.02
Coarse grain	0.80	0.00	0.50	-0.50	0.00	0.00	0.00	0.00	0.00
Sugar	1.00	0.00	0.00	0.00	-0.60	0.00	0.00	0.00	0.50
Dairy products	5.50	0.00	0.00	0.00	0.00	-0.80	0.00	0.00	0.80
Ruminant meat	2.40	0.00	0.00	0.00	0.00	0.00	-0.40	0.08	0.30
Non-ruminant meat	0.70	0.00	0.00	0.00	0.00	0.00	0.25	-0.90	0.60
Brazil									
Rice	6.30	-0.70	0.20	0.10	0.00	0.00	0.00	0.00	0.29
Wheat	6.60	0.25	-0.30	0.04	0.00	0.00	0.00	0.00	0.43
Coarse grain	3.10	0.56	0.16	-0.70	0.00	0.00	0.00	0.00	0.00
Sugar	6.60	0.00	0.00	0.00	-0.60	0.00	0.00	0.00	0.40
Dairy products	10.60	0.00	0.00	0.00	0.00	-0.80	0.00	0.00	0.80
Ruminant meat	2.20	0.00	0.00	0.00	0.00	0.00	-0.70	0.25	0.44
Non-ruminant meat	2.20	0.00	0.00	0.00	0.00	0.00	0.25	-0.90	0.70

Cuba

Rice	0.50	-0.60	0.14	0.04	0.00	0.00	0.00	0.00	0.30
Wheat	1.10	0.15	-0.20	0.00	0.00	0.00	0.00	0.00	0.03
Coarse grain	0.20	0.22	0.02	-0.25	0.00	0.00	0.00	0.00	-0.10
Sugar	0.50	0.00	0.00	0.00	-1.40	0.00	0.00	0.00	1.40
Dairy products	1.70	0.00	0.00	0.00	0.00	-1.00	0.00	0.01	1.00
Ruminant meat	0.10	0.00	0.00	0.00	0.00	0.00	-0.80	0.13	0.66
Non-ruminant meat	0.10	0.00	0.00	0.00	0.01	0.01	0.12	-0.60	0.50

Mexico

Rice	0.30	-0.50	0.20	0.00	0.00	0.00	0.00	0.00	0.27
Wheat	4.20	0.04	-0.35	0.10	0.00	0.00	0.00	0.00	0.20
Coarse grain	12.30	0.00	0.05	-0.85	0.00	0.00	0.00	0.00	0.00
Sugar	3.60	0.00	0.00	0.00	-0.85	0.00	0.00	0.00	0.53
Dairy products	7.50	0.00	0.00	-0.03	0.00	0.50	0.00	0.00	0.04
Ruminant meat	0.70	0.00	0.00	0.00	0.00	0.00	-1.16	0.50	0.65
Non-ruminant meat	1.00	0.00	0.00	0.00	0.00	0.00	0.40	-1.20	0.80

Other Latin America

Rice	3.80	-0.70	0.20	0.10	0.00	0.00	0.00	0.00	0.40
Wheat	6.50	0.13	-0.45	0.12	0.00	0.00	0.00	0.00	0.20
Coarse grain	6.50	0.13	0.21	-0.40	0.00	0.00	0.00	0.00	0.00
Sugar	6.70	0.00	0.00	0.00	-0.60	0.00	0.00	0.00	0.50
Dairy products	12.30	0.00	0.00	0.00	0.00	-0.80	0.00	0.00	0.80
Ruminant meat	2.40	0.00	0.00	0.00	0.00	0.00	-0.80	0.30	0.40
Non-ruminant meat	1.90	0.00	0.00	0.00	0.00	0.00	0.30	-1.00	1.00

Table A5: Livestock feedgrain demand parameters[a]

Proportion of livestock grainfed in:	Dairy cattle		Beef cattle and sheep		Pigs and poultry	
	1982	2000	1982	2000	1982	2000
Industrial market economies						
Australia	0.00	0.00	0.00	0.00	0.95	0.97
Canada	0.87	0.90	0.87	0.90	0.87	0.90
EC-10	0.38	0.42	0.38	0.42	0.38	0.42
EFTA-5	0.58	0.65	0.58	0.65	0.58	0.65
Japan	0.84	0.85	0.84	0.85	0.84	0.85
New Zealand	0.00	0.00	0.00	0.00	0.85	0.89
Spain and Portugal	0.79	0.85	0.79	0.85	0.79	0.85
United States	0.81	0.82	0.81	0.82	0.81	0.82
Centrally planned Europe						
USSR	0.61	0.66	0.61	0.66	0.61	0.66
Other East Europe	0.70	0.75	0.70	0.75	0.70	0.75
Developing economies						
Egypt	0.35	0.42	0.35	0.42	0.35	0.42
Nigeria	0.00	0.00	0.00	0.00	0.31	0.35
South Africa	0.41	0.45	0.41	0.45	1.00	1.00
Other sub-Saharan Africa	0.00	0.00	0.00	0.00	0.24	0.30
Other North Africa & Middle East	0.49	0.54	0.49	0.54	1.00	1.00
Bangladesh	0.00	0.00	0.00	0.00	0.06	0.15
China	0.00	0.34	0.00	0.26	0.29	0.50
India	0.00	0.00	0.00	0.00	0.21	0.26
Indonesia	0.00	0.00	0.00	0.00	0.58	0.65
Korea	0.94	0.95	0.94	0.95	0.94	0.95
Pakistan	0.00	0.00	0.00	0.00	0.40	0.45
Philippines	0.00	0.00	0.00	0.00	0.59	0.69
Taiwan	0.75	0.80	0.75	0.80	0.75	0.80
Thailand	0.00	0.00	0.00	0.00	0.44	0.52
Other Asia	0.00	0.00	0.00	0.00	0.13	0.20
Argentina	0.12	0.15	0.12	0.15	1.00	1.00
Brazil	0.31	0.35	0.31	0.35	1.00	1.00
Cuba	0.00	0.00	0.00	0.00	0.35	0.50
Mexico	0.25	0.30	0.25	0.30	1.00	1.00
Other Latin America	0.00	0.00	0.00	0.00	0.65	0.73

[a] The proportion of livestock grainfed is assumed to increase at a steady rate between 1982 and 2000. For all countries it is assumed that the grain used per unit of livestock product from grainfed animals is 0.40 for dairy cows, 6.0 for beef cattle and sheep and 5.0 for pigs and poultry.

Table A6: Assumed per cent reductions in United States production due to land set-asides and the conservation reserve

	Wheat	Coarse grain	Rice	Dairy products
1980–82 (average)	2	1	2	0
1983	16	39	31	0
1984	8	4	15	0
1985	10	1	22	0
1986	18	7	22	6
1987	15	11	24	6
1988	17	13	24	6
1989	10	9	24	6
1990	4	7	24	6
1991	6	7	24	6
1992	5	5	24	6
1993	3	4	24	6
1994	3	3	24	6
1995	3	3	24	6
1996	3	3	24	6
1997	3	3	24	6
1998	3	3	24	6
1999	3	3	24	6
2000	3	3	24	6

Source: Calculations based on Glaser (1986) and Johnson *et al.* (1986).

Table A7: Exogenous changes in bilateral real exchange rates[a], 1980 to 2000

	1980–82	1983	1984	1985	1986	1987	1988	1989	1990	1995	2000
Industrial market economies											
Australia	100	90	89	78	75	71	74	74	73	72	72
Canada	100	101	97	92	90	93	94	91	91	92	92
EC–10[b]	100	80	72	70	90	102	105	103	102	102	102
EFTA–5[b]	100	83	76	74	97	110	118	122	125	130	130
Japan	100	91	88	87	122	135	142	148	151	152	152
New Zealand	100	85	79	69	78	88	93	93	96	94	94
Spain and Portugal[b]	100	72	68	68	89	101	101	100	99	98	98
United States	100	100	100	100	100	100	100	100	100	100	100
Centrally planned Europe											
USSR	100	85	77	75	87	92	94	96	97	97	97
Other East Europe	100	90	82	75	80	74	76	77	78	78	78
Developing economies											
Egypt	100	95	100	108	115	86	86	86	86	86	86
Nigeria	100	96	97	89	59	22	22	23	23	23	23
South Africa	100	94	79	58	63	76	88	99	109	119	119
Other sub-Sahara Africa[d]	100	86	71	68	72	73	73	73	73	73	73
Other N Africa & Middle East[e]	100	89	80	68	57	69	69	69	69	69	69
Bangladesh	100	71	82	87	78	82	82	82	82	82	82
China	100	79	68	57	49	46	46	46	46	46	46
India	100	91	81	81	81	82	84	84	84	84	84

Indonesia	100	79	75	71	59	50	49	50	51	51	51
Korea	100	89	86	80	79	83	83	84	85	85	85
Pakistan	100	83	83	76	73	68	69	73	72	74	74
Philippines	100	79	76	78	70	72	76	76	79	81	81
Taiwan	100	91	89	87	87	87	88	86	85	85	85
Thailand	100	93	88	75	77	79	79	79	78	79	79
Other Asia[e]	100	92	89	84	80	80	81	81	81	81	81
Argentina	100	54	61	52	58	55	52	49	45	42	42
Brazil	100	74	69	67	67	72	76	72	68	65	65
Cuba[c]	100	85	77	75	87	92	94	96	97	97	97
Mexico	100	67	75	73	53	52	51	51	52	53	53
Other Latin America[e]	100	92	82	75	73	71	67	65	62	59	59

[a] Rates are expressed in $US per local currency and converted into indices with base 100 in 1980–82. Nominal rates are adjusted using GDP deflators, or, where these are inappropriate or unavailable, consumer price indices.

[b] In country groups, the index is based on representative currencies. In the case of the EC, the French Franc is used; for EFTA-5, the Finnish Markkaa; and for Spain and Portugal, the Spanish Peso.

[c] The centrally planned economies, for which no data are readily available, are assigned real exchange rate changes equivalent to the global average (based on the real effective rate for the US).

[d] In the case of 'other sub-Saharan Africa', all African average consumer price indices are used and purchasing power parity is assumed to be retained after 1986, as in the case of Egypt.

[e] Aggregates of developing countries are assigned rates for representative currencies. For 'other North Africa and Middle East', the currency of Iran is used; for 'other Asia', that of India; and for 'other Latin America', that of Chile.

Sources: Values through 1987 are drawn from the International Monetary Fund, *International Financial Statistics*, Washington, D.C., various issues. For later years, the rates are derived from simulations presented in Wharton Econometric Associates, *World Economic Outlook*, May 1986.

Table A8: Share of world production (Q) and net exports (NX) in various food products, individual countries/country groups, 1980 to 1982 (per cent)

		Rice	Wheat	Coarse grain	Sugar	Dairy products	Ruminant meat	Non-ruminant meat	WEIGHTED AVERAGE
Industrial market economies									
Australia	Q	0.2	2.6	0.6	3.2	1.2	4.0	0.7	1.6
	NX	4.2	9.0	1.4	12.2	2.6	15.2	0.3	6.8
Canada	Q	:	5.1	3.5	0.1	1.7	1.9	1.8	2.1
	NX	:	18.0	5.4	-5.0	1.1	-0.3	3.4	5.9
EC-10	Q	0.3	12.3	10.4	13.8	24.7	14.6	18.4	13.5
	NX	-7.5	9.4	-7.4	-6.9	26.1	-2.5	6.4	2.4
EFTA-5	Q	0.0	0.7	1.8	1.0	3.4	1.4	1.9	1.5
	NX	-1.7	-0.1	-0.8	-1.2	3.6	-0.6	0.2	0.0
Japan	Q	3.4	0.1	0.1	0.8	1.4	0.9	3.2	1.9
	NX	3.9	-6.0	-18.4	-11.7	-2.9	-8.0	-5.9	-10.2
New Zealand	Q	:	0.1	0.1	0.0	0.7	0.6	0.1	0.5
	NX	:	-0.1	0.1	-0.8	8.7	13.8	:	2.6
Spain and Portugal	Q	0.1	1.1	1.5	1.1	1.6	1.3	2.8	1.5
	NX	-1.0	-0.4	-9.5	-1.5	-1.6	-0.9	-0.4	-3.0
United States	Q	1.9	15.6	32.0	5.1	12.9	19.9	17.9	15.0
	NX	25.5	41.9	57.0	-21.0	-0.9	-6.7	5.6	19.3
Total	**Q**	**2.9**	**37.5**	**49.8**	**24.4**	**47.0**	**45.5**	**44.3**	**36.0**
	NX	**5.6**	**76.8**	**44.2**	**-27.6**	**37.8**	**16.2**	**11.8**	**31.6**

Centrally planned Europe									
USSR	Q	0.6	19.1	11.8	6.5	19.4	14.3	9.6	11.0
	NX	-10.9	-20.1	-18.9	-27.5	-4.7	-9.3	-8.6	-15.7
Other East Europe	Q	:	7.2	9.6	5.0	9.4	4.8	10.9	7.9
	NX	-4.9	-4.2	-6.6	-3.0	-0.9	1.6	10.0	-1.3
Total	**Q**	**0.7**	**26.3**	**21.4**	**11.5**	**28.8**	**19.2**	**20.5**	**18.9**
	NX	**-15.8**	**-24.3**	**-25.5**	**-30.5**	**-3.7**	**-7.7**	**1.4**	**-17.1**
Developing Economies									
Egypt	Q	0.6	0.4	0.5	0.7	0.4	0.6	0.2	0.5
	NX	0.6	-6.1	-1.4	-0.1	-1.3	-2.2	-1.4	-2.8
Nigeria	Q	0.3	:	0.3	0.1	0.1	0.8	0.3	0.2
	NX	-8.4	-1.6	-0.4	:	0.1	-0.5	-0.3	-1.1
South Africa	Q	:	0.5	1.4	2.0	0.6	1.4	0.4	0.7
	NX	-2.0	-0.1	2.2	4.0	-0.1	0.2	0.2	0.9
Other sub-Saharan	Q	1.3	0.3	2.2	3.1	1.7	4.7	0.9	2.2
	NX	-0.1	-2.0	-1.4	6.2	-2.6	-0.7	-0.8	-0.3
Other N Africa & Middle East	Q	0.5	6.7	2.3	2.5	2.9	3.9	1.5	2.9
	NX	:	-11.0	-8.5	-5.9	-13.4	-10.4	-12.4	-9.8
Bangladesh	Q	5.1	0.2	:	0.6	0.3	0.3	0.1	1.1
	NX	-2.6	-1.3	:	:	-0.3	:	:	-0.5
China	Q	38.2	13.3	10.3	3.6	0.7	1.4	17.4	13.8
	NX	3.1	-14.4	-1.8	-7.7	-0.1	0.3	4.3	-4.9
India	Q	18.9	7.6	1.3	13.8	7.1	1.3	0.3	6.1
	NX	5.0	-1.6	:	0.2	-0.7	1.0	:	-0.1
Indonesia	Q	8.0	:	0.6	1.6	:	0.5	0.4	1.9
	NX	-13.9	-1.6	-0.1	:	-0.9	:	:	-0.8
Korea, Rep.	Q	1.7	:	0.1	:	0.1	0.2	0.5	0.5
	NX	-13.3	-2.1	-3.7	-4.2	:	-0.7	:	-2.7

(continued)

Table A8 *(continued)*

		Rice	Wheat	Coarse grain	Sugar	Dairy products	Ruminant meat	Non-ruminant meat	WEIGHTED AVERAGE
Pakistan	Q	1.2	2.4	0.2	2.6	2.0	1.3	0.1	1.2
	NX	10.2	-0.4			-0.3			0.4
Philippines	Q	1.9		0.5	2.2		0.2	0.7	0.7
	NX	0.6	-1.0	-0.4	6.2	-1.2	-1.0		0.1
Taiwan	Q	0.8			0.8			1.1	0.4
	NX	2.5	-0.7	-3.8	1.6	-0.5	-1.9	0.4	-1.1
Thailand	Q	4.2		0.6	2.3		0.4	0.7	1.0
	NX	33.6	-0.2	2.6	6.2	-0.4	0.1	0.6	2.8
Other Asia	Q	9.9	0.9	0.9	1.2	0.6	1.7	2.1	2.4
	NX	0.2	-2.6	-1.9	-0.5	-2.8	-2.6	-4.5	-1.7
Argentina	Q	0.1	2.3	1.7	1.6	1.2	5.5	0.8	2.0
	NX	0.9	5.6	7.5	2.1	0.1	7.4	-0.3	4.5
Brazil	Q	2.1	0.5	3.3	8.4	2.4	4.3	3.1	2.8
	NX	-2.3	-4.4		9.1	-0.4	1.7	5.6	0.1
Cuba	Q	0.1			7.1	0.2	0.3	0.2	0.9
	NX	-3.0	-1.0	-0.5	34.3	-0.9	-0.7	-0.5	5.6
Mexico	Q	0.1	0.7	1.6	2.7	1.6	1.7	2.3	1.5
	NX	-0.8	-0.8	-3.4	-3.4	-1.9	-0.1	-0.9	-1.8
Other Latin America	Q	1.4	0.3	1.0	7.4	2.2	4.7	2.2	2.5
	NX		-5.2	-3.4	9.9	-4.5	1.9	-3.3	-1.5
Total	**Q**	**96.4**	**36.2**	**28.7**	**64.1**	**24.2**	**35.4**	**35.2**	**45.1**
	NX	**10.2**	**-52.5**	**-18.6**	**58.1**	**-33.9**	**8.4**	**-13.3**	**-14.5**

Table A9: Self-sufficiency in various food products, individual countries/country groups, 1980 to 1982 (production as a percentage of consumption)

	Rice	Wheat	Coarse grain	Sugar	Dairy products	Ruminant meat	Non-ruminant meat	WEIGHTED AVERAGE
Industrial market economies								
Australia	747	353	139	331	123	173	102	187
Canada	–	459	139	12	106	99	113	149
EC-10	76	127	94	93	110	100	103	104
EFTA-5	–	98	97	84	110	97	101	100
Japan	87	10	3	30	86	51	91	62
New Zealand	–	85	126	–	195	353	98	251
Spain and Portugal	87	92	56	81	93	94	99	85
United States	246	313	146	60	102	97	102	121
Total	**138**	**201**	**123**	**85**	**108**	**105**	**102**	**114**
Centrally planned Europe								
USSR	70	83	83	59	98	94	95	88
Other East Europe	27	90	93	91	101	105	106	99
Total	**63**	**85**	**87**	**70**	**99**	**96**	**101**	**92**
Developing economies								
Egypt	104	25	73	99	82	71	70	63
Nigeria	58	2	84	100	38	94	95	66
South Africa	–	103	121	161	99	102	103	114

(continued)

Table A9 *(continued)*

	Rice	Wheat	Coarse grain	Sugar	Dairy products	Ruminant meat	Non-ruminant meat	WEIGHTED AVERAGE
Other sub-Saharan Africa	101	46	94	161	89	99	95	100
Other N Africa & Middle East	101	75	69	72	74	78	70	74
Bangladesh	99	46	91	100	92	100	100	96
China	99	78	94	75	99	102	101	95
India	99	97	100	100	99	109	100	99
Indonesia	97	–	99	100	22	99	100	97
Korea, Rep.	88	4	22	–	97	72	100	67
Pakistan	151	99	100	100	99	100	100	106
Philippines	99	–	90	206	7	66	100	101
Taiwan	124	–	4	162	22	6	102	79
Thailand	141	–	332	195	17	103	105	143
Other Asia	100	64	80	99	73	87	90	93
Argentina	183	237	274	133	101	117	98	135
Brazil	92	35	99	125	99	105	112	100
Cuba	62	–	18	1400	76	79	87	329
Mexico	87	85	78	83	93	99	98	90
Other Latin America	100	24	71	134	87	105	93	95
Total	**100**	**77**	**92**	**122**	**90**	**98**	**98**	**97**

Table A10: Exogenous population and income projections (growth rates, per cent per year)

	Population		GNP	
	1982–87[a]	**1987–2000**	**1982–87[a]**	**1987–2000**
Australia	1.0	1.0	4.0	3.0
Canada	0.9	0.9	4.5	3.0
EC-10	0.2	0.2	2.0	2.6
EFTA-5	0.1	0.1	3.0	2.5
Japan	0.6	0.5	4.5	3.2
New Zealand	0.7	0.7	2.3	2.0
Spain & Portugal	0.6	0.6	3.6	5.0
United States	0.7	0.7	4.4	3.0
USSR	0.7	0.7	2.5	2.3
Other centrally planned Europe	0.3	0.3	3.8	3.5
Egypt	2.1	2.0	2.4	2.0
Nigeria	3.3	3.3	0.2	4.0
South Africa	2.7	2.7	1.5	3.0
Other sub-Saharan Africa	3.0	3.0	0.1	3.0
Other North Africa & Middle East	3.7	3.7	0.2	3.0
Bangladesh	2.5	2.3	3.6	3.5
China	1.3	1.3	6.7	6.0
India	2.3	1.8	4.9	4.3
Indonesia	2.2	1.9	4.1	4.0
Korea	1.5	1.4	7.1	6.5
Pakistan	3.0	2.4	5.7	5.5
Philippines	2.5	2.1	-0.3	3.0
Taiwan	1.7	1.7	7.3	6.6
Thailand	2.0	1.7	5.6	6.0
Other Asia	2.0	2.0	4.7	4.0
Argentina	1.5	1.3	1.8	4.0
Brazil	2.0	1.9	3.9	5.0
Cuba	2.2	2.2	3.6	3.0
Mexico	2.4	2.3	1.6	3.0
Other Latin America	2.2	2.2	2.1	3.0

[a] Actual data are used in this interval. Listed here are period averages only.
Sources: World Bank (1986) and Wharton Econometric Associates (1986).

Table A11: Parameters in stockholding equations

	Constant term, ω	Coefficient of	
	(Fraction of domestic production or consumption)	Departure from trend production (Ω)	Expected unit profit (π) x 1000
Australia			
Rice	0.53	0.19	0.62
Wheat	0.25	0.42	0.34
Coarse grain	0.06	0.06	0.23
Sugar	0.19	0.20	0.30
Dairy products	0.12	0.20	0.10
Canada			
Rice	n.a.	n.a.	n.a.
Wheat	0.37	0.20	0.38
Coarse grain	0.28	0.20	0.30
Sugar	0.08	0.20	0.30
Dairy products	0.13	0.20	0.10
EC-10			
Rice	0.21	0.20	0.00
Wheat	0.15	0.20	0.30
Coarse grain	0.09	0.20	0.25
Sugar	0.25	0.20	0.20
Dairy products	0.09	0.20	0.10
EFTA-5			
Rice	0.10	0.20	0.00
Wheat	0.51	0.20	0.26
Coarse grain	0.21	0.20	0.25
Sugar	0.23	0.20	0.20
Dairy products	0.70	0.20	0.10
Japan			
Rice	0.11	0.14	0.55
Wheat	0.28	0.25	0.18
Coarse grain	0.11	0.25	0.22
Sugar	0.10	0.20	0.20
Dairy products	0.05	0.20	0.10
New Zealand			
Rice	n.a.	n.a.	n.a.
Wheat	0.30	0.40	0.40
Coarse grain	0.40	0.10	0.30
Sugar	0.22	0.20	0.30
Dairy products	0.17	0.20	0.10

	Constant term, ω	Coefficient of	
	(Fraction of domestic production or consumption)	**Departure from trend production (Ω)**	**Expected unit profit (π) x 1000**
Spain and Portugal			
Rice	0.33	0.20	0.10
Wheat	0.34	0.20	0.30
Coarse grain	0.12	0.20	0.30
Sugar	0.10	0.20	0.20
Dairy products	0.09	0.20	0.10
United States			
Rice	0.49	0.30	0.44
Wheat	0.54	0.60	0.46
Coarse grain	0.46	0.50	0.24
Sugar	0.29	0.20	0.20
Dairy products	0.13	0.20	0.10
USSR			
Rice	0.20	0.00	0.20
Wheat	0.30	0.00	0.30
Coarse grain	0.20	0.00	0.30
Sugar	0.24	0.00	0.20
Dairy products	0.06	0.00	0.10
Other centrally planned Europe			
Rice	0.10	0.00	0.20
Wheat	0.12	0.00	0.30
Coarse grain	0.06	0.00	0.30
Sugar	0.32	0.00	0.20
Dairy products	0.02	0.00	0.10
Egypt			
Rice	0.10	0.10	0.20
Wheat	0.04	0.40	0.50
Coarse grain	0.43	0.10	0.40
Sugar	0.16	0.20	0.20
Dairy products	0.01	0.20	0.10
Nigeria			
Rice	0.12	0.30	0.40
Wheat	0.06	0.40	0.40
Coarse grain	0.02	0.10	0.40
Sugar	0.21	0.20	0.20
Dairy products	0.02	0.20	0.10

(continued)

Table A11 *(continued)*

	Constant term, ω	Coefficient of	
	(Fraction of domestic production or consumption)	Departure from trend production (Ω)	Expected unit profit (π) x 1000
South Africa			
Rice	0.06	0.10	0.20
Wheat	0.38	0.60	0.50
Coarse grain	0.07	0.60	0.50
Sugar	0.18	0.20	0.20
Dairy products	0.06	0.20	0.10
Other sub-Saharan Africa			
Rice	0.04	0.10	0.40
Wheat	0.07	0.20	0.40
Coarse grain	0.06	0.40	0.40
Sugar	0.26	0.20	0.20
Dairy products	0.03	0.20	0.10
Other North Africa and Middle East			
Rice	0.10	0.19	0.62
Wheat	0.20	0.42	0.34
Coarse grain	0.11	0.06	0.23
Sugar	0.28	0.20	0.30
Dairy products	0.03	0.20	0.10
Bangladesh			
Rice	0.02	0.03	0.10
Wheat	0.17	0.60	0.62
Coarse grain	0.30	0.00	0.25
Sugar	0.23	0.20	0.20
Dairy products	0.08	0.20	0.10
China			
Rice	0.10	0.00	0.50
Wheat	0.20	0.00	0.50
Coarse grain	0.10	0.00	0.30
Sugar	0.04	0.00	0.20
Dairy products	0.09	0.00	0.10
India			
Rice	0.09	0.45	0.37
Wheat	0.22	0.72	0.31
Coarse grain	0.05	0.05	0.22
Sugar	0.15	0.20	0.20
Dairy products	0.10	0.20	0.10

	Constant term, ω	Coefficient of	
	(Fraction of domestic production or consumption)	Departure from trend production (Ω)	Expected unit profit (π) x 1000
Indonesia			
Rice	0.08	0.20	0.28
Wheat	0.17	0.20	0.00
Coarse grain	0.04	0.00	0.25
Sugar	0.40	0.20	0.20
Dairy products	0.08	0.20	0.10
Korea			
Rice	0.26	1.00	0.23
Wheat	0.09	0.85	0.64
Coarse grain	0.08	1.25	0.49
Sugar	0.17	0.20	0.20
Dairy products	0.01	0.20	0.10
Pakistan			
Rice	0.14	0.05	0.44
Wheat	0.16	0.05	0.34
Coarse grain	0.03	0.00	0.25
Sugar	0.17	0.00	0.20
Dairy products	0.10	0.20	0.10
Philippines			
Rice	0.21	0.50	0.58
Wheat	0.09	0.60	0.00
Coarse grain	0.05	0.85	0.48
Sugar	0.15	0.20	0.20
Dairy products	0.04	0.20	0.10
Taiwan			
Rice	0.20	0.40	0.50
Wheat	0.49	0.50	0.25
Coarse grain	0.10	0.95	0.25
Sugar	0.70	0.60	0.20
Dairy products	0.03	0.20	0.10
Thailand			
Rice	0.09	0.20	0.59
Wheat	0.18	0.60	0.62
Coarse grain	0.05	0.20	0.62
Sugar	0.05	0.20	0.30
Dairy products	0.04	0.20	0.10

(continued)

Table A11 *(continued)*

	Constant term, ω (Fraction of domestic production or consumption)	Coefficient of Departure from trend production (Ω)	Coefficient of Expected unit profit (π) x 1000
Other Asia			
Rice	0.04	0.05	0.46
Wheat	0.02	0.05	0.34
Coarse grain	0.03	0.00	0.25
Sugar	0.17	0.00	0.20
Dairy products	0.03	0.20	0.10
Argentina			
Rice	0.09	0.20	0.20
Wheat	0.07	0.80	0.50
Coarse grain	0.04	0.80	0.30
Sugar	0.20	0.20	0.20
Dairy products	0.05	0.20	0.10
Brazil			
Rice	0.06	0.20	0.20
Wheat	0.09	0.40	0.40
Coarse grain	0.04	1.00	0.50
Sugar	0.24	1.00	0.40
Dairy products	0.10	0.20	0.10
Cuba			
Rice	0.02	0.50	0.58
Wheat	0.10	0.60	0.00
Coarse grain	0.10	0.85	0.48
Sugar	0.17	0.20	0.20
Dairy products	0.10	0.20	0.10
Mexico			
Rice	0.18	0.20	0.20
Wheat	0.10	0.80	0.40
Coarse grain	0.08	0.40	0.40
Sugar	0.04	0.60	0.20
Dairy products	0.06	0.20	0.10
Other Latin America			
Rice	0.29	0.20	0.20
Wheat	0.11	0.40	0.40
Coarse grain	0.09	1.00	0.50
Sugar	0.13	1.00	0.40
Dairy products	0.04	0.20	0.10

Source: Estimation detailed in Appendix 3 of Tyers (1984) and, where data were insufficient, approximations based on similarities across markets and countries.

Appendix 3 Income Distributional Effects of Price-distorting Policies: A General Equilibrium Model[1]

Consider a small, open, three-sector economy producing two sets of tradable final products and one set of non-tradable products (X_j, j = 1,2,3) by combining labour (L), capital (K), imported intermediate inputs (I_i, i = 1,...,m) and some non-tradables (X_3) as intermediate inputs. The economy has a fixed endowment of homogeneous primary factors; capital is immobile between sectors while labour is perfectly mobile; the production function for each sector is of a linear, homogeneous form which exhibits positive and declining marginal products for each factor, and is separable between primary factors, imported intermediate inputs and non-tradable intermediate inputs; tradable product and input prices are given by world markets adjusted according to the country's (initially zero) trade taxes-cum-subsidies (the small country assumption); aggregate product equals aggregate expenditure; there is continual external balance; flexible prices ensure the full employment of all resources; and domestic markets are perfectly competitive so that profits are zero and marginal productivity factor pricing prevails.

If α_{Lj}, α_{Kj}, α_{ij} and α_{nj} represent respectively the quantity of factors L and K, of imported intermediate input I_i (i = 1,...,m) and of non-tradable input X_3 required to produce one unit of X_j (j = 1,2,3), the competitive-equilibrium zero-profit statements are

$$\alpha_{Lj}w + \alpha_{Kj}r + \Sigma_{i=1}^{m} \alpha_{ij}q_i + \alpha_{nj}p_3 = p_j, \quad j=1,2,3 \tag{A3.1}$$

and the full-employment conditions are given by

$$\Sigma_{j=1}^{3} \alpha_{Lj}X_j = L \tag{A3.2}$$

$$\alpha_{Kj}X_j = K_j, \quad j=1,2,3 \tag{A3.3}$$

where w, r_j, q_i and p_j are respectively the labour wage rate, the rental return to capital specific to sector j, and the domestic prices of imported intermediate input Ii and of the product of sector j.

The domestic prices of the two tradable products and the intermediate inputs, p_1, p_2, and q_i ($i = 1,...,m$) are determined by their international prices, p_1^*, p_2^* and q_i^* (which are assumed to be unaffected by this small country's activities and are held constant throughout the analysis) and by any trade taxes-cum-subsidies. The domestic price of the non-tradable product, p_3, is determined endogenously by the equilibrium condition that the domestic demand and supply for that non-tradable are equated. That is,

$$C_3 (p_1, p_2, p_3, Y) = X_3 \qquad (A3.4)$$

where C_3 and X_3 are the quantities of the non-tradable product demanded and supplied and Y is national income.

Equations (A3.1) to (A3.4) can be used as the basis for analysing the effects of a small change in trade taxes-cum-subsidies. Such a change will cause a change in p_3 and in all factor rewards as well as induce a change in techniques (the α's). Differentiating equations (A3.1) and expressing proportional changes by ^ yields

$$\gamma_{Lj}\hat{w} + \gamma_{Kj}\hat{r}_j + \Sigma_{i=1}^{m} \gamma_{ij}\hat{q}_i + \gamma_{nj}\hat{p}_3 = \hat{p}_j, \quad j = 1,2,3 \qquad (A3.5)$$

where the γ's represent distributive shares of the factors and intermediate inputs in the value of sector j's output so that, for example, $\gamma_{Kj} = r_j K_j / p_j X_j$ and their sum is unity for each sector.[2] Dividing all terms in equations (A3.5) by the share of value of output going to primary factors, V_j, where $V_j = 1 - \Sigma_{i=1}^{3} \gamma_{ij}$, and defining θ_{Lj} and θ_{Kj} as the shares of value-added going to labour and specific capital in sector j, yields

$$\theta_{Lj}\hat{w} + \theta_{Kj}\hat{r}_j = (\hat{p}_j - \Sigma_{j=1}^{m} \gamma_{ij}\hat{q}_i - \gamma_{nj}\hat{p}_3)/V_j, \quad j=1,2,3. \qquad (A3.6)$$

For present purposes, attention will focus on the effects of distorting just one of the tradable final product prices, and will assume that the other tradable final product price and the prices of imported intermediate inputs remain at their free-trade level. In this case equations (A3.6), the requirements for the retention of zero profits, reduce to

$$\theta_{Lj}\hat{w} + \theta_{Kj}\hat{r}_j = (\hat{p}_j - \gamma_{nj}\hat{p}_3)/V_j, \quad j=1,2,3. \qquad (A3.7)$$

The requirements for retaining full employment in the factor markets are obtained by differentiating equations (A3.2) and (A3.3) which, since the aggregate supplies of labour and specific capital are assumed fixed, gives

$$\Sigma_{j=1}^{3} \lambda_{Lj}\hat{X}_j + \Sigma_{j=1}^{3} \lambda_{Lj}\,\hat{\alpha}_{Lj} = 0 \tag{A3.8}$$

and

$$\hat{X}_j = -\alpha_{kj}\,\hat{\alpha}_{Kj}, \quad j=1,2,3 \tag{A3.9}$$

where λ_{Lj} is the fraction of the labour force employed in sector j. Given the assumption of separability, so that the ratio of primary factors used in each sector is independent of prices of both imported and non-tradable intermediate inputs, use can be made of the following definition of σ_j, the elasticity of factor substitution:

$$\hat{\alpha}_{Kj} - \hat{\alpha}_{Lj} = \sigma_j\,(\hat{w} - \hat{r}_j), \quad j=1,2,3. \tag{A3.10}$$

Substituting equations (A3.9) and (A3.10) into equation (A3.8) then gives the following requirement for the retention of full employment of labour and capital:

$$\Sigma_{h=1}^{3} \lambda_{Lh}\,\sigma_h\,(\hat{w} - \hat{r}_h) = 0. \tag{A3.11}$$

To ensure the clearance of the domestic market for the non-tradable, as summarized in equation (A3.4), expressions for changes in production and consumption of X_3 are required. The equations for production changes can be obtained by recalling the Wong-Viner envelope theorem (see endnote 2) which reduces to the following, given the separability assumption and the assumption that intermediate input prices do not change:

$$\gamma_{Lj}\,\hat{\alpha}_{Lj} + \gamma_{Kj}\,\hat{\alpha}_{Kj} = 0, \quad j=1,2,3. \tag{A3.12}$$

Substituting equations (A3.10) and (A3.12) into equation (A3.9) yields

$$\hat{X}_j = \theta_{Lj}\,\sigma_j\,(\hat{r}_j - \hat{w}), \quad j=1,2,3. \tag{A3.13}$$

Turning to the consumption changes, the demand for good j is given by $C_j = C_j(p_1, p_2, p_3, Y)$ and hence

$$dC_j = \Sigma_{h=1}^{3} \frac{\partial C_j}{\partial p_h}\,dp_h + \frac{\partial C_j}{\partial Y}\,dY, \quad j=1,2 \tag{A3.14}$$

and

$$dC_3 = \Sigma_{h=1}^{3} \frac{\partial C_3^f}{\partial p_h}\,dp_h + \frac{\partial C_3^f}{\partial Y}\,dY + \Sigma_{h=1}^{3} \frac{\partial C_3^i}{\partial p_h}\,dp_h \tag{A3.15}$$

where C_3^f and C_3^i refer to final and intermediate use of non-tradables, respectively. When the income and price effects are separated in the first term via the Slutsky decomposition, equations (A3.14) and (A3.15) become

$$dC_j = \Sigma_{h=1}^3 \frac{\partial C_j}{\partial p_h}\bigg|_{\overline{U}} \, dp_h + \frac{\partial C_j}{\partial Y}(dY - \Sigma_{h=1}^3 C_h dp_h), \quad j=1,2 \qquad (A3.16)$$

and

$$dC_3 = \Sigma_{h=1}^3 \frac{\partial C_3^f}{\partial p_h}\bigg|_{\overline{U}} \, dp_h + \frac{\partial C_3^f}{\partial Y}(dY - \Sigma_{h=1}^3 C_h^f dp_h)$$

$$+ \Sigma_{h=1}^3 \frac{\partial C_3^i}{\partial p_h} \, dp_h. \qquad (A3.17)$$

National income, Y, is given by

$$Y = \Sigma_{i=1}^3 p_j X_j - \Sigma_{j=1}^m q_i I_i - p_3 C_3^i + \Sigma_{j=1}^2 T_j p_j^* t_j \qquad A3.18)$$

and because the dq_i are assumed to be zero, since profit maximization and separability imply

$$\Sigma_{j=1}^3 p_j dX_j = 0, \; \Sigma_{i=1}^m q_i dI_i = 0 \text{ and } p_3 dC_3^i = 0,$$

and since trade taxes-cum-subsidies are initially zero, it follows from differentiation of equation (A3.18) that

$$dY = \Sigma_{j=1}^3 X_j dp_j - C_3^i \, dp_3 + \Sigma_{j=1}^2 T_j p_j^* dt_j \qquad (A3.19)$$

where T_j is the initial quantity traded and t_j is the proportional trade tax.[3] Since $p_j^* dt_j$ is the same as dp_j for the import-competing sector and minus dp_j for the export sector, and since $X_j + T_j = C_j$ for the import-competing sector and $X_j - T_j = C_j$ for the export sector, and $X_3 = C_3^f + C_3^i$, the substitution of equation (A3.19) into equations (A3.16) and (A3.17) reduces dC_j to

$$dC_j = \Sigma_{h=1}^3 \frac{\partial C_j}{\partial p_h}\bigg|_{\overline{U}} \, dp_h, \quad j=1,2$$

and

$$dC_3 = \Sigma_{h=1}^3 \left(\frac{\partial C_3^f}{\partial p_h}\bigg|_{\overline{U}} + \frac{\partial C_3^i}{\partial p_h}\right) dp_h$$

or, when expressed in proportional form, to

$$\hat{C}_j = \Sigma_{h=1}^3 E_{jh}\hat{p}_h, \quad j=1,2 \qquad (A3.20)$$

and

$$\hat{C}_3 = \Sigma_{h=1}^3 E_h\hat{p}_h \qquad (A3.21)$$

where $E_h = E_{3h}(1-\delta) + E_{3h}^i\delta$ and is the weighted average elasticity of total demand for good 3 with respect to the price of good h, E_{jh} is the income-compensated elasticity of final demand for good j with respect to the price of good h (h,j = 1,2,3), E_{3h}^i is the elasticity of intermediate demand for good 3 with respect to the price of good h, and δ is the proportion of non-tradables' output used as an intermediate input.

The condition for obtaining a new equilibrium in the market for the non-tradable product can now be obtained by differentiating equation (A3.4) to get $\hat{C}_3 = \hat{X}_3$. Then by equating $\hat{C}_3$ from equation (A3.21) with $\hat{X}_3$ from equations (A3.13) one obtains:

$$\theta_{L3}\sigma_3 (\hat{r}_3 - \hat{w}) = \Sigma_{h=1}^{3} E_h\hat{p}_h. \tag{A3.22}$$

The effects of a small change in p_1 or p_2 in response to the imposition of final-product trade taxes-cum-subsidies can now be summarized in the following equations, all of which are derived from the differential forms of equations (A3.1) to (A3.4):

(i)   For competitive-equilibrium zero profits by firms:

$$\theta_{Lj}\hat{w} + \theta_{Kj}\hat{r}_j = (\hat{p}_j - \gamma_{nj}\hat{p}_3)/V_j, \quad j=1,2,3 \tag{A3.7}$$

(ii)   For full employment:

$$\Sigma_{h=1}^{3} \lambda_{Lh}\sigma_h (\hat{w} - \hat{r}_h) = 0 \tag{A3.11}$$

(iii)   For equilibrium in the market for non-tradable products:

$$\theta_{L3}\sigma_3 (\hat{r}_3 - \hat{w}) = \Sigma_{h=1}^{3} E_h\hat{p}_h. \tag{A3.22}$$

These five equations can be solved simultaneously to obtain the following expressions for changes in the five relevant parameters, $\hat{w}, \hat{r}_1, \hat{r}_2, \hat{r}_3$ and $\hat{p}_3$ relative to the change in $\hat{p}_j$ (j = 1,2):

$$Ew_j \equiv \hat{w}/\hat{p}_j = [A_j\theta_{L3}\sigma_3(1 - \gamma_{n3})/V_3 - A_j\,\theta_{K3}E_3 - \theta_{K3}E_j]/\theta_{L3}\sigma_3 \tag{A3.23}$$

$$Er_{jj} \equiv \hat{r}_j/\hat{p}_j = [\theta_{L3}\sigma_3/V_j + \theta_{Lj}\theta_{K3}E_j + A_j\,\theta_{Lj}\theta_{K3}E_3$$

$$-A_j\theta_{Lj}\theta_{L3}\sigma_3 (1 - \gamma_{n3})/V_3 - A_j\gamma_j\theta_{L3}\sigma_3/V_j] \,/\, \theta_{Kj}\theta_{L3}\sigma_3 \tag{A3.24}$$

$$Er_{hj} \equiv \hat{r}_h/\hat{p}_j = Ew_j\theta_{Lh}/\theta_{Kh} - \gamma_hA_j/V_h\theta_{Kh}, \quad h=1,2, h\neq j \tag{A3.25}$$

$$Er_{3j} \equiv \hat{r}_j/\hat{p}_j = [E_j + A_j\sigma_3(1-\gamma_{n3})/V_3 + A_jE_3]/\sigma_3 \tag{A3.26}$$

$$Ep_{3j} \equiv \hat{p}_3/\hat{p}_j \equiv A_j \tag{A3.27}$$

where

$$A_j =$$

$$\frac{B_j\theta_{L3}\sigma_3/V_j+(B_1+B_2+B_3)\,\theta_{K3}E_j}{(B_1+B_2)\theta_{L3}\sigma_3(1-\gamma_{n3})/V_3-(B_1+B_2+B_3)\theta_{K3}E_3+(B_1\gamma_{n1}/V_1+B_2\gamma_{n2}/V_2)\theta_{L3}\sigma_3}$$

$$\text{(A3.28)}$$

and

$$B_j = \lambda_{Lj}\sigma_j/\theta_{Kj}\ \Sigma_{h=1}^{3}\ \lambda_{Lh}\sigma_{h},\quad j{=}1,2,3. \tag{A3.29}$$

These equations summarize the effects of a trade tax-cum-subsidy which changes both the producer price and the consumer price of product j by the same amount. If, instead, a producer price tax-cum-subsidy alone were to be imposed, the equations of change would be the same except the terms with E_j would not appear. Alternatively, if only a consumer tax-cum-subsidy on product j were to be imposed, the equations of change would be as above except the first term in equations (A3.24) and (A3.28) would not appear.

Once these equations are solved, it is possible also to generate the effects on production and consumption of each of the three products, using equations (A3.13) (A3.20) and (A3.21). The effect on a sector's net exports, T_j, where $T_j = X_j - C_j$ ($j = 1,2$) is then given by

$$\hat{T}_j = (\hat{C}_j - s_j\hat{X}_j)/(1 - s_j),\quad j{=}1,2 \tag{A3.30}$$

where s_j is the self-sufficiency ratio for sector j ($s_j = X_j/C_j$). Finally, the effect on the number of workers in each sector can be derived by noting from equation (A3.2) that $L_j = \alpha_{Lj} X_j$, from which it follows after some manipulation that

$$\hat{L}_j = \hat{X}_j/\theta_{Lj},\quad j{=}1,2,3. \tag{A3.31}$$

As noted by Cassing (1981) and others, the effect of trade policies on the real income of a person or group (n) depends not just on the changes in product prices and factor rewards but also on the initial proportions of their income obtained from different factors (a_{Ln}, a_{Kln}, a_{K2n} and a_{K3n}, the sum of which is unity) and the initial proportions of their expenditure on the three products (b_{1n}, b_{2n}, and b_{3n}, the sum of which is also unity). The elasticity of n's real income with respect to p_j is given by

$$EY_{nj} \equiv \hat{Y}_n/\hat{p}_j = a_{Ln}Ew_j + \Sigma_{h=1}^{3}\ a_{Khn}Er_{hj} - b_{jn} - A_jb_{3n} - Z_{nj} \tag{A3.32}$$

where Z_{nj} is the elasticity of n's personal income tax with respect to p_j. Assuming income tax rates are adjusted to keep overall tax revenue constant and all groups face the same average tax rate, then Z_{nj} has the value ρ_j in the case of a price-raising trade tax-cum-subsidy, π_j/V_j in the case of a production subsidy and b_j in the case of a consumption subsidy where ρ_j is the ratio of sector j's net exports to GDP, π_j is sector j's share of GDP and b_j is the share of national expenditure on the output of sector j. However, for the poor agrarian economy, where tax collection costs would outweigh the revenue collected in rural areas, it is necessary to assume farmers are not taxed, so Z_{nj} is omitted from equation (A3.32) for farmers but is divided by $(1 - \pi_1)$ for other groups in the case of the poor country.[4]

There are seven obvious groups of people to consider with this model. Four of them are factor owners, namely farmers, who are assumed to supply all their own labour, land and other forms of capital (although it is a simple matter to alter this assumption to allow, for example, for hired farm labour or land rental); industrial capitalists; other capitalists, whose capital is employed to produce non-tradables; and non-farm workers. The other three groups are bureaucrats in the agricultural and the industrial development ministries, whose career prospects are assumed to be related to output and employment levels in the sectors they serve (changes in which are given by equations (A3.13) and (A3.31)), and bureaucrats in the finance ministry whose prospects are related to the volume of tax revenue (Downs 1967; Niskanen 1971). The latter, though, would be affected only if tax rates were unable to be adjusted.

Unfortunately, equations (A3.23) to (A3.29) are too complex to allow easy examination of the effects of different parameters on the welfare of these groups. It is helpful therefore to select representative parameters for a poor agrarian economy and a rich industrial economy. One such set is provided in Table A.12. Values for the factor intensities of production and value-added shares of output are selected from data in the United Nations' *National Account Statistics: Main Aggregates and Detailed Tables*. (See also Table 2.6 in Chapter 2.) For simplicity, the factor substitution elasticities are assumed to be unity. Tax rates and the intersectoral distribution of labour data (the λ's) are from the World Bank's *World Development Report*. The income-compensated own-price and cross-price elasticities of final demand for non-

Table A12: Assumed parameter values for two representative economies[a]

Parameter/Sector	Poor agrarian economy			Rich industrial economy		
	1	2	3	1	2	3
θ_{Lj}	0.70	0.70	0.70	0.35	0.50	0.60
V_j	0.80	0.60	0.70	0.40	0.50	0.60
λ_{Lj}	0.60	0.10	0.30	0.03	0.30	0.67
σ_j	1.00	1.00	1.00	1.00	1.00	1.00
v_{nj}	0.076	0.150	0.112	0.306	0.255	0.204
E_{1j}	-0.250	0.087	0.164	-0.117	0.035	0.082
E_{2j}	0.318	-0.691	0.373	0.020	-0.515	0.495
E_{3j}	0.300	0.187	-0.487	0.018	0.192	-0.210
E_{3j}^i	0.000	0.000	-0.100	0.000	0.000	-0.100
E_j	0.210	0.131	-0.371	0.001	0.115	-0.166
b_j for farmers	0.58	0.14	0.28	0.14	0.24	0.62
b_j for non-farm capitalists	0.28	0.24	0.48	0.11	0.21	0.68
b_j for non-farm workers	0.58	0.14	0.28	0.17	0.27	0.56
b_j in aggregate	0.55	0.15	0.30	0.14	0.24	0.62
ρ_j	0.20	0.017	0.00	-0.04	0.44	0.00
π_j	0.60	0.10	0.30	0.04	0.34	0.62
η_j	0.65	1.48	1.40	0.20	1.21	1.20

a Parameter values are derived in an internally consistent way. It is also assumed that national taxation amounts to 12.5 per cent of income in the poor country and 25 per cent in the rich country. It follows from the above parameters that δ, the share of non-tradable production used as intermediate inputs, is 0.3 in the poor country and 0.4 in the rich country.

tradables (the E_{3j}'s) are derived from estimates of expenditure shares and income elasticities of demand reported in Lluch, Powell and Williams (1977:Ch. 3) and Theil and Clements (1987:Ch. 2) together with the following formula from Theil and Clements (based on the assumption that the utility function is additive in the three goods):

$$E_{3j} = \phi\eta_3 (\delta_{3j} - b_j\eta_j), \quad j=1,2,3 \tag{A3.33}$$

where η_j is the aggregate income elasticity of final demand, b_j is the aggregate average share of final expenditure on good j, δ_{3j} is the Kronecker delta (=1 if j=3 and =0 otherwise) and ϕ is the income flexibility (the reciprocal of the income elasticity of the marginal utility of income, which Theil and Clements suggest is around -0.6 for both rich and poor countries).[5] The variations in the average expenditure shares (the b's) of different groups around the national aggregates selected from the above-mentioned demand analyses reflect the differences in per capita incomes of those different groups.

Using these assumed parameter values, the effects of a change in p_1 or p_2 on factor rewards, the price of non-tradables, output, employment and the real incomes of the four different groups of factor owners have been calculated and are reported in elasticity form in Table 3.1 of Chapter 3.

Notes to Appendix 3

[1] This appendix is taken from Anderson (1989).

[2] Since the competitive producer takes factor and input prices as given and varies the α's so as to set the derivative of costs equal to zero, it follows that:

$$\gamma_{Lj} \hat{\alpha}_{Lj} + \gamma_{Kj} \hat{\alpha}_{Kj} + \sum_{i=1}^{n} \gamma_{ij} \hat{\alpha}_{ij} = 0, \quad j = 1,2,3.$$

This is the Wong–Viner envelope theorem (Jones 1975).

[3] There is an implicit assumption here that the collection of taxes and dispensing of subsidies is undertaken in a costless and non-distortionary way.

[4] Obviously this is only one of numerous assumptions about the change in tax policy that might accompany a change in price-distorting policies. It assumes that there is an enclave to the economy producing free public goods, the social demand for which is unaffected by such policy changes.

[5] The author is grateful for guidance from Ken Clements in obtaining representative values for these price elasticities of demand.

Appendix 4   The Welfare Incidence of Pure Market Insulation

Consider an open commodity market for a key food commodity, such as rice, which is subject to short-run disturbances originating in domestic production and in the international market. Assume that domestic output and consumption are small by comparison with the quantities exchanged on the world market and that short-run fluctuations in the price of the commodity neither affect industrial output nor the real exchange rate. (See Gibbard and Tyers (1990) for an extension of the model to the large country case.)

To focus on the effects of price stability it is useful to assume further that fluctuations are symmetrical and that stabilization would occur about the mean border price, P_0. Demand and supply schedules are therefore assumed to be linear and risk is introduced through normally distributed random disturbances to production and the border price. Note that commodity storage need not enter this model. The small country assumption ensures that stock changes will not affect prices. They will, of course, affect the variance of net imports or exports, and hence will affect net foreign exchange demands associated with trade in the commodity. But we further assume that this trade is small in relation to the economy as a whole and hence that neither the transaction costs nor the effects on the real exchange rate which are associated with this variance are significant.

The domestic demand for the commodity is divided between rural (farm) households and urban (worker) households.

Workers: $c_W = c_{W0} [1 - \epsilon_W (\frac{P - P_0}{P_0})]$ (A4.1)

Farmers: $c_F = c_{F0} [1 - \epsilon_F (\frac{p - P_0}{P_0})]$ (A4.2)

where ϵ_W and ϵ_F are the price elasticities of demand of workers and farmers, respectively.

Farmers are assumed to be averse to income risk but to make rational risk-neutral production decisions. This apparent contradiction eliminates the responsiveness of mean output to the variance of prices. It therefore causes the underestimation of farmer gains from price stabilization. Since, in the small country case, farmers gain from stabilization in both the examples we consider, this assumption is a small price to pay for analytical simplicity.

Supply: $q = q_0 + v_Q$ (A4.3)

where $v_Q \sim N(0, s_Q^2)$. (A4.4)

Policy intervention is restricted to pure stabilization of the domestic price, about the mean of the international price, through distortions at the border. This might be achieved in practice through the use of specific taxes on trade which are adjusted each year, or through the management of trade by a monopolizing agency to achieve the price stabilization objective. The result is represented by a linear price transmission equation of the type introduced above in Chapter 2. The border price is given by:

$P = P_0 + v_P$ (A4.5)

where $v_p \sim N(0, s_P^2)$. Thus, the price transmission equation is:

$p = P_0 + \phi (P - P_0)$ (A4.6)

where ϕ, the policy variable in this model, is the rate of price transmission—the fraction of any international price change which is transmitted to the domestic market. If equation (A4.6) were expressed in terms of the logarithms of prices, it would be equivalent to ϕ^{SR}, the short-run price transmission elasticity introduced in Chapter 2. Its value ranges between unity in the free-trade case and zero in the case where the domestic market is totally insulated.

Since production decisions are dependent only on the mean price, which is invariant in this model, changes in farm revenue due to disturbances in price or output are translated directly into farm income.

$$Y_F = Y_{F0} + pq - P_0q_0. \tag{A4.7}$$

In any year the revenue position of the government depends upon the border price distortion and the level of net imports:

$$G = (p - P)(c_W + c_F - q). \tag{A4.8}$$

In the case of developing countries, we also assume that the wage bill of industrial workers is adjusted, through indexing or payments in kind, so that worker income is fully compensated for changes in the commodity price. Worker income is then:

$$Y_W = wL = w_0L + c_{W0}(p - P_0) \tag{A4.9}$$

where L is the non-agricultural labour force.

The profits of industrial capital-owners are adjusted accordingly:

$$\pi = \pi_0 - L(w - w_0). \tag{A4.10}$$

This completes the specification of the analytical model. It remains to calculate the income equivalents of the impacts of changes in ϕ, the rate of price transmission, on the welfare of farmers, workers and industrial capital-owners and on government revenue. Consider first the levels of price and income risk implied by the model.

The variance of the domestic price, after stabilization, is obvious from equation (A4.6) as $s_p^2 = \phi^2 s_P^2$. By substituting equations (A4.5) and (A4.6) in (A4.7), the variance of farm income is:

$$\text{Var}\,\{Y_F\} = P_0^2 s_Q^2 + q_0^2 \phi^2 s_P^2 + \phi^2 s_P^2 s_Q^2 \tag{A4.11}$$

To calculate the welfare effect of stabilization on farmers as consumers, the covariance of farm income with price is also needed. Since, by definition, the disturbances to domestic production and the border price are independent, this is

$$\text{Cov}\{p, Y_F\} = q_0 \phi^2 s_P^2 = q_0 s_p^2. \tag{A4.12}$$

Then, for the effect of stabilization on workers with compensated incomes, both the variance of worker income and its covariance with the domestic price are needed. These can be derived from equation (A4.9) as:

$$\text{Var}\,\{Y_W\} = c_{W0}^2 \phi^2 s_P^2 = c_{W0}^2 s_p^2 \tag{A4.13}$$

and

$$\text{Cov} \{p, Y_W\} = c_{W0} \, \phi^2 \, s_P^2 = c_{W0} \, s_P^2 \tag{A4.14}$$

The variance of income to capital-owners is, from equation (A4.10), the same as that of worker income. Since the model is linear in the incomes of both workers and capital-owners, the means of these variables are not affected by insulation policy. Government revenue is quadratic in prices, however. Its mean is therefore not preserved when the value of ϕ changes.

The mean and variance of government revenue are readily derived by substituting equations (A4.1), (A4.2), (A4.3) and (A4.6) into equation (A4.8) so that government revenue, G, is a function of the random variables v_Q and v_P. Taking means and variances of both sides and omitting a term which is fourth-order in σ_P, the following expressions result:

$$E\{G\} = \phi(1 - \phi) \, \sigma_P^2 \, \beta_T \, \epsilon_T \, Y_T \tag{A4.15}$$

and

$$\text{Var}\{G\} = P_0^2 \, q_0^2 \, (1 - \phi)^2 \, \sigma_P^2 \, (s_m^2 + \sigma_Q^2) \tag{A4.16}$$

where Y_T is national income, β_T is the share of that income expended on the commodity, ϵ_T is the price elasticity of aggregate domestic demand and s_m is the level of net imports as a share of domestic production. Note that the expected government revenue from partial insulation rises to a maximum at $\phi = \frac{1}{2}$, but is zero in the extreme cases of free trade and perfect insulation. The variance, however, increases monotonically as the rate of price transmission declines and the degree of insulation increases.

We evaluate the income equivalent of changes in risk by following, with slight modification, the approach of Newbery and Stiglitz (1981:Ch. 9). To simplify the exposition, we ignore cross effects between the focus commodity and others, the prices of which are not to be stabilized, and begin by evaluating the income equivalent of total stabilization around the mean price, P_0. First, equate expected utility without price stabilization and with income Y, to expected utility after stabilization with income Y–B:

$$E\{V(P,Y)\} = E\{V(P_0, Y-B)\} \tag{A4.17}$$

where V is the indirect utility function. By using Taylor Series to expand both sides of this equation around P_0, manageable expressions can be derived for B in terms of the price and income elasticities of demand, the expenditure share and the Arrow-Pratt coefficient of relative risk aversion, R, discussed in Section 3.2 of Chapter 3.

Consider first the effect on consumer welfare. In this case we extend the derivation of Newbery and Stiglitz by avoiding the assumption that the expenditure share on the focus commodity is small. The result is as follows:

$$B_C = \tfrac{1}{2}\, \beta\, Y\, [-\epsilon + \beta\, (R - \eta)]\, \text{Var}\, \{P\}/P^2 - \beta\, (R - \eta)\, \text{Cov}\{Y,P\}/P$$

$$(A4.18)$$

where ϵ is the price elasticity of demand (defined as positive for normal goods), β is the expenditure share, η is the income elasticity of demand and Y is mean income. Note that, where consumer income is correlated with the price, market insulation causes real income to be destabilized. Accordingly, the second term in (A4.18) reduces the gains from stabilization where this is the case and consumers are risk averse.

Equation (A4.18) gives the benefit to consumers of total stabilization. The corresponding effect of a partial stabilization is readily calculated from a comparison of the benefit from a total stabilization which originates at free trade against that from one which originates in a partially stabilized state.

In the case of farmers, who are both producers and consumers, the consumer benefit from price stability, as measured by equation (A4.18), must be added to the welfare effect of the corresponding change in income risk. This also stems from equation (A4.17):

$$B_Y = (Y - Y_0) - \tfrac{1}{2} R\, (\sigma_S^2 - \sigma_0^2)\, Y_0 \qquad\qquad (A4.19)$$

where the first term is the transfer benefit from any change in mean income and σ_0 and σ_S are the coefficients of variation of income before and after stabilization. Note that equation (A4.19) is used to derive the income risk component of the welfare effect on farmers, as well as the welfare effects of changes in the variances of worker and capital-owner incomes and in the mean and variance of government revenue.

The welfare impacts of price stabilization on each group of agents are thus functions of the parameters in the model, specified above, and of each group's average income and their coefficient of relative risk aversion. Expressions for the impact of partial stabilization on the welfare of each group are readily derived from equations (A4.11) through (A4.16), (A4.18) and (A4.19). Each indicates the gain, as a proportion of group income, which would accrue from a partial insulation of the domestic market as characterized by a rate of price transmission, ϕ, less than unity. In the case of farmers,

$$B_F = \tfrac{1}{2}\,(1 - \phi^2)\,\sigma_P^2\,\beta_F\,[R_F(1 + \sigma_Q^2)\,\beta_F/s_F^2 - \epsilon_F + \beta_F(R_F - \eta_F)\,(1 - 2/s_F)]$$
$$(A4.20)$$

where σ_P is the coefficient of variation of the border price (s_P/P_0), σ_Q is the coefficient of variation of production (s_Q/q_0), β_F is the farmers' expenditure share on rice, η_F is their income elasticity of demand and s_F is that share of rice output consumed by farmers (c_{F0}/q_0). The first of the terms in the square brackets relates to the effect of stabilization on income risk, while the latter two stem from its welfare impact on farmers as consumers.

In the case of workers without income compensation,

$$B_W = \tfrac{1}{2}\,(1 - \phi^2)\,\sigma_P^2\,\beta_W\,[-\epsilon_W + \beta_W\,(R_W - \eta_W)] \qquad (A4.21)$$

where the first term in the square brackets relates to the Waugh effect of the downward-sloping demand curve, which is offset by the second term if the level of aversion to risk is high enough.

Workers with income compensation face no welfare-reducing risk. Their welfare effect is:

$$B_{WY} = \tfrac{1}{2}\,(1 - \phi^2)\,\sigma_P^2\,\beta_W[-\epsilon_W + \beta_W\,\eta_W]. \qquad (A4.22)$$

Since the income-compensated price elasticity of demand (the sum in the square brackets) must be negative, price stabilization will in fact reduce this group's welfare.

In the case of industrial capital owners where wages are compensated,

$$B_I = \tfrac{1}{2}\,(1 - \phi^2)\,\sigma_P^2\,\beta_W^2\,R_I\,\delta_W^2 / \delta_I^2 \qquad (A4.23)$$

where δ_W and δ_I are the shares of national income accruing, respectively, to non-agricultural workers and to capital owners.

Finally the effect on government revenue is given by:

$$B_G = \phi(1 - \phi)\,\sigma_P^2\,\beta_T\epsilon_T - \tfrac{1}{2}\,R_G\,(1 - \phi)^2\,\sigma_P^2\,(s_m^2 + \sigma_Q^2)\,\delta_R^2 / \delta_G^2 \qquad (A4.24)$$

where δ_R is the gross revenue from production as a fraction of national income (P_0q_0/Y), δ_G is average government revenue as a fraction of national income, s_m is the ratio of net imports to domestic output, and β_T and ϵ_T are the expenditure share and the price elasticity of aggregate domestic demand. The term R_G is the coefficient of relative risk aversion which reflects preferences for government revenue stability.

Bibliography

Abbott, P.C., 1979. 'Modelling international grain trade with government controlled markets', *American Journal of Agricultural Economics* 61(1): 22–31, February.

Aiyagari, S.R., Eckstein, S.E. and Eichenbaum, M., 1980. 'Rational expectations, inventories and price fluctuations', Discussion Paper No. 363, New Haven, Yale Growth Center.

Alston, J.M., G.W. Edwards and J.W. Freebairn 1988. 'Market distortions and benefits from research'. *American Journal of Agricultural Economics* 70(2): 281–88, May.

—— and Hurd, B.H., 1990. 'Some neglected social costs of government spending in farm programs', *American Journal of Agricultural Economics* 72(1): 149–57, February.

Amat, S., 1982. 'Promoting national food security: the Indonesian experience', in A.H. Chisholm and R. Tyers (eds), *Food Security: Theory, Policy and Perspectives from Asia and the Pacific Rim*, Lexington, D.C. Heath: Ch. 7.

Anderson, J.E., 1988. *The Relative Inefficiency of Quotas*, Cambridge: MIT Press.

Anderson, K., 1978. 'On why rates of assistance differ between Australia's rural industries', *Australian Journal of Agricultural Economics* 22(2): 99–114, August.

——, 1983a. 'The peculiar rationality of beef import quotas in Japan', *American Journal of Agricultural Economics* 65(1): 108–12, February.

——, 1983b. 'Growth of agricultural protection in East Asia', *Food Policy* 8 (4): 327–36, November.

——, 1983c. 'Economic growth, comparative advantage and agricultural trade of Pacific rim countries', *Review of Marketing and Agricultural Economics* 51(3): 231–48, December. [Also published in G.E. Schuh and J.L. McCoy (eds), *Food, Agriculture and Development in the Pacific Basin*, Boulder, Westview Press, 1986: Chapter 2.]

——, 1987. 'On why agriculture declines with economic growth', *Agricultural Economics* 1 (3): 195–207, June.

——, 1989. 'Rent-seeking and price-distorting policies in rich and poor countries', Seminar Paper No. 428, Institute for International Economic Studies, University of Stockholm, January.

——, 1990. *Changing Comparative Advantages in China: Effects on Food, Feed and Fibre Markets*, Paris, Organization for Economic Cooperation and Development.

——, (ed.), 1991a. *New Silk Roads: East Asia and World Textile Markets*, Cambridge, Cambridge University Press.

——, 1991b. 'China's industrialization and fibre self sufficiency', in C. Findlay (ed.), *Economic Reform and Industrial Growth in China: The Wool Textile Case*, London and Sydney, Allen and Unwin: Ch. 5.

——, in press. 'Effects on the environment and welfare of liberalizing food trade: the cases of coal and food', in K. Anderson and R. Blackhurst (eds), *The Greening of World Trade Issues*, London, Harvester Wheatsheaf: Ch. 8.

——, and Baldwin, R., 1987. 'The political market for protection in industrial countries', in A.M. El-Agraa (ed.), *Protection, Cooperation, Development and Integration: Essays in Honour of Kiroshi Kitamura*, London, Macmillan: Ch. 2.

—— and Garnaut, R., 1987. *Australian Protectionism: Extent, Causes and Effects*, London and Sydney, Allen and Unwin.

—— and Hayami, Y. with others 1986. *The Political Economy of Agricultural Protection: East Asia in International Perspective*, London and Sydney, Allen and Unwin.

—— and Tyers, R., 1984. 'European Community grain and meat policies: effects on international prices, trade and welfare', *European Review of Agricultural Economics* 11(4): 367–94.

—— and ——, 1986. 'Agricultural policies of industrial countries and their effects on traditional food exporters', *Economic Record* 62(179): 385–99, December.

—— and ——, 1987a. 'Japan's agricultural policy in international perspective', *Journal of the Japanese and International Economies* 1(2): 131–46, June.

—— and ——, 1987b. 'Economic growth and market liberalization in China: implications for agricultural trade', *The Developing Economies* 25(2): 124–51, June.

—— and ——, 1990. 'How developing countries could gain from agricultural trade liberalization in the Uruguay Round', in I. Goldin and O. Knudsen (eds), *Agricultural Trade Liberalization: Implications for Developing Countries*, Paris, OECD.

—— and ——, 1992. 'Effects of gradual food policy reforms in the 1990s', *European Review of Agricultural Economics* 19 (1): 1–25, January.

Andrews, N., Bowen, B., Gunasekera, D., Haszler, H. and Field, H., 1990. 'Some implications of rebalancing EC agricultural protection', Occasional Paper 96.5, Canberra, Australian Bureau of Agricultural and Resource Economics.

Arrow, K.J., 1965. *Aspects of the Theory of Risk-Bearing*, Helsinki, Academic Bookstore.

Askari, H. and J.T. Cummings, 1977. 'Estimating agricultural supply response with the Nerlove model: a survey', *International Economic Review* 18(2): 257–92.

Australian Bureau of Agricultural Economics, 1985. *Agricultural Policies in the European Community: Their Origin, Nature and Effects on Production and Trade*, Canberra, Australian Government Publishing Service.

Balassa, B, 1965. 'Trade liberalization and "revealed" comparative advantage', *Manchester School of Economic and Social Studies* 33(2): 90–124, May.

——, 1975. *European Economic Integration*, Amsterdam, North Holland.

—— 1979. 'The changing pattern of comparative advantage in manufactured goods', *Review of Economics and Statistics* 61(2): 259–66, May.

—— and Associates, 1971. *The Structure of Protection in Developing Countries*, Baltimore, Johns Hopkins University Press.

—— and Bauwens, L., 1988. *Changing Trade Patterns in Manufactured Goods: An Econometric Investigation*, Amsterdam, North Holland.

Baldwin, R.E., 1982. 'The political economy of protectionism', in J.N. Bhagwati (ed.), *Import Competition and Response*, Chicago, University of Chicago Press: Ch. 10.

——, 1984. 'Rent-seeking and trade policy: an industry approach', *Weltwirtschaftliches Archiv* 120(4):662–77.

——, 1985. *The Political Economy of U.S. Import Policy*, Cambridge, MIT Press.

——, 1989. 'The political economy of trade policy', *Journal of Economic Perspectives* 3(4): 119–35, Fall.

Bale, M.D. and Lutz, E., 1981. 'Price distortions in agriculture and their effects: an international comparison', *American Journal of Agricultural Economics* 63: 8–220.

Balisacan, A.M. and Roumasset, J.A., 1987. 'Public choice of economic policy: the growth of agricultural protection', *Weltwirtschaftliches Archiv* 123(2): 232–47.

Ballinger, N. *et al.*, 1990. *Potential Use of an Aggregate Measure of Support*, Commissioned Paper No. 5 on Bringing Agriculture into the GATT, Columbia, Missouri, International Agricultural Trade Research Consortium.

Bates, R.H., 1981. *Markets and States in Tropical Africa: The Political Basis of Agricultural Policies*, Berkeley, University of California Press.

Baumol, W.J., Batey Blackman, S.A. and Wolff, E.N., 1985. 'Unbalanced growth revisited: asymptotic stagnancy and new evidence', *American Economic Review* 75(4): 806–17, September.

Becker, G.S., 1983. 'A theory of competition among pressure groups for influence', *Quarterly Journal of Economics* 48 (3): 371–400, August.

——, 1985. 'Public policies, pressure groups, and dead weight costs', *Journal of Public Economics* 28 (4): 329–47, December.

——, Mill, E.S. and Williamson, J.G., 1986. 'Modelling Indian migration and city growth 1960–2000', *Economic Development and Cultural Change* 35(1): 1–33.

Bhagwati, J., 1971. 'The generalised theory of distortions and welfare', in J. Bhagwati *et al.* (eds), *Trade, Balance of Payments and Growth*, Amsterdam, North Holland.

Binswanger, H.P., Ruttan, V.W. *et al.*, 1978. *Induced Innovation: Technology, Institutions and Development*, Baltimore, Johns Hopkins University Press.

Blandford, D., 1983. 'Instability in world grain markets', *Journal of Agricultural Economics* 34(3): 379–92, September.

——, Winters, L.A., Munk, K.J., Anderson K. *et. al.*, 1990. 'Discussants' Comments'. in I. Goldin and O. Knudsen (eds), *Trade Liberalization: Implications for Developing Countries*, Paris, OECD: Ch. 16.

Bolin, O., Meyerson, P.M. and Stahl, I.L., 1986. *The Political Economy of the Food Sector: The Case of Sweden*, Stockholm, SNS Forlag.

Booth, A., 1984. 'Survey of recent developments', *Bulletin of Indonesian Economic Studies* 20(3): 1–35.

—— and David, C.C. (eds), 1985. *Food Trade and Food Security in ASEAN and Australia*, Canberra and Kuala Lumpur, ASEAN–Australia Economic Relations Research Project.

Bowen, H.P., 1983. 'On the theoretical interpretation of indices of trade intensity and revealed comparative advantage', *Weltwirtschaftliches Archiv* 119: 464–72.

Bredahl, M.E., Meyers, W.H. and Collins, K.J., 1979. 'The elasticity of foreign demand for U.S. agricultural products: the importance of the price transmission elasticity', *American Journal of Agricultural Economics* 61(1): 58–63, February.

——, Deaton, L., Josling, T., Miekle, K. and Tangermann, S., 1989. *Tariffication and Rebalancing*, Commissioned Paper No. 4 on Bringing Agriculture into the GATT, Columbia, Missouri, International Agricultural Trade Research Consortium.

——, Josling, T., Miner, W., Rossmiller, G.E., Tangerman, S. and Warley, T.K., 1990. *The Comprehensive Proposals for Negotiations in Agriculture*, Commissioned Paper No. 7 on Bringing Agriculture into the GATT, Columbia, Missouri, International Agricultural Trade Research Consortium.

Brennan, G. and Buchanan, J.M., 1985. *The Reason of Rules*, Cambridge, Cambridge University Press.

Brock, W.A. and Magee, S.P., 1978. 'The economics of special interest politics: the case of the tariff', *American Economic Review* 68(2):246–50, May.

—— and ——, 1980. 'Tariff formation in a democracy', in J. Black and B. Hindley (eds), *Current Issues in International Commercial Policy and Diplomacy*, London, Macmillan.

Browning, E.K., 1987. 'On the marginal welfare cost of taxation', *American Economic Review* 77(1): 11–23, March.

Burniaux, J.M. and Waelbroeck, J., 1985. 'The impact of the CAP on developing countries: a general equilibrium analysis', in C. Stevens and J. Verloren van Themaat (eds), *Pressure Groups, Policies and Development*, London, Hodder and Stoughton.

——, Delorme, F., Lienert, I., Martin, J.P. and Hoeller, P., 1988. 'Quantifying the economy-wide effects of agricultural policies: a general equilibrium approach', Working Paper No. 55, Department of Economics and Statistics, Paris, OECD, July.

——, Martin, J.P., Delorme, F., Lienert, I. and van der Mensbrugghe, D., 1990. 'Economy-wide effects of agricultural prices in OECD countries: a GE approach using the WALRAS model', in I. Goldin and O. Knudsen (eds), *Agricultural Trade Liberalization: Implications for Developing Countries*, Paris, OECD: Ch. 10.

Byerlee, D. and Sain, G., 1986. 'Food pricing policy in developing countries: bias against agriculture or for urban consumers?', *American Journal of Agricultural Economics* 68 (4): 961–9, November.

Carter, C. (ed.), 1988. *Elasticities in International Agricultural Trade*, Boulder, Westview Press.

Cassing, J.H., 1981. 'On the relationship between commodity price changes and factor owners' real positions', *Journal of Political Economy* 89 (3): 593–5, June.

—— and Hillman, A.L., 1986. 'Shifting comparative advantage and senescent industry collapse', *American Economic Review* 76(3): 516–23, June.

Chambers, R.G. and Just, R.E., 1979. 'Critique of exchange rate treatment in agricultural trade models', *American Journal of Agricultural Economics* 61(2): 249–257, May.

Chenery, H.B. and Syrquin, M., 1975. *Patterns of Development, 1950–1970*, New York, Oxford University Press for the World Bank.

Chenery, H., Robinson, S. and Syrquin, M., 1986. *Industrialization and Growth: A Comparative Study*, New York, Oxford University Press for the World Bank.

Clark, C., 1957. *The Conditions of Economic Progress*, London, Macmillan (3rd edn).

Corden, W.M., 1971. *The Theory of Protection*, London, Oxford University Press.

——, 1974. *Trade Policy and Economic Welfare*, London, Oxford University Press.

——, 1981. 'Exchange rate protection', in R.N. Cooper *et al.* (eds), *The International Monetary System Under Flexible Exchange Rates*, Cambridge, Mass., Ballinger.

——, 1983. 'The normative theory of international trade', in R.W. Jones and P.B. Kenen (eds), *Handbook of International Economics, Vol. 1*, Amsterdam, North Holland: Ch. 2.

——, 1984. 'Booming sector and Dutch disease economics: survey and consolidation', *Oxford Economic Papers* 36: 359–80.

——. and Findlay, R., 1975. 'Urban unemployment, intersectoral capital mobility and development policy', *Economica* 43(1):59–78, February.

Cornes, R. and Sandler, T., 1986. *The Theory of Externalities, Public Goods and Club Goods*, Cambridge, Cambridge University Press.

Deardorff, A.V., 1984. 'An exposition and exploration of Krueger's trade model', *Canadian Journal of Economics* 17(4): 731–46, November.

——. and Stern, R.M., 1985. *The Michigan Model of World Production and Trade: Theory and Applications*, Cambridge, MIT Press.

Diamond, P.A., 1982. 'Protection, trade adjustment assistance, and income distribution', in J.N. Bhagwati (ed.), *Import Competition and Response*, Chicago, University of Chicago Press: Ch. 5.

Dornbusch, R., 1974. 'Tariffs and nontraded goods', *Journal of International Economics* 4(2): 177–85, May.

Downs, A., 1957. *An Economic Theory of Democracy*, New York, Harper and Row.

——, 1967. *Inside Bureaucracy*, Boston, Little, Brown.

Dries, M.A. and Unnevehr, L.J., 1990. 'Influence of trade policies on price integration in the world beef market', *Agricultural Economics* 4(1): 73–89.

Drysdale, P. and Garnaut, R., 1989. 'A pacific free trade area?' in J. Schott (ed.), *Free Trade Areas and US Trade Policy*, Washington D.C., Institute for International Economics.

Dvoskin, D., 1987. *Excess Capacity in U.S. Agriculture: An Economic Approach to Measurement*, Agricultural Economic Report No. 580, US Department of Agriculture, Washington D.C.

Eaton, J., 1987. 'A dynamic specific-factors model of international trade', *Review of Economic Studies* 54(2): 325–38, April.

—— and Grossman, G., 1985. 'Tariffs as insurance: optimal commercial policy when domestic markets are incomplete', *Canadian Journal of Economics* 18(2): 258–72.

Edirisinghe, N., 1982. 'Food security in Sri Lanka: the historical record', in A.H. Chisholm and R. Tyers (eds), *Food Security: Theory, Policy and Perspectives from Asia and the Pacific Rim*, Lexington, D.C. Heath: Ch. 8.

Field, H., Hearn, S. and Kirby, M.G., 1989. *The 1988 EC Budget and Production Stabilisers*, Occasional Paper 89-3, Canberra, Australian Bureau of Agricultural and Resource Economics.

Findlay, R. and Wellisz, S., 1982. 'Endogenous tariffs, the political economy of trade restrictions, and welfare', in J.N. Bhagwati (ed.),

Import Competition and Response, Chicago, University of Chicago Press: Ch. 8.

—— and ——, 1983. 'Some aspects of the political economy of trade restrictions', *Kyklos* 36 (3): 469–81.

Gardner, B.L., 1983. 'Efficient redistribution through commodity markets', *American Journal of Agricultural Economics* 65 (2): 225–34, May.

——, 1987. 'Causes of US farm commodity programs', *Journal of Political Economy* 95 (2): 290–310, April.

——, 1989. 'Recent studies of agricultural trade liberalisation', in A. Maunder and A. Valdes (eds), *Agricultural and Governments in an Interdependent World,* London, Dartmouth for the IAAE.

Garnaut, R., 1988. 'Asia's giant', *Australian Economic Papers* 27(51): 173–86, December.

——, 1989. *Australia and the Northeast Asian Ascendancy,* Canberra, Australian Government Publishing Service.

—— and Anderson, K., 1980. 'ASEAN export specialization and the evolution of comparative advantage in the Western Pacific region', in R. Garnaut (ed.), *ASEAN in a Changing Pacific and World Economy,* Canberra, Australian National University Press: Ch. 13.

George, A. and Saxon, E., 1986. 'The politics of agricultural protection in Japan', in K. Anderson and Y. Hayami with others, *The Political Economy of Agricultural Protection,* London and Sydney, Allen and Unwin.

Gibbard, P. and Tyers, R., 1990. 'The domestic incidence of commodity price stabilisation in an open economy', Seminar Paper No. 90–04, Centre for International Economic Studies, University of Adelaide.

Gilbert, C.L., 1989. 'The impact of exchange rates and developing country debt on commodity prices', *Economic Journal* 99(397): 773–84, September.

Glaser, L.K., 1986. *Provisions of the Food Security Act of 1985,* Agriculture Information Bulletin No. 498, Washington, D.C., US Department of Agriculture, April.

Grilli, E.R. and Yang, M.C., 1988. 'Primary commodity prices, manufactured goods prices, and the terms of trade of developing countries: what the long run shows', *World Bank Economic Review* 2(1): 1–48, January.

Grossman, G.M., 1983. 'Partially mobile capital: a general approach to two-sector trade theory', *Journal of International Economics* 15(3): 1–17, August.

—— and Helpman, E., 1990. 'Trade, innovation and growth', *American Economic Review* 80(2): 86–91, May.

—— and ——, 1992. 'Comparative advantage and long-run growth', *American Economic Review* 82 (2): 86–91, May.

Gulbrandsen, O. and Lindbeck, A., 1966. 'Swedish agricultural policy in an international perspective', _Skandinaviska Banken Quarterly Review_ 47: 95–107.

—— and ——, 1973. _The Economics of the Agricultural Sector_, Stockholm, Almqvist and Wicksell.

Hamilton, C., 1991. 'The new silk road to Europe: new directions for old trade' in K. Anderson (ed.), _New Silk Roads: East Asia and World Textile Markets_, Cambridge, Cambridge University Press: Ch. 8.

Harris, J.R. and Todoro, M.P., 1970. 'Migration, unemployment and development: a two-sector analysis', _American Economic Review_ 60(1): 126–42.

Hayami, Y., 1988. _Japanese Agriculture Under Siege_, London, Macmillan.

Hayami, Y. and Ruttan, V.W., 1985. _Agricultural Development: An International Perspective_, Baltimore, Johns Hopkins University Press (revised edition).

Hertel, T.W., 1989. 'PSEs and the mix of measures to support farm incomes', _The World Economy_ 12 (1): 17–28.

——, 1990. 'The impact of trade liberalization on low-income, food-deficit countries', in N. Islam and A. Valdes (eds) _The GATT, Agriculture and the Developing Countries_, Washington, D.C., International Food Policy Research Institute: Ch. 5.

Hicks, J.R., 1943. _The Theory of Wages_, London, Macmillan.

Hillman, A.L., 1982. 'Declining industries and political support protectionist motives', _American Economic Review_ 72(3): 1180–7, December.

——, 1989. _The Political Economy of Protection_, New York, Harwood Academic Publishers.

Hong, W., 1979. _Trade Distortions and Employment Growth in Korea_, Seoul, Korea Development Institute Press.

Honma, M. and Hayami, Y., 1986. 'The structure of agricultural protection in industrial countries', _Journal of International Economics_ 20(1/2): 115–29, February.

Houck, J.P. 1986. _Elements of Agricultural Trade Policies_, New York, Macmillan.

IATRC, 1989. _Tariffication and Rebalancing_, Commissioned Paper No. 4 on Bringing Agriculture Into the GATT, Columbia, Missouri, International Agricultural Trade Research Consortium.

——, 1990. _Potential Use of an Aggregate Measure of Support_, Commissioned Paper No. 5 on Bringing Agriculture Into the GATT, Columbia, Missouri, International Agricultural Trade Research Consortium.

Industries Assistance Commission, 1983. _Assistance to Australian Agriculture_, Canberra, Australian Government Publishing Service.

——, 1987. _Assistance to Australian Agricultural and Manufacturing Industries_, Canberra, Australian Government Publishing Service.

International Economic Data Bank (IEDB), 1990. 'World agricultural production and trade: price and quantity data', Technical Paper No. 9, Australian National University.

Johnson, D.G., 1973. *World Agriculture in Disarray*, London, Fontana.

——, 1975. 'World agriculture, commodity policy, and price variability', *American Journal of Agricultural Economics* 57(5): 823–8, December.

Johnson, H.G., 1965. 'An economic theory of protectionism, tariff bargaining and formation of customs unions', *Journal of Political Economy* 73 (3): 256–83, June.

——, 1968. *Comparative Cost and Commercial Policy Theory for a Developing World Economy*, Stockholm, Almqvist and Wicksell.

Johnson, S.R., Meyers, W.N., Womack, A.W., Young, R.E. and Helmar, M.D., 1986. *The Food Security Act of 1985: A Ten-Year Perspective*, FAPRI Staff Report No. 2–86, Ames, Iowa State University, June.

——, Meyers, W.H., Westhoff, P. and Womack, A., 1989. 'Agricultural market outlook and sensitivity to macroeconomic, productivity and policy changes', in A. Maunder and A. Valdes (eds), *Agriculture and Governments in an Interdependent World*, London, Dartmouth for the IAAE.

Jones, R.W., 1971. 'A three-factor model in theory, trade and history', in J. Bhagwati *et al.* (eds), *Trade, Balance of Payments and Growth*, Amsterdam, North Holland: Ch. 1.

——, 1975. 'Income distribution and effective protection in a multicommodity trade model', *Journal of Economic Theory* 11 (1): 1–15, August.

—— and Krueger, A. (eds), 1989. *The Political Economy of International Trade*, Oxford, Basil Blackwell.

Jorgenson, D.W., 1988. 'Productivity and postwar US economic growth', *Journal of Economic Perspectives* 2(4): 23–42, Fall.

Judd, M.A., Boyce, J.K. and Evenson, R.E., 1986. 'Investing in agricultural supply: the determinants of agricultural research and extension', *Economic Development and Cultural Change* 35(1): 77–114, October.

Just, R.E. and Antle, J.M., 1990. 'Interactions between agricultural and environmental policies: a conceptual framework', *American Economic Review* 80(2): 197–202, May.

Just, R.E., Hueth, D.L. and Schmitz, A., 1982. *Applied Welfare Economics and Public Policy*, Englewood Cliffs, Prentice Hall.

Kalt, J.P. and Zupan, M.A., 1984. 'Capture and ideology in the economic theory of politics', *American Economic Review* 74(3): 279–300, June.

Kane, S., Reilly, J. and Bucklin, R., 1989. 'Implications of the greenhouse effect for world agricultural commodity markets', a US Department of Agriculture paper presented at the Western Economic Association Conference, Lake Tahoe, June.

Keesing, D.B. and Sherk, D.R., 1971. 'Population density in patterns of trade and development', *American Economic Review* 61(5): 956-61, December.

Kelley, A.C. and Williamson, J.G., 1984. *What Drives Third World City Growth? A Dynamic General Equilibrium Approach*, Princeton, Princeton University Press.

Kindleberger, C.P., 1951. 'Group behaviour and international trade', *Journal of Political Economy* 59(1): 30-47, February.

——, 1975. 'The rise of free trade in Western Europe, 1820-1875', *Journal of Economic History* 35(1): 20-55, March.

——, 1978. *Government and International Trade*, Essays in International Finance No. 129, Princeton, N.J.

——, 1986. 'International public goods without international government', *American Economic Review* 76(1): 1-3, March.

Knudsen, O., 1990. 'Food security and compensation: the role of the GATT', in N. Islam and A. Valdes (eds) *The GATT, Agriculture and the Developing Countries*, Washington, D.C., International Food Policy Research Institute: Ch. 6.

Koester, U. and Tangermann, S., 1986. 'European agricultural policies and international agriculture', Background Paper for the *World Development Report 1986*, Washington D.C., The World Bank.

Kravis, I.B. and Lipsey, R.E., 1988. 'National price levels and the prices of tradables and nontradables', *American Economic Review* 78(2): 474-8, May.

——, Heston, W. and Summers, R., 1983. 'The share of services in economic growth', in F.G. Adams and B.G. Hickman (eds), *Global Econometrics*, Cambridge, The MIT Press.

Krissoff, B. and Ballinger, N., 1989. 'Agricultural trade liberalization in a multisector world model: implications for select Latin American countries' in B. Greenshields and M. Bellamy (eds), *Government Intervention in Agriculture: Cause and Effect*, International Association of Agricultural Economists. Occasional Paper No. 5, Aldershot, Dartmouth.

Krueger, A.O., 1977. *Growth, Distortions and Patterns of Trade Among Many Countries*, Princeton, N.J., International Finance Section.

——, 1989. 'Some preliminary findings from the World Bank's project on the political economy of agricultural pricing', in A. Maunder and A. Valdes (eds), *Agriculture and Governments in an Interdependent World*, London, Dartmouth for the IAAE.

——, 1990. 'Asian trade and growth lessons', *American Economic Review* 80(2): 108-112, May.

——, Schiff, M. and Valdes, A., 1988. 'Measuring the impact of sector-specific and economy-wide policies on agricultural incentives in LDCs', *World Bank Economic Review* 2(3): 255-72, September.

Krugman, P., 1989. *Is Bilateralism Bad?*, NBER Working Paper No. 2972, Cambridge, Mass., May.

Kuznets, S.S., 1966. *Modern Economic Growth: Rate, Structure and Spread,* New Havan, Yale University Press.

——, 1971. *Economic Growth of Nations: Total Output and Production Structure,* Cambridge, Harvard University Press.

Leamer, E.E., 1984. *Sources of International Comparative Advantage: Theory and Evidence,* Cambridge, MIT Press.

Lerner, A.P., 1936. 'The symmetry between import and export taxes', *Economica* 3 (11): 306–13, August.

Liepmann, H., 1938. *Tariff Levels and Economic Unity in Europe,* London, George Allen and Unwin.

Little, I.M.D., Scitovsky, T. and Scott, M., 1970. *Industry and Trade in Some Developing Countries: A Comparative Study,* London, Oxford University Press for the OECD.

Lloyd, P.J., 1974. 'A more general theory of price distortions in an open economy', *Journal of International Economics* 4(4): 365–86, November.

——. and Procter, R.G., 1983. 'Commodity decomposition of export-import instability', *Journal of Development Economics* 12: 41–57.

Lluch, C., Powell, A.A. and Williams, R.A., 1977. *Patterns in Household Demand and Savings,* New York, Oxford University Press.

Loo, T. and Tower, E., 1989. 'Agricultural protectionism and the less developed countries: the relationship between agricultural prices, debt servicing and the need for development aid', in A. Stoeckel (ed.), *Macroeconomic Consequences of Farm–Support Policies,* Durham, Duke University Press.

—— and ——, 1990. 'Agricultural liberalization, welfare, revenue and nutrition in the developing countries', in I. Goldin and O. Knudsen (eds), *Agricultural Trade Liberalization: Implications For Developing Countries,* Paris, OECD.

Lucas, R.E., 1988. 'On the mechanics of economic development', *Journal of Monetary Economics* 22(1): 3–42.

——, 1990. 'Why doesn't capital flow from rich to poor countries?' *American Economic Review* 80(2): 92–6, May.

Lutz, E. and Scandizzo, P.L., 1980. 'Price distortions in developing countries: a bias against agriculture', *European Review of Agricultural Economics* 7: 5–27.

Mabbs-Zeno, C., *et al.,* 1988. *Estimates of Producer and Consumer Subsidy Equivalents: Government Intervention in Agriculture, 1982–86,* ERS Staff Report No. AGES 880127, Washington, D.C., US Department of Agriculture, April.

McCalla, A.F., 1969. 'Protectionism in international agricultural trade, 1850–1968', *Agricultural History* 43(3): 329–44, July.

—— and Josling, T.E., 1985. *Agricultural Policies and World Markets,* New York, Macmillan.

Magee, S.P., 1980. 'Three simple tests of the Stolper–Samuelson theorem', in P. Oppenheimer (ed.), *Issues in International Economics,* London, Macmillan: 138–55.

——, Brock, W.A. and Young, L., 1989. *Black Hole Tariffs and Endogenous Policy Theory: Political Economy in General Equilibrium*, Cambridge, Cambridge University Press.

Massell, B.F., 1969. 'Price stabilization and welfare', *Quarterly Journal of Economics* 83(2): 284–98, May.

Mayer, W., 1984. 'Endogenous tariff formation', *American Economic Review* 74(5): 970–85, December.

Mussa, M., 1974. 'Tariffs and the distribution of income: the importance of factor specificity, substitutability and intensity in the short and long run', *Journal of Political Economy* 82 (6): 1191–203, December.

Muth, J.F., 1961. 'Rational expectations and the theory of price movements', *Econometrica* 29(3): 315–35, July.

Nam, C.H., 1981. 'Trade and industrial policies and the structure of protection in Korea', in W. Hong and L. Krause (eds), *Trade and Growth of the Advanced Developing Countries*, Seoul, Korea Development Institute Press.

Neary, J.P. and van Wijnbergen, S., 1985. *Natural Resources and the Macroeconomy*, Cambridge, MIT Press.

Nerlove, M., 1972. 'Lags in economic behaviour', *Econometrica* 40(2): 221–52, March.

Newbery, D.M.G., 1987. 'Agricultural taxation: the main issues', in D.M.G. Newbery and N.H. Stern (eds), *The Theory of Taxation in Developing Countries*, New York, Oxford University Press for the World Bank.

——, 1988. 'The analysis of agricultural price reform', *Journal of Public Economics* 35(1): 1–24.

——, 1989. 'The theory of food price stabilisation', *Economic Journal* 99(398): 1065–82, December.

—— and Stiglitz, J.E., 1981. *The Theory of Commodity Price Stabilization*, New York, Oxford University Press.

Niskanen, W.A., 1971. *Bureaucracy and Representative Government*, Hawthorn, NY, Aldine.

OECD, 1983. *Historical Statistics 1960–1981*, Paris, Organisation for Economic Cooperation and Development.

——, 1987. *National Policies and Agricultural Trade*, Paris, Organisation for Economic Cooperation and Development, May.

——, 1988. *Monitoring and Outlook of Agricultural Policies, Markets and Trade*, Paris, Organisation for Economic Cooperation and Development, May.

——, 1990a. *Monitoring and Outlook of Agricultural Policies, Markets and Trade*, Paris, Organisation for Economic Cooperation and Development, May.

——, 1990b. *Modelling the Effects of Agricultural Policies*, OECD Economic Studies No. 13, Paris, Organisation for Economic Cooperation and Development.

Oi, W.Y., 1961. 'The desirability of price instability under perfect competition', *Econometrica* 29(1): 58–64, January.

Olson, M. 1965. *The Logic of Collective Action*, Cambridge, Harvard University Press.

——, M., 1986. 'The exploitation and subsidization of agriculture in the developed and developing countries', in A. Maunder and U. Renborg (eds), *Agriculture in a Turbulent World Economy*, London, Dartmouth for the IAAE: 49–59.

Parikh, K.S., Fischer, G., Frohberg, K. and Gulbrandsen, O., 1988. *Towards Free Trade in Agriculture*, Amsterdam, Mortimers Nijhoff for IIASA.

Peltzman, S., 1976. 'Toward a more general theory of regulation', *Journal of Law and Economics* 19 (2): 211–40, October.

——, 1984. 'Constituent interest and congressional voting', *Journal of Law and Economics* 27(1): 181–210, April.

Perkins, D.H., 1986. *China: Asia's Next Economic Giant?* Seattle, University of Washington Press.

——, 1988. 'Reforming China's economic system', *Journal of Economic Literature* 26(2): 601–45, June.

Perry, G.M., McCarl, B., Rister, M.E. and Richardson, J.W., 1989. 'Modelling government program participation decisions at the farm level', *American Journal of Agricultural Economics* 71(4): 1011–20, November.

Peterson, W.L., 1979. 'International farm prices and the social cost of cheap food policies', *American Journal of Agricultural Economics* 61 (1): 12–21, February.

Pratt, J.W., 1964. 'Risk aversion in the small and in the large', *Econometrica* 32(1): 122–36, January.

Prebisch, R. 1964. *Towards a New Trade Policy for Development*, New York, United Nations.

Riethmuller, P., *et al.*, 1990. *Proposed Strategies for Reducing Agricultural Protection in the GATT Uruguay Round*, Occasional Paper 90.6, Canberra, Australian Bureau of Agricultural and Resource Economics.

Rausser, G.C., 1982. 'Political economic markets: PERTs and PESTs in food and agriculture', *American Journal of Agricultural Economics* 64(5): 821–33, December.

—— and de Gorter, H., 1989. 'Endogenizing policy in models of agricultural markets', in A. Maunder and A. Valdes (eds), *Agriculture and Governments in an Interdependent World*, London, Dartmouth for the IAAE.

Roberts, I., Love, G., Field, H and Klijn, N., 1989. *US Grain Policies and the World Market*, Policy Monograph No. 4, Australian Bureau of Agricultural and Resource Economics, Canberra, Australian Government Publishing Service.

Roe, T., Shane, M. and Vo, D.H., 1986. *Price Responsiveness of World Grain Markets: The Influence of Government Intervention on Import Price*

Elasticity, Technical Bulletin No. 1720, Economic Research Service, Washington, D.C., U.S. Department of Agriculture.

Rojko, A.S., Regier, D., O'Brien, P., Caffing, A. and Bailey, L., 1978. *Alternative Futures for World Food in 1985*. Foreign Agricultural Economic Reports Nos. 146 and 151, Economic Research Service, Washington D.C. US Department of Agriculture.

Romer, P.M., 1990. 'Endogenous technological change', *Journal of Political Economy* 98 (5, Part 2): S71–S101, October.

Roningen, V.O., 1986. *A Static World Policy Simulation (SWOPSIM) Modelling Framework*, ERS Staff Report No. AGES 860625, Washington, D.C., US Department of Agriculture, July.

——, Dixit, P.M. and Seeley, R., 1989. 'Agricultural outlook for the year 2000', in A. Maunder and A. Valdes (eds), *Agriculture and Governments in an Interdependent World*, London, Dartmouth for the IAAE.

Runge, C.F. and von Witzke, H., 1987. 'Institutional change in the Common Agricultural Policy of the European Community', *American Journal of Agricultural Economics* 69(2): 213–22, May.

——, von Witzke, H. and Thompson, S.J., 1989. 'International agricultural policy: a political coordination game', in H. von Witzke, C.F. Runge and B. Job (eds), *Policy Coordination in World Agriculture*, Kiel, Wissenschaftsverlag Vauk, KG.

Rutherford, T.F., Whalley, J. and Wigle, R.M., 1990. 'Capitalization, conditionality and dilution: land prices and the US wheat program', *Journal of Policy Modeling* 12(3): 605–22, Fall.

Ruttan, V.W., 1982. *Agricultural Research Policy*, Minneapolis, University of Minnesota.

Rybczynski, T.M., 1955. 'Factor endowments and relative commodity prices', *Economica* 22: 336–41, November.

Sampson, G. and Snape, R.H., 1980. 'Effect of the EEC's variable import levies', *Journal of Political Economy* 88(5): 1026–40, December.

Sanderson, F., (ed.), 1990. *Agricultural Protectionism in the Industrialized World*, Washington, D.C., Resources for the Future.

Sandrey, R. and Reynolds, R. (eds), 1990. *Farming Without Subsidies: New Zealand's Recent Experience*, Wellington, Ministry of Agriculture and Fisheries.

Sapsford, D., 1985. 'The statistical debate on the net barter terms of trade between primary commodities and manufactures: a comment and some additional evidence', *Economic Journal* 95(379): 781–8, September.

Sarris, A.H. and Freebairn, J.W., 1983. 'Endogenous price policies and international wheat prices', *American Journal of Agricultural Economics* 65(2): 214–24, May.

—— and ——, 1984. 'Domestic price policies and international rice trade', in Storey, A. Schmitz and A.H. Sarris (eds) *International Agricultural Trade*, Boulder, Westview Press.

Saxon, E. and Anderson, K., 1982. *Japanese Agricultural Production in Historical Perspective*, Pacific Economic Papers No. 92, Australia-Japan Research Centre, Canberra, Australian National University.

——, —— and Tyers, R., 1986. 'Historical trends in grain, livestock products and sugar markets: the price data', Annex B to 'Distortions in world food markets: a quantitative assessment' by R. Tyers and K. Anderson, background paper prepared for the World Bank's *World Development Report 1986*, Washington D.C., January.

Schiff, M., 1985. *An Econometric Analysis of the World Wheat Market and Simulation of Alternative Policies, 1960–80*, ERS Staff Report AGES 850827, Washington, D.C., US Department of Agriculture.

Schultz, T.W., 1945. *Agriculture in an Unstable Economy*, New York, McGraw Hill.

——, (ed.), 1978. *Distortions of Agricultural Incentives*, Bloomington, Indiana University Press.

Seitzinger, A.N. and Paarlberg, P.L., 1990. 'A simulation model of the US export enhancement program for wheat', *American Journal of Agricultural Economics* 72(1): 95–103, February.

Setboonsarng, S. and Tyers, R., 1988. *The Effects of the EC's Common Agricultural Policy on Thailand*, Research Report No. 1, Thailand Development Research Institute, Bangkok.

Shoven, J.B. and Whalley, J., 1984. 'Applied general equilibrium models of taxation and international trade', *Journal of Economic Literature* 22(2): 1007–51, September.

Sicular, T., 1989. 'Food pricing policy in China', in T. Sicular (ed.), *Food Pricing Policy in Asia*, Ithaca, Cornell University Press: Ch. 7.

——, 1990. *Ten Years of Reform: Progress and Setbacks in Agricultural Planning and Pricing*, Discussion Paper No. 1474, Harvard Institute of Economic Research, Cambridge, March.

Silberberg, E., 1978. *The Structure of Economics: A Mathematical Analysis*, New York, McGraw Hill.

Sjaastad, L.A., 1989. 'Exchange rates and commodity prices: the Australian case', Seminar Paper 89-10, Centre for International Economic Studies, University of Adelaide, November.

Snape, R.H., 1987. 'The importance of frontier barriers', in H. Kierzkowski (ed.), *Protection and Competition in International Trade: Essays in Honour of W.M. Corden*, Oxford, Basil Blackwell: Ch. 15.

Spraos, J., 1980. 'The statistical debate on the net barter terms of trade between primary commodities and manufactures', *Economic Journal* 90(357): 107–28, March.

Spriggs, J.D., 1990. 'Transparency vs protectionism', Seminar Paper 90-03, Centre for International Economic Studies, University of Adelaide, June.

Stigler, G.S., 1975. *The Citizen and the State*, Chicago, University of Chicago Press.

Stolper, W.F. and Samuelson, P.A., 1941. 'Protection and real wages', *Review of Economic Studies* 9 (1): 58–73, November.

Summers, R., 1985. 'Services in the international economy', in R.P. Inman (ed.), *Managing the Service Economy*, New York, Cambridge University Press.

Suphachalasai, S., 1991. 'Thailand's growth in textile exports', in K. Anderson (ed.), *New Silk Roads: East Asia and World Textile Markets*, Cambridge, Cambridge University Press: Ch. 5.

Thiel, H. and Clements, K.W., 1987. *Applied Demand Analysis: Results from System-Wide Approaches*, Cambridge, Mass., Ballinger.

Thurow, L.C., 1984. *Dangerous Currents: The State of Economics*, London, Oxford University Press.

Tracy, M., 1982. *Agriculture in Western Europe – Challenge and Response 1880–1980*, London, Granada (2nd edn).

Turnovsky, S.J., 1979. 'Futures markets, private storage and price stabilization', *Journal of Public Economics* 12: 310–27.

——, Shalit, H. and Schmitz, A., 1980. 'Consumer surplus, price instability and consumer welfare', *Econometrica* 48(1): 135–52.

Tyers, R., 1984. *Agricultural Protection and Market Insulation: Analysis of International Impacts by Stochastic Simulation*, Pacific Economic Papers No. 111, Australia–Japan Research Centre, Canberra, May.

——, 1985. 'Agricultural protection and market insulation: model structure and results for the European Community', *Journal of Policy Modeling* 7(2): 219–51.

——, 1989. 'Developing country interests in agricultural trade reforms', *Agricultural Economics* 3:169–86.

——, 1990a. 'Implicit policy preferences and the assessment of negotiable trade policy reforms', *European Economic Review* 34(7): 1399–426.

——, 1990b. 'Agricultural trade reform and price risk in domestic and international food markets', *The World Economy* 13(2): 212–29.

——, 1990c. 'Searching under the light: the neglect of dynamics and risk in the analysis of food trade reforms', Centre for International Food and Agricultural Policy, Staff Paper P90–66, University of Minnesota, October.

—— and Anderson, K., 1988a. 'Imperfect price transmission and implied trade elasticities in a multi-commodity world', in C. Carter (ed.), *Elasticities in International Agricultural Trade*, Boulder, Westview Press: Ch. 9.

—— and ——, 1988b. 'Liberalizing OECD agricultural policies in the Uruguay Round: effects on trade and welfare' *Journal of Agricultural Economics* 39 (2): 197–216, May.

—— and ——, 1989. 'Price elasticities in international food trade: synthetic estimates from a global model', *Journal of Policy Modeling* 11(3): 315–44, Fall.

—— and Chisholm, A.H., 1982. 'Agricultural policies in industrialized and developing countries and international food security', in A.H. Chisholm and R. Tyers (eds) *Food Security: Theory, Policy and Perspectives from Asia and the Pacific Rim*, Lexington, D.C. Heath: Ch. 14.

—— and Falvey, R., 1989. 'Border price changes and domestic welfare in the presence of subsidised exports', *Oxford Economic Papers* 41(2): 434–51, April.

—— and Phillips, P., 1986. 'Historical trends in grain, livestock product and sugar markets: the quantity data', Annex A to 'Distortions in world food markets', by R. Tyers and K. Anderson, background paper prepared for the World Bank's *World Development Report 1986*, Washington D.C., January.

US Government, 1987. *Economic Report of the President, 1987*, Government of the United States, January.

Variyam, J.N. Jordan, J.L. and Epperson, J.E., 1990. 'Preferences of citizens for agricultural policies: evidence from a national survey', *American Journal of Agricultural Economics* 72(2): 257–67, May.

Waugh, F.V., 1944. 'Does the consumer benefit from price instability?', *Quarterly Journal of Economics* 58: 602–14.

Wellisz, S. and Findlay, R., 1984. 'Protection and rent-seeking in developing countries', in D.C. Colander (ed.), *Neoclassical Political Economy*, Cambridge, Ballinger: Ch. 10.

Whalley, J., 1984. *Trade Liberalization Among Major World Trading Areas*, Cambridge, MIT Press.

Wharton Econometric Associates, 1986. *World Economic Outlook*, Vol. III No. 1, Philadelphia, May.

Williamson, J.G., 1985. *Did British Capitalism Breed Inequality?* Boston, Allen and Unwin.

——. and Lindert, P.H., 1980. *American Inequality: A Macroeconomic History*, New York, Academic Press.

Winters, L.A., 1987. 'The political economy of the agricultural policy of industrial countries', *European Review of Agricultural Economics* 14: 285–304.

——, 1988. *The So-Called 'Non-Economic' Objectives of Agricultural Policy*, Working Paper CPE/WPI (88)3, Paris, OECD Secretariat, February.

World Bank, 1983. *World Development Report 1983*, New York, Oxford University Press.

——, 1986. *World Development Report 1986*, New York, Oxford University Press.

——, 1988a. *World Development Report 1988*, New York, Oxford University Press.

——, 1988b. *World Tables*, Baltimore, Johns Hopkins University Press (4th edn).

——, 1988c. *Price Prospects for Major Primary Commodities*, World Bank Report No. 814/88, Washington, D.C., November.

——, 1989. *Quarterly Review of Commodity Markets*, December, Washington, D.C., World Bank.

——, 1990. *World Development Report 1990*, New York, Oxford University Press.

Wright, B.D., 1979. 'The effects of ideal production stabilization: a welfare analysis under rational behaviour', *Journal of Political Economy* 87(5): 1011–33.

Yang, Y.Z. and Tyers, R., 1989. 'The economic costs of food self-sufficiency in China', *World Development* 17(2): 237–53, February.

Young, L., and Magee, S.P., 1986. 'Endogenous protection, factor returns and resource allocation', *Review of Economic Studies* 53(3): 407–20, July.

Young, M.D., 1988. 'The integration of agricultural and environmental policies', paper presented to the 18th European Conference of Agricultural Economists, Copenhagen, 1–4 November.

Zietz, J. and Valdes, A., 1985. 'The costs of protectionism to less-developed countries: an analysis for selected agricultural products', Washington, D.C., World Bank and the International Food Policy Research Institute, January (mimeo).

—— and Valdes, A., 1988. *Agriculture in the GATT: An Analysis of Alternative Approaches to Reform*, Research Report 70, Washington D.C., International Food Policy Research Institute.

Zwart, A.C. and Meilke, K.D., 1979. 'The influence of domestic pricing policies and buffer stocks on price stability in the world wheat market', *American Journal of Agricultural Economics* 61(3): 434–47, August.

Index